Ibn Katheer

Life and Times of the Messengers

Taken from
Al-Bidayah wan-Nihayah

1st Edition: October 2010

Supervised by:

Abdul Malik Mujahid

HEAD OFFICE

P.O. Box: 22743, Riyadh 11416 K.S.A.Tel: 00966-1-4033962/4043432 Fax: 4021659
E-mail: darussalam@awalnet.net.sa, riyadh@dar-us-salam.com Website:www.darussalamksa.com

K.S.A. Darussalam Showrooms:
Riyadh
Olaya branch: Tel 00966-1-4614483 Fax: 4644945
Malaz branch: Tel 00966-1-4735220 Fax: 4735221
Suwaydi branch: Tel: 00966 1 4286641
Suwailam branch: Tel & Fax-1-2860422

- **Jeddah**
  Tel: 00966-2-6879254 Fax: 6336270
- **Madinah**
  Tel: 00966-04- 8234446, 8230038
  Fax: 04-8151121
- **Al-Khobar**
  Tel: 00966-3-8692900 Fax: 8691551
- **Khamis Mushayt**
  Tel & Fax: 00966-072207055
- **Yanbu Al-Bahr** Tel: 0500887341 Fax: 04-3908027
- **Al-Buraida** Tel: 0503417156 Fax: 06-3696124

U.A.E
- **Darussalam, Sharjah U.A.E**
  Tel: 00971-6-5632623 Fax: 5632624
  Sharjah@dar-us-salam.com.

PAKISTAN
- **Darussalam,** 36 B Lower Mall, Lahore
  Tel: 0092-42-724 0024 Fax: 7354072
- **Rahman Market, Ghazni Street,**Urdu Bazar Lahore
  Tel: 0092-42-7120054 Fax: 7320703
- **Karachi,** Tel: 0092-21-4393936 Fax: 4393937
- **Islamabad,** Tel: 0092-51-2500237 Fax: 512281513

U.S.A
- **Darussalam, Houston**
  P.O Box: 79194 Tx 77279
  Tel: 001-713-722 0419 Fax: 001-713-722 0431
  E-mail: houston @dar-us-salam.com
- **Darussalam, New York** 486 Atlantic Ave, Brooklyn
  New York-11217, Tel: 001-718-625 5925
  Fax: 718-625 1511
  E-mail: darussalamny@hotmail.com

U.K
- **Darussalam International Publications Ltd.**
  Leyton Business Centre
  Unit-17, Etloe Road, Leyton, London, E10 7BT
  Tel: 0044 20 8539 4885 Fax:0044 20 8539 4889
  Website: www.darussalam.com
  Email: info@darussalam.com
- **Darussalam International Publications Limited**
  Regents Park Mosque, 146 Park Road

AUSTRALIA
- **Darussalam:** 153, Haldon St, Lakemba (Sydney)
  NSW 2195, Australia
  Tel: 0061-2-97407188 Fax: 0061-2-97407199
  Mobile: 0061-414580813 Res: 0061-2-97580190
  Email: abumuaaz@hotmail.com
- **The Islamic Bookstore**
  Ground Floor-165 Haldon Street
  Lakemba, NSW 2195, Australia
  Tel: 0061-2-97584040 Fax: 0061-2-97584030
  Email: info@islamicbookstore.com.au
  Web Site: www.islamicbookstore.com.au

CANADA
- **Nasiruddin Al-Khattab**
  2-3415 Dixie Rd, Unit # 505
  Mississauga
  Ontario L4Y 4J6, Canada
  Tel: 001-416-418 6619

FRANCE
- **Editions & Librairie Essalam**
  135, Bd de Ménilmontant- 75011 Paris
  Tél: 0033-01- 43 38 19 56/ 44 83
  Fax: 0033-01- 43 57 44 31
  E-mail: essalam@essalam com·

MALAYSIA
- **Darussalam**
  Int'l Publishing & Distribution SDN BHD
  D-2-12, Setiawangsa 11, Taman Setiawangsa
  54200 Kuala Lumpur
  Tel: 03-42528200 Fax: 03-42529200
  Email: darussalam@streamyx.com
  Website: www.darussalam.com.my

SRI LANKA
- Darul Kitab 6, Nimal Road, Colombo-4
  Tel: 0094 115 358712 Fax: 115-358713

INDIA
- **Islamic Books International**
  54, Tandel Street (North)
  Dongri, Mumbai 4000 09, INDIA
  Tel: 0091-22-2373 4180
  E-mail: ibi@irf.net

SOUTH AFRICA
- **Islamic Da'wah Movement (IDM)**
  48009 Qualbert 4078 Durban,South Africa

Ibn Katheer

Life and Times of the Messengers

(Stories of Moosa, Samuel, Zakariyya, Yahya, Eesa,
Dhu'l Qarnayn, Luqman, the Children of Israa'eel, Divine
Scriptures and Past Nations)

Taken from

Al-Bidayah wan-Nihayah

Translation and Researched by
Research Department of Darussalam

DARUSSALAM

© **Mak-taba Dar-us-Salam, 2010**

King Fahd National Library Cataloging-in-Publication Data

Ibn Kathir

  Life and times of the messengers. / Ibn Kathir - Riyadh, 2010

  pages: 455 Size: 14x21 cm

  ISBN: 978-603-500-043-7

1- Prophets stories 2-Prophets - Biography 1- Title

229.5 dc   1431/8750

L.D. no. 1431/8750

ISBN: 978-603-500-043-7

Contents

In the Name of Allah, the Most Beneficent, the Most Merciful

Preface to the Revision

All praise and thanks be to Allah, Who revived knowledge of His religion and caused it to blossom forth after it had all but disappeared, and Who demolished the false conjectures of the apostates. I praise Him and I seek refuge with Him from the sins which weigh upon the backs of mankind. I worship Him and seek His aid in removing hindrances and difficulties in the practice of my religion. I bear witness that none has the right to be worshipped except Allah, Alone, without partners and I bear witness that Muhammad – who, by Allah's leave, brought about the dawn of faith to the darkness and misguidance which existed in the hearts of mankind – is the slave and Messenger of Allah. May the Blessings and Peace of Allah be upon him in perpetuity.

O, Allah! We seek Your favor and through You we seek to ward off affliction. We ask You to protect us and to grant us mercy. Our Lord! Make not our hearts deviate after You have already guided us. Make it easy for us to perform our deeds in the way that You have taught us. Make us grateful for what You have given us and make plain a path for us which leads to You. Open up the doors between us and You by which we may arrive before You. To You belong the keys to the heavens and the Earth and You are Most Able to do all things. To proceed:

Among the blessings which Allah has bestowed upon us, the community of Muslims is that He has made it easy for us to follow the path of guidance, and He has opened the doors of knowledge by making available to us these new publications, which present to us the writings of the early scholars and reveal to us what they said regarding legal verdicts, history, events, information and lessons. These scholars opened a clear beacon of light for all those Muslims seeking guidance and they set up for us a signpost in which there is neither deviation nor crookedness. Whoever follows it will arrive safely at his desired destination and whoever diverts from it will be lost forever. They have written these books and treatises and made clear to us therein events, information and virtues. Among such books is this unique work, *Al-Bidayah Wan-Nihayah*, by the Imam, the *Hafiz*, the master scholar of *hadeeth*, 'Imaduddeen Isma'eel Ibn Katheer Al-Qurashi – may Allah have mercy on him. This book was greeted with approval by the vast majority of Muslims. No Islamic library would be complete without it. In it, the author has recorded what Allah, Most High has made easy for him about the history of mankind, from the beginning of creation, starting with the creation of the Throne and the *Kursi* (Footstool), the heavens and the Earth and all that they contain and all that lies between them, such as the angels, the jinn and the devils. He also described how Adam عليه السلام was created, and told the stories of the prophets up to the days of the

Children of Isra'eel and the Days of Ignorance (*Jahiliyyah*), until the advent of Prophet Muhammad ﷺ, which heralded the end of Prophethood. He then recorded his *Seerah*.[1] Then he recorded the events which took place up to his own time. He also spoke of the trials and battles, the signs of the approach of the Hour, then the sending forth of mankind and the terrors of the Resurrection, which he described in detail. He then described the Hell-fire, with all its horrors, and Paradise and all the good things contained therein. He called this particular volume of his book: *An-Nihayah Fil-Fitan Wal-Malahim* (*The Ending in Trials and Battles*). As for the book which is in our hands today, it is *Al-Bidayah*.

By Allah's Grace, I came to know brother Abdul Malik Mujahid, the general manager of Darussalam Publishing in Riyadh. He visited me in my humble office in Damascus and suggested to me the idea of creating a summarised version of this wonderful book. I prayed for Allah's Guidance in the matter and sought help from Him in completing the project. Allah enabled me to make the acquaintance of a number of people of knowledge and experience in this field and a plan of action for the work was written. It consisted of ten principal points and we then started the task, seeking help from the Lord of the heavens and the Earth. All of us exerted our utmost efforts in this task, making repeated revisions and corrections, until we reached the point where, by Allah's Permission, we completed it and it was published in the form which is in your hands today.

The Plan of Action for This Book:

1. Summarization of the text. This was achieved by concentrating on the most important events narrated in the book. In doing so, we took care not to leave out any important details which

---

(1) *Seerah*: Biography, life story, in particular, of Prophet Muhammad ﷺ.

would cause loss of meaning or import.

2. We relied on a number of printed and handwritten copies of the book and in cases where any contradiction or omission was found, we succeeded in establishing the most accurate and authentic text.

3. We left out the *ahadeeth* which proved to be baseless or weak and confined ourselves to the *ahadeeth* which are authentic or *hasan* [1] and those which are acceptable due to the existence of other supporting narrations. On rare occasions, when it was found that there were no other *ahadeeth* in the chapter, we included some weak *ahadeeth* whose weakness was not of an extreme nature.

4. We performed *takhreej* [2] of the *ahadeeth* with ascription of the number of the section and the page, the number of the *hadeeth* and in many cases, the precise location of the *hadeeth* in the original source, then the ruling on its authenticity, if it was not from the *Saheehain*, [3] because the *ahadeeth* therein do not require any ruling on their authenticity and they have been widely accepted by the Muslim *Ummah*. [4] As for the *ahadeeth* in this book, we have relied on the opinions of the Imams and scholars of *hadeeth* – including the earlier scholars, the later scholars and those of the present day. On some occasions, we have recorded the weak *ahadeeth*, while making it plain that they are not authentic. We have not omitted them because the author has included them in order to warn the people against them due to their widespread popularity amongst the Muslims in general. In such cases, we desired not to oppose the author in this effort and so we left them, at the same time making the

---

(1) *Hasan*: Good, sound. An acceptable *hadeeth*, although it does not reach the level of *saheeh* (authentic).

(2) *Takhreej*: Referencing the sources of a *hadeeth* and evaluating them.

(3) *Saheehain*: *Saheeh Al-Bukhari* and *Saheeh Muslim*.

(4) *Ummah*: Nation or people; in this case, what is referred to is the scholars of the *Ummah*.

scholars' ruling on them clear, so as to warn the people against them.

5. We summarised the *asaneed* [1] present in the book, in most cases mentioning only the Companion who narrated the *hadeeth*, or the person who reported it from him.

6. We omitted many of the *Isra'eeliyyat* [2] found in this book which the author referred to in the preface, where he said: "We do not record the *Isra'eeliyyat* except those which the Lawgiver has permitted, i.e., those which do not contradict the Book of Allah and the Sunnah of His Messenger ﷺ. These are stories which are neither believed nor belied and they have been recorded because they provide details of unclarified narratives that we have, or they provide names for people and places that have only been mentioned in passing in our Revelation, due to there being no benefit in specifying them for us. Thus we have reported them in order to provide extra detail and not with the intention of citing them as evidence or placing any reliance on them. Only the Book of Allah and the authentic Sunnah of His Messenger ﷺ may be relied and depended upon. It is from Allah that we seek help and it is He in Whom we place our trust; there is no help and no power except in Allah, the All-Powerful, the Most Wise, the Most High, the Almighty.

7. In some instances, we have referred back to the original manuscript in order to verify the wording of a *hadeeth* from its source. In some cases, the author has combined two narrations of the same *hadeeth* together and so where this has occurred, we have noted it and separated the two narrations, placing our own words between brackets, i.e., (and in another narration...) and we have also identified the source of the addition in the footnotes.

---

(1) *Asaneed* (sing. = *isnad*): Chains of narrators of the *ahadeeth*.

(2) *Isra'eeliyyat*: Narrations of Jewish origin.

8. We have written the Qur'anic Verses in the Uthmani script, in conformity with the copy of the Qur'an published by Al-Madinah Al-Munawwarah Printing Complex.

9. We vowelised the words of many of the *ahadeeth* in the book and, in addition, the poetic verses, wherever possible.

10. We mentioned the meters of the poetic verses between parentheses.

11. We explained the meanings of some difficult or obscure words, relying on dictionaries, books containing *ghareeb* [1] *ahadeeth* and narrations and other sources.

12. We furnished a brief biography of the author, Hafiz Ibn Katheer though in reality, he requires no introduction and no description.

Finally, I ask Allah, Most High, to accept this humble work from us and to acknowledge it as having been done purely and sincerely with the aim of pleasing Him and to grant us and our brothers, who assisted us in the production of this book, pardon and forgiveness in religious and secular matters. In addition, we ask Him that He include this work in the weight of our good deeds on the Day of Resurrection – a Day on which neither wealth nor sons will benefit anyone – except for those whom Allah has blessed with pure hearts.

And our final declaration is that all praise and thanks are due to Allah, and we invoke blessings and peace upon Prophet Muhammad and upon all his righteous family and Companions until the Day of Reckoning.

Yoosuf Al-Hajj Ahmad,
The humble slave of Allah.
Damascus, Ash-Sham (Syria).
2nd of Dhul-Hijjah, 1428 A.H.

---

(1) *Ghareeb:* A *hadeeth* which is reported at one or more stages in its chain of narrators by a single narrator.

Publisher's Preface

Verily, all praise and thanks are due to Allah. We seek His aid and we ask forgiveness of Him. We seek refuge with Allah from the wickedness in ourselves. Whomsoever Allah guides, there is none who can misguide him and whomsoever He sends astray, there is none who can guide him. I bear witness that none is worthy of worship except Allah and that Muhammad is His slave and His Messenger. He sent him with guidance and the true Religion and with the light (of truth), the admonition and wisdom, at a time when no Messengers were sent for a long period, when there was little religious knowledge and the people had gone astray, when the Hour was drawing nearer. Whoever obeys Allah and His Messenger has followed the right course, while whoever disobeys Allah and His Messenger erred from it and gone far astray. To proceed:

The book *Al-Bidayah* (*The Beginning*) by the *Hafiz*, the *Imam*, the scholarly critic, Ibn Katheer is an incomparable work regarding the study of the events and their chronological order, the knowledge of which he strove hard to acquire. He began by describing the start of creation – from the creation of the Throne and the *Kursi* and the heavens and the Earth and all that is in them and all that lies between them, such as the angels, the jinn and the devils and he described the manner of Adam's creation ﷺ. He recounted the stories of the Prophets and the events that took place therein, up to the times of the Children of Isra'eel and the Days of Ignorance, which ended with the advent of the final Prophet, Muhammad ﷺ. Then he gave a detailed description of his life and what happened after that, up to the time in which he lived. He then wrote a separate volume called *An-Nihayah Fil – Fitan Wal-Malahim* (The Ending With Trials and Great Battles).

Furthermore, Allah inspired us to undertake the noble task of making this book easily accessible to both the students and the scholars and then to translate it into several languages, by Allah's Permission.

I suggested to my brother, Yoosuf Al-Hajj, the necessity of summarizing this book in a suitable manner, through the omission of unbeneficial repetition, weak *ahadeeth*, lengthy poems, etc. I am thankful to brother Yoosuf for assembling a team that consisted of Abdul Malik Wadih, Abu Muslim Al-Jaza'iri, Muwaffeq Khaleel Hammad, and himself. Darussalam funded the entire project, paying each team member for his contribution and work. After they completed their portion of the project, the work then went through numerous people in the Research Division of Darussalam, who meticulously went through the work, adding and subtracting materials. After this, the project went through another round of editing of the Arabic material before it was sent to the translation department. The translation was then checked for accuracy and then sent for editing, resulting in the final project that you see before you. All praise and thanks be to Allah for allowing us to produce such a classical work for the first time in the English language.

O Allah! We ask that You bless us with sincerity and success and that You spread goodness through our hands.

'Abdul Malik Mujahid.
Jumadal-Oola 1431 A.H.

Mention of the Story of Moosa, Al-Kaleem عليه السلام

He was Moosa, son of 'Imran, son of Qahith, son of 'Azir, son of Lowi, son of Ya'qoob, son of Ishaq, son of Ibraheem (peace be upon them). Allah, Most High, says, *"And mention in the Book (this Qur'an) Moosa. Verily! He was chosen and he was a Messenger (and) a Prophet. And We called him from the right side of the Mount, and made him draw near to Us for a talk with him (Moosa). And We bestowed on him his brother Haroon (Aaron), (also) a Prophet, out of Our Mercy."* (*Soorah Maryam* 19:51-53) Allah mentions him at different places in the Qur'an and He mentions his story at several places, both in brief as well as in detail. We have spoken about this at relevant places in the *Tafseer* and we shall set forth his life story here from the beginning to the end, as related in the Qur'an and the *Sunnah*. We shall also mention what has been related in the traditions that have been transmitted from *Isra'eeliyyat* – those which were mentioned by the *Salaf* and those mentioned by others – if Allah wills; and in Him we place our trust and on Him we depend.

He, Most High, says, **"Ta Seen Meem.** (These letters are one of the miracles of the Qur'an, and none but Allah, Alone, knows their meanings). *These are Verses of the Book (that makes clear truth from falsehood, good from evil, etc.). We recite to you some of the news of Moosa and Fir'awn in truth, for a people who believe (those who believe in Qur'an, and in the Oneness of Allah). Verily, Fir'awn exalted himself in the land and made its people sects, weakening a group among them, killing their sons, and letting their females live. Verily, he was of the* **mufsidoon** *(i.e. those who commit great sins and crimes, oppressors, tyrants, etc.). And We wished to do a favor to those who were weak (and oppressed) in the land, and to make them rulers and to make them the inheritors, And to establish them in the land, and We let Fir'awn and Haman and their hosts receive from them that which they feared."* (*Soorah Al-Qasas* 28:1-6)

Allah, Most High, mentions the story in brief and then He explains it in detail after that. He mentions that He is relating to His Prophet (Muhammad ﷺ) the story of Moosa الله‎ and Fir'awn in truth; that is, the true facts which were heard and witnessed by those who were present at the time.*"Verily, Fir'awn exalted himself in the land and made its people sects. "* (*Soorah Al-Qasas* 28:4) That is, he behaved tyrannically, was insolent, exceeded all limits, committed outrages, preferred the life of this world (to the life of the Hereafter) and refused to obey his Lord, Most High, ﷻand made its people sects" (*Soorah Al-Qasas* 28:4). That is, he divided his subjects into groups and classes, ﷻweakening a group among them" (*Soorah Al-Qasas* 28:4). The group referred to is the tribe of Banu Isra'eel, who were from the offspring of Prophet Ya'qoob, son of Ishaq, son of Ibraheem, Allah's *Khaleel,* peace be upon them all, who were at that time, the best people on Earth. This unjust, tyrannical, disbelieving, iniquitous king had gained mastery over them, enslaved them and used them to perform vilest, the meanest and the lowest of tasks, in addition to which, he was *"killing their sons, and letting their females live. Verily, he was of the* **mufsidoon.***"* (*Soorah Al-Qasas* 28:4) His justification for doing these wicked things was that the Children of Isra'eel used to study the religious texts that were in their possession, which they had transmitted from Ibraheem عليه السلام; these texts claimed that from his progeny a baby boy would be born at whose hands the king of Egypt would be destroyed. It was said – and Allah knows best the truth of this – that this was revealed to Ibraheem عليه السلام at the time when the king of Egypt attempted to carry out his evil desires with Sarah, the wife of *Al-Khaleel* عليه السلام and Allah protected her from him. These tidings were well-known to the Children of Isra'eel and the Copts spoke of them among themselves until news of them was communicated to Fir'awn by his governors and nobles when they would sit and talk with him in the evenings. Upon hearing this, he ordered that the sons of Banu Isra'eel be killed, in order to prevent that prophesied child from being born, but no precaution can circumvent what has been ordained by Allah.

It means that Fir'awn took every possible precaution to prevent Moosa from growing up to fulfill the prophecy, to such an extent that he appointed men and midwives, whose duty it was to visit the houses of the pregnant women and to find out their expected delivery dates. Then, whenever a woman would give birth to a boy, those slaughterers would kill him at once. According to the People of the Scripture, he ordered the killing of the males in order to weaken the power of the Children of Isra'eel, so that they could not resist them if they fought them. But this claim is doubtful; indeed, it is false, because this order to kill their sons was only given after Moosa عليه السلام was sent, as He, Most High, says,

"Then, when he brought them the Truth from Us, they said, 'Kill the sons of those who believe with him and let their women live'." (*Soorah Ghafir* 40:25) This was because the Children of Isra'eel said to Moosa عليه السلام *"We (the Children of Isra'eel) have suffered troubles before you came to us, and since you have come to us."* (*Soorah Al-A'raf* 7:129) So the truth is that Fir'awn only ordered the killing of their sons at first as a precaution, in order to prevent the coming of Moosa عليه السلام. He did all this, but the Fate said, "O, you tyrannical king, who is deceived by his large army, his great power and his extensive authority! The Greatest (i.e. Allah) – Whom none can defeat and none can resist, Whose Ordainments cannot be contradicted, has decreed that this child against whom you seek to guard yourself, due to which you have killed untold number of innocent souls, will be brought up in none other than your own house and upon your own bed and he will not partake of any food or drink but yours, which is served in your home. It is you who will raise him and educate him, while you are his enemy; yet you will not discover the significance of all this, and then your destruction in this world and in the Hereafter will be at his hands, because of your opposition to the clear truth that he brings and your rejection of the Revelation given to him. This is in order that you and all of the mankind may know that the Lord of the heavens and the Earth is the Doer of what He wills and that He is the All-Powerful, the Stern, Owner of Strength and Power and Will which cannot be opposed.

Allah, Most High, says, *"And We inspired the mother of Moosa, (saying), 'Suckle him (Moosa), but when you fear for him, then cast him into the river and fear not, nor grieve. Verily! We shall bring him back to you, and shall make him one of (Our) Messengers.' Then the household of Fir'awn picked him up, that he might become for them an enemy and a (cause of) grief. Verily! Fir'awn, Haman and their hosts were sinners. And the wife of Fir'awn said, 'A comfort of the eye for me and for you. Kill him* not, perhaps he may be of benefit to us, or we may adopt him as a son.' And they perceived not (the result of that)." (*Soorah Al-Qasas* 28:7-9) This Revelation was an inspiration and spiritual guidance, as He, Most High, says, "*And your Lord inspired the bee, saying, 'Take you habitations in the mountains and in the trees and in what they erect. Then, eat of all fruits, and follow the ways of your Lord made easy (for you)'.*" (*Soorah An-Nahl* 16:68,69) This was not the Revelation of Prophethood, as Ibn Hazm and more than one from among the rationalists claimed. The correct interpretation is the first, as reported by Abul-Hasan Al-Ash'ari from the *madhab*[1] of *Ahlus-Sunnah Wal-Jama'ah.*[2]

Allah placed in her heart and her soul that she should not fear and she should not grieve, because if he went away from her, Allah would return him to her and He would make him a Prophet and Messenger, whose word would be raised high in this life and in the Hereafter. So she did as she was commanded to do and she placed him in a basket in the river, but she neglected to secure the end of the rope to the shore and so the Nile carried him away and the basket passed by the abode of Fir'awn. "*Then they picked him up.*" (*Soorah Al-Qasas* 28:8) He, Most High, says, "*that he might become for them an enemy and a (cause of) grief.*" (*Soorah Al-Qasas* 28:8). Some said that the letter *lam* used in the Verse is *lam al-'aqibah.*[3] And it would appear to be so, although it pertains to the preceding words: "*Then the household of Fir'awn picked him up.*" (*Soorah Al-Qasas* 28:8) But if it is understood to relate to the meaning of the words, which is that the family of Fir'awn were predestined to find him, so that he should become an enemy to them and a (cause of) grief, then the *lam* will be for justification

---

(1)   *Madhab*: Teaching, doctrine, belief, school of thought, etc.

(2)   *Ahlus-Sunnah Wal-Jama'ah*: The followers of the *Sunnah* and the "group" (i.e. the united group of scholars who follow consensus and despise differing).

(3)   *Lam Al-'Aqibah*: Denoting consequences.

or explanation, and Allah knows better. This second supposition is strengthened by the Words of Allah: "Verily! Fir'awn, Haman" (*Soorah Al-Qasas* 28:8) Haman was Fir'awn's wicked *Wazeer "and their hosts"* (*Soorah Al-Qasas* 28:8) That is, those who followed them both *"were sinners"* (*Soorah Al-Qasas* 28:8) It means, they followed what was contrary to the truth, and so they deserved this punishment and pain.

The scholars of *tafseer* mentioned that the servants picked him up from the water and he was in a closed box, but they did not venture to open it until they had placed it in the hands of Fir'awn's wife, whose name was Asiyah, daughter of Muzahim, son of 'Ubaid, son of Ar-Rayyan Ibn Al-Waleed, who had been the Fir'awn of Egypt during the time of Yoosuf عليه السلام. It was said that she was from Banu Isra'eel, from the descendants of Moosa عليه السلام. It was also said that she was his paternal aunt; this was reported by As-Suhaili. And Allah knows better.

We will relate the praises and commendations that have been heaped on her in the story of Maryam, daughter of 'Imran, and how, on the Day of Resurrection, they will be with the wives of the Messenger of Allah ﷺ in Paradise.[1] When she opened the box and removed the covering from him, she saw his face, which was radiant with the light of Prophethood and the Mosaic Illustriousness. When she saw him, she immediately loved him intensely. When Fir'awn came, he said, "What is this?" And he ordered that he be slaughtered; but she snatched the baby from him and pushed him away, saying, *"A comfort of the eye for me and for you."* (*Soorah Al-Qasas* 28:9) But Fir'awn said to her, *"As for you, he may be; but for me, no."* That is, I have no need of him. She said, *"maybe he will profit us..."* (*Soorah Al-Qasas* 28:9)

---

[1] Narrated by At-Tabarani in *Al-Kabeer* (22/451, No. 1100), Ibn 'Asakir (70/119). I say: It was also mentioned by the author in the *Tafseer* (4/391), where he said: "It is weak; it was narrated in a *mursal* form, on the authority of Ibn Abi Dawood.

Allah granted her that benefit which she hoped for: In this world, it was that Allah guided her through him and in the Hereafter, it was that He made her to reside in His Paradise because of him.

"Or we shall adopt him as a son." (*Soorah Al-Qasas* 28:9) This was because they brought him up, as they had no children of their own.

Allah, Most High, says, *"And they perceived not (the result of that"* (*Soorah Al-Qasas* 28:9) means that, they did not know what Allah had willed for them, that He had ordained for them to pick him up as part of His Plan to bring Divine Retribution to Fir'awn and his hosts. *"And the heart of the mother of Moosa became empty. She was very near to disclose him, had We not strengthened her heart (with faith), so that she might remain as one of the Believers. And she said to his (Moosa's) sister, 'Follow him.' So she (his sister) watched him from a* **junub,** *while they perceived not. And We had already forbidden (other) foster suckling mothers for him, until she (his sister came up and) said, 'Shall I direct you to a household who will rear him for you, and sincerely they will look after him in a good manner?' So did We restore him to his mother, that she might be delighted, and that she might not grieve, and that she might know that the Promise of Allah is true. But most of them know not."* (*Soorah Al-Qasas* 28:10-13)

'Abdullah Ibn 'Abbas ﷺ, Mujahid, 'Ikrimah, Sa'eed Ibn Jubair, Abu 'Ubaidah, Al-Hasan, Qatadah, Ad-Dahhak and others all said regarding His Saying: *"And the heart of the mother of Moosa became empty"* (*Soorah Al-Qasas* 28:10) which it means: her heart became empty of all worldly matters, except Moosa ﷺ. *"She was very near to disclose him"* means to disclose his case, namely that the child was her son and to ask about him openly *"had We not strengthened her heart"* means made her patient and strong *"so that she might remain as one of the Believers. And she said to his (Moosa's) sister, 'Follow him'."* She was her grownup daughter. That is, go after him and seek information about him. *"She (his sister) watched him from a* **junub.***"* Mujahid said that it means: from a distance.[1]

Qatadah said, "She began to observe him, (casually,) as if she had no interest in him, which is why Allah, Most High, says, *while they perceived not."* This was because, when Moosa ﷺ was taken to live in Fir'awn's house, they wanted to provide him with a wet-nurse, but he would not accept the breast of any of them, nor would he eat any food. So they felt at a loss as to what to do for him, having exerted all of their efforts to find some way to feed him, but to no avail. As He, Most High, says, "And We had already forbidden (other) foster suckling mothers for him." (*Soorah Al-Qasas* 28:12) So they sent him with the midwives and maids to the marketplace, in the hope that they would find someone whose milk he would accept. While they were standing with him and the people were busy looking at him, his sister espied him, but she did not reveal that she knew him. Instead she said, "Shall I direct you to a household who will rear him for you, and sincerely they will look after him in a good manner?" (*Soorah Al-Qasas* 28:12) According to 'Abdullah Ibn 'Abbas ﷺ, when she said this, they said to her, they had some doubts about her, so they seized her and asked her how she knew these people will be sincere and care for him? She said to them, "They will be sincere and will care for him because they want the king to be happy and because they hope for some reward." So they let her go. After what she said, being safe from their harm, they took her to their house and brought the baby to his mother. She gave him her breast and he accepted it, so they rejoiced and sent the glad tidings to the wife of Fir'awn. She called for Moosa's mother, treating her kindly and rewarding her generously. She did not realize that she was his real mother, but she saw that the baby accepted her breast.

---

(1) 'Abdullah Ibn 'Abbas ﷺ said that it means: from the side.

Then Asiyah asked her to stay with her and nurse the baby, but she refused, saying, "I have a husband and children, and I cannot stay with you, but if you would like me to nurse him in my own home, I will do that." Fir'awn's wife agreed to that, and paid her a regular salary and gave her extra gifts and clothing and treated her kindly. The mother of Moosa عليه السلام came back with her child, happy that after a time of fear Allah granted her security, prestige and ongoing provision. There was only a short time between the distress and the way out, a day and night, or thereabouts. And Allah knows best. Glory be to the One in Whose Hands are all things; what He wills happens and what He does not will does not happen. He is the One Who grants those who fear Him, a way out from every worry and distress, Allah says, *"So did We restore him to his mother, that she might be delighted, and that she might not grieve, and that she might know that the Promise of Allah is true."* (*Soorah Al-Qasas* 28:13) That is, We promised to return him to her and make him a Messenger; so his return to her is proof of the truth of the glad tidings of his status as a Messenger. But most of them know not." (*Soorah Al-Qasas* 28:13)

Allah bestowed this favor on Moosa عليه السلام on the night when He spoke to him, and among the things He said to him was: *"And indeed We conferred a favor on you another time (before). When We inspired your mother with that which We inspired. Saying, 'Put him (the child) into the taboot (a box or a case or a chest) and put it into the river (Nile), then the river shall cast it up on the bank, and there, an enemy of Mine and an enemy of his shall take him.' And I endued you with love from Me, in order that you may be brought up under My Eye."* (*Soorah Ta Ha* 20:37-39) This was that no person saw him except that he loved him. *"that you may be brought up under My Eye."* (*Soorah Ta Ha* 20:39) Qatadah and others among the *Salaf* said that it means: You will be fed and given a pleasant life and you will be given the best foods to eat and the finest garments to wear. All of this is due to My Protection and My Supervision of you in that which I have created in you and for you and the things that I have ordained, which no one besides Me could do. *"When your sister went and said, 'Shall I show you one who will nurse him?' So We restored you to your mother, that she might cool her eyes and she should not grieve. Then you did kill a man, but We saved you from great distress and tried you with a heavy trial."* (*Soorah Ta Ha* 20:40)

He, Most High, says, *"And when he attained his full strength, and was perfect (in manhood), We bestowed on him Hukman (Prophethood, right judgment of the affairs) and religious knowledge (of the Religion of his forefathers i.e. Islamic Monotheism). And thus do We reward the* **muhsinoon** *(i.e. those who do good – see the footnote of V. 9:120). And he entered the city at a time of unawareness of its people, and he found there two men fighting – one of his party (his Religion – from the Children of Isra'eel), and the other of his foes. The man of his (own) party asked him for help against his foe, so Moosa struck him with his fist and killed him. He said, 'This is of Shaitan's doing, verily, he is a plain misleading enemy.' He said, 'My Lord! Verily, I have wronged myself, so forgive me.' Then He forgave him. Verily, He is the Oft-Forgiving, the Most Merciful. He said, 'My Lord! For that with which You have favored me, I will never more be a helper for the* **mujrimoon** *(criminals, those disobedient to Allah, polytheists and sinners, etc.)'!"* (*Soorah Al-Qasas* 28:14-17) Allah, Most High, mentioned that He blessed Moosa's mother by returning him to her and by the Kindness and Grace He bestowed on her following this. Then He described how, when Moosa ﷺ grew up and became a man of fine physique and exemplary character – according to most authorities, he was aged forty years – Allah bestowed wisdom and knowledge on him, i.e. Prophethood and the Message, the glad tidings of which He informed Moosa's mother in His Words: *"Verily! We shall bring him back to you, and shall make him one of (Our) Messengers."* (*Soorah Al-Qasas* 28:7)

Then He, Most High, described the cause of Moosa's departure from Egypt, his journey to the land of Madyan and his residence there for the time ordained for him, and how Allah spoke to him and ennobled him with that which He ennobled him, as we shall make clear. Allah, Most High, says, *"And he entered the city at a time of unawareness of its people."* (*Soorah Al-Qasas* 28:15) 'Abdullah Ibn 'Abbas ﷺ, Sa'eed Ibn Jubair, 'Ikrimah, Qatadah and As-Suddi said that this was in the middle of the day. It was also reported on the authority of 'Abdullah Ibn 'Abbas ﷺ that he said that it was between the two *'isha's*[(1)] *"and he found there two men fighting"* (*Soorah Al-Qasas* 28:15) means exchanging blows and struggling with one another *"one of his party"*. That is, one of them being from among the Children of Isra'eel *"and the other of his foes"*. That is, the other being from among the Copts. This was said by 'Abdullah Ibn 'Abbas ﷺ, Qatadah, As-Suddi and Muhammad Ibn Ishaq. *"The man of his (own) party asked him for help against his foe."* (*Soorah Al-Qasas* 28:15) This was because Moosa ﷵ possessed power in Egypt, due to the fact that he had been adopted and brought up by Fir'awn in his palace. As a result of this, the Children of Isra'eel had gained a degree of strength and respect and they acquired prestige and status due to the fact that one of them had breastfed him, which made them his "uncles", i.e. through a foster relationship. So when that Isra'eelite requested Moosa's help against the Copt, Moosa ﷵ advanced toward him *"so Moosa struck him."* (*Soorah Al-Qasas* 28:15) Mujahid said that it means that he struck him a blow with his fist. Qatadah said that he struck him with a stick that he had with him *"and killed him."* (*Soorah Al-Qasas* 28:15) That is, he died as a result of the blow; and that Copt was a disbeliever, who ascribed partners to Allah, the Almighty. Moosa ﷵ had not intended to kill him; he had only intended to restrain him and curb his aggression. Because of this, Moosa ﷵ said, *"This is of Shaitan's doing, verily, he is a plain misleading enemy.' He said,*

---

(1)   That is, between the time of the *maghrib* prayer and the *'isha'* prayer.

'My Lord! Verily, I have wronged myself, so forgive me.' Then He forgave him. Verily, He is the Oft-Forgiving, the Most Merciful. He said, 'My Lord! For that with which You have favored me, I will never more be a helper for the **mujrimoon** *(criminals, those disobedient to Allah, polytheists, sinners, etc.)!"* (*Soorah Al-Qasas* 28:15-17)

And He, Most High, says, *"So he became afraid, looking about in the city (waiting as to what would be the result of his crime of killing), when, behold, the man who had sought his help the day before, called for his help (again). Moosa said to him, 'Verily, you are a plain misleader!' Then, when he decided to seize the man who was an enemy to both of them, the man said, 'O, Moosa! Is it your intention to kill me as you killed a man yesterday? Your aim is nothing but to become a tyrant in the land, and not to be one of those who do right.' And there came a man running, from the farthest end of the city. He said, 'O, Moosa! Verily, the chiefs are taking counsel together about you, to kill you, so escape. Truly, I am to you of those who give sincere advice.' So he escaped from there, looking about in a state of fear. He said, 'My Lord! Save me from the people who are* **zalimoon** *(polytheists and wrongdoers)'!"* (*Soorah Al-Qasas* 28:18-21)

Allah, Most High, informs us that the following day, Moosa ﷺ was in a state of anxiety in the Egyptian city; i.e. he was fearful that Fir'awn and his council of elders would know that the murder victim, whose case had been submitted to Fir'awn, had been killed by none other than Moosa ﷺ, while supporting a man from among the Children of Isra'eel, for this would strengthen their belief that Moosa ﷺ was one of them – and the consequences of this would be severe. So he began to walk around the city on that morning, *"so he became afraid, looking about."* It means that he started glancing about in all directions. And while he was engorssed, the same Isra'eelite who had sought his help the previous day *"called to him"* (*Soorah Al-*

Qasas 28:18) That is, he shouted to him and requested his help against another man with whom he had picked a fight. But Moosa ﷺ rebuked him and blamed him for his repeated wickedness and argumentativeness, saying to him, *"Verily, you are a plain misleader!"* (*Soorah Al-Qasas* 28:18) Then, when he intended to fight with that Copt – who was the enemy of Moosa ﷺ and of the Isra'eelite – to restrain him and rescue the Isra'eelite from him, he advanced toward the Copt, *"The man said, 'O, Moosa! Is it your intention to kill me as you killed a man yesterday? Your aim is nothing but to become a tyrant in the land, and not to be one of those who do right'."* (*Soorah Al-Qasas* 28:19) Some said that these words were spoken by the Isra'eelite, who was aware of what Moosa ﷺ had done the previous day; and it was as if, when he saw him advancing on the Copt, he thought that Moosa ﷺ wanted to hit him because of his rebuke to him, *"Verily, you are a plain misleader!"* (*Soorah Al-Qasas* 28:18) and so he said those words to Moosa ﷺ (in self-defense). Thus he made known what had transpired the previous day and the Copt went to Fir'awn and incited him against Moosa ﷺ.

What is intended here is that Fir'awn was informed that Moosa ﷺ was the man who had killed the Copt the previous day and so he sent his people out to look for him. But they were preceded by an advisor, who had taken a shortcut to reach him *"And there came a man running, from the farthest end of the city."* (*Soorah Al-Qasas* 28:20). That is, hastening to him, because he was concerned for his safety. He said, *"O, Moosa! Verily, the chiefs are taking counsel together about you, to kill you, so escape"* (*Soorah Al-Qasas* 28:20) means so, you escape from this land. *"Truly, I am to you of those who give sincere advice."* That is, in what I say to you. Allah, Most High, says, *"so he escaped from there, looking about in a state of fear,"* (*Soorah Al-Qasas* 28:21) meaning he left the land of Egypt immediately, being unaware of which road he was taking and not knowing where it would lead him, saying, *"My Lord! Save me from the people who are* **zalimoon.***"* (*Soorah Al-Qasas* 28:21).

And He, Most High, says, *"And when he went toward (the land of) Madyan he said, 'It may be that my Lord guides me to the Right Way.' And when he arrived at the water of Madyan (Midian) he found there a group of men watering (their flocks), and besides them he found two women who were holding back. He said, 'What is the matter with you?' They said, 'We cannot water (our flocks) until the shepherds take (their flocks). And our father is a very old man.' So he watered (their flocks) for them, then he turned back to shade, and said, 'My Lord! Truly, I am in need of whatever good that You bestow on me'!"* (*Soorah Al-Qasas* 28:22-24).

Allah, Most High, informs us about the departure of His slave, His Messenger and His *Kaleem*[1] from Egypt *"looking about in a state of fear."* That is, afraid that one of Fir'awn's men would recognize him, while he had no idea in which direction he was heading, or where his footsteps were taking him. This was due to the fact that he had never before left Egypt. *"And when he went toward (the land of) Madyan"* (*Soorah Al-Qasas* 28:22) means, when he (unknowingly) embarked on the road that led him there, *"He said, 'It may be that my Lord guides me to the Right Way'."* (*Soorah Al-Qasas* 28:22). That is, haply this road will lead to (a good) destination. And that was what happened; it led him to a destination – and what a destination! *"And when he arrived at the water of Madyan"* (*Soorah Al-Qasas* 28:23) it was a well at which the people used to draw water. Madyan was the city whose inhabitants, the companions of the *Aykah*, whom Allah had destroyed. They were the people of Shu'aib ﷺ, and their destruction took place before the time of Moosa ﷺ, according to one of two opinions held by the scholars. When he reached the aforementioned water, *"he found there a group of men watering*

---

(1) Allah's *Kaleem*: The one to whom He spoke.

(their flocks), and besides them he found two women who were holding back." (*Soorah Al-Qasas* 28:23) That is, they were holding back their sheep, to prevent them from becoming mixed with the other peoples' sheep. According to the People of the Scripture, they were seven girls, but this is also a mistake; possibly there were seven daughters, but only two of them were watering the sheep. In this manner, we can reconcile the two sayings, if that is what has been (reliably) reported. Otherwise, (we must say that) it is apparent that he had only two daughters. *"He said, 'What is the matter with you?' They said, 'We cannot water (our flocks) until the shepherds take (their flocks). And our father is a very old man'."* (*Soorah Al-Qasas* 28:23) They said that, we cannot get near to the water until after the shepherds have taken their sheep away, because we are weak; and the reason why we have come here with our sheep is because our father is elderly and weak. Allah, Most High, says, *"So he watered (their flocks) for them."* (*Soorah Al-Qasas* 28:24)

He, Most High, says, *"Then there came to him one of the two women, walking shyly. She said, 'Verily, my father calls you that he may reward you for having watered (our flocks) for us.' So when he came to him and narrated the story, he said, 'Fear you not. You have escaped from the people who are* **zalimoon**.*' And said one of them (the two women), 'O, my father! Hire him! Verily, the best of men for you to hire is the strong, the trustworthy.' He said, 'I intend to wed one of these two daughters of mine to you, on condition that you serve me for eight years, but if you complete ten years, it will be (a favor) from you. But I intend not to place you under a difficulty. If Allah wills, you will find me one of the righteous.' He (Moosa) said, 'That (is settled) between me and you, whichever of the two terms I fulfill, there will be no injustice to me, and Allah is Surety over what we say'."* (*Soorah Al-Qasas* 28:25-28)

When Moosa ﷺ sat in the shade and said, *"O, 'My Lord! Truly,*

I am in need of whatever good that You bestow on me'!" (*Soorah Al-Qasas* 28:24), the two women heard him and they went to their father; it was said that he rebuked them because of their early return and so they told him about Moosa ﷺ and he ordered one of them to go to him and invite him, *"Then there came to him one of the two women, walking shyly,"* (*Soorah Al-Qasas* 28:25) means walking like a free woman. She said, "Verily, my father calls you that he may reward you for having watered (our flocks) for us." (*Soorah Al-Qasas* 28:25) She spoke frankly to him, so that her words should not excite any suspicion in him – and this was a part of her perfect modesty and chastity. *"So when he came to him and narrated the story"* (*Soorah Al-Qasas* 28:25) means, when he told him his story and related to him the events surrounding his departure from Egypt, as he fled from Fir'awn. On hearing his story, the old man said, *"Fear you not. You have escaped from the people who are* **zalimoon.** *"* (*Soorah Al-Qasas* 28:25) It means that you have left the area in which they exercise their authority and you are no longer in their lands. Scholars disagreed as to the identity of this old man; it was said that he was Shu'aib ﷺ and this is widely accepted by many; among those who related it were Al-Hasan Al-Basri and Malik Ibn Anas and he stated it positively in a *Hadith*, but there is some doubt regarding the authenticity of its chain of narrators. Another group declared that Shu'aib ﷺ lived for a very long time after the destruction of his people, so that Moosa ﷺ encountered him and married his daughter.

What is intended is that he offered him his hospitality, gave him a comfortable place to stay and informed him about his situation; he gave him the glad tidings that he was safe. At that point, one of his daughters said to him, *"O, my father! Hire him!"* (*Soorah Al-Qasas* 28:26) so that to herd your sheep; then she praised, him saying that he was strong and trustworthy.

'Abdullah Ibn Mas'ood ؓ said: The most discerning of people are three: The companion of Yoosuf ﷺ (i.e. *Al-'Aziz*), when he said to his wife, *"Make his stay comfortable."* (*Soorah Yoosuf* 12:21), the companion of Moosa, when she said, *"O, my father! Hire him! Verily, the best of men for you to hire is the strong, the trustworthy."* (*Soorah Al-Qasas* 28:26) and Abu Bakr ﷺ when he designated 'Umar Ibn Al-Khattab ﷺ as his successor.

He, Most High, says, *"He (Moosa) said, 'That (is settled) between me and you, whichever of the two terms I fulfill, there will be no injustice to me, and Allah is Surety over what we say'."* (*Soorah Al-Qasas* 28:28) Allah tells us that Moosa ﷺ said to his father-in-law, "The matter will be as you have said and whichever you decide, there will be no sin upon me; and Allah will be the Hearer and Witness to what we agree upon – and He is the Disposer of my affairs and of yours." But though he said this, he completed the ten years in full.

Al-Bukhari narrated on the authority of Sa'eed Ibn Jubair that he said, "A Jew from the people of Al-Hirah asked me which one of the two periods Moosa completed." I said, "I don't know, (but wait) until I see the most learned Arab and enquire him about it." So I went to Ibn 'Abbas ﷺ and asked him. He replied, "Moosa completed the longer and better period." Ibn 'Abbas ﷺ added, "Verily, a Messenger of Allah always does what he says." [1]

He, Most High, says, *"Then, when Moosa had fulfilled the term, and was traveling with his family, he saw a fire in the direction of At-Toor (Mount). He said to his family, 'Wait, I have seen a fire; perhaps I may bring to you from there some information, or a burning fire-brand that you may warm yourselves.' So when he reached it (the fire), he was called from the right side of the valley, in the blessed place from the tree, 'O, Moosa! Verily! I am Allah, the Lord of Al-'Alameen. And throw your stick!' But when he saw it moving as if it were a snake, he turned in flight, and looked not back. (It was said), 'O, Moosa! Draw near, and fear not. Verily,*

---

(1)   Narrated by Al-Bukhari (2684).

you are of those who are secure. Put your hand in your bosom, it will come forth white without a disease, and draw your hand close to your side to be free from fear (that which you suffered from the snake, and also by that your hand will return to its original state). These are two **burhan** *(signs, miracles, evidences and proofs) from your Lord to Fir'awn and his chiefs. Verily, they are the people who are* **fasiqoon** *(rebellious, disobedient to Allah)'."* (*Soorah Al-Qasas* 28:29-32)

We said previously that Moosa صلى الله عليه وسلم completed the longer of the two specified periods (eight years or ten years) and this may be understood from the Words of Allah: *"Then, when Moosa had fulfilled the term."* (*Soorah Al-Qasas* 28:29) It is reported on the authority of Mujahid that he completed ten years of service and another ten after that. Allah says, *"and was traveling with his family"* (*Soorah Al-Qasas* 28:29) means, he had left his father-in-law – according to what more than one of the scholars of *tafseer* and others have said – because he missed his family; so he set out to visit them in secret in Egypt. He was traveling with his family, including his two sons, and some sheep which he had acquired during his time in his father-in-law's service. The scholars said, it was a dark, cold night, due to this, they lost their way and were unable to find the path again. He tried to kindle a fire, but he was unable to do so. The darkness and cold increased and while he was occupied in trying to start a fire, he observed a fire burning at a distance, in the direction of At-Toor, which was a mountain that lay to the west of him, somewhere of to his right. He said to his family, *"Wait! Verily, I have seen a fire."* (*Soorah Ta Ha* 20:10). It was as if – and Allah knows better – he alone saw it, because this fire was from the Light of Truth and it would not be fitting that every person should see it. *"Perhaps I may bring to you from there some information"* (*Soorah Al-Qasas* 28:29) means, perhaps I can ask those whose fire it is on the way to the road. *"...or a burning fire-brand that you may warm yourselves."*

(*Soorah Al-Qasas* 28:29) It is proved that they had lost their way on a cold, dark night, because Allah, Most High, says in another Verse, *"And has there come to you the story of Moosa? When he saw a fire, he said to his family, 'Wait! Verily, I have seen a fire, perhaps I can bring you some burning brand therefrom, or find some guidance at the fire."* (*Soorah Ta Ha* 20:9,10) So this proves that there was darkness and that they had lost their way.

He, Most High, says: *"(Remember) when Moosa said to his household, 'Verily! I have seen a fire, I will bring you from there some information, or I will bring you a burning brand, that you may warm yourselves."* (*Soorah An-Naml* 27:7) So he brought them news from it – and what news he brought them! And he found guidance there – and what guidance he found! And he acquired a light from it – but what a light he acquired! Allah, Most High, says, *"So when he reached it (the fire), he was called from the right side of the valley, in the blessed place from the tree, 'O, Moosa! Verily! I am Allah, the Lord of Al-'Alameen'!"* (*Soorah Al-Qasas* 28:30)

In *Soorah An-Naml*, He Most High, says, *"But when he came to it, he was called, 'Blessed is whosoever is in the fire, and whosoever is round about it! And Glorified be Allah, the Lord of Al-'Alameen."* (*Soorah An-Naml* 27:8) That is, Glory be to Allah, Who does as He wills and decides what He wills. *"And when he came to it (the fire), he was called by name, 'O, Moosa! Verily! I am your Lord! So take off your shoes, you are in the sacred valley, Tuwa. And I have chosen you. So listen to that which is inspired to you. Verily! I am Allah! La ilaha illa Ana (none has the right to be worshipped but I), so worship Me, and perform as-salah (iqamat as-salah – Prayer) for My Remembrance. Verily, the Hour is coming and My Will is to keep it hidden that every person may be rewarded for that which he strives. Therefore, let not the one who believes not therein (i.e. in the Day of Resurrection, Reckoning, Paradise and Hell, etc.), but follows his own lusts, divert you therefrom, lest you perish'."* (*Soorah Ta Ha* 20:11-16)

More than one of the scholars of *tafseer* from among the earlier and the later generations have said that when Moosa عليه السلام walked toward that fire which he had seen, and when he reached it, he found that it was burning in a green boxthorn tree. The more the fire burned, the more the greenness of the tree increased and he stood in amazement. The tree was at the foot of a mountain, which lay west of him, to his right, as He, Most High, says, *"And you (O, Muhammad) were not on the western side (of the Mount), when We made clear to Moosa the Commandment, and you were not among those present."* (*Soorah Al-Qasas* 28:44) Moosa عليه السلام was in a valley named *Tuwa* and he was facing the *Qiblah* and that tree was on his right, in the West. His Lord called to him in the Sacred Valley of *Tuwa* and He commanded him first of all to remove his shoes, out of reverence and respect for that blessed location – and especially on that blessed night. According to the People of the Scriptures, he placed his hand on his face in awe and in fear for his sight, due to the intensity of the light. Then Allah, Most High, addressed him as He willed, saying to him, *"Verily! I am Allah, the Lord of* **Al-'Alameen!***"* (*Soorah Al-Qasas* 28:30) and *"Verily! I am Allah!* **La ilaha illa Ana** *(none has the right to be worshipped but I), so worship Me, and perform* **as-salah (iqamat as-salah)** *for My Remembrance."* (*Soorah Ta Ha* 20:14). That is, I am the Lord of the Worlds, besides Whom none has the right to be worshipped – and worship devoted to any other deity cannot benefit.

Then He informed him that the life of this world is only temporary and that the permanent abode is that of the Day of Resurrection, whose establishment is inevitable *"that every person may be rewarded for that which he strives."* (*Soorah Ta Ha* 20:15) That is, whether good or evil. He encouraged him and incited him to work for it and to avoid those who do not believe in it, such as those who disobey their Lord and follow their own vain desires.

Then He informed him that He is able to do all things, saying to a thing, "Be!" and it is: *"And what is that in your right hand, O, Moosa?"* (*Soorah Ta Ha* 20:17) means that, is this not your stick, which We have known since you had it. This is an interrogative, used for the purpose of affirmation. *"He said, 'It is my stick upon which I lean, with which I beat down branches for my sheep and for which I find other uses'."* (*Soorah Ta Ha* 20:18) That is, it is my stick which I know and of which I am sure. *"(Allah) said, 'Cast it down, O, Moosa!' He cast it down, and behold! It was a snake, moving quickly."* (*Soorah Ta Ha* 20:19,20)

This was a great miracle and an irrefutable proof that when the One Who was speaking to him says to something, "Be!" it is – and that He does as He wills.

This serpent combined huge size with lightning speed and when Moosa ﷺ saw it *"he turned in flight"* (*Soorah An-Naml* 27:10) means, he fled in fear from the snake, because it was a natural human reaction to do so, *"and did not look back."* (*Soorah An-Naml* 27:10). That is, he did not turn around; so his Lord called him, saying, "O, Moosa! Draw near, and fear not. Verily, you are of those who are secure." (*Soorah Al-Qasas* 28:31) When he returned, Allah, Most High, commanded him to take hold of it: *He said, "Grasp it, and fear not, We shall return it to its former state."* (*Soorah Ta Ha* 20:21) It was said that he feared it greatly and so he placed his hand in the sleeve of his garment and then placed his hand inside its mouth. According to the People of the Scriptures, he grasped it by its tail and when he held it firmly, it became a stick once again, with two branches. So Glory be to Allah, the Omnipotent, Almighty, Lord of the two Easts and the two Wests. Then He, Most High, commanded him to place his hand inside his garment and then to remove it, upon which he saw that it was shining white, like the moon *"without any disease"* means without leprosy or *bahaq*,[1] which is why He says, *"Put your hand in your bosom, it will come forth white, without a disease, and draw your hand close to your side to be free from fear (that which you suffered from the snake, and also by that your hand will return to its original state)."* (*Soorah Al-Qasas* 28:32)

What is meant is that when Allah, Most Glorified, commanded Moosa ﷺ to go to Fir'awn, *"He said, 'My Lord! I have killed a man among them, and I fear that they will kill me. And my brother Haroon (Aaron), he is more eloquent in speech than I, so send him with me as a helper to confirm me. Verily! I fear that they will belie me.' Allah said, 'We will strengthen your arm through your brother, and give you both power, so they shall not be able to harm you, with Our Ayat, you two as well as those who follow you will be the victors'."* (*Soorah Al-Qasas* 28:33-35)

Allah, Most High, informs us about Moosa ﷺ and his reply to his Lord, the Almighty, the All-Powerful, when He told him to go to his enemy, from whose power and injustice in the lands of Egypt he had fled, after he had killed the Copt. He said, *"He said, 'My Lord! I have killed a man among them, and I fear that they will kill me. And my brother Haroon he is more eloquent in speech than I, so send him with me as a helper to confirm me. Verily! I fear that they will belie me'."* (*Soorah Al-Qasas* 28:33,34) That is, make along with me a helper, an adviser and a supporter, who will aid me in delivering Your Message to them, because he is more eloquent in speech than I am and better able to elucidate.

Allah, Most High, says in reply to his question, *"Allah said, 'We will strengthen your arm through your brother, and give you both power'."* (*Soorah Al-Qasas* 28:35). That is proof and evidence *"So they shall not be able to harm you, with our Ayat".* That is, so they will not be able to inflict any harm on you because of your

---

(1)   *Bahaq*: Tetter, *vitiligo alba* (a mild form of leprosy).

acting upon Our *Ayat* (fulfilling Our Commands), or it was said, due to the blessing of Our *Ayat*. *"You two as well as those who follow you will be the victors."*

In *Soorah Ta Ha*, He says, *"Go to Fir'awn! Verily, he has transgressed (all bounds in disbelief and disobedience, and has behaved arrogantly and as a tyrant)." (Moosa) said, "O, my Lord! Open for me my chest (grant me self-confidence, contentment, and boldness). And ease my task for me; and make loose the knot (the defect) from my tongue, (i.e. remove my speech defect), that they may understand my speech."* (*Soorah Ta Ha* 20:24-28) It was said that he was afflicted by a speech impediment as a result of putting a burning coal in his mouth when he was a small child. This was due to Fir'awn, wanting to test his intelligence when, as a small child, he seized his beard. Fir'awn wanted to kill him (for pulling his beard), but Asiyah, fearing for him, said, "He is a baby!" So Fir'awn tested him by placing a date and a burning coal in front of him; Moosa ﷺ tried to take the date, but Fir'awn directed his hand to the coal and he took it and placed it on his tongue, as a result of which he was afflicted with a speech defect. So he asked Allah to remove a part of it – sufficient that the people might understand his speech – and he did not ask Him to completely remove it.

Al-Hasan Al-Basri said, "Messengers only ask for what is sufficient for their needs; for this reason, a little of the defect remained on his tongue. This is why Fir'awn – may Allah's curse be upon him – claimed concerning Moosa ﷺ, *"...and (he) can scarcely express himself clearly." (Soorah Az-Zukhruf* 43:52) It means that he cannot convey his meaning and express what is in his mind and his heart. Then Moosa ﷺ said, *"And appoint for me a helper from my family, Haroon, my brother; increase my strength with him, and let him share my task (of conveying Allah's Message and Prophethood), that we may glorify You much and remember You much, verily! You are of us Ever All-Seeing."*

(Allah) said, "You are granted your request, O, Moosa!" (Soorah Al-Qasas 20:29-36) That is, We have granted everything that you asked and given you all that you requested – and it was due to the high estimation in which his Lord, the Almighty, the All-Powerful held him that when he asked Allah to grant Prophethood to his brother, He did so. And this is indicative of great rank. He, Most High, says, *"and he was honorable before Allah." (Soorah Al-Ahzab* 33:69)

He, Most High, says, *"And We bestowed on him his brother Haroon, (also) a Prophet, out of Our Mercy." (Soorah Maryam* 19:53)

The Mother of the Believers, 'A'ishah, may Allah be pleased with her, heard a man saying to some people when they were traveling on the road for *Hajj* (in Makkah), "Which brother was most benevolent toward his brother?" The people remained silent, but 'A'ishah, may Allah be pleased with her, said to those around her *howdah*, "It was Moosa, son of 'Imran, when he asked for Prophethood to be bestowed on his brother, Haroon, and Allah did so. This is why Allah, Most High, says, *'And We bestowed on him his brother, Haroon, (also) a Prophet, out of Our Mercy'." (Soorah Maryam* 19:53)

He, Most High, says in *Soorah Ash-Shu'ara'*, *"And (remember) when your Lord called Moosa (saying), 'Go to the people who are* **zalimoon** *(polytheists and wrongdoers), The people of Fir'awn. Will they not fear Allah and become righteous?' He said, 'My Lord! Verily, I fear that they will belie me, and my breast straitens, and my tongue expresses not well. So send for Haroon (to come along with me). And they have a charge of crime against me, and I fear they will kill me.' Allah said, 'Nay! Go you both with Our Signs. Verily! We shall be with you, listening. And when you both come to Fir'awn, say, We are the Messengers of the Lord of* **Al-'Alameen,** *so allow the Children of Isra'eel to go with us'." (Fir'awn) said* *(to Moosa), 'Did we not bring you up among us as a child? And you did dwell many years of your life with us. And you did your deed, which you did. And you are one of the ingrates'."* (*Soorah Ash-Shu'ara'* 26:10-19) And the meaning of these Words is: So they went to Fir'awn and spoke these words to him, conveying to him the Message they had been given, which was to call him to the worship of Allah, Most High, Alone, without ascribing partners to Him; to free the slaves, the Children of Isra'eel, from his grip and his subjugation and allow them to worship their Lord as and when they wished; let them be free to declare His Oneness, invoke Him and humble themselves before Him. But Fir'awn responded with arrogance, insolence and oppression, looking on Moosa عليه السلام with contempt and scorn, saying to him, *"Did we not bring you up among us as a child? And you did dwell many years of your life with us."* (*Soorah Ash-Shu'ara'* 26:18) That is, was it not you whom we brought up in our house, to whom we showed kindness, and on whom we bestowed favors for so many years? This proves that the Fir'awn to whom Moosa عليه السلام was sent was the same Fir'awn from whom he fled. This contradicts the claim of the People of the Scriptures, who said that the Fir'awn from whom he fled died while he was living in Madyan and that the person to whom he was sent was another Fir'awn.

He, Most High, says, *"And you did your deed, which you did. And you are one of the ingrates"* (*Soorah Ash-Shu'ara'* 26:19). means, you killed the Coptic man and fled from us and were ungrateful for the favors we bestowed on you. *Moosa said, "I did it then, when I was ignorant (as regards my Lord and His Message)."* (*Soorah Ash-Shu'ara'* 26:20). That is, before my Lord inspired me and sent down Revelation to me. *"So I fled from you when I feared you. But my Lord has granted me* **Hukman** *(i.e. religious knowledge, right judgment of the affairs and Prophethood), and appointed me as one of the Messengers."* (*Soorah Ash-Shu'ara'* 26:21) Then he replied to Fir'awn regarding the favors he had given him, such as bringing him up and showing kindness to him, *"And this is the past favor with which you reproach me, that you have enslaved the Children of Isra'eel."* (*Soorah Ash-Shu'ara'* 26:22) It means that, this favor which you have mentioned, which was that you treated me with kindness – and I am one man from among the Children of Isra'eel – does it compare with the manner in which you have used this entire great nation and enslaved them with a view to making them carry out your works and serve you. *Fir'awn said, "And what is the Lord of the* **Al-'Alameen?***" Moosa said, "Lord of the heavens and the Earth, and all that is between them, if you seek to be convinced with certainty." Fir'awn said to those around, "Do you not hear (what he says)?" Moosa said, "Your Lord and the Lord of your ancient fathers!" Fir'awn said, "Verily, your Messenger who has been sent to you is a mad man!" Moosa said, "Lord of the East and the West, and all that is between them, if you did but understand!"* (*Soorah Ash-Shu'ara'* 26:23-28)

Allah, Most High, informs us of the discussion, the dispute and the debate which took place between Fir'awn and Moosa الله and the proof (of disbelief) which *Al-Kaleem* confirmed against the wicked Fir'awn, including the rational and spiritual proofs and then the tangible, perceptible proofs. This was because Fir'awn – may Allah have curse on him – demonstrated his rejection of the Creator, Most Blessed, Most High, and claimed that he was the (only) deity. *"Then he gathered his people and cried aloud, saying, 'I am your lord, most high'."* (*Soorah An-Nazi'at* 79:23,24) And he said, *"O, chiefs! I know not that you have an* **ilah** *(god) other than me."* (*Soorah Al-Qasas* 28:38) He was just being stubborn in this dispute and he knew that he was a slave, subject to Allah's Mastery and Lordship and that He is the Creator, the Inventor of all things, the Bestower of forms, the true God, as He, Most High, says, *"And they belied them (those* **Ayat***) wrongfully and arrogantly, though their ownselves were convinced thereof [i.e.*

those (**Ayat**) *are from Allah, and Moosa is the Messenger of Allah in truth, but they disliked to obey Moosa, and hated to believe in his Message of Monotheism]. So see what was the end of the* **mufsidoon** *(disbelievers, those disobedient to Allah, evildoers, liars)."* (*Soorah An-Naml* 27:14)

This is why he said to Moosa عليه السلام by way of rejection of his Message and evincing his belief that there is no lord who had sent him, *"And what is the Lord of the* **Al-'Alameen**?*"* (*Soorah Ash-Shu'ara'* 26:23) That is, the Lord of the Worlds, the Creator of these heavens and this Earth, which are visible (to all) and every oft-created thing in between them, such as the clouds, the winds, the rains, the plants and the animals, which every rational person knows, do not create themselves and require a Creator – and that is Allah, besides Whom none has the right to be worshipped, the Lord of the Worlds. *"He said"*, that is, Fir'awn said *"to those around him"*. Such as his princes, his provincial governors and his ministers, by way of mockery and ridicule of what Moosa عليه السلام had related, *"Do you not hear?"* means these words of his. Moosa عليه السلام said, addressing both Fir'awn and those around him, *"Your Lord and the Lord of your ancient fathers!"* (*Soorah Ash-Shu'ara'* 26:26). It means, it is He Who created you and your fathers, your grandparents and all of the previous generations, because every person knows that he did not create himself nor did his father and mother create themselves; and he (i.e. everybody) was not brought into being without a Creator – he was only brought into being and created by the Lord of the Worlds. And it is these two aspects that are referred to in the Words of Allah, Most High: *"We will show them Our Signs in the universe, and in their own selves, until it becomes manifest to them that this (the Qur'an) is the truth."* (*Soorah Fussilat* 41:53) But in spite of all this, Fir'awn did not wake up from his sleep, nor did he divest himself of his errors. Instead, he persisted in his transgression, stubbornness and rejection. "Fir'awn said, 'Verily, your Messenger who has been sent to you is a madman!' Moosa said, 'Lord of the East and the West, and all that is between them, if you did but understand'!'" (*Soorah Ash-Shu'ara'* 26:27,28) That is, it is He Who subjugates these shining stars and causes the celestial bodies to remain in their orbits. He created the darkness and the light. He is the Lord of the Earth and the heaven. He is the Lord of the first created people and the last. He created the sun, the moon and the moving and the fixed celestial bodies. He created the night with its darkness and the day with its light. All are under His Subjugation and Control and all of their movements are ordained by Him and follow courses decreed by Him at all times, for He, Most High, is the Creator, the Owner, and He disposes of the affairs of His creation as He wills.

When the proofs were established against Fir'awn and his specious arguments had been refuted and no words remained for him except words of obstinacy, he gave up arguing and used his authority, his rank and his power, saying, *"If you choose an **ilah** (god) other than me, I will certainly put you among the prisoners." Moosa said, "Even if I bring you something manifest (and convincing)?" Fir'awn said, "Bring it forth then, if you are of the truthful!" So (Moosa) threw his stick, and behold, it was a serpent, manifest. And he drew out his hand, and behold, it was white to all beholders!"* (*Soorah Ash-Shu'ara'* 26:29-33)

These were the two proofs with which Allah had supported him: the stick and the hand. In this situation, he displayed the great miracle, which dazzled their eyes and their minds when he threw the stick and lo, it became a serpent, manifest, i.e. with a huge body, terrifying and hideous to the beholders.

Allah, Most High, says in *Soorah Ta Ha*, *"When your sister went and said, 'Shall I show you one who will nurse him?' So We restored you to your mother, that she might cool her eyes and she should not grieve. Then you did kill a man, but We saved you from great distress and tried you with a heavy trial. Then you stayed a number of years with the people of Madyan. Then you came here according to a fixed term. And I have* **Istana'tuka** *for Myself. Go you and your brother with My* **Ayat**, *and do not taniya in My Remembrance. Go, both of you, to Fir'awn, verily, he has transgressed (all bounds in disbelief and disobedience and behaved as an arrogant man and as a tyrant). And speak to him mildly, perhaps he may accept admonition or fear Allah." They said, "Our Lord! Verily! We fear lest he should hasten to punish us or lest he should transgress (all bounds against us)." He (Allah) said, "Fear not, verily! I am with you both, hearing and seeing."* (*Soorah Ta Ha* 20:40-46)

Allah, Most High, addressed Moosa ﷺ on the night when He inspired him and conferred Prophethood on him, and informed him that He was a Witness when he was in the house of Fir'awn and that He was guarding him, protecting him and bestowing His Kindness on him. Then He reminded him of how He removed him from Egypt to Madyan by His Will, His Power and His Disposal and how he remained there for a number of years. *"Then you came here according to a fixed term."* (*Soorah Ta Ha* 20:40). That is, according to the fixed term ordained by Me. *"And I have* **Istana'tuka** *for Myself."* (*Soorah Ta Ha* 20:41) That is, I have chosen you for Myself, to convey My Message and to hear My Speech. *"Go you and your brother with My* **Ayat**, *and do not taniya in My Remembrance"* (*Soorah Ta Ha* 20:42) means, do not be weak or slack in remembering Me when you approach him, for that will be a support for you when addressing him, answering him, offering him advice and establishing the evidence against him.

Allah, Most High, says, *"O, you who believe! When you meet (an enemy) force, take a firm stand against them and remember the Name of Allah much (both with tongue and mind), so that you may be successful."* (*Soorah Al-Anfal* 8:45) Then He, Most High, says, *"Go, both of you, to Fir'awn, verily, he has transgressed (all bounds in disbelief and disobedience and behaved as an arrogant man and as a tyrant). And speak to him mildly, perhaps he may accept admonition or fear Allah."* (*Soorah Ta Ha* 20:43,44) This was from Allah's Gentleness, Generosity, Compassion and Mercy toward His creation, in spite of His Knowledge of Fir'awn's disbelief, his arrogance and his tyranny; and at that time, he was the worst of Allah's creation, yet Allah sent one who was the best of His creation at that time to him. Nevertheless, He commanded them to call Fir'awn to Allah in the best way, with kindness and gentleness and to treat him as one who it is hoped may remember Allah or fear Him, as He, Most High, said to His Messenger 🕮, *"Invite (mankind, O, Muhammad,) to the Way of your Lord (i.e. Islam) with wisdom (i.e. with the Divine Inspiration and the Qur'an) and fair preaching, and argue with them in a way that is better."* (*Soorah An-Nahl* 16:125).

He, Most High, says, *"And argue not with the people of the Scriptures (Jews and Christians), unless it be in (a way) that is better (with good words and in good manner, inviting them to Islamic Monotheism with His Verses), except with such of them as do wrong."* (*Soorah Al-'Ankaboot* 29:46) Al-Hasan Al-Basri said, regarding the Words of Allah: "And speak to him mildly" (*Soorah Ta Ha* 20:44) means, be tolerant and forbearing with him and say to him, "Verily, you have a Lord and you have a Hereafter – and before you are a Garden and a Fire."

He, Most High, says, *"So go you both to him, and say, 'Verily, we are Messengers of your Lord, so let the Children of Isra'eel go with us, and torment them not; indeed, we have come with a sign from your Lord! And peace will be upon him who follows the guidance! Truly, it has been revealed to us that the punishment will be for him who denies (believes not in the Oneness of Allah and in His Messengers, etc.), and turns away (from the truth and obedience to Allah)."* (*Soorah Ta Ha* 20:47,48) Allah, Most

High, tells us that He commanded them both to go to Fir'awn and to call him upon him to believe in Allah, Most High, and worship Him, Alone, without ascribing partners to Him, and to ask him also to cease tormenting the Children of Isra'eel; free them from their enslavement and allow them to leave with Moosa and Haroon,may Allah be pleased with them both. *"And peace will be upon him who follows the guidance!"* (*Soorah Ta Ha* 20:47) That is, peace will be on you if you follow the guidance. Then they warned him against rejecting their Message, saying, *"Truly, it has been revealed to us that the punishment will be for him who denies (believes not in the Oneness of Allah and in His Messengers, etc.), and turns away (from the truth and obedience to Allah)."* (*Soorah Ta Ha* 20:48) That is, rejects the truth in his heart and turns away from acting upon it. He, Most High, says, regarding Fir'awn, *Fir'awn said, "Who then, O, Moosa, is the Lord of you two?" (Moosa) said, "Our Lord is He Who gave to each thing its form and nature, then guided it aright." (Fir'awn) said, "What about the generations of old?" (Moosa) said, "The knowledge thereof is with my Lord, in a Record. My Lord is neither unaware nor does He forget." Who has made earth for you like a bed (spread out); and has opened roads (ways and paths, etc.) for you therein; and has sent down water (rain) from the sky. And We have brought forth with it various kinds of vegetation. Eat and pasture your cattle, (therein); verily, in this are proofs and signs for men of understanding. Thereof (the earth) We created you, and into it We shall return you, and from it We shall bring you out once again."* (*Soorah Ta Ha* 20:49-55)

Allah, Most High, informs us that Fir'awn refused to confirm the existence of the Creator, saying, *"Who then, O, Moosa, is the Lord of you two?" (Moosa) said, "Our Lord is He Who gave to each thing its form and nature, then guided it aright."* (*Soorah Ta Ha* 20:49,50) That is, it is He Who created mankind and ordained for them their deeds, their sustenance and their lifespans; He recorded all of these things with Him, in His Book, *Al-Lawh Al-Mahfooz* (the Preserved Tablet). This Verse is like the Words of Him, Most High, *"Glorify the Name of your Lord, the Most High, Who has created (everything), and then proportioned it. And Who has measured; then guided (i.e. showed mankind the right as well as wrong paths, and guided the animals to pasture.)* (*Soorah Al-A'la* 87:1-3) That is, He ordained preordainments and guided His creations to them. Fir'awn said to Moosa عليه السلام, "Then if your Lord is the Creator, Who ordains everything and guides His creatures to that which He has ordained, in which case, none would have the right to be worshipped but He, then why did the earlier peoples worship deities other than Him, ascribing partners and rivals to Him from such things as the stars, as you know? Why were the earlier generations not guided to that which you have mentioned?" *"(Moosa) said, 'The knowledge thereof is with my Lord, in a Record. My Lord is neither unaware nor does He forget'."* (*Soorah Ta Ha* 20:52) That is, even if they worshipped other deities besides Allah, that is not an argument or an authorization for you to do likewise, nor does it prove anything that contradicts what I say, because they were ignorant, like you. They will be held accountable for everything that they did and they will be recompensed accordingly, by my Lord, the Almighty, the All-Powerful and He does not wrong anyone, even as little as an atom's weight, because all of the deeds of the slaves are recorded with Him in a Record and He is not unaware of any of their doeds, nor dies He forget anything.

Then he spoke to him of Allah's Greatness and His Ability to create (all) things; he described to him how Allah made the Earth a resting place and the sky a ceiling, safe and well-guarded, and He subjugated the clouds and the rains to provide sustenance to His slaves and their livestock and (other) animals, as He, Most High, says, *"Eat and pasture your cattle (therein); verily, in this are proofs and signs for men of understanding."* (*Soorah Ta Ha* 20:54)

That is, for those who possess rational minds and sound innate character, for He, Most High is the Creator and the Sustainer, as He says, *"O, mankind! Worship your Lord (Allah), Who created you and those who were before you so that you may become* **Al-Muttaqoon**. *Who has made the Earth a resting place for you, and the sky as a canopy, and sent down water (rain) from the sky and brought forth therewith fruits as a provision for you. Then do not set up rivals unto Allah (in worship) while you know (that He Alone has the right to be worshipped)."* (*Soorah Al-Baqarah* 2:21,22). And after Allah had described how He gave life to the Earth with rain and caused thereby the plants and crops to burst forth from it, He called attention to the ultimate destination (on the Day of Resurrection), saying *"Thereof"* i.e. from the Earth *"We created you, and into it We shall return you, and from it We shall bring you out once again."* (*Soorah Ta Ha* 20:55), as He, Most High, says, *"As He brought you (into being) in the beginning, so shall you be brought into being (on the Day of Resurrection) (in two groups, one as a blessed one [Believers], and the other as a wretched one [disbelievers])."* (*Soorah Al-A'raf* 7:29)

He, Most High, says, *"And He it is Who originates the creation, then will repeat it (after it has been perished), and this is easier for Him. His is the highest description (i.e. none has the right to be worshipped but He, and there is nothing comparable unto Him) in the heavens and in the Earth. And He is the Almighty, the Most Wise."* (*Soorah Ar-Room* 30:27) Then He, Most High, says, *"And indeed We showed him (Fir'awn) all Our Signs and Evidences, but he denied and refused. He (Fir'awn) said, 'Have you come to drive us out of our land with your magic, O, Moosa? Then verily, we can produce magic the like thereof; so appoint a meeting between us and you, which neither we, nor you shall fail to keep, in an open wide place where both shall have a just and equal chance (and beholders could witness the competition).' (Moosa) said, "Your appointed meeting is the day of the festival, and let the people assemble when the sun has risen."* (*Soorah Ta Ha* 20:56-59)

Allah, Most High, informs us about the wretchedness and sheer ignorance of Fir'awn, the meanness of his intellect in denying Allah's Signs, his arrogant refusal to follow them and his saying to Moosa ﷺ, *"Verily, what you have brought is no more than magic and we shall oppose you with its like."* Then he asked Moosa ﷺ that he appoint a meeting between them at a fixed time and in a designated place. And this was one of Moosa's major objectives – to show Allah's Signs and His Proofs openly to an assembly of the people, which is why he said, *"Your appointed meeting is the day of the festival."* (*Soorah Ta Ha* 20:59) That was the day of their New Year celebration and a day on which it was their custom to gather. *"And let the people assemble when the sun has risen."* (*Soorah Ta Ha* 20:59) That is, in the late morning, just before noon, when the light of the sun was very bright; in this way, the truth would be clearer and more obvious to them; and he did not request that the meeting be held at night, so that they might not be deceived by trickery and falsehood in the darkness of night. Instead, he requested that it be held in daylight and openly, because he had insight from his Lord and he had certainty that Allah would make His Word and His Religion triumphant, even though the Copts might dislike it.

Allah, Most High, says, *"So Fir'awn withdrew, devised his plot and then came back. Moosa said to them, 'Woe unto you! Invent not a lie against Allah, lest He should destroy you completely by a punishment. And surely, he who invents a lie (against Allah) will fail miserably.' Then they debated with one another what they must do, and they kept their talk secret. They said, 'Verily! These are two magicians. Their object is to drive you out from your land with magic, and overcome your chiefs and nobles. So devise your plot, and then assemble in line. And whoever overcomes this day will be indeed successful'."* (*Soorah Ta Ha* 20:60-64)

Allah, Most High, informs us about Fir'awn and how he went and gathered the magicians in his land – Egypt at that time was filled with magicians who excelled in their art – so they gathered before him from all corners of the land and they were very large in numbers.

Fir'awn came along with his princes and the governors of his provinces without exception. This was because Fir'awn had ordered their presence at this unprecedented meeting; they came out, saying, *"That we may follow the sorcerers (who were on Fir'awn's religion of disbelief) if they are the winners."* (*Soorah Ash-Shu'ara'* 26:40). Moosa ﷺ advanced toward the magicians and he admonished them and rebuked them for practicing vain and false magic, which contradicts Allah's Signs and His Proofs, saying, *"Woe unto you! Invent not a lie against Allah, lest He should destroy you completely by a punishment. And surely, he who invents a lie (against Allah) will fail miserably." Then they debated with one another what they must do.* (*Soorah Ta Ha* 20:61,62) It was said that it means that they disagreed among themselves and one of them said, "This is the speech of a Prophet and not magic," while another said, "Nay, it is magic." And Allah knows better. They spoke these words and others secretly, among themselves. *They said: "Verily! These are two magicians. Their object is to drive you out from your land with magic"* (*Soorah Ta Ha* 20:63) They said, "This man, Moosa and his brother are skilled magicians and their aim is to gather the people on their side and to attack the King and his entourage and expel you from your abodes; and they are scheming against you by this magic. *"So devise your plot, and then assemble in line. And whoever overcomes this day will be indeed successful."* (*Soorah Ta Ha* 20:64) They only said these first words in order to prepare, encourage one another and bring forth all of the tricks, deceptions, cheating, sorcery and falsehood. But how far from the truth were their beliefs and how wrong were their ideas! How could their falsehood, their sorcery and their folly oppose the proofs which Moosa ﷺ, Allah's slave, His *Kaleem* and His Messenger brought; proofs which dazzled the eyes and confused the minds. They said, *"and then assemble in line."* (*Soorah Ta Ha* 20:64) As the assembled all together they incited each other to advance in this position, because Fir'awn had promised them and caused them to hope for a great reward; but that which Satan promises them is naught but illusion. *They said, "O, Moosa! Either you throw first or we will be the first to throw." (Moosa) said, "Nay, throw you (first)!" Then behold, their ropes and their sticks, by their magic, appeared to him as though they moved fast. So Moosa conceived a fear in himself. We (Allah) said, "Fear not! Surely, you will have the upper hand. And throw that which is in your right hand! It will swallow up that which they have made. That which they have made is only a magician's trick, and the magician will never be successful, no matter whatever amount (of skill) he may attain."* (*Soorah Ta Ha* 20:65-69)

When the magicians lined up and Moosa and Haroon, peace be upon them, stood before them and they said to Moosa ﷺ, "Either you throw before us, or we will throw before you." *(Moosa) said, "Nay, throw you (first)!"* They had taken ropes and sticks and placed in them quicksilver and other substances, which would cause them to twist and turn in a manner that would make them appear to be moving of their own accord. But they only moved because of these tricks and thus they deceived the eyes of the people and terrified them. As they threw their ropes and their sticks, they chanted, *"By the might of Fir'awn, it is we who will certainly win!"* (*Soorah Ash-Shu'ara'* 26:44). He, Most High, says, *"So when they threw, they bewitched the eyes of the people, and struck terror into them, and they displayed a great magic."* (*Soorah Al-A'raf* 7:116) He, Most High, says, *"Then behold, their ropes and their sticks, by their magic, appeared to him as though they moved fast. So Moosa conceived a fear in himself."* (*Soorah Ta Ha* 20:66,67) That is, he feared for the people that they would be seduced by their sorcery and their trickery before he could throw what was in his hand, for he would not do anything before Allah commanded him and inspired him to throw at the fixed time: *"Fear not! Surely, you will have the upper hand. And throw that which is in your right hand! It will swallow up that which they have made. That which they have made is only a magician's trick, and the magician will never be successful, no matter whatever amount (of skill) he may attain."* (*Soorah Ta Ha* 20:68,69) On hearing this, Moosa ﷺ threw his stick and he said, *"What you have brought is sorcery, Allah will surely make it of no effect. Verily, Allah does not set right the work of mufsidoon (the evildoers, corrupt ones, etc.). And Allah will establish and make apparent the truth by His Words, however much the mujrimoon (criminals, disbelievers, polytheists, sinners, etc.) may hate it."* (*Soorah Yoonus* 10:81,82). He, Most High, says, *"Then Moosa threw his stick, and behold, it swallowed up all the falsehoods which they showed!"* (*Soorah Ash-Shu'ara'* 26:45)

He, Most High, says, *"Thus truth was confirmed, and all that they did was made of no effect. So they were defeated then and there, and were returned disgraced. And the sorcerers fell down in prostration. They said, 'We believe in the Lord of the* **Al-'Alameen** *– the Lord of Moosa and Haroon'."* (*Soorah Al-A'raf* 7:118-122). This was because when Moosa ﷺ threw his stick, it became a huge serpent with feet – according to what has been reported from more than one scholars from among the *Salaf* – and it also had a large neck and a gigantic, terrifying body, which caused scare among the people and forced them flee, in awe and fear, from the spot. The serpent advanced upon the ropes and sticks they had thrown and began to devour them, one after another, moving very rapidly. The people looked at it in sheer amazement. As for the magicians, they saw something that terrified them and confused them, and they beheld a thing the like of which they had never seen and never imagined, and was beyond their comprehension and devoid of capabilities to reproduce. At this point, with the knowledge of magic they possessed, they realized that this was not magic, nor was it sleight of hand, nor trickery, nor imagination, nor falsehood, nor lies, nor misguidance. Rather, it was real and none could do it except Allah, Who sent it to support the truth. Allah lifted the cover of foolishness from their hearts and illuminated them with the guidance that He had created; and He banished the hardness from them, causing them to turn to their Lord in repentance and throw themselves down in prostration before Him. They said loudly for all those present to hear, without fearing any punishment or affliction, "We have believed in the Lord of Moosa and Haroon," as Allah, Most High, says, *"So the magicians fell down in prostration. They said, 'We believe in the Lord of Haroon and Moosa.' (Fir'awn) said, 'Believe you in him (Moosa) before I give you permission? Verily! He is your chief who taught you magic. So I will surely cut off your hands and feet on opposite sides, and I will surely crucify you on the trunks of date-palms, and you shall surely know which of us (I, [Fir'awn]) or the Lord of Moosa [i.e. Allah]) can give the severe and more lasting punishment.' They said, 'We prefer you not over the clear signs that have come to us, and to Him (Allah) Who created us. So decree whatever you desire to decree, for you can only decree (regarding) the life of this world. Verily! We have believed in our Lord, that He may forgive us our faults, and the magic to which you did compel us. And Allah is better as regards reward in comparison to your (Fir'awn's) reward, and more lasting (as regards punishment in comparison to your punishment).' Verily! Whoever comes to his Lord as a* **mujrim** *(criminal, polytheist, disbeliever in the Oneness of Allah and His Messengers and sinner, etc.), then surely, for him is Hell, therein he will neither die nor live. But whoever comes to Him (Allah) as a Believer (in the Oneness of Allah, etc.), and has done righteous good deeds, for such are the high ranks (in the Hereafter), the Gardens of* **'Adn**

(Eden) (everlasting Gardens), under which rivers flow, wherein they will abide forever: such is the reward of those who purify themselves (by abstaining from all kinds of sins and evil deeds which Allah has forbidden and by doing all that which Allah has ordained)." (*Soorah Ta Ha* 20:70-76) Sa'eed Ibn Jubair, 'Ikrimah, Al-Qasim Ibn Abi Burdah, Al-Awza'i and others said that when the magicians prostrated, they saw their houses and their palaces in Paradise prepared and decorated for their arrival and for this reason, they did not pay any heed to Fir'awn's threats. This was because, when Fir'awn saw that the magicians had publicly embraced Islam and that the people were saying good things about Moosa and Haroon, peace be upon them, this made him alarmed and he saw something that confused him, robbed him of his perception and took away his sight. He was a sly, cunning and deceptive man, highly skilled in avoiding Allah's Path and so he said, addressing the magicians before the assembled crowd, *"Believe you in him (Moosa) before I give you permission?"* (*Soorah Ta Ha* 20:71). That is, did you not think to consult me before doing this terrible thing that you have done in front of my assembled subjects? Then he resorted to threats, intimidation, ranted and raved and lied and made far-fetched claims, saying, *"Verily! He is your chief who taught you magic."* (*Soorah Ta Ha* 20:71). And in another Verse, he said, *"Surely, this is a plot which you have plotted in the city to drive out its people, but you shall come to know."* (*Soorah Al-A'raf* 7:123) These words which he spoke were false, and every rational person acknowledges the disbelief, untruthfulness and folly in them; indeed, a child would not believe them, for all of those present, including the people of his country and others knew that these (magicians) had never met Moosa ﷺ before, so how could he be their chief, who had taught them magic? In addition to this, it was not he who had gathered them and he knew nothing of their gathering. It was Fir'awn who invited them and selected them from every deep mountain pass and valley, from the farthest corners of Egypt, from the cities and

from the countryside. He, Most High, says in *Soorah Al-A'raf*, *Then after them We sent Moosa with Our Signs to Fir'awn and his chiefs, but they wrongfully rejected them. So see how was the end of the* **mufsidoon**. *And Moosa said, 'O, Fir'awn! I am a Messenger from the Lord of* **Al-'Alameen***. Proper it is for me that I say nothing concerning Allah but the truth. Indeed I have come unto you from your Lord with a clear proof. So let the Children of Isra'eel go along with me.' (Fir'awn) said, 'If you have come with a sign, show it forth - if you are one of those who tell the truth.' Then he (Moosa) threw his stick and behold! It was a serpent, manifest! And he drew out his hand, and behold! It was white (with radiance) for the beholders. The chiefs of the people of Fir'awn said, 'This is indeed a well-versed sorcerer; he wants to get you out of your land, so what do you advise?' They said, 'Put him and his brother off (for a time), and send callers (men) to the cities to collect (and) that they bring up to you all well-versed sorcerers.' And so the sorcerers came to Fir'awn. They said, 'Indeed there will be a (good) reward for us if we are the victors.' He said, 'Yes, and moreover you will (in that case) be of the nearest (to me).' They said, 'O, Moosa! Either you throw (first), or shall we have the (first) throw?' He (Moosa) said, 'Throw you (first).' So when they threw, they bewitched the eyes of the people, and struck terror into them, and they displayed a great magic. And We inspired Moosa (saying), 'Throw your stick,' and behold! It swallowed up straight away all the falsehoods which they showed. Thus truth was confirmed, and all that they did was made of no effect. So they were defeated then and there, and were returned disgraced. And the sorcerers fell down prostration. They said, 'We believe in the Lord of* **Al-'Alameen***, the Lord of Moosa and Haroon.' Fir'awn said, 'You have believed in him (Moosa) before I give you permission. Surely, this is a plot which you have plotted in the city to drive out its people, but you shall come to know. Surely, I will cut off your hands and your feet on opposite sides, then I will crucify you all.' They said, 'Verily, we are returning to our Lord.*

And you take vengeance on us only because we believed in the **Ayat** *of our Lord when they reached us! Our Lord! Pour out on us patience, and cause us to die as Muslims'."* (*Soorah Al-A'raf* 7:103-126)

What is meant is that Fir'awn rejected everything, invented lies and evinced extreme disbelief in his words: *"Verily! He is your chief who taught you magic."* (*Soorah Ta Ha* 20:71) He brought forth a statement so patently false that its untruthfulness was clear to all. He said, *"Surely, this is a plot which you have plotted in the city to drive out its people, but you shall come to know."* (*Soorah Al-A'raf* 7:123) And he said, *"Surely, I will cut off your hands and your feet on opposite sides."* (*Soorah Al-A'raf* 7:124). This way he threatened to cut off their right hands and their left feet. *"Then I will crucify you all."* (*Soorah Al-A'raf* 7:124). He said that he would make an example of them and a warning to others among his subjects against emulating them, which is why he said, *"and I will surely crucify you on the trunks of date-palms."* (*Soorah Ta Ha* 20:71) He said he would place them on the trunks of date-palms because they are the highest and most visible *"and you shall surely know which of us (I, [Fir'awn] or the Lord of Moosa [i.e. Allah]) can give the severe and more lasting punishment."* (*Soorah Ta Ha* 20:71) means in the life of this world. *They said, "We prefer you not over the clear signs that have come to us."* (*Soorah Ta Ha* 20:72) That is, we will not obey you and abandon the faith in the clear signs and irrefutable proofs that has become firmly set in our hearts *"and to Him (Allah) Who created us."* (*Soorah Ta Ha* 20:72). It was said that the letter "*waw*" in this Verse means "and", and it was said that it implies an oath. *"So decree whatever you desire to decree"* (*Soorah Ta Ha* 20:72) means do whatever you are able to do *"for you can only decree (regarding) the life of this world."* (*Soorah Ta Ha* 20:72). It means that, your jurisdiction over us is limited to this Earthly life and when we move on from it to the abode of the Hereafter, we will be under the Jurisdiction of Him to Whom we have submitted and Whose Messengers we have obeyed. *"Verily! We have believed in our Lord, that He may forgive us our faults, and the magic to which you did compel us. And Allah is better as regards reward in comparison to your (Fir'awn's) reward, and more lasting (as regards punishment in comparison to your punishment)."* (*Soorah Ta Ha* 20:73) That is, His Reward is better than that which you promised us and made us aspire to and *"more lasting"* (*Soorah Ta Ha* 20:72) means more permanent than this transient, Earthly life. In another Verse, He says: *They said, "No harm! Surely, to our Lord (Allah) we are to return; verily! We really hope that our Lord will forgive us our sins"* (*Soorah Ash-Shu'ara'* 26:50,51) means He will forgive us for the sins and unlawful deeds we committed. *"As we are the first of the believers (in Moosa and in the Monotheism which he has brought from Allah)."* That is, we are the first from among the Copts to believe in Moosa and Haroon, peace be upon them both.

They also said to him, *"And you take vengeance on us only because we believed in the* **Ayat!***"* (*Soorah Al-A'raf* 7:126). That is, we are not guilty of any sin in your eyes except that we have believed in our Messenger and obeyed the Signs of our Lord, when they came to us. *"Our Lord! pour out on us patience"* (*Soorah Al-A'raf* 7:126). means to make us steadfast in the face of the punishment that this obstinate tyrant, this ruthless ruler may inflict on us *"and cause us to die as Muslims."* (*Soorah Al-A'raf* 7:126). They also said, seeking to warn him and make him fear the Punishment of his Lord, the Great, *"Verily! Whoever comes to his Lord as a* **mujrim,** *then surely, for him is Hell, therein he will neither die nor live."* (*Soorah Ta Ha* 20:74) They said to him, "So take care not to be one of them," but he was one of them. *"But whoever comes to Him (Allah) as a believer (in the Oneness of Allah, etc.), and has done righteous good deeds, for such are the high ranks (in the Hereafter)."* (*Soorah Ta Ha* 20:75) That is, the elevated abodes (in Paradise) *"The Gardens of* **'Adn**

(Eden) (everlasting Gardens), under which rivers flow, wherein they will abide forever: such is the reward of those who purify themselves (by abstaining from all kinds of sins and evil deeds which Allah has forbidden and by doing all that which Allah has ordained)." (Soorah Ta Ha 20:76) So beware of being among them. But those pre ordainments – which none can overcome and none can prevent – came between him and that (i.e. Paradise) and the Judgment of Allah, Most High, was that he would be among the inhabitants of the blazing Fire, so that he should feel the agonizing punishment that would be poured on his head from above, and that is *al-hameem*[1] and the painful humiliation. It will be said to him by way of rebuke and censure – and he is disgraced, *manbooh,*[2] wretched and base: *"Taste you (this)! Verily, you were (pretending to be) the mighty, the generous!"* (Soorah Ad-Dukhan 44:49)

It is apparent from these words that Fir'awn – may Allah's Curse be on him – crucified them and tortured them – may Allah be pleased with them all. 'Abdullah Ibn 'Abbas ﷺ and 'Ubaid Ibn 'Umair said that at the start of the day, they were magicians and by the end of it, they were pious martyrs. This is supported by their saying: *"Our Lord! Pour out on us patience, and cause us to die as Muslims."* (Soorah Al-A'raf 7:126)

When this momentous event transpired, i.e. the defeat which was inflicted on the Copts in that place and the magicians who sought help from their Lord embraced Islam, it did not increase in them in anything except disbelief, stubbornness and remoteness from the truth. Allah, Most High, says, after relating the above mentioned story in *Soorah Al-A'raf, The chiefs of Fir'awn's people said, "Will you leave Moosa and his people to spread mischief in the land, and to abandon you and your gods?" He said, "We*

---

(1) *Al-Hameem*: A boiling fluid.
(2) *Manbooh*: One who is likened to a dog, because of his wretchedness.

will kill their sons, and let their women live, and we have indeed irresistible power over them." Moosa said to his people, "Seek help in Allah and be patient. Verily, the Earth is Allah's. He gives it as a heritage to whom He wills of His slaves, and the (blessed) end is for the **muttaqoon**.*" They said, "We (Children of Isra'eel) had suffered troubles before you came to us, and since you have come to us." He said, "It may be that your Lord will destroy your enemy and make you successors on the Earth, so that He may see how you act."* (*Soorah Al-A'raf* 7:127-129)

Allah, Most High, informs us that the chiefs among the people of Fir'awn – and they were the governors and the powerful and influential – incited Fir'awn to inflict harm on the Prophet of Allah, Moosa عليه السلام, and to respond to the Message he brought with disbelief, rejection and harm, rather than belief. They said, *"Will you leave Moosa and his people to spread mischief in the land, and to abandon you and your gods?"* (*Soorah Al-A'raf* 7:127) They – may Allah humiliate them – meant that his call to worship Allah, Alone, without ascribing partners to Him, and his prohibition of worshipping deities other than Him was a corruption in comparison to the beliefs of the Copts – may Allah's Curse be on them. Some of them said, *"and to abandon you and your* **ilahah?***"* (*Soorah Al-A'raf* 7:127) means their worship of you. It is possible to understand this in two ways; one of them is "and to abandon your religion" and this is strengthened by the other recitation. The second is "and to abandon worship of you," because he used to claim that he was a god – may Allah's Curse be on him. *He said, "We will kill their sons, and let their women live."* (*Soorah Al-A'raf* 7:127) so that their fighters should not become great in numbers *"and we have indeed irresistible power over them."* (*Soorah Al-A'raf* 7:127). That is, to overcome them. *Moosa said to his people, "Seek help in Allah and be patient. Verily, the Earth is Allah's. He gives it as a heritage to whom He wills of His slaves, and the (blessed) end is for the*

muttaqoon." (*Soorah Al-A'raf* 7:128). That is, if they are bent on harming you and murdering you, then seek refuge with your Lord and bear patiently your tribulation.   *"Verily, the Earth Is Allah's. He gives it as a heritage to whom He wills of His slaves, and the (blessed) end is for the* **muttaqoon.**" It means that you be of those pious people, so that the blessed end may be yours, as He, Most High, says in another Verse, *And Moosa said, "O, my people! If you have believed in Allah, then put your trust in Him, if you are Muslims (those who submit to Allah's Will)." They said, "In Allah, we put our trust. Our Lord! Make us not a trial for the folk who are* **zalimoon** *(i.e. do not make them overpower us). And save us by Your Mercy from the disbelieving folk."* (*Soorah Yoonus* 10:84-86)

As for their saying: *"We (Children of Isra'eel) had suffered troubles before you came to us, and since you have come to us."* (*Soorah Al-A'raf* 7:129) That is, our sons were killed before you came to us and after you came to us. *He said, "It may be that your Lord will destroy your enemy and make you successors on the earth, so that He may see how you act."* (*Soorah Al-A'raf* 7:129)

Allah, Most High, says in *Soorah Ha Meem Al-Mu'min*, *"And indeed We sent Moosa with Our* **Ayat,** *and a manifest authority, to Fir'awn, Haman and Qaroon (Korah), but they called (him) 'a sorcerer, a liar'!"* (*Soorah Ghafir* 40:23,24). Fir'awn was the king and Haman was his minister; Qaroon was an Isra'eelite from among the people of Moosa ﷺ, yet he followed the religion of Fir'awn and his notables. He possessed great wealth, as we shall show in his story, which we shall relate later, if Allah, Most High, wills. *Then, when he brought them the Truth from Us, they said, "Kill the sons of those who believe with him and let their women live," but the plots of disbelievers are nothing but errors!* (*Soorah Ghafir* 40:25). The sole purpose of this killing of the male infants after the start of Moosa's mission was to humiliate, degrade and diminish the Children of Isra'eel, so that they would not have the courage to defend themselves or to attack the Copts. There were among the Copts those who warned them, but this did not benefit them and it did not deflect from the Ordainment of the One Who, (when He wills something,) simply says, "Be!" And it is. *Fir'awn said, "Leave me to kill Moosa, and let him call his Lord (to stop me from killing him)! I fear that he may change your religion, or that he may cause mischief to appear in the land!"* (*Soorah Ghafir* 40:26)

This is why the people said, by way of mockery: Fir'awn has become a "reminder", because Fir'awn, according to his claim, feared for the people that Moosa ﷺ would cause them to go astray. Moosa said, *"Verily, I seek refuge in my Lord and your Lord from every arrogant person who believes not in the Day of Reckoning!"* (*Soorah Ghafir* 40:27). That is, I have sought refuge and recourse with Allah against Fir'awn or anyone else assailing me with evil. His saying: *"from every arrogant person..."* (*Soorah Ghafir* 40:27). That is, every obstinate tyrant who will not desist or cease and fears not the Punishment of Allah, because he does not believe in the Return (to Allah, on the Day of Resurrection) or the Recompense, which is why he said, *"...from every arrogant person who believes not in the Day of Reckoning!"* (*Soorah Ghafir* 40:27)

He, Most High, says, *And a believing man of Fir'awn's family, who hid his faith said, "Would you kill a man because he says, 'My Lord is Allah', and he has come to you with clear Signs (proofs) from your Lord? And if he is a liar, upon him will be (the sin of) his lie. But if he is telling the truth, then some of that (calamity) wherewith he threatens you will fall on you. Verily, Allah guides not one who is a* **musrif** *(a polytheist, or a murderer who sheds blood without a right, or the one who commits major sins, an oppressor, or a transgressor), a liar! O, my people! Yours is the kingdom this day, you are uppermost in the land. But who will save us from the Punishment of Allah, should it befall us?"*

Fir'awn said, "I show you only that which I see, and I guide you only to the path of right policy!" (Soorah Ghafir 40:28,29)

This man was a paternal cousin of Fir'awn and he concealed his faith from his people out of fear for his own safety.

What is meant is that this man hid his belief and when Fir'awn – may Allah's curse be on him – made his intention clear to kill Moosa عليه السلام, he consulted his notables regarding this matter, the believer feared for Moosa عليه السلام and so he responded gently to Fir'awn, with words that contained a mixture of encouragement (to do good) and warning (against doing evil); he spoke in the manner of one who is asking for advice and seeking an opinion – and it has been confirmed in the *Hadith* from the Messenger of Allah ﷺ that he said, "The best *jihad* is to speak words of truth before an unjust ruler."[1]

This was the highest level of such kind of a *jihad*, because Fir'awn was the most tyrannical and oppressive of rulers; and there was nothing truer or more just than this speech, because in it there was protection of the blood of a Prophet. It is also possible that he argued with them by revealing his faith and making plain to them that which he had formerly concealed. But the first explanation appears more likely, and Allah knows better. He said, *"Would you kill a man because he says, 'My Lord is Allah'." (Soorah Ghafir* 40:28) It means that simply due to his saying that "My Lord is Allah" you would kill him. If so, this is not a just cause for killing a man; rather it is a reason to treat him with honor, respect, gentleness and forsake vengeance, i.e. especially since *"he has come to you with clear Signs (proofs) from your Lord?" (Soorah Ghafir* 40:28). That is, with miracles that prove the truth of that which he has brought from Him Who

---

(1) This is an authentic *Hadith* narrated by Abu Dawood (4344), At-Tirmidhi (2174) and Ibn Majah (4011), on the authority of Abu Sa'eed Al-Khudri رضي الله عنه.

sent him. So if you deal gently with him, you will be safe, because *"if he is a liar, upon him will be (the sin of) his lie."* (*Soorah Ghafir* 40:28). That is, that will not harm you, *"but if he is telling the truth,"* (*Soorah Ghafir* 40:28) – and you have opposed him, *"then some of that (calamity) wherewith he threatens you will fall on you."* (*Soorah Ghafir* 40:28) – and you fear that even the lightest punishment from that which he has warned you of may befall you, then what will you do if the whole punishment is inflicted on you? These words in this situation are at the highest levels of courteousness, carefulness and perfect logic. His saying: *"O, my people! Yours is the kingdom this day, you are uppermost in the land"* (*Soorah Ghafir* 40:29) was a warning that they might be deprived of this mighty kingdom, because states never oppose Allah's Religion except that they lose their dominion and are humbled after having possessed great power. And this is what befell the people of Fir'awn; they continued to doubt, oppose and resist the Message brought by Moosa عليه السلام until Allah removed them from the authority they had enjoyed, expelled them from their houses and their palaces and took away their blessings and their pleasures. Then they were cast into the sea, humiliated; and their souls were transferred from their former state of greatness and high rank to that of the lowest. This is why the believing, righteous, rightly-guided man, follower of the truth, adviser to his people and possessor of perfect understanding said, *"O, my people! Yours is the kingdom this day, you are uppermost in the land."* That is, you are in authority over the people, rulers over them. *"But who will save us from the Punishment of Allah, should it befall us?"* (*Soorah Ghafir* 40:29) means even if possessed double the numbers, preparedness, strength and power that you do, this would not avail us anything and it would not protect us from Allah's Punishment. *Fir'awn said* (*Soorah Ghafir* 40:29), in answer to all of this, *"I show you only that which I see."* (*Soorah Ghafir* 40:29). That is, I only say unto you that which I consider to be true. *"and I guide you only to the path of right policy!"*

(*Soorah Ghafir* 40:29). And he lied in both of these statements, because in his heart, he knew that what Moosa ﷺ had brought was the truth from Allah, without any doubt. He only displayed opposition to it due to sinfulness, enmity, arrogance and disbelief.

As for his saying: *"and I guide you only to the path of right policy!"* (*Soorah Ghafir* 40:29). He lied in this also, because he was not following right guidance in the matter; on the contrary, he was following foolishness, error, stupidity and vain fancy. He was one of the first to worship idols and graven images, then he called upon his ignorant, misguided people to follow him and believe his claim that he was their lord.

What is intended is to make clear the untruthfulness of his saying: *"I show you only that which I see."* (*Soorah Ghafir* 40:29) and his saying: *"and I guide you only to the path of right policy!"* (*Soorah Ghafir* 40:29)

He, Most High, says, *And he who believed said, "O, my people! Verily, I fear for you a fate like that day (of disaster) of the Confederates (of old)! Like the fate of the people of Nooh, and 'Ad and Thamood and those who came after them. And Allah wills no injustice for (His) slaves. And, O, my people! Verily! I fear for you the Day when there will be mutual calling (between the people of Hell and of Paradise)." A Day when you will turn your backs and flee, having no protector from Allah. And whomsoever Allah sends astray, for him there is no guide. And indeed Yoosuf did come to you, in times gone by, with clear signs, but you ceased not to doubt in that which he did bring to you, till when he died you said, "No Messenger will Allah send after him." Thus Allah leaves astray him who is a* **musrif** *(a polytheist, oppressor, criminal, sinner, who commit major sins) and a* **murtab** *(one who doubts Allah's Warning and His Oneness). Those who dispute about the* **Ayat** *of Allah, without any authority that has come to them, it is greatly hateful and disgusting to Allah and to those who believe.*

Thus does Allah seal up the heart of every arrogant tyrant (so they cannot guide themselves to the Right Path). (*Soorah Ghafir* 40:30-35)

Allah's *Wali* (friend) warned them that if they belied Allah's Messenger, Moosa ﷺ, the same punishments that were inflicted on the people of Nooh ﷺ, 'Ad, Thamood and those who came after them, up to the time of Fir'awn's people, would be inflicted on them. By these exemplary punishments, Allah established the proofs for all of the people of the Earth in the truth of the Messages that the Prophets brought, which showed how He exacted retribution on their rejecters and saved the *Awliya'*[1] who followed them. Furthermore, He made them fear the Day of Resurrection, which is the Day of the Gathering, i.e. when He will call the people in successive groups and they will turn on their heels in an attempt to flee, but they will find no way to do so. *On that day man will say, "Where (is the refuge) to flee?" No! There is no refuge! Unto your Lord (Alone) will be the place of rest that day.* (*Soorah Al-Qiyamah* 75:10-12)

He, Most High, informs us about the inhabitants of Egypt at that time, i.e. about their natural inclination to reject the truth and oppose the Messengers, which is why He says, *but you ceased not to doubt in that which he did bring to you, till when he died you said, "No Messenger will Allah send after him."* (*Soorah Ghafir* 40:34). That is, you continued to reject it, which is why he said, *Thus Allah leaves astray him who is a* **musrif** *(a polytheist, oppressor, a criminal, sinner who commit major sins) and a* **murtab** *(one who doubts Allah's Warning and His Oneness). Those who dispute about the* **Ayat** *of Allah, without any authority that has come to them, it is greatly hateful and disgusting to Allah and to those who believe. Thus does Allah seal up the heart of every arrogant, tyrant. (So they cannot guide*

---

(1)   *Awliya'*: Plural of *wali* (friend).

themselves to the Right Path) (*Soorah Ghafir* 40:34,35) That is, they reject Allah's Proofs and the evidences of His Oneness, and they do not have any proof or evidence from Allah. This is a thing that is absolutely abhorrent to Allah, i.e. He hates those of mankind who possess such characteristics, which is why he says, *Thus does Allah seal up the heart of every arrogant tyrant (so they cannot guide themselves to the Right Path). (Soorah Ghafir* 40:35). The first word in the Verse (*kadhalika*) has been read as meaning "likewise" and also as "thus" – and both of them are inseparable: That is, thus, if the hearts oppose the truth and do so without any evidence from Allah, He seals them.

He, Most High, says, *And Fir'awn said, "O, Haman! Build me a tower that I may arrive at the ways, the ways of the heavens, and I may look upon the **Ilah** (God) of Moosa but verily, I think him to be a liar." Thus it was made fair-looking, in Fir'awn's eyes, the evil of his deeds, and he was hindered from the (Right) Path, and the plot of Fir'awn led to nothing but loss and destruction (for him). (Soorah Ghafir* 40:36,37) Fir'awn belied Moosa ﷺ in his assertion that Allah had sent him and falsely claimed to his people that *"I know not that you have an **ilah** (a god) other than me, so kindle for me (a fire), O, Haman, to bake (bricks out of) clay, and set up for me a **Sarhan** (a lofty tower, or palace, etc.) in order that I may look at (or look for) the **Ilah** (God) of Moosa; and verily, I think that he (Moosa) is one of the liars." (Soorah Al-Qasas* 28:38). And here He says, *"...that I may arrive at the ways, the ways of the heavens." (Soorah Ghafir* 40:36,37). That is, the paths or roads. *"...and I may look upon the **Ilah** (God) of Moosa but verily, I think him to be a liar." (Soorah Ghafir* 40:37). It is possible to infer two meanings from this Verse; one of them is: I think that he is a liar when he says that there is a Lord of this world other than me. The second is in his claim that Allah sent him. The first appears more likely, based on what is known of Fir'awn's nature, because he used to deny the existence of the

Creator. However, the second is closer to the wording, since he said, *"...and I may look upon the Ilah (God) of Moosa."* (*Soorah Ghafir* 40:37). That is, so that I might see if He sent him or not. *"...but verily, I think him to be a liar."* (*Soorah Ghafir* 40:37). But Fir'awn's intention was no more than to discourage his people from believing in Moosa ﷺ and to encourage them to reject him.

Let us return to the advice of the believer and the arguments he advanced. Allah, Most High, says, *And the man who believed said, O, my people! Follow me, I will guide you to the way of right conduct (i.e. guide you to Allah's Religion of Islamic Monotheism with which Moosa has been sent). O, my people! Truly, this life of the world is nothing but a (quick passing) enjoyment, and verily, the Hereafter that is the home that will remain forever. Whosoever does an evil deed will not be requited except the like thereof, and whosoever does a righteous deed, whether male or female and is a true believer (in the Oneness of Allah), such will enter Paradise, where they will be provided therein (with all things in abundance) without limit.* (*Soorah Ghafir* 40:38-40)

He – may Allah be pleased with him – called them to the path of right guidance and truth, which is following the Prophet of Allah, Moosa ﷺ, and believing in the Message that he brought from his Lord. Then he induced them to give up the pleasures of this temporary Earthly life, which must, without doubt, come to an end. He encouraged them to seek the reward which is with Allah, with Whom no deed is lost. He is the Omnipotent, in Whose Hands is the dominion of all things. It is He Who gives a great reward for few deeds and it is from His Justice that He does not recompense an evil deed except with its like. He (the believer) informed them that the Hereafter is an everlasting abode, which He will grant to the believer, who performs righteous deeds. Such will be admitted to the highest Gardens of Paradise and Halls of Tranquility, and they will have many superior good things, everlasting blessings which will never perish or pass away. And the goodness that they will have will be more than they require.

Then he began to invalidate their beliefs and to cause them to fear the end to which they were heading, saying, *"And O, my people! How is it that I call you to salvation while you call me to the Fire! You invite me to disbelieve in Allah (and in His Oneness), and to join partners in worship with Him; of which I have no knowledge, and I invite you to the Almighty, the Oft-Forgiving! No doubt you call me to (worship) one who cannot grant (me) my request (or respond to my invocation) in this world or in the Hereafter. And our return will be to Allah, and* **musrifoon!** *They shall be the dwellers of the Fire! And you will remember what I am telling you, and my affair I leave it to Allah. Verily, Allah is the All-Seeing of (His) slaves."* So Allah saved him from the evils that they plotted (against him), while an evil punishment encompassed Fir'awn's people. *The Fire; they are exposed to it morning and afternoon, and on the day when the Hour will be established (it will be said to the angels), "Cause Fir'awn's people to enter the severest punishment!"* (*Soorah Ghafir* 40:41-46)

He had called them to the worship of the Lord of the heavens and Earth, Who says to a thing, "Be!" and it is, while they called him to the worship of Fir'awn, the ignorant man, the misguided, the cursed, which is why he said to them by way of rebuke, *"And O, my people! How is it that I call you to salvation while you call me to the Fire! You invite me to disbelieve in Allah (and in His Oneness), and to join partners in worship with Him; of which I have no knowledge, and I invite you to the Almighty, the Oft-Forgiving!"* (*Soorah Ghafir* 40:41,42). Then he made clear to them the futility of worshipping anything other than Allah, such as idols and graven images and he further explained that they have no power to benefit or harm, saying, *"No doubt you call me to (worship) one who cannot grant (me) my request (or respond to my invocation) in this world or in the Hereafter. And our return will be to Allah, and* **musrifoon!** *They shall be the dwellers of the*

Fire!" (*Soorah Ghafir* 40:43)

Then he warned them what would happen if they continued in their obstinacy, saying, *"And you will remember what I am telling you, and my affair I leave it to Allah. Verily, Allah is the All-Seeing of (His) slaves."* (*Soorah Ghafir* 40:44) Allah, Most High, says, *So Allah saved him from the evils that they plotted (against him)* (*Soorah Ghafir* 40:45) means, because of his rebuke to them, Allah saved him from the punishment that befell them, because of their disbelief in Allah and the plots they hatched in order to prevent people from reaching the Path of Allah, such as vain fancies and tricks which they imposed on the common people, which is why He said, *"encompassed"*. That is, surrounded. *So Allah saved him from the evils that they plotted (against him), while an evil punishment encompassed Fir'awn's people. The Fire; they are exposed to it morning and afternoon."* (*Soorah Ghafir* 40:45,46). That is, their souls are exposed night and day in their *barzakh*[1] to the Fire. *"And on the day when the Hour will be established (it will be said to the angels), 'Cause Fir'awn's people to enter the severest punishment'!"* (*Soorah Ghafir* 40:46). And we have already discussed the evidence in this Verse for the punishment of the grave in the *Tafseer*. All praise and thanks be to Allah.

What is meant is that Allah, Most High, did not destroy them until after the proofs had been established against them, including the sending of Messengers to them and the removal of doubts from them. And the establishment of the proofs against them was achieved sometimes by instilling fear in them and at other times by encouragement, as He Most High, says, *And indeed We punished the people of Fir'awn with years of drought and shortness of fruits, that they might remember (take heed). But whenever good came to them, they said, "Ours is this." And if evil afflicted them, they ascribed it to evil omens connected with Moosa and those with*

---

(1)   *Barzakh*: The period between death and the Resurrection.

*him. Be informed! Verily, their evil omens are with Allah but most of them know not. They said (to Moosa), "Whatever **Ayat** you may bring to us, to work therewith your sorcery on us, we shall never believe in you." So We sent on them the flood, the locusts, the lice, the frogs, and the blood: (as a succession of) manifest signs, yet they remained arrogant, and they were of those people who were **mujrimoon**." (Soorah Al-A'raf 7:130-133)*

Allah, Most High, informs us how He tried the people of Fir'awn, i.e. the Copts, with the years; and these were the years of drought during which the crops failed and no entreaty was of benefit. He says, *"and shortness of fruits"* (*Soorah Al-A'raf* 7:130) is referred to the fruits of the trees. *That they might remember (take heed). (Soorah Al-A'raf 7:130).* But they did not benefit from it, nor did they take heed; instead, they remained arrogant and persisted in their disbelief and obstinacy. *But whenever good came to them (Soorah Al-A'raf* 7:131) means abundance of crops and the like. *They said, "Ours is this." (Soorah Al-A'raf* 7:131) means this is what we deserve and what is fitting for us. *And if evil afflicted them, they ascribed it to evil omens connected with Moosa and those with him. (Soorah Al-A'raf* 7:131) That is, they would say, "This has befallen us because of their evil portents, yet they would not say regarding their good fortune that it was their blessing (from Allah) and due to their (the Copts') proximity to Moosa ﷺ and his people. Instead, their hearts were filled with rejection and arrogance and were averse to the truth. When evil befell them, they ascribed it to Moosa ﷺ and when good came their way, they ascribed it to themselves. He, Most High, says, *Be informed! Verily, their evil omens are with Allah (Soorah Al-A'raf* 7:131) means Allah will recompense them with the fullest recompensation for this. *But most of them know not. They said (to Moosa), "Whatever **Ayat** you may bring to us, to work therewith your sorcery on us, we shall never believe in you." (Soorah Al-A'raf* 7:131-132). That is, no matter what *Ayat* (i.e. miracles) you may bring, we will not believe in you, we will not follow you and we will not obey you – even if you were to bring every *Ayah*. Likewise, Allah informs us in His Saying: *Truly! Those, against whom the Word (Wrath) of your Lord has been justified, will not believe. Even if every sign should come to them – until they see the painful torment.* (*Soorah Yoonus* 10:96-97). He, Most High, says, *So We sent on them the flood, the locusts, the lice, the frogs and the blood: (as a succession of) manifest signs, yet they remained arrogant, and they were of those people who were* **mujrimoon.** (*Soorah Al-A'raf* 7:133)

Allah, Most High, says, *And when the punishment fell on them they said, "O, Moosa! Invoke your Lord for us because of His Promise to you. If you will remove the punishment from us, we indeed shall believe in you, and we shall let the Children of Isra'eel go with you." But when We removed the punishment from them to a fixed term, which they had to reach, behold! They broke their word! So We took retribution from them. We drowned them in the sea, because they belied Our* **Ayat** *and were heedless about them.* (*Soorah Al-A'raf* 7:134-136)

He, Most High, informs us about their disbelief, their arrogance and their determination to continue in their error, ignorance and refusal to follow Allah's *Ayat* and to believe in His Messenger, in spite of the great and clear signs and the profound and overwhelming proofs which Allah allowed them to witness with their own eyes. But the more signs they witnessed, and the more they weakened them and exhausted them, the more they swore to Moosa عليه السلام and promised him that if he relieved them of these (afflictions), they would surely believe in him and they would definitely send with him his followers. But every time they were relieved of these signs, they returned to the evil they had formerly practiced and they rejected the truth that he had brought to them and did not pay any heed to it. And so Allah would send upon them another sign, more severe than the last and more powerful.

So they would speak, but they would lie, and they would promise, but they would not keep their promise. *"If you will remove the punishment from us, we indeed shall believe in you, and we shall let the Children of Isra'eel go with you."* (*Soorah Al-A'raf* 7:134). So they would be relieved of the calamitous punishment, after which they would return to their vast and deep ignorance. And Allah, the Mighty, the Gentle, the Omnipotent would grant them a respite; He would not hurry them. Instead He would defer their punishment. Then He seized them after the evidence was established against them and they had received the warning. He seized them with the Seizure of the Almighty and made them a warning and an example to those disbelievers who resemble them and a lesson to those believers among His slaves who allow themselves to be admonished by them, as He, Most Blessed, Most High, says – and He is the Most Truthful of speakers – in *Soorah Ha Meem Wal-Kitab Al-Mubeen*: *And indeed We did send Moosa with Our Ayat to Fir'awn and his chiefs (inviting them to Allah's Religion of Islam) He said, "Verily, I am a Messenger of the Lord of* **Al-'Alameen.** *" But when he came to them with Our* **Ayat,** *behold! They laughed at them. And not an* **Ayah** *(sign, etc.) We showed them but it was greater than its fellow, and We seized them with torment, in order that they might turn (from their polytheism to Allah's Religion [Islamic Monotheism]). And they said (to Moosa), "O, you sorcerer! Invoke your Lord for us according to what He has covenanted with you. Verily, We shall guide ourselves (aright)." But when We removed the punishment from them, behold! They broke their covenant (that they will believe if We remove the punishment for them). And Fir'awn proclaimed among his people, saying, "O, my people! Is not mine the dominion of Egypt, and these rivers flowing underneath me. See you not then? Am I not better than this one (Moosa), who is maheen (has no honor nor any respect, and is weak and despicable) and can scarcely express himself clearly? Why then are not golden bracelets bestowed on him, or angels sent along*

*with him?" Thus he (Fir'awn) befooled and misled his people,
and they obeyed him. Verily, they were ever a people who were*
fasiqoon *(rebellious, disobedient to Allah). So when they angered
Us, We punished them and drowned them all. And We made them
a precedent and an example to later generations.* (*Soorah Az-
Zukhruf* 43:46-56)

Allah, Most High, describes how He sent His slave, *Al-Kaleem*,
the noble, to Fir'awn, the despicable, the vile; and how He,
Most High, supported him with clear and obvious signs, which
deserved to be received with exaltation and belief, abandonment
of the pagan beliefs that they followed and a return to the truth
and the Straight Path. Whereas instead of that, they laughed at
them and mocked at and they rejected Allah's Path and declined
to follow the truth. So Allah sent upon them the *Ayat*, one after
another; and each *Ayah* was greater than the one that preceded it,
because confirmation was more profound than that which came
before it. *And not an* **Ayah** *(sign, etc.) We showed them but it
was greater than its fellow, and We seized them with punishment,
in order that they might turn (from their polytheism to Allah's
Religion [Islamic Monotheism]). And they said (to Moosa), "O,
you sorcerer! Invoke your Lord for us according to what He has
covenanted with you. Verily, We shall guide ourselves (aright)."*
(*Soorah Az-Zukhruf* 43:48,49) The word "sorcerer" at that time
did not have any negative connotations, because the learned
men at that time were sorcerers, which is why they addressed
him thus when they needed him and implored him. Allah, Most
High, says, *But when We removed the punishment from them,
behold! They broke their covenant (that they will believe if We
remove the punishment for them).* (*Soorah Az-Zukhruf* 43:50)
Then He, Most High, informs us about Fir'awn's bragging of
his kingdom, the vastness of his land, of its beauty and of the
waterways which traverse it, i.e. the canals which they dug for
minimizing the effect of the Nile's flood and to make use of its

waters for irrigation purposes. Then he boasted about himself and his jewelry and began to belittle the Messenger of Allah, Moosa عليه السلام , and to ridicule him, saying that he *"can scarcely express himself clearly"* (*Soorah Az-Zukhruf* 43:52) means his speech was not clear due to the remainder of that tongue impediment, which in him was a sign of nobility, perfection and beauty and it did not prevent him from being spoken to by Allah and receiving Revelation from Him; and after that, He revealed the Tawrah to him, yet Fir'awn belittled him – may Allah's curse be upon him – because he did not wear bracelets on his arms and bore no adornments. And yet (in fact) such adornments are for women and are unbefitting an ordinary man, so what then of the Messengers, who possess the most complete discernment and understanding and the highest intentions, and are the most abstemious people on Earth, and know best what Allah has prepared for His *Awliya'* in the Hereafter.

And He, Most High, says, *"...or angels sent along with him?"* (*Soorah Az-Zukhruf* 43:53) But the matter does not require that; if the idea was that the angels would glorify and exalt him, the angels glorify and display humility toward much lesser men than Moosa عليه السلام, according to the *Hadith* which states, "Verily, the angels lower their wings for the seeker of knowledge, out of pleasure for what he is doing."[1] So what would be the manner of their humility and glorification toward Moosa عليه السلام, *Al-Kaleem*? And if the idea was that they might bear witness to the truth of his Message, then Allah has already supported him with miracles, which prove indisputably to those with good hearts and those who are seeking truth and that which is right and proper. But those who look at the outer covering and ignore what is inside it are blind to the clear proofs and plain evidences that he brought; and the Lord of lords has sealed their hearts, because of the doubt and uncertainty they feel, as was the

---

(1)   This *Hadith*, which has been graded *hasan,* was narrated by Imam Ahmad (17623) and At-Tirmidhi (3535 and 3536).

case with Fir'awn, the Copt, the blind man (i.e. blind to the truth), the liar. Allah, Most High, says, *Thus he (Fir'awn) befooled and misled his people, and they obeyed him"* (*Soorah Az-Zukhruf* 43:54) means, he deceived their hearts and minds and turned them from one state to another, until they believed his claim that he was their lord – may Allah's curse be on him and disgrace them. *Verily, they were ever a people who were* **fasiqoon** *(rebellious, disobedient to Allah). (Soorah Az-Zukhruf 43:54) So when they angered Us, We visited vengeance on them. (Soorah Az-Zukhruf 43:55)* That is, by drowning, debasement and deprivation of power, replacing might with humiliation, blessings with punishment, luxury with poverty and fine living with the Fire – we seek refuge with Allah from that. *And We made them a precedent (Soorah Az-Zukhruf 43:56)* means as a lesson for those who possessed similar characteristics. *And an example (Soorah Az-Zukhruf 43:56).* That is to those who take warning from them and fear the evil consequences that befell them, as He, Most High, says, *Then, when Moosa came to them with Our Clear* **Ayat,** *they said, "This is nothing but invented magic. Never did we hear of this among our fathers of old." Moosa said, "My Lord knows him best who came with guidance from Him, and whose will be the happy ending in the Hereafter. Verily, the* **zalimoon** *will not be successful." Fir'awn said, "O, chiefs! I know not that you have an* **ilah** *(a god) other than me, so kindle for me (a fire), O, Haman, to bake (bricks out of) clay, and set up for me a* **Sarhan** *(a lofty tower, or palace, etc.) in order that I may look at (or look for) the* **Ilah** *(God) of Moosa; and verily, I think that he (Moosa is one of the liars." And he and his hosts were arrogant in the land, without right, and they thought that they would never return to Us. So We seized him and his hosts, and We threw them all into the sea (and drowned them). So behold (O, Muhammad) what was the end of the* **zalimoon.** *And We made them leaders inviting to the Fire, and on the Day of Resurrection, they will not be helped. And We made a curse to follow them in this world, and on the Day of Resurrection, they will be among* **maqboohoon** *(those who are* *prevented from receiving Allah's Mercy or any good, despised or destroyed, etc.).* (*Soorah Al-Qasas* 28:36-42)

Allah, Most High, informs us that when they arrogantly refused to follow the truth and their king made his false claim, and they agreed upon it and obeyed him in it, the Anger of the Lord, the Omnipotent – the Almighty, Whom none can overcome and none can resist – increased upon them, and He inflicted the severest of punishments on them and He drowned Fir'awn and his followers on one morning, so that not a single one of them escaped. In fact, all of them died and entered the Fire and they continue to be cursed by the people in this world, and on the Day of Resurrection, wretched will be the state of the supporters and the supported (Fir'awn) and on that Day they will be the most abject and debased.

The Story of the Destruction of Fir'awn and His Armies

When the Copts of Egypt persisted in their disbelief, arrogance and obstinacy, in obedience to Fir'awn and disobedience to Allah's Prophet and Messenger and His *Kaleem*, Moosa عليه السلام, son of 'Imran, and Allah, Most High, bared the solid proofs against the people of Egypt and showed them the miracles which dazzled their eyes and bewildered their minds, they paid no heed; in spite of all this, they would not stop their nasty activities, would not desist and would not return (to belief) – none but a few of them believed. It was said only three, Fir'awn's wife – and the People of the Scriptures have no information about her – the Believer from Fir'awn's family whose story we have already told, and the man who came running to advise Moosa عليه السلام from the farthest side of the city, saying, *"O, Moosa! Verily, the chiefs are taking counsel together about you, to kill you, so escape. Truly, I am to you of those who give sincere advice."* (*Soorah Al-Qasas* 28:20) This was said by 'Abdullah Ibn 'Abbas ﷺ, according to what was narrated by Ibn Abi Hatim from him; and he was referring to other than the magicians, for they were from the Copts.

They kept their faith concealed because of the fear of Fir'awn and his power, his tyranny and his authoritative rule, and also that news of their accepting Islam would be conveyed to him by his chiefs, which would result in him preventing them from practicing their religion.

Allah, Most High, says, *and verily, Fir'awn was an arrogant tyrant on the Earth.* (*Soorah Yoonus* 10:83) He was an obstinate oppressor, determined to practice falsehood. *He was indeed one of the* **musrifoon** *(polytheists, sinners and transgressors, those who give up the truth and follow the evil, and commit all kinds of great sins).* (*Soorah Yoonus* 10:83) He was a disease the time for whose eradication had come, an evil fruit whose time to be destroyed had arrived and an evil soul whose destruction had been ordained.

On this, Moosa ﷺ said, *"O, my people! If you have believed in Allah, then put your trust in Him if you are Muslim (those who submit to Allah's Will)." They said, "In Allah we put our trust. Our Lord! Make us not a trial for the folk who are* **zalimoon** *(i.e. do not make them overpower us). And save us by Your Mercy from the disbelieving folk."* (*Soorah Yoonus* 10:84-86) He ordered them to put their trust in Allah and seek help from Him and to seek refuge with Him and they complied with his orders, so Allah made for them a release and a way of escape from the situation they were in. *And We inspired Moosa and his brother (saying), "Take dwellings for your people in Egypt, and make your dwellings as a* **qiblah,** *and perform* **as-Salah (iqamat us-Salah)***, and give glad tidings to the believers."* (*Soorah Yoonus* 10:87). Allah revealed to Moosa ﷺ and his brother, Haroon ﷺ that they should tell the Children of Isra'eel to take houses that were separate from the houses of the Copts, so that they might be ready to leave in case they were commanded to do so, and in that case, they would know each other's houses. As for His Saying: *"and make your dwellings as a* **qiblah***..." (Soorah Yoonus* 10:87), it was said that it means as places of worship and it was also said that it means as places in which you offer frequent prayers; this latter opinion was held by Mujahid, Abu Malik, Ibraheem An-Nakha'i, Ar-Rabee', Ad-Dahhak, Zaid Ibn Aslam, his son, 'Abdur Rahman and others.

Based on this understanding, the meaning of the Verse would be that they should seek help from Allah against the pain, misery and oppression to which they were being subjected by offering frequent prayers, as He, Most High, says, *And seek help in patience and* **as-Salah** *(the prayer) and truly it is extremely heavy and hard except for* **al-khashi'oon** *(i.e. the true Believers in Allah – those who obey Allah with full submission, fear much from His Punishment, and believe in His Promise [Paradise, etc.] and in His Warnings [Hell, etc.]). (Soorah Al-Baqarah* 2:45) And whenever the Messenger of Allah ﷺ was beset by any problem, he would pray.

Sa'eed Ibn Jubair said that *"and make your dwellings as a* **qiblah***..." (Soorah Yoonus* 10:87) means make them facing each other.

And He, Most High, says, *And Moosa said, "Our Lord! You have indeed bestowed on Fir'awn and his chiefs splendor and wealth in the life of this world. Our Lord! That they may lead men astray from Your Path. Our Lord! Destroy their wealth, and harden their hearts, so that they will not believe until they see the painful punishment." Allah said, "Verily, the invocation of you both is accepted. So keep you both to the Straight Way (i.e. keep on doing good deeds and preaching Allah's Message with patience), and follow not the path of those who know not (the* truth, *i.e. to believe in the Oneness of Allah, and also to believe in the Reward of Allah: Paradise, etc.)* (*Soorah Yoonus* 10:88,89)

This was a great and momentous invocation which Allah's *Kaleem*, Moosa عليه السلام , made against his enemy, Fir'awn, out of anger for Allah's sake, because of his arrogant refusal to follow the truth, his turning away from Allah's Path, his obstinacy, his recalcitrance, his disobedience, his dogged insistence on adhering to follow that which is false and invalid and his disdain for the clear, plain and perceptible truth and the indisputable evidence, which is why he said, *"Our Lord! You have indeed bestowed on Fir'awn and his chiefs"* (*Soorah Yoonus* 10:88) (on his followers among the Copts and those who professed and practiced his religion) *"splendor and wealth in the life of this world, our Lord! That they may lead men astray from Your Path."* (*Soorah Yoonus* 10:88). It means that those who exalt the importance of the life of this world are bedazzled by this, causing the ignorant among them to think that they are following what is correct, because of the fine things, such as garments, ships, houses and palaces, foodstuffs, beautiful landscapes, great power, etc., that they possess, but these things were theirs in the life of this world, not in the Hereafter. *Our Lord! Destroy their wealth.* (*Soorah Yoonus* 10:88). 'Abdullah Ibn 'Abbas رضي الله عنهما and Mujahid said that it means, eradicate it. As for His Saying: *"and harden their hearts, so that they will not believe until they see the painful punishment"* (*Soorah Yoonus* 10:88), according to 'Abdullah Ibn 'Abbas رضي الله عنهما, it means seal them; and this invocation was made out of anger for Allah's sake, for His Religion and for His Proofs. And Allah, Most High, accepted it and implemented it, just as He accepted the invocation of Nooh عليه السلام against his people, when he said, *"My Lord! Leave not one of the disbelievers on the Earth!"* (*Soorah Nooh* 71:26). This is why Allah, Most High, says, addressing Moosa عليه السلام when he made his invocation against Fir'awn and his chiefs and his invocation was affirmed by Haroon عليه السلام and so he was described as a supplicator also: Allah said *"Verily, the invocation of you both is accepted. So you both keep to the Straight Way (i.e. keep on doing good deeds and preaching Allah's Message with patience), and follow not the path of those who know not (the truth i.e. to believe in the Oneness of Allah, and also to believe in the Reward of Allah: Paradise, etc.)."* (**Soorah Yoonus** 10:89)

And He, Most High, says, *And We inspired Moosa, saying, "Take away My slaves by night, verily, you will be pursued." Then Fir'awn sent callers to (all) the cities, (saying), "Verily! These indeed are but a small band. And verily, they have done what has enraged us; But we are host all assembled, amply forewarned." So, We expelled them from gardens and springs, treasures and every kind of honorable place. Thus (We turned them [Fir'awn's people] out) and We caused the Children of Isra'eel to inherit them. So they pursued them at sunrise. And when the two hosts saw each other, the companions of Moosa said, "We are sure to be overtaken." (Moosa) said, "Nay, verily! With me is my Lord, He will guide me." Then We inspired Moosa (saying), "Strike the sea with your stick." And it parted, and each separate part (of that seawater) became like the huge, firm mass of a mountain. Then We brought near the others (Fir'awn's party) to that place. And We saved Moosa and all those with him. Then We drowned the others. Verily! In this is indeed a sign (or a proof), yet most of them are not believers. And verily, your Lord! He is truly the Almighty, the Most Merciful.* (**Soorah Ash-Shu'ara'** 26:52-68). The scholars of *tafseer* said that when Fir'awn and his army set out in pursuit of the Children of Isra'eel, he headed a large force.

What is meant is that Fir'awn and his army caught up with them at sunset and the two hosts saw one another and there remained no doubt and no confusion. They looked across at each other and it seemed that naught remained except for them to fight each other. At that point, Moosa's companions said fearfully to him, *"We are sure to be overtaken."* (**Soorah Ash-Shu'ara'** 26:61). This was they had had to follow a path to the sea and they had no way to go except into the sea – and none of them could do this. To their left and to their right lay mountains – and they were of towering heights. Fir'awn had trapped them and now faced them; they saw him before him at the head of his soldiers and they observed their great numbers and their preparedness (weapons, chariots, armor, etc.) and they were in a state of extreme fear and terror, because of the humiliation and deception they had experienced under his rule. So they complained to the Prophet of Allah ﷺ of their situation; but the Messenger, the honest and trustworthy said to them, *"Nay, verily! With me is my Lord, He will guide me."* (*Soorah Ash-Shu'ara'* 26:62)

Then, when the matter came to a head and the situation became critical and Fir'awn advanced with his armies, intent on their task, bearing their arms and filled with anger and resentment and the eyes (of the Children of Isra'eel) were turned away and their hearts were in their throats, at that moment, the Most Gentle, the Mighty, the Omnipotent, Lord of the Noble Throne revealed to Moosa, *Al-Kaleem* ﷺ: *"Strike the sea with your stick."* (*Soorah Ash-Shu'ara'* 26:63). And when he struck the sea, it was reported that he said to it, "Split, by Allah's Permission."

Allah, Most High, says, *Then We inspired Moosa (saying), "Strike the sea with your stick." And it parted, and each separate part (of that seawater) became like the huge, firm mass of a mountain.* (*Soorah Ash-Shu'ara'* 26:63). It was said that it parted revealing twelve paths, one for each tribe to proceed. It was even said that Allah caused apertures (like windows) to appear so that they might see each other, but this statement requires verification, because water is a transparent substance when there is light behind it. So the water was standing still, like mountains, held back by the Mighty Power which emanates from the One Who says to a thing, "Be!" and it is. And He, Most High, commanded the west wind and it burned the black clay of the sea, so that it became dry and did not stick to the hooves of their horses and the feet of their camels.

Allah, Most High, says, ❨ And indeed We inspired Moosa (saying), "Travel by night with *'ibadi* (My slaves) and strike a dry path for them in the sea, fearing neither to be overtaken (by Fir'awn [Fir'awn]) nor being afraid (of drowning in the sea)." Then Fir'awn pursued them with his hosts, but the seawater completely overwhelmed them and covered them up. And Fir'awn led his people astray, and he did not guide them ❩ (*Soorah Ta Ha* 20:77-79)

And what is meant is that when the sea was transformed in this manner by the Permission of the Lord, the Mighty, the Powerful, He commanded Moosa صلى to cross it with the Children of Isra'eel, and so they went down to it in haste, filled with happiness. And they had seen that amazing sight, which bedazzled those who saw it and guided the hearts of the Believers. Then, when they had crossed it and the last of them had emerged from it, they departed from it. This happened as the first of Fir'awn's army arrived at the path across the sea, and Moosa صلى intended to strike the sea with his staff again, so that it would return to its former state, in order to prevent Fir'awn and his army from reaching them. But Allah, the Omnipotent, Owner of Majesty ordered him to leave the sea in this state, as He, the Truthful says in His Words: ❨ And indeed We tried before them Fir'awn's people, when there came to them a noble Messenger (i.e. Moosa [Moosa] saying, "Restore to me the slaves of Allah (i.e. the Children of Isra'eel). Verily! I am to you a Messenger worthy of all trust. And exalt not (yourselves) against Allah. Truly, I have come to you with a manifest authority. And truly, I seek refuge in my Lord and your Lord, lest you stone me (or call me a sorcerer or kill me). But if you believe me not, then keep away from me and leave me alone. (But they were aggressive), so he (Moosa) called upon his Lord (saying), "These are indeed the people who are *mujrimoon* (disbelievers, polytheists, sinners, criminals, etc.). (Allah said), "Depart you with My slaves by night. Surely, you will be pursued. And leave the sea as it is. Verily, they are a host to be drowned. How many of gardens and springs have they (Fir'awn's) people left. And green crops (fields, etc.) and goodly places, and comforts of life wherein they used to take delight! Thus (it was)! And We made other people inherit them (i.e. We made the Children of Isra'eel to inherit the kingdom of Egypt). And the heavens and the Earth wept not for them, nor were they given a respite. And indeed We saved the Children of Isra'eel from the humiliating punishment, from Fir'awn. Verily! He was arrogant and was of the *musrifoon* (those who transgress all bounds in spending and other things and commit great sins). And We chose them (the Children of Isra'eel) above the *'Alameen* (during the time of Moosa [Moosa]) with knowledge, and granted them signs in which there was a plain trial ⦂ (*Soorah Ad-Dukhan* 44:17-33). The meaning of His Words: ⦂ "And leave the sea as it is" ⦂ (*Soorah Ad-Dukhan* 44:24) is: still, as it is, do not change it from this state. This was said by 'Abdullah Ibn 'Abbas ﷺ, Mujahid, 'Ikrimah, Ar-Rabee', Ad-Dahhak, Qatadah, Ka'b Al-Ahbar, Simak Ibn Harb, 'Abdur-Rahman Ibn Zaid Ibn Aslam and others.

When he left it as it was, and Fir'awn reached it and saw what he saw and witnessed what he witnessed, he was alarmed at the sight and he acknowledged what he had secretly acknowledged before, which was that this was the Work of the Lord of the Noble Throne and he recoiled and did not advance. In his heart, he regretted that he had set out in pursuit of them; but at such a time and in such circumstances, his regret profited him nothing. However, he showed a brave front to his troops and he dealt with them in an aggressive manner. But his disbelieving soul and his sinful nature caused him to say to those who scorned and despised them and obeyed him and followed him in his falsehood, "See how the sea has rolled up so that I may overtake my slaves who have run away

from my authority, abandoned obedience to me and left my land!"
And he told himself that he should go after them and he hoped
that he would be safe, but how far he was from that!

Allah, Most High, says, *And We saved Moosa and all those*
with him. Then We drowned the others. Verily! In this is indeed a
sign (or a proof), yet most of them are not believers. And verily,
your Lord! He is truly the Almighty, the Most Merciful. (Soorah
Ash-Shu'ara' 26:65-68) That is, in His saving of His *Awliya'* –
for not a single one of them was drowned – and His drowning
of His enemies – for not a single one of them was saved. And
this was a great sign and an indisputable proof of His Mighty,
the Omnipotence and of the truthfulness of His Messenger with
regard to the noble law and the righteous system of jurisprudence
that he brought from his Lord. And He, Most High, says, *And We*
took the Children of Isra'eel across the sea, and Fir'awn with his
hosts followed them in oppression and enmity, till when drowning
overtook him, he said, "I believe that **La ilaha illa (Allah)***:*
(none has the right to be worshipped but [Allah]), in Whom the
Children of Isra'eel believe, and I am one of the Muslims (those
who submit to Allah's Will)." Now (you believe) while you refused
to believe before and you were one of the **mufsidoon.** *So this day*
We shall deliver your (dead) body (out from the sea) that you may
be a sign to those who come after you! And verily, many among
mankind are heedless of Our **Ayat.** *(Soorah Yoonus 10:90-92)*

Allah, Most High, informs us how Fir'awn, the leader of the
disbelieving Copts, was drowned and how the waves plunged
him down and then raised him up, while the Children of Isra'eel
looked at him and at his troops and the great punishment which
Allah had inflicted on them, in order to gladden the eyes of the
Children of Isra'eel and heal their hearts. When Fir'awn saw the
destruction and the agony of death approached him, he regretted
and repented (of his disbelief) and at that moment, he believed,
when his belief no longer availed him, as Allah, Most High, says,

Truly! Those against whom the Word (Wrath) of your Lord has been justified will not believe. Even if every sign should come to them – until they see the painful punishment. (*Soorah Yoonus* 10:96,97) And He, Most High, says, *So when they saw Our punishment, they said, "We believe in Allah, Alone, and reject (all) that we used to associate with Him as (His) partners. Then their Faith (in Islamic Monotheism) could not avail them when they saw Our Punishment. (Like) this has been the way of Allah in dealing with His slaves. And there the disbelievers lost utterly (when Our Punishment covered them).* (*Soorah Ghafir* 40:84,85) And thus did Moosa ﷺ supplicate against Fir'awn and his chiefs, that Allah destroy their wealth and harden their hearts, *"...so that they will not believe until they see the painful punishment."* (*Soorah Yoonus* 10:88) That is, when it would no longer avail them and it would be a cause of regret for them. And Allah, Most High, had said to them both, i.e. Moosa ﷺ and Haroon ﷺ when they made this supplication, *"Verily, the invocation of you both is accepted."* (*Soorah Yoonus* 10:89). So this proves that Allah, Most High, accepted and answered the supplication of His *Kaleem*, Moosa ﷺ and his brother, Haroon ﷺ.

It is also clear from the *Hadith* narrated by Imam Ahmad, on the authority of 'Abdullah Ibn 'Abbas ﷺ, who said, "The Messenger of Allah ﷺ said, "(Regarding) when Fir'awn said, *"I believe that* **La ilaha illa (Allah):** *(none has the right to be worshipped but [Allah]), in Whom the Children of Isra'eel believe, and I am one of the Muslims (those who submit to Allah's Will)."* (*Soorah Yoonus* 10:90), Jibraeel said to me, "If you had seen me... when I thrust the mire of the sea into his mouth in order to prevent the Mercy (of Allah) reaching him."[1]

And He, Most High, says, *"Now (you believe) while you refused to believe before and you were one of the* **mufsidoon?***"* (*Soorah*

---

(1)   This is an authentic *Hadith* narrated by Imam Ahmad (2816).

Yoonus 10:91). This is a rhetorical question, implying censure and rebuke and it proves that Allah, Most High, did not accept his repentance, because – and Allah knows better – if he were returned to the life of this world, he would have returned to what he was doing before, as Allah, Most High, says, regarding the disbelievers, when they see the Fire, that they will say, *"Would that we were but sent back (to the world)! Then we would not deny the **Ayat** of our Lord, and we would be of the believers!"* (*Soorah Al-An'am* 6:27)

And He, Most High, says, *"So this day We shall deliver your (dead) body (out from the sea) that you may be a sign to those who come after you!"* (*Soorah Yoonus* 10:92). 'Abdullah Ibn 'Abbas ﷺ and more than one scholars said that some of the Children of Isra'eel doubted that Fir'awn was dead, indeed some of them even went so far as to say, "Fir'awn does not (i.e. cannot) die." So Allah commanded the sea to raise him up high, or it was said, onto the surface of the water, or it was also said, onto an elevated piece of land – and he was wearing his armor, which they recognized and by which they were able to confirm that he was dead and to realize Allah's Omnipotence over him. This is why He says, *"So this day We shall deliver your (dead) body (out from the sea)..."* (*Soorah Yoonus* 10:92) means with your armor on your body by which you will be recognized *"...that you may be a sign."* (*Soorah Yoonus* 10:92) That is, you are a sign *"... to those who come after you!"* (*Soorah Yoonus* 10:92). That is, from the Children of Isra'eel, as evidence of Allah's Ability to destroy him. For this reason, some of the *Salaf* recited *"...that you may be a sign to those who come after you!"* (*Soorah Yoonus* 10:92), meaning: We shall deliver you along with your armor, in order that your armor may be a sign to those who come after you from the Children of Isra'eel, by which they may recognize you and know that you are dead. And Allah knows better. The destruction of Fir'awn and his army took place on the·Day of

'Ashurah, according to what Imam Al-Bukhari has narrated in his *Saheeh*, on the authority of 'Abdullah Ibn 'Abbas ⁕, who said, "When the Prophet ﷺ arrived in Madinah, the Jews were fasting on the Day of 'Ashurah and they said, "This is the day on which Moosa defeated Fir'awn." The Prophet ﷺ said (to the Muslims), "You have more right to celebrate Moosa's victory than they have. So observe the fast on this day."[1] The essence of this *Hadith* is recorded in the *Saheehain* and in other compilations.[2] And Allah knows better.

Chapter Regarding the Events Surrounding the Children of Isra'eel After the Destruction of Fir'awn

Allah, Most High, says, *So We took retribution from them. We drowned them in the sea, because they belied Our* **Ayat** *and were heedless about them. And We made the people who were considered weak to inherit the eastern parts of the land and the western parts thereof which We have blessed. And the fair Word of your Lord was fulfilled for the Children of Isra'eel, because of their endurance. And We destroyed completely all the great works and buildings which Fir'awn and his people had erected. And We brought the Children of Isra'eel (with safety) across the sea, and they came upon a people devoted to some of their idols (in worship). They said, "O, Moosa! Make for us an* **ilah** *(a god) as they have* **alihah** *(gods)." He said, "Verily, you are a people who know not (the Majesty and Greatness of Allah and what is obligatory upon you, i.e. to worship none but Allah Alone,*

---

(1)   Narrated by Al-Bukhari (4680).

(2)   Narrated by Al-Bukhari (3397), Muslim (1130), Abu Dawood (2444), Ibn Majah (1734) and Imam Ahmad (3154).

the One and the Only God of all that exists)." (Moosa added,) *"Verily, these people will be destroyed for that in which they are engaged (idol worship). And all that they are doing is in vain."* *He said, "Shall I seek for you an ilah (a god) other than Allah, while He has given you superiority over* **Al-'Alameen?***" And (remember) when We rescued you from Fir'awn's people, who were subjecting you to the worst kind of torment, killing your sons and letting your daughters live? And in that was a great trial from your Lord.* (*Soorah Al-A'raf* 7:136-141). Allah, Most High, mentions what happened to Fir'awn and his army, how they were drowned and how He took away their power, their wealth and their lives and caused the Children of Isra'eel to inherit all of their wealth and property, as He, Most High, says, *Thus (We turned them [Fir'awn's people] out) and We caused the Children of Isra'eel to inherit them.* (*Soorah Ash-Shu'ara'* 26:59). And He, Most High says, *And We wished to do a favor to those who were weak (and oppressed) in the land, and to make them rulers and to make them the inheritors.* (*Soorah Al-Qasas* 28:5). And (in *Soorah Al-A'raf*) He, Most High, says, *And We made the people who were considered weak to inherit the eastern parts of the land and the western parts thereof which We have blessed. And the fair Word of your Lord was fulfilled for the Children of Isra'eel, because of their endurance. And We destroyed completely all the great works and buildings which Fir'awn and his people had erected.* (*Soorah Al-A'raf* 7:137). He demolished all of that and took from them their great and vast power in the world and destroyed the king, his followers, his governors and his troops and none remained in Egypt except the common folk. Ibn 'Abdul-Hakam reported in his *Tareekh Misr* (History of Egypt) that from that time onward, the women of Egypt enjoyed dominance over men, due to the fact that the wives of the governors and the aristocracy married men of lesser social status from among the general populace and so they had power over them; and this has continued to be the custom of women in Egypt to this day.

And they (the scholars) mentioned that when they (the Children of Isra'eel) crossed the sea and headed toward Ash-Sham (Syria), they remained for three days without finding any water. Some of them began to talk due to this and they found some salty water which they were unable to drink, but Allah commanded Moosa عليه السلام to place a piece of wood in it and he did so; and it became sweet and drinkable. And there the Lord taught him the religious obligations and supererogatory practices and taught him a number of Commandments. He, Most High, says in His Noble Book, *And We brought the Children of Isra'eel (with safety) across the sea, and they came upon a people devoted to some of their idols (in worship). They said, "O, Moosa! Make for us an* **ilah** *(a god) as they have* **alihah** *(gods)." He said, "Verily, you are a people who know not (the Majesty and Greatness of Allah and what is obligatory upon you, i.e. to worship none but Allah Alone, the One and the Only God of all that exists)." (Moosa added,) "Verily, these people will be destroyed for that which they are engaged in (idol worship). And all that they are doing is in vain."* (*Soorah Al-A'raf* 7:138,139)

They spoke these words of ignorance and misguidance after they had already witnessed Allah's *Ayat* and His Ability to do all things, which demonstrated to them the truth of what Allah's Messenger صلى الله عليه وسلم brought to them from the Owner of Majesty and Honor. This occurred when they passed by a people who were worshipping idols – it was said that they were in the form of cows – and it appears as if they asked them why they were worshipping them and they replied that they had the ability to benefit them and harm them, and they said that they sought sustenance through them in times of need. It appears as if some of the ignorant ones among them believed these claims of theirs and so they asked their Prophet, *Al-Kaleem*, the noble, the great, to make for them deities, like the deities of these people. And he said to them, in order to make clear to them that they had no sense and were not rightly guided, *"Verily, these people will be destroyed for that which they are engaged in (idol worship). And all that they are doing is in vain."* (*Soorah Al-A'raf* 7:139). Then he reminded them of the blessings that Allah had bestowed on them and of how He had favored them over all of the peoples of their time with knowledge, the Law, the Messenger in their midst, His Kindness toward them and the Graces that He bestowed on them, such as their deliverance from the grasp of Fir'awn, the obstinate tyrant and his subsequent destruction, which they witnessed. He also reminded them of how He had made them to inherit the wealth and prosperity that Fir'awn and his chiefs had gathered and the buildings that they had erected. And he made clear to them that no worship Allah is of benefit except that of Allah, Alone, without ascribing partners to Him, because He is the Creator, the Sustainer and the Subduer. Not all of the Children of Isra'eel asked this question; rather, the name "Children of Isra'eel" is used in Allah's Words: *And We brought the Children of Isra'eel (with safety) across the sea, and they came upon a people devoted to some of their idols (in worship). They said, "O, Moosa! Make for us an* **ilah** *(a god) as they have* **alihah** *(gods)."* (*Soorah Al-A'raf* 7:138) to refer to those who asked the question, without indicating that all of them are included, i.e. some of them said it, as in His Saying: *And we shall gather them all together so as to leave not one of them behind. And they will be set before your Lord in (lines as) rows, (and Allah will say), "Now indeed, you have come to Us as We created you the first time. Nay, but you thought that We had appointed no meeting for you (with Us)."* (*Soorah Al-Kahf* 18:47,48)

Imam Ahmad narrated on the authority of Abu Waqid Al-Laithi ﷺ that he said, "We set out with the Messenger of Allah ﷺ for Hunain and we passed by a lote tree and we said, "O, Messenger of Allah! Make for us a *Dhat Anwat*, like that of the disbelievers." The pagans had a lote tree on which they used to hang their weapons and they used to stay around it. On hearing this, the Prophet of Allah ﷺ said, "*Allahu Akbar*! This is similar to what the Children of Isra'eel said to Moosa ﷺ: *"Make for us an ilah (a god) as they have alihah (gods)."* (*Soorah Al-A'raf* 7:138)! Verily, you are following the ways of those who went before you!" [1]

What is meant is that when Moosa ﷺ departed from Egypt and headed for Bait Al-Maqdis (the Holy Land), he found there arrogant people from among the Hittites, the Cananites, the Perizzites and others and Moosa ﷺ commanded the Children of Isra'eel to make war on them and drive them out of Jerusalem, because Allah had ordained that for them and promised it for them through Revelation given to Ibraheem, *Al-Khaleel* ﷺ and Moosa, *Al-Kaleem* ﷺ. But they refused and recoiled from *jihad* and so Allah caused fear to overpower them and cast them into the desert, where they wandered here and there, back and forth for forty long years, as He, Most High, says, *And (remember) when Moosa said to his people, "O, my people! Remember the Favor of Allah to you, when He made Prophets among you, made you kings, and gave you what He had not given to any other among the Al-'Alameen. O, my people! Enter the Holy Land (Palestine) which Allah has assigned to you, and turn not back for then you will be returned as losers." They said, "O, Moosa! In it (this Holy Land) are a people of great strength, and we shall never enter it, till they leave it; when they leave, then we will enter." Two men of those who feared and on whom Allah had bestowed His Grace (they were Yeshua [Joshua] and Kalab [Caleb]) said, "Assault them through the gate, for when you are in, victory will be yours, and put your trust in Allah if you are indeed Believers." They said, "O Moosa! We shall never enter it as long as they are there. So go you and your Lord and fight you two, we are sitting right here." He (Moosa) said, "O, my Lord! I have power only*

---

(1)   This is an authentic *Hadith* narrated by Imam Ahmad (21393).

over myself and my brother, so separate us from the people who are the **fasiqoon** *(rebellious and disobedient to Allah)!" (Allah) said, "Therefore it (this Holy Land) is forbidden to them for forty years; in distraction they will wander through the land. So be not sorrowful over the people who are the* **fasiqoon.**" (*Soorah Al-Ma'idah* 5:20-26)

The Prophet of Allah ﷺ reminded them of the Blessings that Allah had bestowed on them and the Kindness He had shown them by granting them worldly and religious favors and he ordered them to make *jihad* in Allah's Cause and to fight His enemies; he said, *"O, my people! Enter the holy land (Palestine) which Allah has assigned to you, and turn not back",* (*Soorah Al-Ma'idah* 5:21) means do not turn on your heels and refuse to fight your enemies *"for then you will be returned as losers."* (*Soorah Al-Ma'idah* 5:21). It means that you will lose after your previous gains and you will be diminished after having been complete. *They said, "O, Moosa! In it (this Holy Land) are a people of great strength."* (*Soorah Al-Ma'idah* 5:22) That is, they are fierce and arrogant disbelievers. *"and we shall never enter it, till they leave it; when they leave, then we will enter."* (*Soorah Al-Ma'idah* 5:22). They feared these strong, aggressive people, even though they had witnessed the destruction of Fir'awn, who was more tyrannical than they, sterner in punishment, commanding more people and with a stronger force at his disposal. This proves that they were rebuked due to saying these words and censured because of them. This was due to their cowardice in the face of the enemy's aggression and their refusal to fight them.

Regarding the Saying of Allah, Most High: *Two men of those who feared said* (*Soorah Al-Ma'idah* 5:23) means, feared Allah, though some recited it as "who were feared". *On whom Allah had bestowed His Grace* (*Soorah Al-Ma'idah* 5:23) means with Islam, faith, obedience and courage. *...said, "Assault them through the gate, for when you are in, victory will be yours, and put your* *trust in Allah if you are indeed Believers."* (*Soorah Al-Ma'idah* 5:24). That is, if you have put your trust in Allah, sought help from Him and protection from Him, He will help you against your enemy, help you against them and make you victorious over them. They said, *"O Moosa! We shall never enter it as long as they are there. So go you and your Lord and fight you two, we are sitting right here."* (*Soorah Al-Ma'idah* 5:24). Their elders were determined to refrain from engaging in *jihad* in Allah's Cause and a serious situation developed. It was said that when Yoosha' and Kalab heard these words, they tore their garments and Moosa عليه السلام and Haroon عليه السلام sat down in shock at these words and they became angry for Allah's sake and they also felt compassion for them, because of the awful consequences for them of their words: *He (Moosa) said, "O, my Lord! I have power only over myself and my brother, so separate us from the people who are the* **fasiqoon!***"* (*Soorah Al-Ma'idah* 5:25). 'Abdullah Ibn 'Abbas رضي الله عنه said, "Judge between me and them." *(Allah) said, "Therefore it (this Holy Land) is forbidden to them for forty years; in distraction they will wander through the land. So be not sorrowful over the people who are the* **fasiqoon** *(rebellious and disobedient to Allah)."* (*Soorah Al-Ma'idah* 5:26) They were punished for their refusal to do *jihad* by being made to wander aimlessly night and day, morning and evening in the desert.

Imam Ahmad narrated on the authority of Al-Miqdad that he said to the Messenger of Allah ﷺ on the day of the Battle of Badr, "O, Messenger of Allah! We will not say to you, as the Children of Isra'eel said to Moosa عليه السلام, *"So go you and your Lord and fight you two, we are sitting right here."* (*Soorah Al-Ma'idah* 5:24).' But (we will say), "Go you and your Lord and fight; we are with you fighting."[1] This chain of narrators is good from this source and it is narrated from other sources. 'Abdullah Ibn Mas'ood said that Al-Miqdad went to the Messenger of Allah ﷺ and found him

---

(1)   This is an authentic *Hadith* narrated by Imam Ahmad (18348).

invoking Allah against the pagans and he said, "By Allah, O, Messenger of Allah, we will not say to you as the Children of Isra'eel said to Moosa, *"So go you and your Lord and fight you two, we are sitting right here."* (*Soorah Al-Ma'idah* 5:24). Rather, we will fight on your right, on your left, in front of you and behind you," and I saw the Messenger of Allah's face beaming when he heard this and he was extremely happy."[1]

---

(1)   This is an authentic *Hadith* narrated by Imam Ahmad (3690).

Chapter Concerning the Children of Isra'eel's Wandering in the Wilderness

We have already discussed the Children of Isra'eel's refusal to fight against the giants and how Allah, Most High, punished them by causing them to wander in the wilderness and He ordained that they would not leave it for forty years.

According to the scholars of *tafseer*, the Children of Isra'eel camped around Mount Sinai and Moosa ﷺ ascended the mountain and his Lord spoke to him and commanded him to remind the Children of Isra'eel of the Blessings that Allah had bestowed on them, such as how He had delivered them from Pharaoh and his people … and He told him that on the third day, they must assemble around the mountain, but that none of them should approach it, for anyone who did so would be killed. He even forbade that any of their livestock should come near so long as they could hear the sound of the horn, but that once the horn was silent, it was lawful for them to approach it. The Children of Isra'eel heard these Words of Allah, but they did not understand until Moosa ﷺ made them understand. Then they said to Moosa ﷺ, "Convey to us what the Lord, the Almighty, the All-Powerful has told you, for we fear to die." So Moosa ﷺ conveyed to them what Allah had told him and he spoke these Ten Commandments:

1. That they should worship Allah, Alone, without ascribing partners to Him.

2. That they should not swear falsely by Allah.

3. That they should preserve the sanctity of the Sabbath, meaning that they should devote themselves on one day in the week to the worship of Allah – and this occurs (now) on Friday, the day which Allah selected to replace the abrogated day, Saturday.

4. That they should honor their fathers and their mothers, in order that they might enjoy a long life in this world which Allah, their Lord, had given them.

5. That they should not commit murder.

6. That they should not commit adultery or unlawful sexual intercourse.

7. That they should not steal.

8. That they should not bear false witness against their neighbors.

9. That they should not covet their neighbors' houses.

10. That they should not covet their neighbors' wives, or male or female slaves, or oxen, or donkeys, or anything that belonged to their neighbors.

All of this is a prohibition of envy. Many of the scholars from among the *Salaf* and others said that these Ten Commandments are all implied in two Qur'anic Verses; and they are the Words of Allah, Most High, in *Soorah Al-An'am*:

Say (O, Muhammad). "Come, I will recite what your Lord has prohibited to you: Join not anything in worship with Him; be good and dutiful to your parents; kill not your children because of poverty – We provide sustenance for you and for them; come not near to fawahish (shameful sins, illegal sexual intercourse, etc.) whether committed openly or secretly, and kill not anyone whom Allah has forbidden, except for a just cause (according to Islamic law). This He has commanded you that you may understand. And come not near to the orphan's property, except to improve it, until he (or she) attains the age of full strength; and give full measure and full weight with justice. We burden not any person, but that which he can bear. And whenever you give your word (i.e. judge between men or give evidence, etc.), say the truth even if a near relative is concerned, and fulfill the Covenant of Allah, This He commands you, that you may remember. And verily, this (i.e. Allah's Commandments mentioned in the above two Verses 151 and 152) *is my Straight Path, so follow it, and follow not (other) paths, for they will separate you away from His Path. This He has ordained for you that you may become* **muttaqoon.** *" (Soorah Al-An'am 6:151-153)*

In addition to these Ten Commandments, they mentioned many other counsels and rulings which have come and gone and which were acted upon for a time, until they were disobeyed by those who were charged with the duty of fulfilling them. Then they set about changing them, distorting them and misinterpreting them. Then after all this, they abandoned them and they became abrogated and replaced with others, after having been prescribed and executed. And the whole affair – both past and present – is in Allah's Hands; and He commands what He wills and does as He wants. Surely, His is the Creation and Commandment. Blessed be Allah, the Lord of *Al-'Alameen!*[1]

---

(1)   See *Soorah Al-A'raf* 7:54

And He, Most High, says, *O, Children of Isra'eel! We delivered you from your enemy, and We made a covenant with you on the right side of the Mount, and We sent down to you* **al-manna** *and quails, (saying) eat of the* **Tayyibat** *(good and lawful things) wherewith We have provided you, and commit no oppression therein, lest My Anger should justly descend on you. And he on whom My Anger descends, is indeed destroyed. And verily, I am indeed Forgiving to him who repents, believes (in My Oneness, and associates none in worship with Me) and does righteous good deeds, and then remains constant in doing them, (till his death).* (*Soorah Ta Ha* 20:80-82)

Allah, Most High, reminds the Children of Isra'eel the Grace and Kindness that He has shown to them, by saving them from their enemies and delivering them from hardship and oppression. And He reminds them that He promised them the company of their Prophet – His *Kaleem* – to the right side of the mountain, i.e. to the right of them, in order that He might send down the great Commandments to him – and in these Commandments was great benefit for them – both in the life of this world and in the Hereafter. He also calls upon them to bring to mind how He sent down *manna* to them from the heaven when they were traveling throughout the Earth, in places where there were no crops and no livestock. They would awake each morning and find it around their tents and they would take from it for that day, sufficient for their needs until the same time the next day. And if anyone stored up more than that, he would find that it had gone bad, but if anyone took a little from it, he would find that it was enough for him. They used to make from it something resembling bread, which was just white and very sweet. Then in the afternoon, quails would descend on them and they would avail themselves of them without difficulty, as much as they needed, according to what was sufficient for their dinner.

And during the summer months, Allah would shade them

with clouds, which protected them from the heat and dazzling brightness of the sun, as He, Most High, says in *Soorah Al-Baqarah, O, Children of Isra'eel! Remember My Favor which I bestowed upon you, and fulfill (your obligations to) My Covenant (with you) so that I fulfill (My Obligations to) your covenant (with Me), and fear none but Me. And believe in what I have sent down (this Qur'an), confirming that which is with you, (the Tawrah and the Injeel), and be not the first to disbelieve therein, and buy (get) not with My Verses (the Tawrah and the Injeel) a small price (i.e. getting a small gain by selling My Verses), and fear Me and Me Alone.* **(Tafseer At-Tabari, Vol. I, page 253). (Soorah Al-Baqarah 2: 40,41)** *up to His words: And (remember) when We delivered you from Fir'awn's people, who were subjecting you to horrible torment, killing your sons and sparing your daughters, and therein was a mighty trial from your Lord. And (remember) when We separated the sea for you and saved you and drowned Fir'awn's people while you were looking (at them, when the seawater covered them). And (remember) when We appointed for Moosa forty nights, and (in his absence) you took the calf (for worship), and you were* **zalimoon.** *Then after that We forgave you so that you might be grateful. And (remember) when We gave Moosa the Scripture (the Tawrah) and the criterion (of right and wrong) so that you may be guided aright. And (remember) when Moosa said to his people, "O, my people! Verily, you have wronged yourselves by worshipping the calf. So turn in repentance to your Creator and kill yourselves (the innocent kill the wrongdoers among you), that will be better for you with your Lord." Then He accepted your repentance. Truly, He is the One Who accepts repentance, the Most Merciful. And (remember) when you said, "O, Moosa! We shall never believe in you till we see Allah plainly." But you were seized with a thunderbolt (lightning) while you were looking. Then We raised you up after your death, so that you might be grateful. And We shaded you with clouds and sent down on you* **al-manna** *and the quails, (saying), "Eat of the good* *lawful things We have provided for you," (but they rebelled). And they did not wrong Us but they wronged themselves.* **(Soorah Al-Baqarah 2:49-57) – up to His Words:** *And (remember) when Moosa asked for water for his people, We said, "Strike the stone with your stick." Then twelve springs gushed forth therefrom. Each (group of) people knew its own place for water. "Eat and drink of that which Allah has provided and do not act corruptly, making mischief on the Earth." And (remember) when you said, "O Moosa! We cannot endure one kind of food. So invoke your Lord for us to bring forth for us of what the earth grows, its herbs, its cucumbers, its foom,*[1] *its lentils and its onions." He said, "Would you exchange that which is better for that which is lower? Go you down to any town and you shall find what you want!" And they were covered with humiliation and misery, and they drew on themselves the Wrath of Allah. That was because they used to disbelieve the* **Ayat** *of Allah and killed the Prophets wrongfully. That was because they disobeyed and used to transgress the bounds (in their disobedience to Allah, i.e. commit crimes and sins) (Soorah Al-Baqarah 2:60,61)*

So Allah, Most High, reminded them of the Blessings that He had bestowed on them and the Kindness He had shown to them, which made their lives easier, such as the *manna* and the quails – two pleasant foods, which they obtained without difficulty or effort on their part; indeed, Allah used to send down the *manna* in the early morning and the quails in the afternoon and He caused the water to gush forth in springs for them. Moosa عليه السلام struck a rock which they had been carrying with them with his stick, upon

---

(1) Ibn Abi Hatim said that Ibn 'Abbas رضى الله عنه said that *foom* means *thaom* (garlic). Ibn Jareer At-Tabari commented, "If this is correct, then '*foom*' is one of those words whose pronunciation was altered, the letter '*fa*'' was replaced by the letter *tha*`, since they are similar in sound." And Allah knows better. Others said that *foom* is wheat, the kind used for bread. Al-Bukhari said, "Some of them said that *foom* includes all grains or seeds that are eaten."

which twelve springs gushed forth, one surging spring for each tribe. Then the flow became cold and they drew water, drank and watered their riding beasts, after which they kept what sufficed to supply their needs. In addition, He shaded them with the clouds from the heat (of the sun).

These were a plenty of blessings and valuable gifts from Allah, but they did not give them the attention or respect that they deserved, nor did they give thanks or observe worship for them. Then many of them became dissatisfied and bored with them and so they asked to be given something else in their place, from the produce of the land, such as herbs, cucumbers, *foom*, lentils and onions.

Al-Kaleem rebuked them, scolded them and reprehended them for these words and berated them, saying, *"Would you exchange that which is better for that which is lower? Go you down to any town and you shall find what you want!"* (*Soorah Al-Baqarah* 2:61) It means that which you request and desire, in place of these blessings which you are enjoying may be found with the inhabitants of large and small towns; so if you go to them, i.e. and you give up this privilege – which you do not deserve – you will find there (in the towns) all those inferior foods that you mentioned, which you desire and yearn for. But I will not accede to your request, nor will I convey to you the fate which you bring upon yourselves.

And all of these characteristics which they displayed prove that they did not desist from what they were forbidden to do, as He, Most High, says, *...and commit no oppression therein, lest My Anger should justly descend on you. And he on whom My Anger descends, he is indeed perished.* (*Soorah Ta Ha* 20:81) That is, he is surely destroyed and he is most deserving of that; and Allah is the Destroyer, the Annihilator, Whose Anger rightly befalls such a person.

The Request to See Allah

Allah, Most High, says, *And We appointed for Moosa thirty nights and added (to the period) ten (more), and he completed the term, appointed by his Lord, of forty nights. And Moosa said to his brother Haroon, "Replace me among my people, act in the Right Way (by ordering the people to obey Allah and to worship Him Alone) and follow not the way of the* **mufsidoon** *(mischief-makers)." And when Moosa came to the meeting appointed by Us, and his Lord spoke to him, he said, "O, my Lord! Show me (Yourself), that I may look upon You." Allah said, "You cannot see Me, but look upon the mountain, if it stands still in its place, then you shall see Me." So when his Lord appeared to the mountain, He made it collapse to dust, and Moosa fell down unconscious. Then, when he recovered his senses he said, "Glory be to You, I turn to You in repentance and I am the first of the Believers." He (Allah) said, "O, Moosa I have chosen you above men by My Messages, and by My speaking (to you). So hold that which I have given you and be of the grateful." And We wrote for him on the Tablets the lesson to be drawn from all things and the explanation of all things (and said), "Hold unto these with firmness, and* *enjoin your people to take the better therein. I shall show you the home of* **fasiqoon.** *I shall turn away from My* **Ayat** *those who behave arrogantly on the Earth, without a right, and (even) if they see all the* **Ayat,** *they will not believe in them. And if they see the way of righteousness (Monotheism, piety, and good deeds), they will not adopt it as the way, but if they see the way of error (polytheism, crimes and evil deeds), they will adopt that way, that is because they have rejected Our* **Ayat** *and were heedless (to learn a lesson) from them. Those who deny Our* **Ayat** *and the Meeting in the Hereafter (Day of Resurrection,), vain are their deeds. Do they expect to be rewarded with anything except what they used to do?"* (*Soorah Al-A'raf* 7:142-147)

A number of the *Salaf*, including 'Abdullah Ibn 'Abbas ﷺ, Masrooq and Mujahid said that the thirty nights referred to were the whole month of *Dhul-Qa'dah* and he completed forty days by remaining for ten days of *Dhul-Hijjah*; based on this reckoning, Allah's Words would have been spoken to him on the day of *'Eid An-Nahr*.[1] And on the same day, Allah, the Almighty, the All-Powerful, completed for Muhammad ﷺ His Religion and confirmed His Evidence and His Proof. What is meant is that when Moosa ﷺ had completed the appointed time period, during which he fasted – it was said that he did not taste food and when the month was over, he took some tree bark and chewed it in order to improve the smell of his breath. Then Allah commanded him to remain for a further ten nights, making a total of forty nights; this is why it was authentically reported in the *Hadith*: "The smell of the fasting person's breath is sweeter to Allah than the odour of musk." [2]

Before leaving, Moosa ﷺ had appointed his beloved, respected and honored brother, Haroon ﷺ, to be leader of the Children

---

(1) *'Eid An-Nahr*: The Festival of Sacrifice, which is the culmination of the *Hajj*.

(2) Narrated by Al-Bukhari (1894), Muslim (1151), At-Tirmidhi (764), An-Nasa'i (2215), Ibn Majah (1638) and Ahmad (7636).

of Isra'eel in his absence; Haroon ﷺ was his full brother and his minister in supplicating to Allah, and so he advised him and commanded him – and his status as a Prophet does not make this incompatible or incongruous – Allah, Most High, says, *And when Moosa came to the meeting appointed by Us* (*Soorah Al-A'raf* 7:143) means at the time he was commanded to attend *and his Lord spoke to him.* (*Soorah Al-A'raf* 7:143). That is, Allah spoke to him from behind a screen, which allowed him to hear what was said to him, and He called him, confided in him and brought him near. This was indeed, a high rank, a strong position, a noble office and an exalted station – may abundant blessings and peace be upon him in the life of this world and in the Hereafter. When he was given this elevated status and sublime rank and he heard the (Divine) Speech, he asked Allah to raise the screen, saying to the Almighty, Whom no eyes may behold and Whose Evidence is Strong, *"O, my Lord! Show me (Yourself), that I may look upon You." Allah said, "You can not see Me"* (*Soorah Al-A'raf* 7:143). Then Allah, Most High, explained to him that he could not withstand Allah's revealing Himself, because the mountain, which was stronger, of greater size and firmer than a human being, could not withstand His revealing Himself to it, which is why He says, *"...but look upon the mountain, if it stands still in its place, then you shall see Me."* (*Soorah Al-A'raf* 7:143)

'Abdullah Ibn 'Abbas ﷺ said, regarding the Words of Allah, Most High: *No vision can grasp Him* (*Soorah Al-An'am* 6:103), "This refers to His Light; it is His Light which, if it is revealed to anything, it cannot withstand it." This is why He, Most High, said to Moosa ﷺ, *So when his Lord appeared to the mountain, He made it collapse to dust, and Moosa fell down unconscious. Then, when he recovered his senses he said, "Glory be to You, I turn to You in repentance and I am the first of the Believers."* (*Soorah Al-A'raf* 7:143)

Mujahid said, regarding the Words of Him, Most High: *"...*

but look upon the mountain, if it stands still in its place, then you shall see Me." (*Soorah Al-A'raf* 7:143), "(It means:) Because it (the mountain) is larger than you and stronger; but when his Lord revealed Himself to the mountain, and he saw that the mountain could not withstand it and collapsed into dust, he fell to the ground unconscious."

We have mentioned in the *Tafseer* the narration of Imams Ahmad and At-Tirmidhi – which was declared authentic by Ibn Jareer At-Tabari and Al-Hakim – on the authority of Anas ﷺ, who reported that the Messenger of Allah ﷺ recited *So when his Lord appeared to the mountain, He made it collapse to dust.* He indicated by placing his thumb on the top joint of his little finger (how much of Himself Allah had revealed to the mountain) and this caused the mountain to sink to the ground."[1]

As-Suddi narrated on the authority of 'Ikrimah, who reported on the authority of 'Abdullah Ibn 'Abbas ﷺ that he said that what Allah revealed of Himself it was no more than the extent of a little finger and it caused the mountain to turn to dust. *...and Moosa fell down unconscious.* That is, it caused him to swoon. Qatadah said, "(He fell down) dead." But the first interpretation is the correct one, because He says, *Then, when he recovered his senses...* (*Soorah Al-A'raf* 7:143) – and one can only recover or awake from a faint (not from death) – he (Moosa عليه السلام) said, *"Glory be to You..."* (*Soorah Al-A'raf* 7:143). This is an acknowledgement that Allah is Above such a thing (as being seen by His creation) and glorification and exaltation of Him. *"I turn to You in repentance..."* (*Soorah Al-A'raf* 7:143). That is, I shall not ask to see You again after this. *"...and I am the first of the Believers"* (*Soorah Al-A'raf* 7:143) means, the first to believe that You cannot be seen by any living thing without it being killed and (You cannot be revealed

---

(1) This is an authentic *Hadith* narrated by Imam Ahmad (3/209, No. 12766), At-Tirmidhi (3074), Ibn Jareer At-Tabari in his *Tafseer* (9/53) and Al-Hakim in *Al-Mustadrak* (2/630, No. 4104).

to) any dry (inanimate) thing without it tumbling to the ground.

And it has been authentically reported in the *Saheehain* on the authority of Abu Sa'eed Al-Khudri ☞ that he said, "The Messenger of Allah ﷺ said, 'Do not ascribe to me superiority over the other Prophets, for on the Day of Resurrection the people will become unconscious and I will (feel that) I am the first to regain consciousness. Then I will see Moosa holding one of the legs of the Throne. I will not know whether he has come to his senses before me or that the shock he had received at the Mountain, (during his worldly life) was sufficient for him'."[1]

And He, Most High, says, *He (Allah) said, "O, Moosa I have chosen you above men by My Messages, and by My speaking (to you)." (Soorah Al-A'raf 7:144).* That is, in that time, not the times before him, because Ibraheem, *Al-Khaleel* عليه السلام was superior to him, as we made clear earlier, in the story of Ibraheem عليه السلام. Nor does it include the time after him, because Muhammad ﷺ is superior to both of them, as evinced by the story of *Al-Isra,* where his superiority over all of the Messengers and Prophets was made clear. And it was also confirmed that he said, "The entire creation will turn to me, including even Ibraheem عليه السلام (for intercession)."[2]

And He, Most High, says, *"So hold that which I have given you and be of the grateful" (Soorah Al-A'raf 7:144)* means, so take what I have given you of the Message and (My) Speech and do not ask for more than that, and be grateful for it.

And He, Most High, says, *And We wrote for him on the Tablets the lesson to be drawn from all things and the explanation of all things. (Soorah Al-A'raf 7:145).* The Tablets were of precious stone; and it has been reported in the *Saheeh* that Allah wrote for him the Tawrah with His Hand and in it there are admonitions

---

(1)   Narrated by Al-Bukhari (4638) and Muslim (2374).

(2)   Narrated by Muslim (820).

against sin and details of all that they needed to know regarding what is lawful and what is unlawful, punishments and rulings.[1] *"Hold unto these with firmness."* (*Soorah Al-A'raf* 7:145). That is, with a firm resolve and a sincere intention. *"...and enjoin your people to take the better therein."* (*Soorah Al-A'raf* 7:145) means, to take them and act upon them in the best manner. *"I shall show you the home of* **fasiqoon.** *"* (*Soorah Al-A'raf* 7:145). That is, you (Children of Isra'eel) will see the consequences for those who turn away from obedience to Allah, disobey His Commands and belie His Messengers. *I shall turn away from My* **Ayat** *(Verses of the Qur'an)* (*Soorah Al-A'raf* 7:146) It means that, I shall deprive the hearts of those who are too proud to obey Me, and arrogant with people without right, from understanding the Signs and proofs that testify to My Might, Law and Commandments. *Those who behave arrogantly on Earth, without a right, and (even) if they see all the* **Ayat,** *they will not believe in them.* (*Soorah Al-A'raf* 7:146) That is, no matter what miracles and supernatural phenomena they witnessed, they would not agree to be guided by them. *And if they see the way of righteousness (monotheism, piety, and good deeds), they will not adopt it as the Way.* (*Soorah Al-A'raf* 7:146) That is, they will not travel it or follow it. *...but if they see the way of error (polytheism, crimes and evil deeds), they will adopt that way, that is because they have rejected Our* **Ayat** *and were heedless (to learn a lesson) from them* (*Soorah Al-A'raf* 7:146) means We have turned them away from following the Straight Path because of their rejection of Our *Ayat,* their disregard of them, their refusal to believe in them, reflect on their meaning and act upon them. *Those who deny Our* **Ayat** *and the Meeting in the Hereafter (Day of Resurrection,), vain are their deeds. Do they expect to be rewarded with anything except what they used to do?* (*Soorah Al-A'raf* 7:147)

---

(1)   Narrated by Al-Bukhari (6614), Muslim (2652), Abu Dawood (4701), Ibn Majah (80) and Ahmad (7340), on the authority of Abu Hurairah ☞.

The Story of Their Worship of the Calf During the Absence of Allah's Kaleem From Them

Allah, Most High, says, *And the people of Moosa made in his absence, out of their ornaments, the image of a calf (for worship). It had a sound (as if it was mooing). Did they not see that it could neither speak to them nor guide them to the way? They took it for worship and they were **zalimoon** (wrongdoers). And when they regretted and saw that they had gone astray, they (repented and) said, "If our Lord has not Mercy upon us and forgives us not, we shall certainly be of the losers." And when Moosa returned to his people, angry and grieved, he said, "What an evil thing is that which you have done (i.e. worshipping* *the calf) during my absence. Did you hasten and go ahead as regards the matter of your Lord (you left His worship)?" And he threw down the Tablets and seized his brother by (the hair of) his head and dragged him toward him. Haroon said, "O, son of my mother! Indeed the people judged me weak and were about to kill me, so make not the enemies rejoice over me, nor put me amongst the people who are* **zalimoon***." Moosa said, "O, my Lord! Forgive me and my brother, and make us enter into Your Mercy, for you are the Most Merciful of those who show mercy." Certainly, those who took the calf (for worship), wrath from their Lord and humiliation will come upon them in the life of this world. Thus do We recompense those who invent lies. But those who committed evil deeds and then repented afterward and believed, verily, your Lord after (all) that is indeed Oft-Forgiving, Most Merciful. And when the anger of Moosa was subsided, he took up the Tablets, and in their inscription was guidance and mercy for those who fear their Lord.* (**Soorah Al-A'raf** 7:148-154)

Allah, Most High, informs us about the affair of the Children of Isra'eel and how, when Moosa ﷺ departed from them for the appointment with his Lord and remained on the mountain, where his Lord confided in him and he asked Him about many things and He answered him, a man from among the Children of Isra'eel, whose name was Haroon (Aaron) As-Samiri, took some jewelry that that he had borrowed and fashioned a calf from it; in it he cast some dust which he had taken from the trace of Jibraeel's steed, when he saw him on the day when Allah drowned Pharaoh at Jibraeel's hand. When he cast it, the calf lowed as a real calf lows. It was said that it was transformed into a living, flesh-and-blood calf and that it lowed. This was said by Qatadah and others. It was also said that it was only the wind, when it entered it from the rear and exited from its mouth, making the lowing sound, in the manner in which a cow lows. Upon this, they began to dance around it and celebrate. *They said, "This is your* **ilah** *(god), and the* **ilah** *(god) of Moosa, but (Moosa) has forgotten."* (*Soorah Ta Ha* 20:88). It means that Moosa has forgotten his "Lord", which is with us and he has gone off to seek him, when he is here. Exalted is He above what they say, hallowed be His Names and His Attributes and multiplied be His Blessings and His Promised Rewards. Allah, Most High, says, making clear the falseness of their claims, *Did they not see that it could not return them a word (for answer), and that it had no power either to harm them or to do them good?* (*Soorah Ta Ha* 20:89). And He says, *Did they not see that it could neither speak to them nor guide them to the way? They took it for worship and they were* **zalimoon**. (*Soorah Al-A'raf* 7:148). So He said that the animal could not speak and could not reply to them, nor did it possess the power to inflict harm on them or benefit them, nor could it guide them to right conduct. They took it as a deity to be worshipped and thus they wronged themselves, knowing within themselves that what they were doing was falsehood, ignorance and plain error. *And when they regretted* (*Soorah Al-A'raf* 7:149) means, when they repented of what they had done *...and saw that they had gone astray, they (repented and) said, "If our Lord has not Mercy upon us and forgives us not, we shall certainly be of the losers."* (*Soorah Al-A'raf* 7:149). Then, when Moosa returned to them, and saw that they were worshipping the calf, and he had with him the Tablets containing the Towrah, he threw them down and it was said that he broke them.

Then he advanced upon them and reprimanded them, rebuked them and disparaged them for their wicked deed and they offered an invalid excuse for their action, saying, *"...we were made to carry the weight of the ornaments of the (Fir'awn's) people, then we cast them (into the fire), and that was what As-Samiri suggested."* (*Soorah Ta Ha* 20:87). They said that they found it difficult to carry the people of Pharaoh's jewelry – and they were the soldiers; Allah had commanded them to take it and made it lawful for them. They did not seek to excuse themselves for having worshipped the calf, which had a body and which lowed, besides Allah, the One, *As-Samad*,[1] the Subduer, because of their ignorance, lack of knowledge and intelligence. Then Moosa ادلّٰهعليه went to his brother, Haroon ادلّٰهعليه, and said to him, *"O, Haroon! What stopped you when you saw them going astray, that you followed me not (according to my advice to you)?"* (*Soorah Ta Ha* 20:92,93). That is, why, when you saw what they were doing, did you not obey me and inform me of what they were doing? *"Verily, I feared lest you should say, "You have caused a division among the Children of Isra'eel,"* (*Soorah Ta Ha* 20:94). means you have left them and come to me, when you had been appointed to take my place as their leader in my absence. *He (Moosa) said, "O, my Lord! Forgive me and my brother, and make us enter into Your Mercy, for you are the Most Merciful of those who show mercy."* (*Soorah Al-A'raf* 7:151). Haroon ادلّٰهعليه had indeed forbidden them to do this wicked deed in the sternest of terms and strongly rebuked them for it. Allah, Most High, says, *And Haroon indeed had said to them beforehand, "O, my people! You are being tried in this..."* (*Soorah Ta Ha* 20:90). That is, Allah has ordained this calf for you and made it low as a trial and a test for you. *"... and verily, your Lord is (Allah) the Most Beneficent"* (*Soorah Ta Ha* 20:90) means not this calf; *"...so follow me."* (*Soorah Ta Ha* 20:90). That is, in what I say to you. *and obey my order."* They *said, "We will not stop worshipping it (i.e. the calf), until Moosa returns to us."* (*Soorah Ta Ha* 20:90-91) Allah bears witness on behalf of Haroon ادلّٰهعليه – and Allah, Most High, is Sufficient as a Witness – that he forbade them to do that and rebuked them for it, but they did not obey him and they did not follow him. Then Moosa ادلّٰهعليه approached As-Samiri. *"And what is the matter*

---

(1) *As-Samad*: The Self-Sufficient Master, Whom all creatures need, Who neither eats nor drinks.

with you, O, Samiri?" (*Soorah Ta Ha* 20:95) That is, what made you do what you did? *He (As-Samiri) said, "I saw what they saw not"* (*Soorah Ta Ha* 20:96) means I saw Jibraeel ﷺ when he was riding his steed *"...so I took a handful (of dust) from the (hoof) prints of the messenger."* (*Soorah Ta Ha* 20:96) - the hoof prints of Jibraeel's steed.

And some of the scholars mentioned that he saw it and every time it placed its hooves on the ground, the place became green and grass grew; so he took some dust from its hoof prints and he threw it onto the calf which had been manufactured from gold, that which we have mentioned happened. This is why Allah, Most High, says, *"...and I threw it (into the fire in which were put the ornaments of the Fir'awn's people, or into the calf). Thus my inner-self suggested to me." He (Moosa) said, "Then go away! And verily, your (punishment) in this life will be that you will say, "Touch me not (i.e. you will live alone exiled away from mankind)."* (*Soorah Ta Ha* 20:96,97). This was a supplication against him, that he might not touch anyone, as a punishment for touching that which he had no right to touch. This was a punishment for him in this world; then he informed him of what awaited him in the Hereafter, saying, *"...and verily (for a future punishment), you have a promise that will not fail."* (*Soorah Ta Ha* 20:97) It was also recited as: that We will not fail (to fulfill). *"And look at your **ilah** (god), to which you have been devoted. We will certainly burn it, and scatter its particles in the sea."* (*Soorah Ta Ha* 20:97). It was said that Moosa ﷺ went to the calf and burned it in fire; this was said by Qatadah and others. It was also said that it was filed down; this was said by 'Ali ﷺ, 'Abdullah Ibn 'Abbas ﷺ and others and it was the version according to the People of the Scriptures. Then he scattered it into the sea. After that, he commanded the Children of Isra'eel to drink from it and when those who had worshipped the calf drank of it, the sand stuck to their lips, as proof of their guilt. It was also said that their skin became yellow. Then Allah, Most High, tells us that Moosa ﷺ said to them, *"Your* **Ilah** *(God) is only Allah, the One* **(La ilaha illa Huwa)** *(none has the right to be worshipped but He). He has full knowledge of all things."* (*Soorah Ta Ha* 20:98) *And He, Most High, says, Certainly, those who took the calf (for worship), wrath from their Lord and humiliation will come upon them in the life of this world. Thus do We recompense those who invent lies.* (*Soorah Al-A'raf* 7:152). And that is what happened. Some of the *Salaf* said that Allah's Saying: *Thus do We recompense those who invent lies* (*Soorah Al-A'raf* 7:152) applies to all those who innovate in religious matters until the Day of Resurrection. Then He, Most High, informs us of His Gentleness and Mercy toward His creation and His Kindness toward His slaves, in accepting the repentance of those who turn in repentance to Him. He says, *But those who committed evil deeds and then repented afterward and believed, verily, your Lord after (all) that is indeed Oft-Forgiving, Most Merciful.* (*Soorah Al-A'raf* 7:153). But Allah, Most High, did not accept the repentance of those who worshipped the calf, except by their being killed, as He, Most High, says, *And (remember) when Moosa said to his people, "O, my people! Verily, you have wronged yourselves by worshipping the calf. So turn in repentance to your Creator and kill yourselves (the innocent kill the wrongdoers among you), that will be better for you with your Lord." Then He accepted your repentance. Truly, He is the One Who accepts repentance, the Most Merciful.* (*Soorah Al-Baqarah* 2:54)

Then He, Most High, says, *And when the anger of Moosa subsided, he took up the Tablets, and in their inscription was guidance and mercy for those who fear their Lord.* (*Soorah Al-A'raf* 7:154) Some of the scholars cited His Saying: *and in their inscription* (*Soorah Al-A'raf* 7:154) as evidence that they were destroyed; but there is some doubt about this claim; there is nothing in the wording to suggest that they were broken. And

Allah knows better. 'Abdullah Ibn 'Abbas ﷺ said in the *Hadith* of the trial that their worship of the calf was soon after their emergence from the sea and this is not improbable, because when they came out from it, *They said, "O, Moosa! Make for us an* **ilah** *(a god) as they have* **alihah** *(gods)."* (*Soorah Al-A'raf* 7:138)

And He, Most High, says, *And Moosa chose out of his people seventy (of the best) men for Our appointed time and place of meeting, and when they were seized with a violent earthquake, he said, "O, my Lord, if it had been Your Will, You could have destroyed them and me before; would You destroy us for the deeds of the foolish ones among us? It is only Your Trial by which You lead astray whom You will, and keep guided whom You will. You are our* **Wali** *(Protector), so forgive us and have Mercy on us, for You are the Best of those who forgive. And ordain for us good in this world, and in the Hereafter. Certainly we have turned unto You." He said, "(As to) My Punishment I afflict therewith whom I will and My Mercy embraces all things. That (Mercy) I shall ordain for those who are the* **muttaqoon,** *and give* **zakah;** *and those who believe in Our* **Ayat;** *those who follow the Messenger, the Prophet who can neither read nor write (i.e. Muhammad) whom they find written with them in the Tawrah (Deut, xviii, 15) and the Injeel (John xiv, 16), – he commands them for* **al-ma'roof** *(i.e. Islamic Monotheism and all that Islam has ordained); and forbids them from* **al-munkar** *(i.e. disbelief, polytheism of all kinds, and all that Islam has forbidden); he allows them as lawful* **Tayyibat** *(i.e. all good and lawful as regards things, deeds, beliefs, persons, foods, etc.), and prohibits them as unlawful* **khaba'ith** *(i.e. all evil and unlawful as regards things, deeds, beliefs, persons, foods, etc.), he releases them from their heavy burdens (of Allah's Covenant), and from the fetters (bindings) that were upon them. So those who believe in him (Muhammad), honor him, help him, and follow the Light (the Qur'an) which has been sent down with him, it is they who will be successful.* (*Soorah Al-A'raf* 7:155-157)

As-Suddi, 'Abdullah Ibn 'Abbas ﷺ and others said that these seventy were scholars from among the Children of Isra'eel and with them was Moosa ﷺ, Haroon ﷺ, Yoosha', Nadab and Abihu. They went with Moosa ﷺ to ask for forgiveness for the Children of Isra'eel for their worship of the calf. They had been commanded to bathe, purify themselves and wear perfume and when they went with him and approached the mountain, it was covered with clouds and there was a column of brilliant light emanating from them. Moosa ﷺ went up the mountain. The Children of Isra'eel said that they heard the Speech of Allah and this corresponds with what was said by a group of the scholars of *tafseer* and they understood Allah's Saying: *...a party of them (Jewish rabbis) had heard the Word of Allah (the Tawrah), then they changed it knowingly after they had understood it.* (*Soorah Al-Baqarah* 2:75) in light of it. But this is not necessarily so, because He, Most High, says, *...then grant him protection, so that he may hear the Word of Allah (the Qur'an).* (*Soorah At-Tawbah* 9:6). That is, conveyed to him. In the same way, those (from the Children of Isra'eel) heard it from Moosa ﷺ.

Muhammad Ibn Ishaq said, "Moosa ﷺ selected from among the Children of Isra'eel seventy of the best men. He said to them, "Go to the meeting with Allah and repent for what you committed. Beg His Forgiveness for those of your people whom you left behind. Fast, purify yourselves and clean your clothes." So, he went with them to Mount Toor in Sinai for the meeting place and time designated by his Lord. He went there only with the leave and knowledge of Allah.

The seventy requested that they might hear the Speech of Allah and he (Moosa) said, "I will do so." (i.e. I will submit your request to Allah). Then, when Moosa ﷺ approached the mountain, a column of clouds came down over it and the mountain was covered. Moosa ﷺ approached and entered the clouds and he said to the people, "Approach." When Allah spoke to Moosa ﷺ,

his cloak was surrounded by a brilliant light which no human could bear to look at, so below him a barrier was placed and the people approached. When they entered the cloud they fell in prostration and they heard Him while he was speaking to Moosa علیه السلام, commanding him and forbidding him, saying what to do and what not to do. When He completed commanding him, and removed the cloud from Moosa علیه السلام, he faced the people and they said, "O, Moosa! We will not believe in you unless we see Allah directly." So the thunder shook them, their souls were captured and they all died.

Moosa علیه السلام stood up invoking, begging and supplicating to his Lord, *"O, My Lord, if it had been Your will, you could have destroyed them and me before; would you destroy us for the deeds of the foolish ones among us."* (*Soorah Al-A'raf* 7:55). But the thunderbolt seized them and their souls were destroyed and all of them died. Then Moosa علیه السلام stood up and implored his Lord, saying, *"O, my Lord, if it had been Your Will, You could have destroyed them and me before; would You destroy us for the deeds of the foolish ones among us?"* (*Soorah Al-A'raf* 7:155). That is, do not blame us because of the actions of those foolish people among us who worshipped the calf, for we are innocent of what they did. 'Abdullah Ibn 'Abbas رضي الله عنه, Mujahid, Qatadah and Ibn Juraij said that the thunderbolt only took them because they did not forbid their people to worship the calf. As for Allah's Saying: *"It is only Your Trial"* (*Soorah Al-A'raf* 7:155), the meaning is: Your Test (of the Children of Isra'eel). This was said by 'Abdullah Ibn 'Abbas رضي الله عنه, Sa'eed Ibn Jubair, Abul 'Aliyah, Ar-Rabee' Ibn Anas and more than one of the earlier and the later scholars. That is, it is You Who ordained this and created the affair of the calf in order to test them thereby, as Haroon علیه السلام said to them before, *"O, my people! You are being tried in this"* (*Soorah Ta Ha* 20:90) means you are being tested by this; this is why Allah tells us that Moosa علیه السلام said, *"...by which You lead astray whom You will, and keep guided whom You will."* (*Soorah Al-A'raf* 7:155). That is, You cause to go astray whom You will by Your Trial and You guide whom You will thereby. The Judgment and the Decision belongs to You and no one can prevent or repel what You have decided and ordained. *"You are our Wali (Protector), so forgive us and have Mercy on us, for You are the Best of those who forgive."* (*Soorah Al-A'raf* 7:155)

And He, Most High, says, *"And ordain for us good in this world, and in the Hereafter. Certainly we have turned unto You."* (*Soorah Al-A'raf* 7:156) It means that we have repented to You, returned to You and sought forgiveness from You. This was said by 'Abdullah Ibn 'Abbas ☻, Mujahid, Sa'eed Ibn Jubair-Abul 'Aliyah, Ibraheem At-Taimi, Adh-Dahhak, As-Suddi, Qatadah and a number of others and it is also linguistically correct. *He said: "(As to) My Punishment I afflict therewith whom I will and My Mercy embraces all things."* (*Soorah Al-A'raf* 7:156) That is, I punish whomsoever I will, with whatever punishment I will from among the things that I have created and ordained. *"...and My Mercy embraces all things."* (*Soorah Al-A'raf* 7:156) – as confirmed in the *Saheehain*, from the Messenger of Allah ﷺ, who said, "When Allah created the Creation, He wrote in His Book – and He wrote (that) about Himself, and it is placed with Him on the Throne – 'Verily My Mercy overcomes My Anger'."[1] *"That (Mercy) I shall ordain for those who are the* **muttaqoon,** *and give* **zakah;** *and those who believe in Our* **Ayat**" (*Soorah Al-A'raf* 7:156) means I shall definitely ordain it for those who possess these attributes. *Those who follow the Messenger, the Prophet who can neither read nor write (i.e. Muhammad).* (*Soorah Al-A'raf* 7:157) In this there is confirmation that Muhammad ﷺ and his nation were mentioned by Allah to Moosa ﷺ among the things which He confided to him, taught him and apprised him of.

---

(1)   Narrated by Al-Bukhari (7404) and Muslim (2751), on the authority of Abu Hurairah ☻.

Al-Hafiz Abu Hatim Muhammad Ibn Hatim Ibn Hibban said in his *Saheeh*, on the authority of Al-Mugheerah Ibn Shu'bah who reported on the authority of the Prophet while standing on the pulpit, "Verily, Moosa asked his Lord, the Almighty, the All-Powerful, 'Which of the inhabitants of Paradise will have the least rank?' He said, 'A man will come after the people of Paradise have entered it and it will be said to him, Enter Paradise. He will say, 'How shall I enter Paradise when the people have entered their abodes and taken what is theirs?' It will be said to him, 'Would you be happy to have of Paradise what one of the kings of the Earth had?' He will say, 'Yes, O, my Lord!' So it will be said to him, 'This is yours, plus the like of it, plus the like of it again.' He will say, 'O, my Lord! I am well-pleased.' It will be said to him, 'In addition to this, yours is whatever your heart desires and whatever pleases your eye.' And he asked his Lord, 'Which of the people of Paradise occupy the highest position in Paradise?' Allah said, 'I will tell you about them: I have fixed their nobility with My Own Hands and sealed it and no eye has seen Paradise, no ear has heard it and it cannot be imagined by the mind of any human being'."[1]

Ibn Hibban said, on the authority of Abu Hurairah , that he reported from the Prophet that he said, "Moosa asked his Lord, the Almighty, the All-Powerful about six qualities which he believed belonged to him, and a seventh, which Moosa did not like. He said, "O, my Lord! Which of your slaves is the most pious?" He said, "The one who remembers (Allah) and does not forget (Him)." Moosa then asked, "And which of Your slaves is most rightly guided?" Allah said, "He who follows the (Divine) guidance." Moosa then asked, "And which of Your slaves is most judicious?" Allah said, "The one who judges for the people as he judges for himself." Moosa

_____

(1) Narrated by Ibn Hibban in his *Saheeh* (99/14, No. 6216) and it is supported by an authentic narration. See the following *Hadith*.

said, "And which of Your slaves is most knowledgeable?" Allah said, "The scholar whose appetite for knowledge is never satisfied; he combines the knowledge of the people with his (own) knowledge." Moosa then said, "And which of Your slaves is most mighty?" Allah replied, "He who, when he is master, displays forgiveness." Moosa then asked, "And which of Your slaves is wealthiest?" Allah answered, "He who is happy with what he is given." Moosa then said, "And which of Your slaves is poorest?" Allah said, "The one who possesses *manqoos*." The Messenger of Allah said, "(True) wealth is not that which is apparent; it is only wealth of the soul. And when Allah wills something good for a slave, He places his wealth in his soul and his piety in his heart. But if He wills something bad for a slave, He places his poverty in front of his eyes (i.e. He makes him feel it and he is always discontented)."[1]

Ibn Hibban said that the possessor of "*manqoos*" means the one who is dissatisfied with his circumstances; he regards what he has been given as insufficient and seeks more.

Ibn Hibban said, "Allah's *Kaleem* asked his Lord to teach him something by which he might remember Him". It was reported on the authority of Abu Sa'eed Al-Khudri from the Prophet that he said, "Moosa said, 'O, my Lord! Teach me something by which I might remember You and supplicate You.' Allah said, 'Say, O, Moosa, '*La ilaha ill-Allah* (none has the right to be worshipped except Allah)'." Moosa said, "O, my Lord! All of your slaves say this." Allah said, "Say, '*La ilaha ill-Allah* (none has the right to be worshipped except Allah)'." Moosa said, "I only want You to give something special for me." Allah said, "O, Moosa! If all of the inhabitants of the seven heavens and the seven earths were placed in a scale and '*La ilaha ill-Allah,* was placed in

---

(1)   This *Hadith* is *hasan*; it was narrated by Ibn Hibban in his *Saheeh* (14/100-101, No. 6217).

(the other side of) it, '*La ilaha ill-Allah* (none has the right to be worshipped except Allah)' would be heavier than they." [1]

This *Hadith* is supported by the *Hadith* of *Al-Bitaqah*[2] and the nearest thing to its meaning is the *Hadith* narrated in the *Sunan* from the Prophet ﷺ, in which it is reported that he said, "The best invocation is the invocation on 'Arafah and the best thing that I and the Prophets who came before me have said is: '*La ilaha ill-Allah Wahdahu la shareeka Lahu; Lahul-mulku wa Lahul-hamdu wa Huwa 'ala kulli shay'in Qadeer* (none has the right to be worshipped except Allah, Alone, without partners; His is the Kingdom and to Him belongs all praise and He is Able to do all things)'." [3]

Ibn Abi Hatim said, in the explanation of "*Ayat Al-Kursi*", "It is reported on the authority of 'Abdullah Ibn 'Abbas ﷺ that the Children of Isra'eel asked Moosa ﷺ, "Does your Lord sleep?" He said, "Fear Allah!" Then his Lord, the Almighty, the All-Powerful called him (saying), "O, Moosa! They asked you if your Lord sleeps; take two bottles in your hands and stand for the whole night." So Moosa ﷺ did so, and when a third of the night had passed, he became drowsy and fell to his knees; then he recovered and retained his grip on them. But toward the end of the night, he became drowsy and the two bottles fell and smashed. Then Allah said, "O, Moosa! If I were to sleep, the heavens and the Earth would fall and be destroyed, just as the two bottles in your hands were destroyed." Ibn 'Abbas ﷺ said, "So Allah sent down to His

---

(1) The *isnad* of this *Hadith* is weak; it was narrated by Ibn Hibban in his *Saheeh* (14/102, No. 6218).

(2) The author has referred here to a long *Hadith* in which it is mentioned that while reckoning a person's deeds, a card will be placed in the balance on which the *kalimah* "*La ilaha ill-Allah* (none has the right to be worshipped except Allah)" will be written. This card will weigh more than a heap of bad deeds.

(3) This *Hadith* is *hasan* and it was narrated by At-Tirmidhi. (3585).

Messenger ﷺ *Ayat Al-Kursi."*

And He, Most High, says, *"And (remember) when We raised the mountain over them as if it had been a canopy, and they thought that it was going to fall on them. (We said), 'Hold firmly to what We have given you (i.e. the Tawrah), and remember that which is therein (act on its Commandments), so that you may fear Allah and obey Him."* (*Soorah Al-A'raf* 7:171)

'Abdullah Ibn 'Abbas ﷺ and more than one of the *Salaf* said, "When Moosa ﷺ came to them with the Tablets on which was written the Tawrah, he ordered them to accept them and hold onto them with strength and determination, but they said, "Announce them to us, and if their commands and prohibitions are easy, we will accept them." He said, "Nay, you must accept them with all that they entail." But they examined them over and over again, until Allah raised the mountain over their heads, so that it became like a canopy over them, i.e. like a cloud over their heads and it was said to them, "If you do not accept them and all that they entail, this mountain will fall on you." So they accepted that and then they were commanded to prostrate, which they did. But they began to look toward the mountain, from the sides of their faces and this became a *Sunnah* for the Jews until this day. They say, "There is no prostration greater than the prostration in which the punishment was lifted from us." Sunaid Ibn Dawood reported on the authority of Hajjaj Ibn Muhammad, who in turn reported on the authority of Abu Bakr Ibn 'Abdullah that he said, "When he proclaimed them (the Commandments) to them, there was not a mountain, a tree or a rock on the face of the Earth that did not shake and there is not a Jew on the face of the Earth – whether great or small – who does not tremble when the Tawrah is recited to him and shake his head." Allah, Most High, says, *"Then after that you turned away"* (*Soorah Al-Baqarah* 2:64) means then after witnessing this great covenant and this momentous matter, you violated your oaths and your covenants. *"Had it not been for the Grace and Mercy of Allah upon you"* (*Soorah Al-Baqarah* 2:64) means that He sent to you a succession of Messengers and sent down to you His Books *"indeed you would have been among the losers."* (*Soorah Al-Baqarah* 2:64)

The Story of the Cow of the Children of Isra'eel

Allah, Most High, says, *"And (remember) when Moosa said to his people, 'Verily, Allah commands you that you slaughter a cow.' They said, 'Do you make fun of us?' He said, 'I take Allah's Refuge from being among* **Al-Jahiloon** *(the ignorant or the foolish).' They said, 'Call upon your Lord for us that He may make plain to us what it is!' He said, 'He says, 'Verily, it is a cow neither too old nor too young, but (it is) between the two conditions', so do what you are commanded.' They said, 'Call upon your Lord for us to make plain to us its color.' He said, 'Allah says, 'It is a yellow cow, bright in its color, pleasing to the beholders'.' They said, 'Call upon your Lord for us to make plain to us what it is. Verily, to us all cows are alike, and surely, if Allah wills, we will be guided.' He (Moosa) said, 'He says, 'It is a cow neither trained to till the soil nor water the fields, sound, having no other color except bright yellow'.' They said, 'Now you have brought the truth.' So they slaughtered it though they were near to not doing it. And (remember) when you killed a man and fell into dispute* *among yourselves as to the crime. But Allah brought forth that which you were hiding. So We said, 'Strike him (the dead man) with a piece of it (the cow).' Thus Allah brings the dead to life and shows you His Ayat so that you may understand." (Soorah Al-Baqarah* 2:67-73)

They were commanded to slaughter a cow which was *'awan*, i.e. halfway between old and young. This was said by 'Abdullah Ibn 'Abbas ☙, Mujahid, Abul-'Aliyah 'Ikrimah, Al-Hasan, Qatadah and a number of others. Then they became more demanding and made things more difficult for themselves, asking about its color. They were then commanded to slaughter a yellow cow, whose color was bright, i.e. mixed with redness, which was pleasing to those who saw it; and this color is hard to find.

Then they became even more demanding, *They said, "Call upon your Lord for us to make plain to us what it is. Verily, to us all cows are alike, and surely, if Allah wills, we will be guided." (Soorah Al-Baqarah* 2:70) And in the *Hadith* traceable to the Prophet ﷺ which was narrated by Ibn Abi Hatim and Ibn Marduyah, it was reported: "Had not the Children of Isra'eel said that they would be guided if Allah willed, they would not have been granted guidance."[1] But there is some doubt about its authenticity – and Allah knows better. *He (Moosa) said, "He says, 'It is a cow neither trained to till the soil nor water the fields, sound, having no shiyah in it'." They said, "Now you have brought the truth." So they slaughtered it though they were near to not doing it. (Soorah Al-Baqarah* 2:71) This description was more difficult than what had preceded it, since they were now commanded to slaughter a cow which had not been trained to plough the earth or irrigate the soil with a water scoop, being *musallamah*, i.e. sound in body, without any defects. This was said by Abul-'Aliyah and Qatadah. Allah's Saying: *"...having no*

---

(1) As-Suyooti ascribed it to Ibn Abi Hatim and Ibn Marduyah in *Ad-Durr Al-Manthoor* and the author declared it to be weak.

shiyah *in it"* (*Soorah Al-Baqarah* 2:71) means: having no other color besides yellow. Rather, it was free from any defect and free from having any other colors mixed with its yellow color. When he had determined its description in such great detail, *They said, "Now you have brought the truth."* (*Soorah Al-Baqarah* 2:71) It was said that they did not find a cow matching this description except with a man from among them who was dutiful to his father and they requested it from him, but he refused to give it to them. So they asked him to suggest a price for it, even offering to pay him its weight in gold, according to As-Suddi, but he still refused to give it to them unless they agreed to give him ten times its weight in gold. They did so and he then sold it to them, after which Allah's Prophet ﷺ commanded them to slaughter it. *"So they slaughtered it though they were near to not doing it."* (*Soorah Al-Baqarah* 2:71) That is, they were uncertain regarding it. Then he conveyed to them from Allah that they should strike the body of the murdered man with a part of it. It was said that that part was the meat of its thigh and it was also said that it was the bone that adjoins the cartilage. It was also said that they struck him with the part that is between the shoulders. When they struck him with a part of it, Allah, Most High, brought him back to life and he stood up and the blood was flowing from his jugular veins. Then the Prophet of Allah ﷺ asked him, "Who killed you?" He replied, "My brother's son killed me." Then he became dead once more. Allah, Most High, says, *"Thus Allah brings the dead to life and shows you His Ayat so that you may understand."* (*Soorah Al-Baqarah* 2:73) It means that as you have witnessed the bringing back to life of this murdered man, as a result of Allah's Command to him, likewise it is the case regarding all people who die; if Allah wills to revive them, He revives them in a single hour, as He, Most High, says, "The creation of you all and the resurrection of you all are only as (the creation and resurrection of) a single person." (*Soorah Luqman* 31:28)

The Story of Moosa and Al-Khidr

Allah, Most High, says, *"And (remember) when Moosa said to his servant, 'I will not give up (traveling) until I reach the junction of the two seas or (until) I spend years and years in traveling.' But when they reached the junction of the two seas, they forgot their fish, and it took its way through the sea as in a tunnel. So when they passed further on (beyond that fixed place), Moosa said to his servant, 'Bring us our morning meal; truly, we have suffered much fatigue in this, our journey.' He said, 'Do you remember when we betook ourselves to the rock? I indeed forgot the fish; none but* **Shaitan** *made me forget it. It took its course into the sea in a strange (way)!' (Moosa) said, 'That is what we have been seeking.' So they went back retracing their footsteps. Then they found one of Our slaves, unto whom We had bestowed Mercy from Us, and whom We had taught knowledge from Us. Moosa said to him (Al-Khidr), 'May I follow you so that you teach me something* *of that knowledge (guidance and true path) which you have been taught (by Allah)?' He (Al-Khidr) said, 'Verily! You will not be able to have patience with me! And how can you have patience about a thing which you know not?' Moosa said, 'If Allah wills, you will find me patient, and I will not disobey you in aught.' He (Al-Khidr) said, 'Then, if you follow me, ask me not about anything till I myself mention it to you.' So they both proceeded, till, when they boarded the ship, he (Al-Khidr) scuttled it. Moosa said, 'Have you scuttled it in order to drown its people? Verily, you have committed a thing* **imran** *(a* **munkar** *- evil, bad, dreadful thing).' He (Al-Khidr) said, 'Did I not tell you that you would not be able to have patience with me?' (Moosa) said, 'Call me not to account for what I forgot, and be not hard upon me for my affair (with you).' Then they both proceeded, till they met a boy, and he (Al-Khidr) killed him. Moosa said, 'Have you killed an innocent person who had killed none? Verily, you have committed a thing* **nukran** *(a great* **munkar** *- prohibited, evil, dreadful thing)!' (Al-Khidr) said, 'Did I not tell you that you would not be able to have patience with me?' (Moosa) said, 'If I ask you anything after this, keep me not in your company, you have received an excuse from me.' Then they both proceeded till, when they came to the people of a town, they asked them for food, but they refused to entertain them. Then they found therein a wall about to collapse and he (Al-Khidr) set it up straight. (Moosa) said, 'If you had wished, surely, you could have taken wages for it!' (Al-Khidr) said, 'This is the parting between me and you; I will tell you the interpretation of (those) things regarding which you were unable to have patience: As for the ship, it belonged to* **masakeen** *(poor people) working in the sea. So I wished to make a defective damage in it, as there was a king after them who seized every ship by force. And as for the boy, his parents were Believers, and we feared lest he should oppress them by rebellion and disbelief. So we intended that their Lord should change him for them for one better in righteousness and near to mercy. And as for the wall, it belonged to two orphan* *boys in the town; and there was under it a treasure belonging to them; and their father was a righteous man, and your Lord intended that they should attain their age of full strength and take out their treasure as a Mercy from your Lord. And I did it not of my own accord. That is the interpretation of those (things) regarding which you could not be patient'."* (*Soorah Al-Kahf* 18:60-82)

And Al-Bukhari narrated on the authority of Sa'eed Ibn Jubair that he said, "I said to 'Abdullah Ibn 'Abbas ﵁, 'Nawf Al-Bikali claims that Moosa of the Children of Isra'eel was not Moosa, the companion of Al-Khidr'." Ibn 'Abbas ﵁ said, "Allah's enemy tells a lie! Ubayy Ibn Ka'b narrated to us that Allah's Messenger ﷺ said, "Moosa got up to deliver a sermon before the Children of Isra'eel and he was asked, "Who is the most learned person among the people?" Moosa replied, "I (am the most learned)." Allah then admonished Moosa for he did not ascribe all knowledge to Allah only. (Then) came the Divine Inspiration: "Yes, one of Our slaves at the junction of the two seas is more learned than you." Moosa said, "O, my Lord ! How can I meet him?" Allah said, "Take a fish in a basket and wherever the fish is lost, follow it (you will find him at that place). So Moosa set out along with his slave, Yoosha' Ibn Noon, and they carried with them a fish till they reached a rock and rested there. Moosa put his head down and slept. (Sufyan, a sub-narrator said that somebody other than 'Amr said:) "At the rock there was a water spring called *'Al-Hayat'* and none came in touch with its water but became alive. Some of the water of that spring fell over that fish, so it moved and slipped out of the basket and entered the sea. When Moosa woke up, he said to his servant, *"Bring us our morning meal."* (*Soorah Al-Kahf* 18:62) The narrator added: Moosa did not suffer from fatigue except after he had passed the place he had been ordered to observe. His servant, Yoosha' (Joshua) said to him, *"Do you remember when we betook ourselves to the rock? I indeed forgot the fish; none but **Shaitan** made me forget it. It took its course into the sea in a strange* *(way)!"* (*Soorah Al-Kahf* 18.63) The narrator added, "So they came back, retracing their steps and then they found in the sea, the way of the fish looking like a tunnel. So there was an astonishing event for his slave, and there was a tunnel for the fish. When they reached the rock, they found a man covered with a garment. Moosa greeted him. The man said astonishingly, "Is there any such greeting in your land?" Moosa said, "I am Moosa." The man said, "Moosa of the Children of Isra'eel?" Moosa said, "Yes," and added, *"May I follow you so that you teach me something of that knowledge (guidance and true path) which you have been taught (by Allah)?"* (18.66) Al-Khidr said to him, "O, Moosa! You have something of Allah's knowledge which Allah has taught you and which I do not know; and I have something of Allah's knowledge which Allah has taught me and which you do not know." Moosa said, "But I will follow you." Al-Khidr said, *"Then if you follow me, ask me no question about anything until I myself speak to you concerning it."* (*Soorah Al-Kahf* 18:70) After that both of them proceeded along the seashore. There passed by them a boat whose crew recognized Al-Khidr and received them on board free of charge. So they both got on board. A sparrow came and sat on the edge of the boat and dipped its beak unto the sea. Al-Khidr said to Moosa, "My knowledge and your knowledge and all the creation's knowledge compared to Allah's knowledge is not more than the water taken by this sparrow's beak." Then Moosa was startled by Al-Khidr's action of taking an *adze* and scuttling the boat with it. Moosa said to him, "These people gave us a free lift, but you intentionally scuttled their boat so as to drown them. *"In order to drown its people? Verily, you have committed a thing* **imran** *(a* **munkar** *– evil, bad, dreadful thing) He (Al-Khidr) said, Did I not tell you, that you would not be able to have patience with me? Moosa said, "call me not to account for what I forgot, and be not haved upon me for my affair (with you)."* (*Soorah Al-Kahf* 18:71-73) Then they both proceeded and found a boy playing with other boys. Al-Khidr took hold of him by the head

and cut it off. Moosa said to him, *"Have you killed an innocent person who had killed none? Verily, you have committed a thing* **nukran** *(a great* **munkar** *– prohibited, evil, dreadful thing)!"* (*Soorah Al-Kahf* 18:74) He said, *"Did I not tell you that you would not be able to have patience with me?"* – up to *"...but they refused to entertain them. Then they found therein a wall about to collapse."* (*Soorah Al-Kahf* 18:75-77) Al-Khidr moved his hand thus and set it upright (repaired it). Moosa said to him, "When we entered this town, they neither gave us hospitality nor fed us; if you had wished, you could have taken wages for it," Al-Khidr said, *"This is the parting between me and you; I will tell you the interpretation of (those) things regarding which you were unable to have patience."* (*Soorah Al-Kahf* 18:78)

Allah's Messenger ﷺ said, "We wished that Moosa could have been more patient so that He (Allah) could have described to us more about their story."

Sa'eed Ibn Jubair said that 'Abdullah Ibn 'Abbas ﷺ used to recite, *"as there was a king before them who seized every ship by force."* (*Soorah Al-Kahf* 18:79) and he used to recite, *"And as for the boy, he was a disbeliever and his parents were Believers."* (*Soorah Al-Kahf* 18:80)."[1]

And He, Most High, says, *"And as for the wall, it belonged to two orphan boys in the town; and there was under it a treasure belonging to them; and their father was a righteous man, and your Lord intended that they should attain their age of full strength and take out their treasure as a Mercy from your Lord. And I did it not of my own accord. That is the interpretation of those (things) regarding which you could not be patient."* (*Soorah Al-Kahf* 18:82) As-Suhaili said that they were Asram and Sareem, the sons of Kashih. *"...and there was under it a treasure belonging to them."* (*Soorah Al-Kahf* 18:82) According to 'Ikrimah, it

---

(1) Narrated by Al-Bukhari (4725).

was gold. 'Abdullah Ibn 'Abbas 🙵 said that it was knowledge. What appears most likely is that it was a golden tablet on which knowledge was written.

He, Most High, says, *"...and their father was a righteous man."* (*Soorah Al-Kahf* 18:82) It was said that he was the seventh father and it was also said that he was the tenth. At all events, in it there is evidence that the righteous man is protected in his offspring and Allah is the One Whose Help is sought. And He, Most High, says, *"...as a Mercy from your Lord."* (*Soorah Al-Kahf* 18:82) This proves that he was a Prophet and that he did nothing of his own accord; rather, he acted in accordance with the Command of his Lord, which means that he was a Prophet. It was also said that he was a Messenger and also that he was a *Wali*. But stranger than that is the claim of those who said that he was an angel.

The Story of the Building of the Tabernacle of Time

The People of the Scripture said that Allah commanded Moosa 🙶🙶 to make a tent from cedar wood, leather and sheepskin; and He commanded him to embellish it with dyed silk, gold and silver, using intricate designs, according to the People of the Scripture. This Tabernacle of Time was with the Children of Isra'eel in the wilderness and they used to pray toward it, so it was their *Qiblah* and their Ka'bah; and their *Imam* was Allah's *Kaleem*, Moosa 🙶🙶, while the one who offered the sacrifices was his brother, Haroon 🙶🙶. When Haroon and then Moosa (peace be upon them both) died, the sons of Haroon 🙶🙶 continued to follow what their father had practiced with regard to the sacrifice – and they still practice it until this day. They undertook the burden of Prophethood after Moosa 🙶🙶 and the responsibility of leadership after him was given to his slave, Yoosha', and it was he who brought them into Bait Al-Maqdis (the Holy Land).

What is meant here is that when he became ruler of Bait Al-Maqdis, this Tabernacle was erected on the rock of Bait Al-Maqdis and they used to pray toward it. After it had gone, they prayed toward its former place, i.e. the rock. This is why it was the *Qiblah* of the Prophets who came after him, until the time of the Messenger of Allah ﷺ – and he prayed toward it prior to the migration to Madinah, though he would pray with the Ka'bah directly in front of him. After he had migrated to Madinah, he was commanded to pray toward Bait Al-Maqdis and he did so for sixteen or seventeen months. Then the *Qiblah* was changed to the Ka'bah – and that was the *Qiblah* of Ibraheem – in the month of Sha'aban, in the year 2 A.H., at the time of the *'Asr* prayer, or, it was said, the *Zuhr* prayer.[1]

---

(1)   See *Saheeh Al-Bukhari* (40).

The Story of Qaroon with Moosa

Allah, Most High, says, *"Verily, Qaroon (Korah) was of Moosa's people, but he behaved arrogantly toward them. And We gave him the treasures, that of which the keys would have been a burden to a body of strong men. When his people said to him, 'Do not exult; verily! Allah likes not those who exult. But seek, with that (wealth) which Allah has bestowed you, the home of the Hereafter, and forget not your portion of legal enjoyment in this world, and be generous as Allah has been Generous to you, and seek not mischief in the land. Verily, Allah likes not the* **mufsidoon** *(those who commit great crimes and sins, oppressors, tyrants, mischief-makers and corrupt people).' He said, 'This has been given to me only because of knowledge I possess.' Did he not know that Allah had destroyed before him generations, men who were stronger than him in might and greater in the amount (of riches) they had collected. But the* **mujrimoon** *(criminals,* *disbelievers, polytheists and sinners, etc.) will not be questioned of their sins (because Allah knows them well, so they will be punished without account). So he went forth before his people in his pomp. Those who were desirous of the life of the world, said, 'Ah, would that we had the like of what Qaroon has been given! Verily! He is the owner of a great fortune.' But those who had been given (religious) knowledge said, 'Woe to you! The Reward of Allah is better for those who believe and do righteous good deeds, and this none shall attain except those who are patient (in following the truth).' So We caused the earth to swallow him and his dwelling place. Then he had no group or party to help him against Allah, nor was he one of those who could save themselves. And those who had desired (a position like) his position the day before, began to say, 'Know you not that it is Allah Who enlarges the provision or restricts it to whomsoever He pleases of His slaves? Had it not been that Allah was Gracious to us, He could have caused the earth to swallow us up (also)! Know you not that the disbelievers will never be successful? That home of the Hereafter (i.e. Paradise), We shall assign to those who rebel not against the truth with pride and oppression in the land nor do mischief by committing crimes. And the good end is for the muttaqoon'.*" (*Soorah Al-Qasas* 28:76-83)

It is reported on the authority of 'Abdullah Ibn 'Abbas ﷺ that he said, "Qaroon was Moosa's cousin. Qatadah said that he was called *An-Noor* (the Light) because of his pleasant voice when reciting the Tawrah. But the enemy of Allah was guilty of hypocrisy, like the hypocrisy of As-Samiri, and he was destroyed by his wrongdoing, because of his wealth.

Allah, Most High, described his enormous wealth to the extent that a group of strong men would have found the keys to his treasures heavy to carry. It was also said that his wealth was in animal skins and that it was carried on sixty mules. And Allah knows better. The advisers among his people had admonished him, saying, *"Do not exult. Verily! Allah likes not those who exult"* (*Soorah Al-Qasas* 28:76) means do not be proud because of what you have been given and do not behave arrogantly toward others. *"But seek, with that (wealth) which Allah has bestowed on you, the home of the Hereafter."* (*Soorah Al-Qasas* 28:77) They were saying, "Let your priority be the attainment of Allah's Reward in the abode of the Hereafter, because it is better than and more lasting." And at the same time, *"...and forget not your portion of legal enjoyment in this world."* (*Soorah Al-Qasas* 28:77) That is, take from your property what Allah has made lawful to you and enjoy yourself with it in a lawful manner. *"...and be generous as Allah has been Generous to you"* (*Soorah Al-Qasas* 28:77) means be good to Allah's creation, just as their Creator has been good to you. *"...and seek not mischief in the land."* (*Soorah Al-Qasas* 28:77) It means that do not act meanly toward them, do not spread corruption among them and do not treat them in a manner contrary to that which you were commanded to do, for (if you do that), He will punish you and take what He has given you away from you. *"Verily, Allah likes not the* **mufsidoon**. *"* (*Soorah Al-Qasas* 28:77) But his reply to this correct and eloquent advice from his people was naught but to say, *"This has been given to me only because of knowledge I possess."* (*Soorah Al-Qasas* 28:78) That is, I have no need to act upon what you have mentioned or what you have indicated, because Allah has only given me this (wealth) because He knows that I deserve it and am worthy of it; and if I was not beloved by Him, He would not have given me what He has given me. But Allah answered him, saying, *"Did he not know that Allah had destroyed before him generations, men who were stronger than him in might and greater in the amount (of riches) they had collected. But the* **mujrimoon** *will not be questioned of their sins (because Allah knows them well, so they will be punished without account)"* (*Soorah Al-Qasas* 28:78) means We have destroyed previous generations because of their sins and offenses – and they possessed much greater power and wealth and more children than Qaroon. So if what he says is correct; We would not punish anyone who had more wealth than he. His wealth is not a proof of Our Love for him or Our Care for him, as He, Most High, says, *"And it is not your wealth, nor your children that bring you nearer to Us (i.e. pleases Allah), but only he (will please Us) who believes (in Islamic Monotheism), and does righteous deeds; as for such, there will be twofold reward for what they did, and they will reside in the high dwellings (Paradise) in peace and security."* (*Soorah Saba'* 34:37) And He, Most High says, *"Do they think that We enlarge them in wealth and children, We hasten unto them with good things (in this worldly life so that they will have no share of good things in the Hereafter)? Nay, but they perceive not."* (*Soorah Al-Mu'minoon* 23:55,56)

Allah, Most High, says, *"So he went forth before his people in his pomp."* (*Soorah Al-Qasas* 28:79) Many of the scholars of *tafseer* said that he would set out with great pomp and ceremony, wearing fine clothes and riding in a beautiful carriage, with servants and retinue and when those who are impressed by the splendor of the life of this world saw him, they wished that they had wealth like his and were envious of his situation. When the scholars – those who possessed correct understanding, the intelligent and ascetic – heard their words, they said to them, *"Woe to you! The Reward of Allah is better for those who believe and do righteous good deeds."* (*Soorah Al-Qasas* 28:80) That is, Allah's Reward in the abode of the Hereafter is better, more lasting, more splendid and more exalted. Allah, Most High, says, *"...and this none shall attain except those who are patient (in following the truth)"* (*Soorah Al-Qasas* 28:80) means none shall attain this advice, this statement and this high-mindedness zeal for the abode of the Hereafter, which is much superior when compared to the embellishments of this inferior, Earthly life – except those whose hearts Allah guides and makes firm, whose understanding He supports and whose aims and goals He causes to be achieved.

And how fine is the saying of one of the *Salaf*, who said, "Verily, Allah loves penetrating insight in cases of doubt or obscurity and perfect rationality in cases of vain desire." Allah, Most High, says, *"So We caused the earth to swallow him and his dwelling place. Then he had no group or party to help him against Allah, nor was he one of those who could save themselves." (Soorah Al-Qasas* 28:81) After describing how he would set out with his pomp and his pride therein, showing disdain toward the people because of it, Allah said, *"So We caused the earth to swallow him and his dwelling place."*

As narrated in *Saheeh Al-Bukhari* in the *Hadith* of Az-Zuhri, who reported on the authority of Salim, who in turn reported on the authority of his father, who reported from the Prophet ﷺ that he said, "While a man was dragging his *izar* (lower garment) on the ground (behind him), suddenly Allah made him sink into the earth and he will go on sinking into it till the Day of Resurrection."[1]

And Allah, Most High, says, *"Then he had no group or party to help him against Allah, nor was he one of those who could save themselves." (Soorah Al-Qasas* 28:81) There was no one to help him – neither he himself nor any other, as Allah says, *"Then will (man) have no power, nor any helper." (Soorah At-Tariq* 86:10) And when the swallowing of the earth, the loss of his wealth, the ruin of his house and the destruction of him, his family and his landed property befell him, those who had wished for wealth such as he had been given repented and thanked Allah, Who organizes the affairs of His slaves as He wills, in the best way. This is why they said, *"Had it not been that Allah was Gracious to us, He could have caused the earth to swallow us up (also)! Know you not that the disbelievers will never be successful?" (Soorah Al-Qasas* 28:82)

Then He, Most High, informs us of that *"That home of the*

_____

(1)   Narrated by Al-Bukhari (3485).

Hereafter (i.e. Paradise)" (*Soorah Al-Qasas* 28:83) – and that is the everlasting abode, the abode which those who are given it will be happy and will be comforted by the (beautiful) women therein. And it is only prepared for those who desire not grandeur and greatness in this world, nor corruption. Grandeur is pride, arrogance and insolence and corruption is acts of disobedience, such as taking the wealth of the people by force, corrupting their way of life, treating them badly and not advising them. Then He, Most High, says, *"And the good end is for the* **muttaqoon** *(pious)."* (*Soorah Al-Qasas* 28:83)

Allah, Most High, has described the censure of Qaroon in more than one Verse of the Qur'an: He, Most High, says, *"And indeed We sent Moosa with Our* **Ayat***, and a manifest authority, to Fir'awn, Haman and Qaroon, but they called (him) "a sorcerer, a liar!"* (*Soorah Ghafir* 40:23,24)

And Imam Ahmad has narrated on the authority of 'Abdullah Ibn 'Amr ﷺ from the Prophet ﷺ that one day he mentioned the prayer, saying, "Whoever observes it (regularly and conscientiously) will have a light, a proof and salvation on the Day of Resurrection. But he who does not observe it will have no light, no proof and no salvation; and on the Day of Resurrection, he will be with Qaroon, Fir'awn, Haman and 'Ubayy Ibn Khalaf."[1] Imam Ahmad was alone in narrating this.

---

[1] This is an authentic *Hadith* narrated by Imam Ahmad (2/1169, No. 6540).

Description of the Virtues, Good Qualities and Characteristics of Moosa and His Death

Allah, Most High, says, *"And mention in the Book (this Qur'an) Moosa. Verily! He was chosen and he was a Messenger (and) a Prophet. And We called him from the right side of the Mount, and made him draw near to Us for a talk with him (Moosa). And We bestowed on him his brother Haroon, (also) a Prophet, out of Our Mercy."* (*Soorah Maryam* 19:51-53)

And He, Most High, says, *(Allah) said, "O, Moosa! I have chosen you above men by My Messages, and by My speaking (to you)."* (*Soorah Al-A'raf* 7:144)

And we have mentioned previously that it is recorded in the *Saheehain* from the Messenger of Allah ﷺ that he said, "Do not ascribe to me superiority over the other Prophets, for on the Day of Resurrection the people will become unconscious and I will (feel that) I am the first to regain consciousness. Then I will see Moosa holding one of the legs of the Throne. I will not know whether he has come to his senses before me or that the shock he had received at the Mountain, (during his worldly life) was sufficient for him."[1]

And Imam Abu 'Abdullah Al-Bukhari narrated on the authority of Abu Hurairah ؓ that he said, "The Messenger of Allah ﷺ said, '(Prophet) Moosa was a shy person and used to cover his body completely because of his extensive shyness. One of the Children of Isra'eel hurt him by saying, He covers his body in this way only because of some defect in his skin, either leprosy or scrotal hernia, or he has some other defect. Allah wished to clear Moosa of what they said about him, so one day while Moosa was in seclusion, he took off his clothes and put them on a stone and started taking a bath. When he finished the bath, he moved toward his clothes so as to take them, but the stone took his clothes and fled; Moosa picked up his stick and ran after the stone saying, 'O, stone! Give me my garment!' Till he reached a group of the Children of Isra'eel who saw him naked then, and found him the best of what Allah had created, and Allah cleared him of what they had accused him of. The stone stopped there and Moosa took and put his garment on and started hitting the stone with his stick. By Allah, the stone still has some traces of the hitting, three, four or five marks. This was what Allah refers to in His Saying: *"O, you who believe! Be you not like those who annoyed Moosa, But Allah cleared him of that which they alleged, and he was honorable in Allah's Sight."* (*Soorah Al-Ahzab* 33.69)

And it is reported in the *Saheehain* in the narration of Qatadah, on the authority of Anas, who reported on the authority of Malik

---

(1)   Narrated by Al-Bukhari (4638) and Muslim (2374).

Ibn Sa'sa'ah, who reported from the Prophet ﷺ that on the night when he was raised up to the heavens, he met Moosa ﷺ in the sixth heaven and Jibraeel ﷺ said to him, "This is Moosa." So he greeted him with salutations of peace; he said, "I greeted him with salutations of peace and he said, 'Welcome to the righteous Prophet and righteous brother.' When I proceeded on, he started weeping and when he was asked why he was weeping, he said, 'I am weeping because followers of this youth who was sent after me will enter Paradise in greater number than my followers'."[1]

Allah, Most High, has mentioned Moosa ﷺ in the Qur'an in many places, praised him and related his story in His Noble Book a number of times and He has repeated it at length and in brief. He has praised him eloquently and in many places, He has coupled mention of him and his Book (the Towrah) with the mention of Muhammad ﷺ and His Book (the Qur'an), as in *Soorah Al-Baqarah*, where *He says, "And when there came to them a Messenger from Allah (i.e. Muhammad) confirming what was with them, a party of those who were given the Scripture threw away the Book of Allah behind their backs as if they did not know!"* (*Soorah Al-Baqarah* 2:101)

And He, Most High, says *"And indeed We granted to Moosa and Haroon the criterion (of right and wrong), and a shining light (i.e. the Tawrah) and a Reminder for* **Al-Muttaqoon**. *Those who fear their Lord without seeing Him, while they are afraid of the Hour. And this is a blessed Reminder (the Qur'an) which We have sent down, will you then (dare to) deny it?"* (*Soorah Al-Anbiya'* 21:48-50)

And He, Most High, says, *"Let the people of the Injeel (Gospel) judge by what Allah has revealed therein. And whosoever does not judge by what Allah has revealed (then) such (people) are the* **Fasiqoon** *(the rebellious i.e. disobedient (of a lesser degree)*

---

(1)   Narrated by Al-Bukhari (3207) and Muslim (164).

to Allah. And We have sent down to you (O, Muhammad,) the Book (this Qur'an) in truth, confirming the Scripture that came before it and muhaiminan (trustworthy in highness and a witness) over it (old Scriptures)." (Soorah Al-Ma'idah 5:47,48) So He has made the Qur'an as a judge over all of the previous Scriptures, a confirmation of them and an explanation of the alterations and substitutions that have occurred therein, because the People of the Scripture were entrusted with the Scriptures that were in their hands, but they were unable to preserve them, retain them and protect them. This is why alterations and substitutions occurred therein – because of their poor understanding, their deficient knowledge, their bad intentions and their betrayal of their Deity – may Allah's Curse remain upon them until the Day of Resurrection. This is why their books contain clear errors regarding Allah and His Messengers – errors which are innumerable and indescribable, the like of which are not to be found and are unknown elsewhere.

In short, the law of Moosa ﷺ was great and the people of his nation were in large numbers; among them were Prophets, learned men, those who were devoted to worshipping Allah, ascetics, men of understanding, kings, princes, leaders and nobles. But they passed away and were replaced, and they altered their law and were turned into apes and swine. Then they abrogated them after all of the accounting of their nation and misadventures too numerous to mention befell them. However, we shall relate those which contain convincing arguments for those who wish to know it, if Allah wills. On Him we depend and on Him we rely.

Mention of the Pilgrimage of Moosa to the Ancient House and the Description of It

Imam Ahmad narrated on the authority of 'Abdullah Ibn 'Abbas that the Messenger of Allah   passed by Al-Azraq Valley and he asked, "Which valley is this?" They said, "It is Al-Azraq Valley." He said, "It is as if I am now looking at Moosa coming down from the mountain track and he is calling upon Allah, the Almighty, the All-Powerful in a loud voice, saying, 'Here I am, at Your service, O, Allah!' – until he reached the mountain track of Harsha'."[1] He then asked them, "Which mountain track is this?" They said, "This is the mountain track of Harsha'." He said, "It is as if I am now looking at Yoonus, son of Matta, riding on a red she-camel, with a cloak of wool around him and the reins of his she-camel are made from *khulbah*." Hushaim said, "It (*khulbah*) means date-palm fibers – and he was calling upon Allah, saying, 'Here I am, at Your service, O, Allah'!"[2]

Imam Ahmad narrated on the authority of Mujahid that he said, "We were with Ibn 'Abbas   and someone mentioned *Ad-Dajjal* and it was said, "It is written between his eyes: '*Kaf, Fa', Ra'*'."[3] He said, "What do they say?" He said, "They say, "It is written between his eyes: '*Kaf, Fa', Ra'*." Ibn 'Abbas   then said, "I did not hear him (i.e. the Prophet) say that, but he said, "As for Ibraheem, look at your companion (i.e. look at me), while as for Moosa, he was a well-built man, with curly hair and he rode a red camel, whose reins were made of *khulbah*. It is as if I am seeing him now going down into the valley and calling out, 'Here I am, at Your service, O, Allah!'."[4] Hushaim said that *khulbah* means date-palm fibers.

---

(1)   Harsha': A mountain track between Makkah and Madinah.

(2)   This is an authentic *Hadith* narrated by Imam Ahmad (1857).

(3)   These three Arabic letters spell the root verb *kafara*, which means to disbelieve.

(4)   This is an authentic *Hadith* narrated by Imam Ahmad (2497).

Description of Moosa's Death

Al-Bukhari narrated in his *Saheeh* on the authority of Abu Hurairah ؓ that he said, "The Angel of Death was sent to Moosa ﷺ. When he came to Moosa, he struck him. The angel returned to his Lord and said, "You have sent me to a slave who does not want to die." Allah said, "Return to him and tell him to put his hand on the back of an ox and for every hair that will come under it, he will be granted one year of life." Moosa said, "O, Lord! What will happen after that?" Allah replied, "Then death." Moosa said, "Let it come now!" Moosa then requested Allah to let him die close to the Holy Land so that he would be at a stone's throw distance from it." Abu Hurairah ؓ added, "The Messenger of Allah ﷺ said, 'If I were there, I would show you his grave below the red sand dune at the side of the road'." [1]

Imam Ahmad narrated on the authority of Abu Hurairah ؓ that he said, The Angel of Death came to Moosa ﷺ and he said,

_____

(1)   Narrated by Al-Bukhari (3407).

"Answer your Lord." But Moosa struck the Angel of Death in the eye and knocked it out. The angel returned to Allah and said, "You sent me to a slave of Yours who does not wish to die." He added, "And he has knocked out my eye!" Allah then restored his eye and said, "Return to My slave and say to him, 'Is it life you desire? If you desire to live, then place your hand on the back of the bull. Then you will live as many years as the number of hairs covered by your hand'." Moosa ﷺ asked, "Then what?" He was told, "Then death." He said, "Then now, O, my Lord, or soon!"[1] Imam Ahmad was alone in narrating this and it is *mawqoof* with this wording. It was narrated by Ibn Hibban in his *Saheeh*, on the authority of Abu Hurairah ﷺ from the Messenger of Allah ﷺ.[2] Ibn Hibban was doubtful about it, and he explained it, saying, "When the Angel of Death said this, Moosa ﷺ did not know him, because he came to him in a form which Moosa ﷺ did not recognize, just as Jibraeel ﷺ came to the Prophet ﷺ in the form of a Bedouin[3] and the angels came to Ibraheem ﷺ and Lot ﷺ in the form of young men and Ibraheem ﷺ and Lot ﷺ did not recognize them at first. Similarly, it seems likely that Moosa ﷺ did not recognize him for the same reason, and so he struck him and knocked out his eye, because he entered his house without seeking permission. This is in agreement with our law, which permits the removal of the eye of one who looks at you in your house without permission."

Then he related the *Hadith* via 'Abdur-Razzaq, on the authority of Ma'mar, who reported on the authority of Hammam, who in turn reported on the authority of Abu Hurairah ﷺ that he said, The

---

(1) This is authentic, but *mawqoof* – and it was narrated by Imam Ahmad (8402).

(2) This is an authentic *Hadith* narrated by Ibn Hibban in his *Saheeh* (14/112, No. 6223).

(3) Narrated by Muslim (8), Abu Dawood (4695), At-Tirmidhi (2610), An-Nasa'i (4990), Ibn Majah (63) and Ahmad (185), on the authority of 'Umar Ibn Al-Khattab ﷺ.

Messenger of Allah ﷺ said, "The Angel of Death came to Moosa in order to take his soul and he said to him, 'Answer your Lord.' But Moosa struck the Angel of Death in the eye and knocked out his eye."[1]

It was as if he did not recognize him in that form; he did not know that the angel was speaking the truth, since at that time, he had not established that it was a noble angel, for there were many things that he hoped to see occur in his lifetime, such as their departure from the wilderness and their entry into the Holy Land. But it had already been ordained by Allah that he should die in the wilderness, after his brother, Haroon عليه السلام, as we shall make clear, if Allah, Most High, wills.

Some of them claimed that it was Moosa عليه السلام who led them out of the wilderness and into the Holy Land – and this contradicts what the People of the Scripture and the majority of the Muslims believe.

Among the proofs for this is the saying of Moosa عليه السلام, when he chose death, saying, "My Lord! Bring as close as a stone's throw to the Holy Land," and if he had entered it, he would not have said that. But when he was with his people in the wilderness and the time of his death drew near, he wished to be close to the land to which he had migrated and he encouraged his people to go there. But fate intervened between them and it by a stone's throw.

Imam Ahmad narrated on the authority of Anas Ibn Malik ؓ that he said, "The Messenger of Allah ﷺ said, "When I was raised up to the heaven, I passed by Moosa and he was standing in prayer in his grave, near the red sand dune."[2]

---

(1) This is an authentic *Hadith* narrated by Ibn Hibban in his *Saheeh* (14/116, No. 6224).

(2) This is an authentic *Hadith* narrated by Imam Ahmad (13181).

The Story of Yoosha'

Prophethood and His Undertaking of the Burdens of the Children of Isra'eel After the Deaths of Moosa and Haroon

He was Yoosha', son of Noon, son of Afrayeem, son of Yoosuf, son of Ya'qoob, son of Ishaq, son of Ibraheem, *Al-Khaleel* (peace be upon them all). The People of the Scriptures say that he was the cousin of Hood عليه السلام and Allah has mentioned him in the Qur'an, without specifying his name, in the story of Al-Khidr, as we mentioned previously: *"And (remember) when Moosa said to his servant."* (*Soorah Al-Kahf* 18:60) *"So when they had passed further on (beyond that fixed place), Moosa said to his servant..."* (*Soorah Al-Kahf* 18:62) And we have mentioned previously the authentic narration of Ubayy Ibn Ka'b ﷺ from the Prophet ﷺ, in which he stated that he was Yoosha', son of Noon عليه السلام and the People of the Scriptures concur with the view that he was a Prophet.

Imam Ahmad narrated on the authority of Abu Hurairah ﷺ that he said, The Messenger of Allah ﷺ said, "One of the Prophets fought in a battle and he said to his people, 'Let no man follow me who has married a woman and wishes to consummate the marriage but has not yet done so, nor one who has built a house and has not yet erected its roof, nor one who has bought a sheep or a she-camel and he is waiting for it to deliver its young.' So he set out to do battle and neared the town at the time for *'Asr* prayer, or thereabouts and he said to the sun, "You are commanded (by Allah) and I am commanded (by Allah). O, Allah! hold it (the sun) back for me for a little while." So it was held back for him until Allah granted him victory. Then they gathered the booty they had won and the fire came to burn it, but it refused to consume it. So he said, "Among you there is someone who has stolen something from the booty. So let one man from every tribe swear an oath of allegiance to me. The hand of one of them stuck to his hand and he said, "Among you are the ones who have stolen something from the booty. Let your tribe swear an oath of allegiance to me." So his tribe swore an oath of allegiance to him and the hands of two or three men stuck to his hand and he said, "Among you are those who have stolen the booty. You are the thieves who have stolen the booty." Then they produced for him the equivalent of a cow's head in gold and they put it with the wealth and it was on a plateau. Then the fire accepted it and consumed it. The Prophet ﷺ added, "The spoils of war were not made lawful for any people before us. This is because Allah saw our weakness and humility and made them lawful for us." Muslim was alone in narrating it from this source.[1]

What is meant is that when he led them through the gate of the city, they were commanded to enter it while bowing in submission and thanks to Allah, the Almighty, the All-Powerful for the great victory which He had bestowed on them, and which

---

[1] Narrated by Muslim (1747).

He had promised them. And they were commanded to say as they entered the city, *hittatun*. That is, remove from us the sins that we committed in the past, i.e. our refusal to fight. This is why, when the Messenger of Allah ﷺ entered Makkah on the day of the conquest, he entered it – and he was riding his she-camel – in a state of submission, in order to express praise and thanks to Allah. In fact, so low did he bow his head that the tip of his beard touched the saddle of his riding beast. And with him were the soldiers, in particular, the green regiment, of whom nothing was visible except their eyes (because of their armor). When he entered it, he first bathed and then prayed eight *rak'ahs*.[1]

As for the Children of Isra'eel, they disobeyed the command given to them in word and in deed: They entered the gate, crawling on their posteriors and saying, "*Habbatun fee sha'rah* (a seed in a hair)," or, according to another narration, "*Hintatun fee sha'rah* (a grain of wheat in a hair)." In short, they altered what they had been commanded to do and mocked it, as Allah, Most High, says about them in *Soorah Al-A'raf*, which is a Makkan *Soorah*, *And (remember) when it was said to them, "Dwell in this town (Jerusalem) and eat therefrom wherever you wish, and say, '(O, Allah) forgive our sins.' And enter the gate in prostration (bowing with humility). We shall forgive you your wrongdoings. We shall increase (the reward) for those who do good." But those among them who did wrong changed the word that had been told to them. So We sent on them a punishment from heaven in return for their wrongdoings.* (*Soorah Al-A'raf* 7:161-162)

And He, Most High, says in *Soorah Al-Baqarah* – which is a Madinan *Soorah* – addressing them, *And (remember) when We said, "Enter this town (Jerusalem) and eat bountifully therein*

---

(1) Narrated by Al-Bukhari (1176), Muslim (336), Abu Dawood (1290), At-Tirmidhi (474), An-Nasa'i (225), Ibn Majah (614), Ahmad (26347), Malik (359) and Ad-Darimi (1452), on the authority of Umm Hani (may Allah be pleased with her).

with pleasure and delight wherever you wish, and enter the gate in prostration (or bowing with humility) and say, 'Forgive us', and We shall forgive you your sins and shall increase (reward) for those who do good." But those who did wrong changed the word from that which had been told to them for another, so We sent upon the wrongdoers **rijzan** *(a punishment) from the heaven because of their refusal to obey Allah.* (*Soorah Al-Baqarah* 2:58-59) (*Tafseer At-Tabari*, Vol. 1, Page 305)

Mention of the Stories of Al-Khidr and Ilyas (Elias)

As for Al-Khidr عليه السلام, we have already said that Moosa عليه السلام traveled to him in order to seek the hidden knowledge that he possessed; and Allah relates their stories in His Book, in *Soorah Al-Kahf*, which we have spoken of in the *tafseer* of that *Soorah*. And here we relate the *Hadith* which clearly mentions Al-Khidr عليه السلام and describes how Moosa عليه السلام, son of 'Imran, the Prophet of the Children of Isra'eel, to whom the Towrah was sent down, traveled to see him.[1]

Scholars have continued to disagree regarding his name, his lineage and whether or not he was a Prophet until now, voicing a number of opinions, which I will mention to you here, if Allah wills, by His Strength and His Power. Al-Hafiz Ibn 'Asakir said, "It is said that he was Al-Khidr, son of Adam عليه السلام, i.e. the fruit of his loins." Then he narrated a *Hadith* from Ad-Daraqutni, on the authority of 'Abdullah Ibn 'Abbas رضي الله عنه, who said, "Al-Khidr is the son of Adam, the fruit of his loins. And Allah has prolonged his lifespan until the day when he will belie the *Dajjal*.

Ibn Qutaibah mentioned in *Al-Ma'arif*, on the authority of

---

(1) The *takhreej* for this *Hadith* has been given previously.

Wahb Ibn Munabbih that Al-Khidr's name was Balya. It was also said that he was Eelya, son of Malkan, son of Falagh, son of 'Abir, son of Shalakh, son of Arfakhshadh, son of Sham, son of Nooh ﷺ. Isma'eel Ibn Abi Uwais said, "According to what has been conveyed to us, Al-Khidr's name was Al-Mu'ammar, son of Malik, son of 'Abdullah, son of Nasr, son of Al-Azad – and Allah knows better."

And Al-Bukhari narrated on the authority of Abu Hurairah ﷺ from the Prophet ﷺ that he said, "He was only known as Al-Khidr because when he sat upon a piece of white, barren land, it became green with plantation (after he sat on it)."[1]

The context of the story proves that he was a Prophet from a number of aspects; one of them is the Saying of Allah, Most High: *Then they found one of Our slaves, unto whom We had bestowed mercy from Us, and whom We had taught knowledge from Us.* (*Soorah Al-Kahf* 18:65) Another is when Moosa ﷺ said to him, *"May I follow you so that you teach me something of that knowledge (guidance and true path) which you have been taught (by Allah)?" He (Al-Khidr) said, "Verily! You will not be able to have patience with me! And how can you have patience about a thing which you know not?" Moosa said, "If Allah wills, you will find me patient, and I will not disobey you in aught." He (Al-Khidr) said, "Then, if you follow me, ask me not about anything till I myself mention it to you."* (*Soorah Al-Kahf* 18:66-70) Now if he was a *Wali* and not a Prophet, Moosa ﷺ would not have addressed him in this manner and he would not have answered Moosa ﷺ in this way. Moosa ﷺ only asked to accompany him in order to acquire the knowledge with which Allah had favored him, and not Moosa ﷺ. And if he was not a Prophet, he would not have been infallible and Moosa ﷺ – who was also a great Prophet and a noble Messenger and necessarily infallible – would

---

(1)   Narrated by Al-Bukhari (3402).

not have felt any great need to acquire knowledge from a *Wali*, who was not necessarily infallible and he would not have decided to go to him and remain with him for an extended period of time – it was said that it was eighty years – and when he met with him, he behaved with humility toward him and followed in him in a manner that enabled him to benefit from him. This proves that he was a Prophet, like him and that he received Revelation, like him. And he was favored with hidden knowledge and Prophetic secrets which Moosa, *Al-Kaleem*, the noble Prophet عليه السلام had not been made privy to. Ar-Rummani cited this as evidence of Al-Khidr's Prophethood. The third aspect is that Al-Khidr killed the boy and he would not have done so unless he had been ordered to do so via Revelation from an angel. This is a separate proof of his Prophethood and a clear evidence of his infallibility, because it is not permissible for a *Wali* to embark on killing individuals simply based on what might enter his mind, because his notions are not infallible, since it is possible for him to make mistakes, according to the consensus of the scholars. And when Al-Khidr resolved to kill that boy, who had not yet reached maturity, it was because he knew that if he reached maturity, he would become a disbeliever and his parents might follow him into disbelief, because of their great love for him. So in killing him there was a great benefit for them, since it prevented them from falling into disbelief and being punished for that. This proves that he was a Prophet, and that he was supported by Allah with infallibility. I have seen Shaikh Abul Faraj Ibn Al-Jawzi following this path in citing the evidence for Al-Khidr's Prophethood and it was declared authentic and cited as evidence by Ar-Rummani as well. The fourth aspect is that when Al-Khidr explained the reasons for his actions to Moosa عليه السلام and made clear to him the truth of the matter, after all that, he said, *"...as a Mercy from your Lord. And I did it not of my own accord."* (*Soorah Al-Kahf* 18:82) That is, I did not do those things of my own accord; rather, I was commanded to do them and I received Revelation regarding them. These aspects prove that he was a Prophet and his attainment of the status of *Wali*, or even Messenger does not invalidate that, as others have said. As for the view that he was one of the angels, it is very strange. And if it is established that he was a Prophet, as we have mentioned, then those who claimed that he was a *Wali* have nothing to support their claim – although a *Wali* might become acquainted with the truth in matters, without being a Prophet or Messenger.

As for the difference of opinion regarding his existence in our time, the majority of scholars hold that he remains alive to this day. It was said that because Adam عليه السلام was buried after they escaped from the flood, he was included in the supplication of his father, Adam عليه السلام, requesting long life. It was said that his longevity was due to the fact that he drank from the spring of life and so he lives on. They also mentioned reports which they cited as evidence that he remains alive until now and we shall relate them if Allah wills. And this was his advice to Moosa عليه السلام, when he said this, *(Al-Khidr) said, "This is the parting between me and you, I will tell you the interpretation of (those) things over which you were unable to hold patience."* (*Soorah Al-Kahf* 18:78)

Numerous traditions which are *munqati'ah*[1] have been narrated in this regard.

Shaikh Abul-Faraj Ibn Al-Jawzi – may Allah have Mercy on him – has dealt with the *Ahadeeth* related in this regard that are *marfoo'ah*[2] in his book *Ujalatul-Muntaziri Fee Sharhi Halat Al-Khidr* and he has made clear that they are fabricated. As to the traditions from the Companions (رضي الله عنهم) and the *Tabi'oon*, he has shown that their *asaneed* are weak, by explaining them and the ignorance of their narrators and he has succeeded in this very well and delivered an expert critique.

---

(1)   *Munqati'ah*: Broken, incomplete.

(2)   *Marfoo'ah*: Ascribed to the Prophet ﷺ.

As for those who claimed that he has died, they include Al-Bukhari, Ibraheem Al-Harbi, Abul-Husain Al-Munadi and Ibn Al-Jawzi, who supported the idea and wrote a *Ujalatul-Muntaziri Fee Sharhi Halat Al-Khidr*. And he argued on their behalf, citing a number of proofs, including the Words of Allah, Most High: *And We granted not to any human being immortality before you (O, Muhammad) (Soorah Al-Anbiya' 21:34)* So if Al-Khidr was human, then he must necessarily be included in the generality of this statement; and it is not permissible to exclude him from it without some authentic proof – and the basic principle is non-existence, unless until it is proven otherwise. And nothing has been reported from any infallible source that contains evidence that he is so excluded, which would necessitate acceptance. Another of the proofs cited by Ibn Al-Jawzi is the Saying of Allah, Most High: *And (remember) when Allah took the Covenant of the Prophets, saying, "Take whatever I gave you from the Book and* **Hikmah** *(understanding of the Laws of Allah, etc.), and afterward there will come to you a Messenger (Muhammad) confirming what is with you; you must, then, believe in him and help him." Allah said, "Do you agree (to it) and will you take up My Covenant (which I conclude with you)?" They said, "We agree." He said, "Then bear witness; and I am with you among the witnesses (for this)."* (*Soorah Ali 'Imran 3:81*) 'Abdullah Ibn 'Abbas ﷺ said, "Allah did not send a Prophet except that He took from him a Covenant that if Muhammad ﷺ should be sent while he was alive, he would certainly believe in him and support him. And He commanded each Prophet to take from his nation a covenant that if Muhammad ﷺ was sent during their lifetime, they would believe in him and support him. Al-Bukhari narrated this from him.[1] Now if Al-Khidr was a Prophet or a *Wali*, he would be included in this covenant and if he had been alive during the time of the Messenger of Allah ﷺ,

---

(1) This is an authentic *Hadith*; see *Fath Al-Bari* (The Book of the *Ahadeeth* Pertaining to the Prophets, Chapter: The *Hadith* of Al-Khidr With Moosa).

he would have come to him and believed in what Allah revealed to him, and would have helped prevent any of his enemies reaching him, for if he was a *Wali*, then Abu Bakr As-Siddeeq was better than he; and if he was a Prophet, then Moosa صلى was better than he. Imam Ahmad has narrated on the authority of Jabir Ibn 'Abdullah صلى that the Messenger of Allah صلى said, "By Him in Whose Hand is my soul, If Moosa صلى was alive, he would have no alternative but to follow me."[1] And this is conclusive argument. And this Verse has proved that if it had happened that all of the Prophets were alive and *mukallafoon*[2] during the time of the Messenger of Allah صلى, all of them would have followed him and would have been under his orders, and they would have been obliged to live in accordance with the law that he was given, just as when he met with them on the night of *Al-Isra* (the Night Journey), he was raised above all of them and when they descended with him to Bait Al-Maqdis, and the time for prayer came, Jibraeel صلى conveyed to them Allah's Command that he should lead them in the prayer, which he did, in the place of their *wilayah* (responsibility) and the abode in which they had lived. This proves that he is the greatest *Imam* and the Seal of the Messengers, who has been given precedence over all of them – may Allah's choicest Blessings and Peace be upon him and upon all of them. If this is known – and it is something known to every Believer – then it must be accepted that if Al-Khidr صلى was alive, he would have been one of the nation of Muhammad صلى and among those who followed his Law and he would have had no alternative but to do so. And when 'Eesa, the son of Mary, صلى will descend at the end of time, he will judge in accordance with this pure Law and he will not depart from it or deviate from it; and he is one of the five Messengers known as *Ulul-'Azm*[3] and the Seal of the

---

(1)   Narrated by Imam Ahmad (14736) and declared authentic by the author. I say: In its chain of narrators is one Mujahid Ibn Sa'eed (Al-Hamdani, who has been declared weak by scholars of *Hadith*).

(2)   *Mukallafoon*: (sing. *mukallaf*) meaning legally capable.

(3)   *Ulul-'Azm*: Possessor of strong will and perseverance; they are mentioned

Prophets of Banu Isra'eel. And it is well-known that it has not been transmitted in any authentic or *hasan* narration that Al-Khidr المعلا met with the Messenger of Allah ﷺ on even a single day, or that he fought with him in any battle; and on the day of the Battle of Badr, the Prophet ﷺ invoked his Lord, asking Him for help and victory against the disbelievers, saying, "O, Allah! If this small band of Muslims is destroyed, You will not be worshipped on this Earth."[1] This small band of Muslims included the leaders of the Muslims and the leaders of the angels, including Jibraeel المعلا, as Hassan Ibn Thabit said in a Verse of one of his poems which has been called "the most splendid verse spoken by the Arabs":

"And (remember) the Battle of Badr,

When they were repelled by Jibraeel,

(Fighting) under our banner, and Muhammad."

Now if Al-Khidr had been alive, his standing under this banner would have been the noblest position he had ever occupied and the greatest battle in which he had ever fought. Also, if he had still been alive after that, he would have transmitted the Prophetic *Ahadeeth* and Qur'anic Verses that he heard from the Messenger of Allah ﷺ and he would have denounced the fabricated *Ahadeeth*, the narrations that were *maqloobah*,[2] the innovated opinions and the fanatical heresies. And he would have fought alongside the Muslims in their battles, attended their Friday prayers and their gatherings and benefited them (with his knowledge and wisdom) and repelled the harm that the disbelievers desired to inflict on them. He would have supported the scholars and lawmakers and corroborated their proofs and rulings. This would have the

---

in the Qur'an, in *Soorah Al-Ahqaf* (46:35). According to scholars of *tafseer*, the Verse refers to Nooh, Ibraheem, Moosa, 'Eesa and Muhammad (peace be upon them all).

(1)   Narrated by Muslim (1763), At-Tirmidhi (3081) and Ahmad (208).

(2)   *Maqloobah*: Those whose words were mixed up or reversed.

best thing said of him regarding his existence throughout time, his traversing of the deserts and tracts of land, his meetings with peoples, many of whose circumstances are unknown. No one has any doubts regarding these things that we have mentioned after he has been made to understand – and Allah guides whom He wills to the Straight Path.

And it has been authentically reported in the *Saheehain* and elsewhere on the authority of 'Abdullah Ibn 'Umar ﷺ that the Messenger of Allah ﷺ performed the *'Isha'* prayer one night and then he said, "Do you know the importance of this night? Nobody present on the face of the Earth tonight will be living after one hundred years from this night."[1] In another version, it was reported that he said, "no eye will be moving...."[2]

Ibn Al-Jawzi said, "These authentic *Ahadeeth* prove conclusively that the claim that Al-Khidr is alive is incorrect. The scholars said that if Al-Khidr did not reach the era of the Messenger of Allah ﷺ – as appears most apparent – then there is no ambiguity in the matter. And if he reached his era, then this *Hadith* must mean that he was not alive a hundred years after that night, in which case, he must now be dead, because he is included in the generality of this statement; and the fundamental principle is that there is no exception to such a general statement, unless it is confirmed by some authentic proof which must be accepted. And Allah knows better.

---

(1) Narrated by Al-Bukhari (564), Muslim (2537), Abu Dawood (4348), At-Tirmidhi (2251) and Ahmad (5585).

(2) This is an authentic *Hadith* narrated by Imam Ahmad, on the authority of 'Ali Ibn Abi Talib ﷺ.

As For Ilyas ... (Elias)

Allah, Most High, says, after relating the story of Moosa and Haroon (peace be upon them both) in *Soorah As-Saffat*, *And verily, Ilyas was one of the Messengers. When he said to his people, "Will you not fear Allah? Will you call upon* **Ba'l** *(a well- known idol of his nation whom they used to worship) and forsake the Best of creators, Allah, your Lord and the Lord of your forefathers?" But they denied him (Ilyas), so they will certainly be brought forth (to the punishment), except the chosen slaves of Allah. And We left for him (a goodly remembrance) among generations (to come) in later times.* **Salamun** *(peace) be upon Ilyaseen (Ilyas)!" Verily, thus do We reward the* **Muhsinoon** *(those who do good, who perform good deeds totally for Allah's sake only). Verily, he was one of Our believing slaves.* (*Soorah As-Saffat* 37:123-132)

The scholars of genealogy said that he was Ilyas Ibn Tusba. It was also said that he was the son of Ya Seen, son of Finhas, son of Al-'Eezar, son of Haroon ﷺ.

And it was said that he was Ilyas, son of Al'azir, son of Al-'Eezar, son of Haroon ﷺ, son of 'Imran. They (the scholars) said that he was sent to the people of Ba'labak, which lies to the east of Damascus. He called upon them to believe in Allah, the Almighty, the All-Powerful and to abandon the worship of their idol, which they called *Ba'l*.

It was said that the idol was a woman called *Ba'l*, but the first explanation is more correct. This is why he said to them, *"Will you not fear Allah? Will you call upon Ba'l and forsake the Best of creators, Allah, your Lord and the Lord of your forefathers?"* (*Soorah As-Saffat* 37:124-126) But they belied him and opposed him and attempted to kill him. It was said that he fled from them and that he hid from them.

Makhool narrated on the authority of Ka'b that he said, "Four Prophets are living: two of them are on Earth – Ilyas and Al-Khidr – and two of them are in the heavens – Idrees and 'Eesa (peace be upon them all)."

Mention of a Number of Prophets From Banu Isra'eel After Moosa

Ibn Jareer At-Tabari said in his *Tareekh*, "There is no disagreement among the scholars of the history of the people of the past and their affairs from among our nation and others, that the one who took over the affairs of Banu Isra'eel after Yoosha' عليه السلام (Joshua) was Caleb (Kalab), son of Yuafanna, i.e. one of the companions of Moosa عليه السلام and his brother-in-law. He was one of the two men from among those who feared Allah – Joshua and Caleb – and it was they who said to the Children of Isra'eel, when they refused to fight in Allah's Cause, *"Assault them through the gate, for when you are in, victory will be yours, and put your trust in Allah if you are indeed Believers."* (*Soorah Al-Ma'idah* 5:23)

Ibn Jareer At-Tabari said, "Then after him, the one who undertook responsibility for the affairs of Banu Isra'eel was (Hizqeel) Ezekiel عليه السلام, son of Boozi, and it was he who invoked Allah and He revived *...those who went forth from their homes in thousands, fearing death. (Soorah Al-Baqarah* 2:243)

The Story of Hizqeel (Ezekiel)

Allah, Most High, says, *Did you (O Muhammad,) not think of those who went forth from their homes in thousands, fearing death? Allah said to them, "Die". And then He restored them to life. Truly, Allah is full of Bounty to mankind, but most men thank not.* (*Soorah Al-Baqarah* 2:243)

And Muhammad Ibn Ishaq reported on the authority of Wahb Ibn Munabbih that he said, "When Allah took Kalab, the son of Yoofanna to Him after Yoosha', he appointed as his successor to lead the Children of Isra'eel, Hizqeel, son of Boozi, who was the son of Al-'Ajooz and it was he who supplicated for the people whom Allah mentioned in His Book, according to what has been conveyed to us: *those who went forth from their homes in thousands, fearing death...* (*Soorah Al-Baqarah* 2:243) Ibn Ishaq said, "They fled from the plague and they camped on a raised area of land; and Allah said to them, "Die," and they all died."

And it was reported on the authority of As-Suddi, who in turn reported on the authority of 'Abdullah Ibn 'Abbas ♦ and 'Abdullah Ibn Mas'ood and on the authority of other Companions that they said regarding Allah's Words: *Did you (O Muhammad,) not think of those who went forth from their homes in thousands, fearing death? Allah said to them, "Die". And then He restored them to life.* (*Soorah Al-Baqarah* 2:243) that they were the people of a town known as Dawardan, in the direction of Wasit, where the plague broke out. As a result of that, the majority of the population fled and camped in an area near to it. And (most of) those who remained in the town were destroyed, while others were saved and not many of them died. When the plague ended, they returned safely and (those who still lived from) those who had remained alive said, "These companions of ours were more prudent than we; had we done as they did, we would (all) have survived. And if the plague returns, we shall certainly leave with them." So when the plague returned, they fled and they numbered more than thirty thousand and they camped in a place which was a wide valley. There, an angel called them from the floor of the valley and another from the top of it, saying, "Die!" And they died. Then, when they were dead and their bodies remained lying there (decomposed), a Prophet named Hizqeel ﷺ passed by them and when he saw them, he stopped and began to think about them, twisting the corners of his mouth and his fingers. Then Allah revealed to him, "Do you wish Me to show you how I will return them to life?" He said, "Yes," thinking only of his amazement at Allah's Power over them. It was said to him, "Call!" So he called, "O, you bones! Allah commands you to unite!" upon which, the bones flew together until they became skeletal bodies. Then Allah revealed to him that he should call, "O, you bones! Allah commands you to be clothed in flesh!" upon which, they became covered with flesh and blood and (even) the garments in which they had died. Then it was said to him, "Call." So he called, "O, you bodies! Allah commands you to stand up!" upon which, they stood up. Some said that Mansoor claimed, on the authority of Mujahid, that when they were brought back to life, they said, "Glorified be You, O Allah, and all praise and thanks be to You. None has the right to be worshipped except You." Then they returned to their people alive, and their people knew that they had been dead, for they had the pallor of death on their faces and they were wearing rotted garments. Then they lived on until the time written for them. Imam Ahmad and the compilers of the *Saheehain* (Al-Bukhari and Muslim) narrated on the authority of 'Abdullah Ibn 'Abbas ؓ that 'Umar Ibn Al-Khattab ؓ set out for Ash-Sham (Syria) and when he reached Sargh, the Commanders of the (Muslim) army, Abu 'Ubaidah Ibn Al-Jarrah ؓ and his Companions met him and told him that an epidemic had broken out in Ash-Sham. 'Umar ؓ said, "Call for me the early emigrants." So 'Umar ؓ called them, consulted them and informed them that an epidemic had broken out in Ash-Sham. Those people differed in their opinions. Some of them said, "We have come out for a purpose and we do not think that it is proper to give it up," while others said (to 'Umar), "You have along with you other people and the Companions of the Messenger of Allah ﷺ, so do not advise that we take them to this epidemic." 'Umar said to them, "Leave me now." Then he said, "Call the *Ansar* for me." I called them and he consulted them and they followed the way of the emigrants and differed as they did. He then said to them, "Leave me now," and added, "Call for me the old people of Quraish who emigrated in the year of the Conquest of Makkah." I called them and they gave a unanimous opinion saying, "We advise that you should return with the people and do not take them to that (place) of epidemic." So 'Umar ؓ made an announcement, "I will ride back to Madinah in the morning, so you should do the same." Abu 'Ubaidah Ibn Al-Jarrah said (to 'Umar), "Are you running away from what Allah has ordained?" 'Umar ؓ said, "Would that someone else had said such a thing, O Abu 'Ubaidah! Yes, we are running from what Allah has ordained to what Allah has ordained. Don't you agree that if you had camels that went down a valley having two places, one green and the other dry, you would graze them on the green one only if Allah had ordained that, and you would graze them on the dry one only if Allah had ordained that?" At that time 'Abdur-Rahman Ibn 'Awf, who had been absent because of some job, came and said, "I have some knowledge about this. I have heard the Messenger of Allah ﷺ say, 'If you hear about it (an outbreak of plague) in a land, do not go to it; but if plague breaks out in a country where you are staying, do not run away from it.' 'Umar ﷺ thanked Allah and returned to Madinah." [1]

I say: We have already related the story of Ilyas ﷺ (Elias) following on from the story of Al-Khidr ﷺ, because they are frequently mentioned together and because their story is after the story of Moosa ﷺ in *Soorah As-Saffat* and so we have advanced his story because of this. And Allah knows better. It has been reported that Muhammad Ibn Ishaq narrated on the authority of Wahb Ibn Munabbih that he said, "Then Ilyas' successor, Al-Yasa' (Elisha) ﷺ was raised to Prophethood after him and this is his story:

The Story of Al-Yasa'a (Elisha)

Allah has mentioned him among the Prophets in *Soorah Al-An'am* in His Saying: *And Isma'eel (Ishmael) and Al-Yasa'a (Elisha), and Yoonus (Jonah) and Loot (Lot), and each one of them We preferred above* **Al-'Alameen** *(of their times).* (*Soorah Al-An'am* 6:86) And He, Most High says in *Soorah Sad, And remember Isma'eel, Al-Yasa'a, and Zul-Kifl (Isaiah), all are among the best.* (*Soorah Sad* 38:48). Ishaq Ibn Bishr Abu Huzaifah said, "Sa'eed informed us on the authority of Qatadah, who reported on the authority of Al-Hasan that he said, "After Ilyas ﷺ was Al-Yasa'a ﷺ and he remained for as long as Allah willed, calling them to Allah and holding fast to the teachings of Ilyas ﷺ and the law given to him until Allah, the Almighty, the

---

[1]   This is an authentic *Hadith* narrated by Imam Ahmad (1685), Al-Bukhari (5729) and Muslim (2219).

All-Powerful took him. After that, changes and corruption spread among them, innovations and sins became widespread, tyrants became numerous and they killed the Prophets. Among them was a willful, obstinate and despotic king.

Al-Hafiz Abul-Qasim Ibn 'Asakir said in "the letter *Ya'*" in his *Tareekh*, "Al-Yasa'a – and he was Al-Asbat, son of 'Adiyy, son of Shootlam, son of Afratheem, son of Yoosuf, son of Ya'qoob, son of Ishaq, son of Ibraheem, *Al-Khaleel* (peace be upon them all). It was also said that he was the paternal cousin of Ilyas عليه السلام. And it was said that he hid with him on the mountain known as Qasiyoon, from the king of Ba'labak, that then he went with him to that land and that when Ilyas عليه السلام was raised up, Al-Yasa'a عليه السلام succeeded him as leader of his people and Allah appointed him as a Prophet after him.

The Story of Shamweel (Samuel)

And Therein Begins the Case of Dawood (David)

He was Shamweel (Samuel), son of Bali, son of 'Al-Qamah, son of Yarkham, son of Aleehoo, son of Tahoo, son of Zoof, son of 'Al-Qamah, son of Mahath, son of Amusa, son of Ezria. Muqatil said that he was descended from Haroon ﷺ, while Mujahid said that he was Asamweel, son of Halfaqa, but he did not give details of his lineage more than this. And Allah knows better.

Allah, Most High, says in His Noble Book, *Have you not thought about the group of the Children of Isra'eel after (the time of) Moosa? When they said to a Prophet of theirs, "Appoint for us a king and we will fight in Allah's Cause." He said, "Would you then refrain from fighting, if fighting was prescribed for you?" They said, "Why should we not fight in Allah's Cause, while we have been driven out of our homes and our children (families have been taken as captives)?" But when fighting was ordered for them, they turned away, all except a few of them. And Allah is Aware of the* **Zalimoon**. *And their Prophet (Samuel) said to them, "Indeed Allah has appointed Taloot (Saul) as a king over you."*

They said, "How can he be a king over us when we are better fitted than he for the kingdom, and he has not been given enough wealth?" He said, "Verily, Allah has chosen him above you and has increased him abundantly in knowledge and body. And Allah grants His Kingdom to whom He wills. And Allah is Sufficient for His creature' needs, All-Knowing." And their Prophet (Samuel) said to them, "Verily! The sign of His Kingdom is that there shall come to you **At-Taboot** *(a wooden box), wherein is* **Sakeenah** *(peace and reassurance) from your Lord and a remnant of that which Moosa and Haroon left behind, carried by the angels. Verily, in this is a sign for you if you are indeed Believers." Then, when Taloot set out with the army, he said, "Verily! Allah will try you by a river. So whoever drinks thereof, he is not of me, and whoever tastes it not, he is of me, except him who takes (thereof) in the hollow of his hand." Yet they drank thereof, all except a few of them. So when he had crossed it (the river), he and those who believed with him, said, "We have no power this day against Jaloot (Goliath) and his hosts." But those who knew with certainty that they were to meet their Lord, said, "How often a small group overcame a mighty host by Allah's Leave?" And Allah is with* **As-Sabireen** *(the patient, persevering ones). And when they advanced to meet Jaloot (Goliath) and his forces, they invoked (Allah, saying), "Our Lord! Pour forth on us patience and make us victorious over the disbelieving people." So they routed them by Allah's Leave and Dawood (David) killed Jaloot, and Allah gave him (Dawood) the kingdom (after the death of Taloot and Samuel) and* **Al-Hikmah** *(Prophethood) and taught him of that which He willed. And if Allah did not check one set of people by means of another, the Earth would indeed be full of mischief. But Allah is full of Bounty to* **Al-'Alameen**. (*Soorah Al-Baqarah* 2:246-251)

Most of the scholars of *tafseer* said that the Prophet of the people mentioned in this story is Shamweel عليه السلام. It was also said that it is Sham'oon and it was said they are one and the same person. And it was also said that it is Yoosha' ﷺ, but this is very improbable, according to what Imam Abu Ja'afar Ibn Jareer At-Tabari has narrated in his *Tafseer*, which states that between the death of Yoosha' ﷺ and the sending of Shamweel ﷺ was a period of four hundred and sixty years. And Allah knows better.

What is meant by this is that when these people had become exhausted by wars and they had been vanquished by enemies, they asked the Prophet of Allah ﷺ at that time to appoint for them a king to whom they would pledge their obedience and alongside whom they would fight their enemies. He said to them, *"Would you then refrain from fighting, if fighting was prescribed for you? They said,"Why should we not fight in Allah's way".* (*Soorah Al-Baqarah* 2:246) That is, what prevents you from fighting? *"...while we have been driven out of our homes and our children (families have been taken as captives)?"* (*Soorah Al-Baqarah* 2:246) They said, "We have been fought against and wronged and so it is only fitting that we should fight in defense of our children who have been taken by force and the weak among them and those who have taken away by them. He, Most High, says, *But when fighting was ordered for them, they turned away, all except a few of them. And Allah is Aware of the* **Zalimoon**. (*Soorah Al-Baqarah* 2:246). As Allah says at the end of the story, none crossed the river with the king except a few, while the rest returned and refused to fight.

And their Prophet (Samuel) said to them, "Indeed Allah has appointed Taloot as a king over you." (*Soorah Al-Baqarah* 2:247) 'Ikrimah and As-Suddi said that he was a water carrier. Wahb Ibn Munabbih said that he was a tanner. Others mentioned other occupations. And Allah knows better. This is why they said, *"How can he be a king over us when we are better fitted than he for the kingdom, and he has not been given enough wealth?"* (*Soorah Al-Baqarah* 2:24) *He said, "Verily, Allah has chosen him above you and has increased him abundantly in knowledge..."* (*Soorah Al-Baqarah* 2:247) It was said that the knowledge was in matters pertaining to warfare; and it was said that rather, it was in all matters. *"...and body."* (*Soorah Al-Baqarah* 2:247) It was said that it means in height and also that it means in handsomeness. But it would appear from the context that he was the most handsome of them and the most knowledgeable of them after their Prophet ﷺ. *"And Allah grants His Kingdom to whom He wills."* (*Soorah Al-Baqarah* 2:247) Judgment is for Him, as is the creation and all matters. *"And Allah is Sufficient for His creature needs, All-Knowing."* And their Prophet (Samuel) said to them, *"Verily! The sign of His Kingdom is that there shall come to you at-taboot (the wooden box), wherein is* **Sakeenah** *(peace and reassurance) from your Lord and a remnant of that which Moosa and Haroon left behind, carried by the angels. Verily, in this is a sign for you if you are indeed Believers."* (*Soorah Al-Baqarah* 2:247,248) This is also from the blessing of the appointment of this righteous man over them and good fortune bestowed on them, that Allah returned to them the *Taboot*, which had been forcibly taken from them by their enemies. And aforetimes, they had been aided in achieving victory over their enemies because of it. *"...wherein is* **Sakeenah** *from your Lord and a remnant of that which Moosa and Haroon (Aaron) left behind."* (*Soorah Al-Baqarah* 2:248) It was said that in it were pieces of the Tablets (on which the Ten Commandments were written) and some of the *manna* that had descended on them when they were in the wilderness. *"...carried by the angels"* (*Soorah Al-Baqarah* 2:248) means the angels will come to you bearing it and you will witness that with your own eyes, so that it will be a proof from Allah against you and a clear evidence of the truth of what I say to you and of the correctness of the appointment of this righteous king over you. This is why he said, *"Verily, in this is a sign for you if you are indeed Believers."* (*Soorah Al-Baqarah* 2:248) It was said that the Amalekites had seized this box, which contained the things we have mentioned, such as the *Sakeenah* and the blessed remnants.

And it was said that it also contained the Towrah and while it was in their possession, they placed it under an idol belonging to them in their land and in the morning they found it on the head of the idol, so they placed it under it again, but on the following day, they found the box on top of the idol. When this was repeated, they realized that it was the Work of Allah, Most High, and so they sent it out of their city, to one of their villages. But a disease afflicted their necks. When this situation had persisted for some time, they put it in a cart and tied two cows to it and sent them forth. It was said that the angels gave them water until they came to the leaders of the Children of Isra'eel, who were waiting for it, in according with the information given to them by their Prophet regarding it.

And He, Most High, says, *Then, when Taloot set out with the army, he said, "Verily! Allah will try you by a river. So whoever drinks thereof, he is not of me, and whoever tastes it not, he is of me, except him who takes (thereof) in the hollow of his hand."* (*Soorah Al-Baqarah* 2:249) 'Abdullah Ibn 'Abbas and several scholars of *tafseer* said that it was the River Jordan, which was known as Ash-Sharee'ah. One of the commands given by Taloot to his army at the edge of the river – which was conveyed to him by the Prophet of Allah as a test and a trial – was that if any of them drank from the river, he could not accompany Taloot into battle, except those who only took a handful of water.

Allah, Most High, says, *Yet, they drank thereof, all except a few of them.* (*Soorah Al-Baqarah* 2:249) As-Suddi said, "The army consisted of eighty thousand men and seventy-six thousand of them drank from it, leaving only four thousand men remaining with Taloot." And Al-Bukhari narrated in his *Saheeh*, on the authority of Al-Bara' Ibn 'Azib that he said, "We, the Companions of Muhammad, used to say that the number of the warriors of

Badr was the same as the number of Taloot's companions who crossed the river (of Jordan) with him, and none crossed the river with him but a Believer, and they were over three hundred and more than ten Believers."[1]

As-Suddi's claim that the number of soldiers was eighty thousand is questionable, because it is not likely that an army of warriors reaching eighty thousand could have assembled in the land of Bait Al-Maqdis. And Allah knows better. Allah, Most High, says, *So when he had crossed it (the river), he and those who believed with him, they said, "We have no power this day against Jaloot and his hosts."* (*Soorah Al-Baqarah* 2:249). That is, they deemed themselves too few in numbers and too weak to stand against their enemies, when they compared their own small force with the huge numbers of their enemies. *But those who knew with certainty that they were to meet their Lord, said, "How often has a small group overcome a mighty host by Allah's Leave!" And Allah is with* **As-Sabiroon** *(the patient ones, etc.)."* (*Soorah Al-Baqarah* 2:249. Meaning the cavalry among them; and the cavalry were those who possessed faith and certainty and they were patient in the face of argument and abuse. *And when they advanced to meet Jaloot (Goliath) and his forces, they invoked, "Our Lord! Pour forth on us patience and make us victorious over the disbelieving people."* (*Soorah Al-Baqarah* 2:250) They asked Allah to pour on them patience, i.e. to immerse them in it from above, so that their hearts would remain steadfast and they would not fear, make their feet firm on the battlefield and strengthen the brave ones in the turmoil of battle. So they asked Allah to grant them steadfastness, both open and hidden, that He grant them victory against their enemies and His enemies among the disbelievers and the rejecters of His Signs and His Blessings and He, the Almighty, the Omnipotent, the All-Hearing, the All-Seeing, the Most Wise, the All-Knowing granted their request and

---

(1)   Narrated by Al-Bukhari (3957, 3958 and 3959).

caused them to achieve their objectives. This is why He says, *So they routed them by Allah's Leave.* (*Soorah Al-Baqarah* 2:251) That is, by Allah's Power, not by their own power and by Allah's Strength and Help, not by their own strength and their numbers; and they won this victory in spite of the great numbers of the enemy, as Allah, Most High, says, *And Allah has already made you victorious at Badr, when you were a weak little force. So, fear Allah much (abstain from all kinds of sins and evil deeds which He has forbidden and love Allah much, perform all kinds of good deeds which He has ordained) that you may be grateful.* (*Soorah Aal 'Imran* 3:123) And in the Words of Him, Most High: *...and Dawood killed Jaloot, and Allah gave him (Dawood) the kingdom (after the death of Taloot and Samuel) and* **Al-Hikmah** *(Prophethood), and taught him of that which He willed.* (*Soorah Al-Baqarah* 2:251) There is evidence of the bravery of Dawood ﷺ and that he killed Jaloot and humiliated thereby his army and broke it; and there is no greater battle than the one in which a king kills his enemy and due to that, he captures (as booty) a huge amount of wealth, their champions are taken as captives, the word of faith is elevated over the idols, Allah's *Awliya'* are given ascendancy over His enemies and the Religion of Truth is made victorious over falsehood and its adherents.

The Story of Dawood (David)

He was Dawood, son of 'Eesha, son of Uwaid, son of Ba'az, son of Salmoon, son of Nahshoon, son of 'Uwainazab, son of 'Iram, son of Hisroon, son of Faras, son of Yahooza, son of Ya'qoob, son of Ishaq, son of Ibraheem, *Al-Khaleel* (peace be upon them): Allah's slave and His Prophet, and His *Khaleefah* in the land of Bait Al-Maqdis. Allah combined in him kingship and Prophethood, the best of this earthly life and the Afterlife. Kings belonged to one lineage and Prophets to another, but in the case of Dawood علیه السلام, both were combined in him. This is as Allah, Most High, says, *...and Dawood killed Jaloot, and Allah gave him (Dawood) the kingdom (after the death of Taloot and Samuel) and* **Al-Hikmah** *(Prophethood), and taught him of that which He willed. And if Allah did not check one set of people by means of another, the Earth would indeed be full of mischief. But Allah is full of Bounty to* **Al-'Alameen**. (*Soorah Al-Baqarah* 2:251) It means that if kings were not set up to rule over the people, the strong would devour the weak. And Allah says, *And* *indeed We bestowed Grace on Dawood from Us (saying), "O, you mountains! Glorify (Allah) with him! And you birds (also)! And We made the iron soft for him." Saying, "Make you perfect coats of mail, balancing well the rings of chain armor, and work you (men) righteousness. Truly, I see all that you do."* (*Soorah Saba'* 34:10,11) And He, Most High, says, *And We subjected the mountains and the birds to glorify Our Praises along with Dawood, And it was We Who was the doer (of all these things). And We taught him the making of metal coats of mail (for battles), to protect you in your fighting. Are you then grateful?* (*Soorah Al-Anbiya'* 21:79,80) Allah helped him in the making of iron coats of mail, to strengthen them against their enemies and He guided him as to how to make them. He says, *"...balancing well the rings of chain armor."* (*Soorah Saba'* 34:11) That is, do not make the rivets too loose that the rings (of chain mail) will shake, or make them too tight that they will not be able to move at all, but make it just right. This was said by Mujahid, Qatadah, Al-Hakam and 'Ikrimah.

And it has been confirmed in an authentic *Hadith*: "The best thing that a man can eat is that which he has earned by working with his own hands. The Prophet of Allah, Dawood, used to eat from the earnings of his own hands."[1]

And He, Most High, says, *and remember Our slave Dawood,* **Dhul-Aydi***. Verily, he was ever oft-returning in all matters and in repentance (toward Allah). Verily, We made the mountains to glorify Our Praises with him (Dawood) in the* **'ashiyy** *(i.e. after midday till sunset) and* **ishraq** *(i.e. after sunrise till midday). And (so did) the birds assemble, all with him (Dawood) did turn (to Allah i.e. glorified His Praises). We made his kingdom strong and gave him* **Al-Hikmah** *and sound judgment in speech and decision.* (*Soorah Sad* 38:17-20) 'Abdullah Ibn 'Abbas ﷺ

---

(1)   Narrated by Al-Bukhari (2072).

and Mujahid said that *Dhul-Aydi* (literally, the Owner of Hands) means possessor of strength in obedience (to Allah); i.e. strong in worship and the performance of righteous deeds. Qatadah said, "He was given strength in worship and understanding of Islam." He added, "And it was reported to us that he used to stand at night (in prayer) and he would fast half of the time." And it has been confirmed in the *Saheehain* that the Messenger of Allah ﷺ said, "The prayer most beloved by Allah is the prayer of Dawood ﷺ and the fast most beloved by Allah is the fast of Dawood ﷺ: he used to sleep for half of the night, then he would stand (in prayer) for a third of it and then sleep for a sixth of it. And he would fast for a day and break his fast for a day and he would not flee if he encountered (an enemy)."[1]

And He, Most High, says, *Verily, We made the mountains to glorify Our Praises with him (Dawood) in the* **'ashiyy** *and* **ishraq**. *And (so did) the birds assemble: all with him (Dawood) did turn (to Allah i.e. glorified His Praises).* (*Soorah Sad* 38:18,19) This is, like His Saying: *"O, you mountains! Glorify with him! And you birds (also)!"* (*Soorah Saba'* 34:10) This was said by 'Abdullah Ibn 'Abbas ﷺ, Mujahid and others in the explanation of this Verse. *Verily, We made the mountains to glorify Our Praises with him (Dawood) in the* **'ashiyy** *and* **ishraq** (*Soorah Sad* 38:18) means at the end of the forenoon and at the start of it. This was because Allah had bestowed on him a beautiful voice, the like of which He had not given to anyone before him, so that whenever he recited His Book (the *Zaboor* [Psalms]), the birds would stop in the air and sing with him and glorify (Allah) with him, and likewise, the mountains responded to him and glorified (Allah) with him, singing praises with him every morning and evening – may the blessings and peace of Allah be upon him.

---

[1] Narrated by Al-Bukhari (*Book of Tahajjud, Hadith* No. 231 – English translation).

Imam Ahmad narrated on the authority of 'A'ishah, may Allah be pleased with her, that she said, "The Messenger of Allah ﷺ heard the voice of Abu Moosa Al-Ash'ari ﷺ when he was reciting (the Qur'an) and he said, "Abu Moosa has been given one of the Psalms of the people of Dawood ﷺ."[1] And this is in accordance with the conditions for acceptance stipulated by the two *Shaikhs* (Al-Bukhari and Muslim), though they did not narrate it via this route. In addition to his pleasant voice, he was swift in reciting the Psalms, according to the narration of Imam Ahmad on the authority of Abu Hurairah ﷺ, who said, The Messenger of Allah ﷺ said, "Recitation was made easy for Dawood ﷺ; he used to order that his riding beast be saddled and he would finish his recitation before it was saddled and he would not eat except from the fruits of his own labor."[2]

And He, Most High, says, *We made his kingdom strong and gave him* **Al-Hikmah** *and sound judgment* (*Soorah Sad* 38:20) means, We gave him a great kingdom and insightful judgment.

As to His Saying: *...and gave him* **Al-Hikmah**. (*Soorah Sad* 38:20) That is, Prophethood. *...and sound judgment.* Shuraih Al-Qadi, Ash-Sha'bi and Qatadah said that *and sound judgment* is testimony and oaths. Qatadah said, "Two witnesses for the plaintiff or an oath on the part of the defendant is meaning of sound judgment." This is the sound judgment which the Prophets and Messengers judged and the believers and righteous accepted. This is the basis of this *Ummah's* judicial system until the Day of Resurrection. This was the view of Abu 'Abdur-Rahman As-Sulami. Mujahid and As-Suddi said that it means passing the right judgment and understanding the case. Mujahid also said, "It is soundness in speech and in judgment, and this includes all of the above." This is what is meant, and it is the view favored by Ibn

---

(1) This is an authentic *Hadith* narrated by Imam Ahmad (24815).

(2) Narrated by Al-Bukhari (3417) and by Imam Ahmad (27377).

Jareer At-Tabari.

And Allah, Most High, says, *And has the news of the litigants reached you? When they climbed over the wall into (his)* **mihrab** *(a praying place or a private room). When they entered upon Dawood, he was terrified of them, they said, "Fear not! (We are) two litigants, one of whom has wronged the other, therefore judge between us with truth, and treat us not with injustice, and guide us to the Right Way. Verily, this my brother (in religion) has ninety-nine ewes, while I have (only) one ewe, and he says, "Hand it over to me, and he overpowered me in speech." (Dawood) said (immediately without listening to the opponent), "He has wronged you in demanding your ewe in addition to his ewes. And, verily, many partners oppress one another, except those who believe and do righteous good deeds, and they are few." And Dawood guessed that We had tried him and he sought Forgiveness of his Lord, and he fell down prostration and turned (to Allah) in repentance. So We forgave him that, and verily, for him is a near access to Us and a good place of (final) return (Paradise).* (*Soorah Sad* 38:21-25)

Many of the scholars of *tafseer* from among the earlier and later scholars have related stories and reports in explanation of these Verses, but most of them are *Isra'eeliyyat* and they include fabricated stories which we have no alternative but to omit from our book. So it is better to speak briefly of this story and refer knowledge of it to Allah, may He be exalted. And Allah guides whom He wills to the Straight Path.

Allah, Most High, says, *So We forgave him that, and verily, for him is a near access to Us and a good place of (final) return (Paradise).* (*Soorah Sad* 38:25) That is, on the Day of Resurrection, he will be brought close to Allah by virtue of his good deeds, as confirmed in the *Hadith*: "Behold! the Dispensers of Justice will be seated on pulpits of light, on the right side of the Merciful, Exalted and Glorious. Either side of Him is the right side, both being equally meritorious. (The Dispensers of Justice are) those who do justice in their rules, in matters relating to their families and in all that they undertake to do."[1]

Scholars have differed regarding whether the prostration of *Soorah Sad* is obligatory or one of thanks. There are two opinions in this matter:

Al-Bukhari narrated on the authority of Al-'Awwam that he said, "I asked Mujahid about the prostration of *Soorah Sad* and he said, "I asked Ibn 'Abbas ﷺ, "Why do you prostrate?" He said, "Have you not read *...and among his progeny Dawood, Sulaiman. (Soorah Al-An'am* 6:84) (and) *They are those whom Allah had guided. So follow their guidance. (Soorah Al-An'am* 6:90) So Dawood ﷺ was one of those whom your Prophet was commanded to follow. Dawood ﷺ prostrated here so the Messenger of Allah ﷺ also prostrated here."

Imam Ahmad narrated on the authority of 'Abdullah Ibn 'Abbas ﷺ that he said regarding the prostration in *Soorah Sad*, "It is not one of the obligatory prostrations, but I have seen the Messenger of Allah ﷺ prostrating in it."

Al-Bukhari, Abu Dawood, At-Tirmidhi and An-Nasa'i narrated likewise on the authority of Ayyoob and At-Tirmidhi said that it is *hasan-saheeh*. An-Nasa'i said, "Ibraheem Ibn Al-Hasan Al-Maqsami told me: 'Hajjaj Ibn Muhammad related to us on the authority of 'Umar Ibn Dharr, who in turn reported on the authority of his father, who likewise reported on the authority of Sa'eed Ibn Jubair, on the authority of 'Abdullah Ibn 'Abbas ﷺ that the Prophet ﷺ prostrated in *Soorah Sad* and he said, Dawood ﷺ performed this prostration out of repentance and we perform it out of thanks'." Ahmad was alone in narrating this, but all of the men (in the chain of narrators) are trustworthy.

---

(1)   Narrated by Muslim (1827).

Ibn Abi Hatim said, "It was reported on the authority of Malik Ibn Deenar that he said regarding the Words of Allah: *...and verily, for him is a near access to Us and a good place of (final) return (Paradise).* (*Soorah Sad* 38:25) "Dawood will stand on the Day of Resurrection at the foot of the Throne and Allah will say, "O, Dawood! Glorify Me on this Day with that fine and pleasant voice with which you used to glorify Me in the life of the world." Dawood ﷺ will say, "How, when You have taken it?" Then Allah will say, "Verily, I return it to you." Then Dawood ﷺ will lift up his voice in a manner that will bring forth all of the felicities and delights of the Gardens (of Paradise)." *O, Dawood! Verily! We have placed you as a successor on Earth, so judge you between men in truth (and justice) and follow not your desire for it will mislead you from the Path of Allah. Verily! Those who wander astray from the Path of Allah (shall) have a severe punishment, because they forgot the Day of Reckoning.* (*Soorah Sad* 38:26) This was an address from Allah, Most High, to Dawood ﷺ and what is meant by this is the rulers and governors of the people; He commanded them to be just and to follow the truth sent down from Allah and no other opinions or fancies. And He warned those who follow something other than that and judge according to something other than that, of a severe punishment. And Dawood ﷺ was the model at that time of justice and frequent worship and all deeds through which one may draw near to Allah (*taqarrubat*), to such a degree that he would pass an hour of the day or night without the members of his household being engaged in acts of worship, as He, Most High, says, *"Work you, O, family of Dawood, with thanks!" But few of My slaves are grateful.* (*Soorah Saba'* 34:13)

Al-Hafiz Ibn 'Asakir reported many pleasant and agreeable things in *The Biography of Dawood* ﷺ, such as his saying: "Be toward the orphan as a compassionate father." And: "Know that as you sow, so shall you reap." And he narrated with a chain of narrators that is *ghareeb* and *marfoo'* that Dawood ﷺ said, "O, you sower of evil deeds! You shall reap their thorns and their *hasak*."[1] And it was reported from Dawood عليه السلام that he said, "The likeness of a foolish orator in the meeting place of the people is as the likeness of the one who sings at the head of a dead person." He also said, "How ignominious is poverty after wealth, yet how much worse than that is error after guidance." And he said, "Think of something that you would hate to be said of you in the meeting place of the people and do not do it when you are alone." And he said, "Never promise your brother that which you do not fulfill for him, for that is enmity between you and him."

And the Messenger of Allah ﷺ said, "The best fast is the fast of Dawood عليه السلام."[2] He used to recite the *Zaboor* in seventy different recitations… and he used to bow in prayer at night and weep in it and everything would weep along with him; and his voice would alleviate the troubled and the sick.

---

(1) *Hasak*: A plant which has a fruit that is rough and clings to the wool of the sheep.

(2) The *takhreej* for this has been given previously.

A Description of Dawood's Death

As for his death – may Allah's Peace be upon him – Imam Ahmad narrated in his *Musnad,* on the authority of Abu Hurairah عنه‌الله that the Messenger of Allah ﷺ said, "Dawood عليه‌السلام was intensely protective and solicitous of his family and whenever he went out, he would lock the door and no one would visit his family until he returned. He went out one day and the house was locked. His wife happened to look out and saw a man standing in the middle of the courtyard. She said to those within in the house, "From where did this man enter when the house is locked? By Allah, we will bring disgrace on Dawood." Then Dawood عليه‌السلام arrived and found the man standing in the middle of the house and he said to him, "Who are you?" He said, "I am the one who fears not the kings and who may not be prevented by a barrier." Dawood عليه‌السلام said, "Then by Allah, you are the Angel of Death; I welcome Allah's Commandment." Then he remained until his soul had been taken. When he had been washed and shrouded and all matters pertaining to him had been completed, the sun rose upon him and Sulaiman عليه‌السلام said to the birds, "Shade Dawood," so they shaded him until the earth covered him. Then Sulaiman عليه‌السلام

said to the birds, "Grasp your wings." Abu Hurairah ﷺ said that at this point in the story, the Messenger of Allah ﷺ grasped his hand to show them what the birds did. On that day, most of the shade was provided by falcons with large wingspans.[1]

The Story of Sulaiman (Solomon), Son of Dawood

Al-Hafiz Ibn 'Asakir said that he was Sulaiman, son of Dawood, son of 'Eesa, son of 'Owaid, son of Ba'az, son of Salmoon, son of Nahshoon, son of Aminazab, son of Iram, son of Hasroon, son of Faras, son of Yahooda, son of Ya'qoob, son of Ishaq, son of Ibraheem, Abur-Rabee' (peace be upon them), the Prophet of Allah, son of the Prophet of Allah.

Allah, Most High, says, *And Sulaiman inherited Dawood. He said, "O, mankind! We have been taught the language of birds, and on us have been bestowed all things. This, verily, is an evident Grace."* (*Soorah An-Naml* 27:16) That is, he inherited Prophethood and the throne of his father. It does not refer to wealth, because Dawood ﷺ had other sons and he would not favor him over the others. It has been confirmed in authentic *Ahadeeth* from more than one source, on the authority of a number of the Companions that the Messenger of Allah ﷺ said, "We do not bequeath our property to anyone; what we leave is given in charity."[2] And in another version: "We, the community of Prophets, are not inherited."[3] So the Prophet ﷺ has informed us that the Prophets' wealth is not inherited from them, as other people's wealth is inherited. Rather, their wealth is given in charity after their death to the poor and needy. It is not given to their kin, because the life of this world was considered of too little value

---

(1) This is an authentic *Hadith* narrated by Imam Ahmad (2/419, No. 9148).

(2) Narrated by Al-Bukhari (3093) and Muslim (1757) and (1759).

(3) This is an authentic *Hadith* narrated by Imam Ahmad (2/463, No. 27238).

by them for them to do that, as it was in the Sight of Him Who sent them, chose them and preferred them. He says, *"O, mankind! We have been taught the language of birds."* (*Soorah An-Naml* 27:16) This means that Sulaiman ﷺ understood the language by which the birds used to converse with each other and was able to interpret for the people their meanings and their desires.

And He, Most High, says, *"...and on us have been bestowed all things."* (*Soorah An-Naml* 27:16) That is, everything that the king needs, including numbers, materials, troops, armies, hosts from among the Jinn and mankind, birds, wild animals, free roaming devils, knowledge, understanding and the ability to read the minds of Allah's creatures, both those that speak and those that do not.

Then He says, *"This, verily, is an evident Grace"* (*Soorah An-Naml* 27:16) means from the Originator of all creatures and the Creator of the heavens and the Earth, as He, Most High says, *And there were gathered before Sulaiman his hosts of Jinn and men and birds, and they all were set in battle order (marching forward). Till when they came to the valley of the ants, one of the ants said, "O, ants! Enter your dwellings, lest Sulaiman and his hosts crush you, while they perceive not." So he (Sulaiman) smiled, amused at her speech and said, "My Lord!* **Awzi'nee** *that I may be grateful for Your Favors which You have bestowed on me and on my parents, and that I may do righteous good deeds that will please You, and admit me by Your Mercy among Your righteous slaves."* (*Soorah An-Naml* 27:17-19)

Allah, Most High, informs us about His Prophet, the son of His Prophet, Sulaiman, son of Dawood, of how he rode with his army one day, all of them from the jinn, mankind and the birds; the jinn and men marched with him, while the birds flew over him, shading him and the others with their wings from the heat of the sun. And there were three men charged with the task of keeping each row straight, i.e. officers who organized the ranks into straight lines, so that no one advanced from his designated marching place or lagged behind it. Allah, Most High, says, *Till when they came to the valley of the ants, one of the ants said, "O, ants! Enter your dwellings, lest Sulaiman and his hosts crush you, while they perceive not."* (*Soorah An-Naml* 27:18) So it commanded and warned and excused Sulaiman ﷺ and his armies, due to the fact that they were unaware (of the ants' presence). Wahb said that he (Sulaiman) was sitting on a carpet in a valley in At-Ta'if and that this ant's name was Jarsa and that it belonged to a colony called Banu Shaisaban, that she was lame and that she was the same size as a wolf, but these claims are doubtful. Indeed, the wording of the Verse indicates that he was riding with his army at the time, not, as some claimed, sitting on a carpet. This is because, if it had been as they said, the ants would not have been harmed in any way by him, nor would they have been trampled.

What is intended is that Sulaiman ﷺ understood the words of good advice which that ant addressed to its community and he smiled at that, out of a feeling of delight and happiness at the gift which Allah had bestowed on him alone. It is not as some of the foolish people claim, that before Sulaiman ﷺ, the animals of the earth used to converse with mankind, until Sulaiman, son of Dawood took from them a covenant which silenced them, after which they did not converse with mankind. All of this is only claimed by those who do not know. If it were so, Sulaiman ﷺ would not have any superiority over others due to his understanding of their languages, since all of mankind – according to their claim – would have understood them. And if he had taken a covenant from them not to speak to anyone other than him, while he understood them, there would have been no benefit in this either. This is why he said, *My Lord* **"Awzi'nee…"** (*Soorah An-Naml* 27:19). That is, inspire me and guide me *"…that I may be grateful for Your Favors which You have bestowed on me and* *on my parents, and that I may do righteous good deeds that will please You, and admit me by Your Mercy among Your righteous slaves.* " (*Soorah An-Naml* 27:19) So he asked Allah to ordain for him gratitude for the Blessing that He had bestowed on him and the superiority that He had granted to him over other men. He also asked Him to make it easy for him to perform righteous deeds and to gather him when he should, with His righteous slaves. And Allah, Most High, acceded to his supplication. What is meant by his parents is his father, Dawood صلى and his mother, who was one of the righteous slaves (of Allah).

He, Most High, says, *He inspected the birds, and said, "What is the matter that I see not the hoopoe? Or is he among the absentees? I will surely punish him with a severe punishment, or slaughter him, unless he brings me a clear reason." But the hoopoe stayed not long, he said, "I have grasped that which you have not grasped and I have come to you from Saba' (Sheba) with sure news. I found a woman ruling over them, and she has been given all things and she has a great* **'arsh***. I found her and her people worshipping the sun instead of Allah, and* **Shaitan** *has made their deeds fair-seeming to them, and has barred them from (Allah's) Way, so they have no guidance* **Al-la** *(this word has two interpretations)* **(a)** *(as* **Shaitan** *has barred them from Allah's Way) so that they do not worship (prostrate before) Allah, or* **(b)** *So that they may worship (prostrate before) Allah, Who brings to light what is hidden in the heavens and the Earth, and knows what you conceal and what you reveal." (Tafseer At-Tabari,* Vol. 19, page 149*) Allah,* **la ilaha illa Huwa** *(none has the right to be worshipped but He), the Lord of the Supreme Throne! (Sulaiman) said, "We shall see whether you speak the truth or you are (one) of the liars. Go you with this letter of mine, and deliver it to them, then draw back from them, and see what (answer) they return." She said, "O, chiefs! Verily! Here is delivered to me a noble letter. Verily, it is from Sulaiman, and verily! It (reads),* **"In the Name of***

Allah, the Most Gracious, the Most Merciful: "Be you not exalted against me, but come to me as Muslims (true Believers who submit to Allah with full submission)." She said, "O, chiefs! Advise me in (this) case of mine. I decide no case till you are present with me." They said, "We have great strength, and great fortitude, but it is for you to command; so think over what you will command." She said, "Verily! kings, when they enter a town (country), they despoil it, and make the most honorable amongst its people low. And thus they do. But verily, I am going to send him a present, and see with what (answer) the messengers return." So when (the messengers with the present) came to Sulaiman, he said, "Will you help me in wealth? What Allah has given me is better than that which He has given you! Nay, you rejoice in your gift!" (Then Sulaiman said to the chief of her messengers who brought the present), "Go back to them. We verily shall come to them with hosts that they cannot resist, and we shall drive them out from there in disgrace, and they will be abased." (Soorah An-Naml 27:20-37)

Allah, Most High, tells us about the affair of Sulaiman عليه السلام and the hoopoe, describing how the birds of all kinds came, fulfilling what he requested from them and coming to him in rotation, as is the custom of armies with kings. And the job of the hoopoe – according to what Ibn 'Abbas رضي الله عنه and others said – was, when they were in need of water in the deserts during their travels, it would come and see if there was water for them in a certain spot. It had an ability given to it by Allah, Most High, which allowed it to see water underground. When it had shown them where to find it, they would dig for it, find it, extract it and use as much of it as they needed. So when Sulaiman عليه السلام called for it one day, he did not find it in its place of service. *He inspected the birds, and said, "What is the matter that I see not the hoopoe? Or is he among the absentees?" (Soorah An-Naml* 27:20) means why is he missing from here? Has he absented himself from my sight, so that I do not see him before me? *"I will surely punish him with a*

severe punishment." (*Soorah An-Naml* 27:21). He threatened him
with some kind of punishment. Scholars disagreed as to what the
nature of that punishment was, but the result is the same, no matter
what kind of punishment it was. *"...or slaughter him, unless he
brings me a clear reason"* (*Soorah An-Naml* 27:21) means a
reason that saves him from this predicament. Allah, Most High
says, *But the hoopoe stayed not long.* (*Soorah An-Naml* 27:22).
That is, the hoopoe remained absent for only a short time, then
he came back and he said to Sulaiman ﷺ, *"I have grasped that
which you have not grasped..."* (*Soorah An-Naml* 27:22) That
is, I have obtained information of something which is unknown
to you. *"...and I have come to you from Saba' (Sheba) with sure
news"* (*Soorah An-Naml* 27:22) meaning with true information.
*"I found a woman ruling over them, and she has been given all
things that could be possessed by any ruler of the Earth, and she
has a great throne."* (*Soorah An-Naml* 27:23) He described the
great kingdom ruled over by the kings of Saba' in Yemen. At
that time, the crown had been inherited by a woman from among
them, who was the daughter of a king who had not left any other
heir besides her, so they made her their queen.

Ath-Tha'labi narrated on the authority of Abu Bakrah that he
said, "I mentioned Bilqees in the presence of the Messenger of
Allah ﷺ and he said, "Any people who appoint a woman to rule
over them will not be successful."[1] Isma'eel Ibn Muslim (one
of the narrators) is Al-Makki and he is weak. But it has been
confirmed in *Saheeh Al-Bukhari* on the authority of Abu Bakrah
ﷺ that when the Messenger of Allah ﷺ was informed that the
people of Persia had crowned the daughter of Kisra (Khosrau)

---

[1] Narrated by Ath-Tha'labi in *'Ara'is Al-Majalis* (279) with an abridged
chain of narrators; and it says, "It was reported on the authority of
Abu Bakr ﷺ..." instead of Abu Bakrah ﷺ. And this book is filled with
Isra'eeliyyat, which do not benefit the reader and in which there is noth-
ing authentic. See also the comment of the author after mentioning the
Hadith.

as their queen he said, "A people who appoint a woman as their leader will never be successful."[1]

And He, Most High, says, *"...and she has been given all things."* (*Soorah An-Naml* 27:23) That is, everything that kings are given. *"...and she has a great 'arsh"* (*Soorah An-Naml* 27:23) means the throne of her kingdom, which was inlaid with all kinds of precious stones, pearls, gold and dazzling gems. Then he mentioned their disbelief in Allah, their worship of the sun, to the exclusion of Allah, Shaitan's misguidance of them and his hindering of them from worshipping Allah, Alone, without partners *Who brings to light what is hidden in the heavens and the earth, and knows what you conceal and what you reveal.* (*Soorah An-Naml* 27:25) It means that He knows everything that is hidden in the heavens and on earth and He knows what His servants say and do in secret, and what they say and do openly. *Allah,* **la ilaha illa Huwa** *(none has the right to be worshipped but He), the Lord of the Supreme Throne!* (*Soorah An-Naml* 27:26) That is, to Him belongs the Supreme Throne, besides which there is no greater throne among the created things. On hearing this, Sulaiman صلى الله عليه وسلم sent with him a letter containing an invitation to declare their obedience to Allah and to His Messenger صلى الله عليه وسلم, to turn to Him in repentance and to submit in humility to His Dominion and His Authority, which is why He said to them, *"Be you not exalted against me..."* (*Soorah An-Naml* 27:31) That is, do arrogantly refuse to obey me and follow my commands. *"...but come to me as Muslims (true Believers who submit to Allah with full submission)."* (*Soorah An-Naml* 27:31) That is, come to me as those who hear and obey, without argument or hesitation. When the letter came to them with the bird, then the people took the letter but what has the ground to do with the Pleiades?[2] This paper

---

(1) Narrated by Al-Bukhari (4425). It was also narrated by At-Tirmidhi (2262) and An-Nasa'i (5388).

(2) This is an Arabic expression used to describe things of disproportionate

was with a bird who heard and obeyed, who understood and had knowledge of what was said. And more than one of the scholars of *tafseer* and other scholars have mentioned that the hoopoe bore the letter and arrived at her palace, where he dropped it on her while she was alone. Then he stood at one side and waited to see what her reply to the letter would be. She gathered her governors, ministers and the leading members of the country in order to seek their advice. *She said, "O, chiefs! Verily, here is delivered to me a noble letter."* (*Soorah An-Naml* 27:29) Then she read the first line of the letter to them: *"Verily, it is from Sulaiman."* (*Soorah An-Naml* 27:30) Then she read the letter: *"In the Name of Allah, the Most Beneficent, the Most Merciful, Be you not exalted against me, but come to me as Muslims (true believers who submit to Allah with full submission)."* (*Soorah An-Naml* 27:30) Then she asked their advice regarding the letter and what had befallen her. She behaved courteously toward them and addressed them and they listened to her. *She said, "O, chiefs! Advise me in (this) case of mine. I decide no case till you are present with me."* (*Soorah An-Naml* 27:32) That is, I do not settle or determine any matter unless you are present. *They said, "We have great strength and great fortitude"* (*Soorah An-Naml* 27:33) means, we possess (military) strength and have the ability to fight and oppose their warriors, so if you desire us to do that, we are fully able to do so. *"...but it is for you to command; so think over what you will command."* (*Soorah An-Naml* 27:33) So they expressed their commitment to hear and obey and they informed her of their readiness for war, but they left it to her to decide what the best guidance for her and for them was. Her opinion was better and more correct than theirs, for she realized that the writer of this letter could not be defeated, thwarted, opposed or deceived. *She said, "Verily! kings, when they enter a town (country), they despoil it, and make the most honorable amongst its people low. And thus they do."* (*Soorah An-Naml* 27:34) She gave her sensible opinion, which was that if

---

value.

this king defeated her kingdom, the responsibility would be hers alone and their enmity would be mainly directed toward her, as the ruler. *"But verily, I am going to send him a present, and see with what (answer) the messengers return."* (*Soorah An-Naml* 27:35). She decided to cooperate with him, in order to protect herself and her people, by sending a gift to Sulaiman ﷺ, but she did not know that Sulaiman ﷺ would not accept a gift from them in such circumstances, because they were disbelievers and he and his armies were able to defeat them, which is *why when (the messengers with the present) came to Sulaiman, he said, "Will you help me in wealth? What Allah has given me is better than that which He has given you! Nay, you rejoice in your gift!"* (*Soorah An-Naml* 27:36) This was in spite of the fact that those gifts were magnificent, according to what the scholars of *tafseer* have said.

Then he said to her messenger and the delegation she had sent to him – while the people were gathered and were listening – *"Go back to them. We verily shall come to them with hosts that they cannot resist, and we shall drive them out from there in disgrace, and they will be abased."* (*Soorah An-Naml* 27:37) He said: Return with the gifts that you have presented to me to the one who bestowed them, for the wealth, gifts and men with which Allah has blessed me are better and more numerous than that which pleases you so much and due to which you glory over the rest of mankind. *"We verily shall come to them with hosts that they cannot resist."* (*Soorah An-Naml* 27:37) It means that I will surely send upon them armies against which they will be unable to defend themselves and I will surely expel them from their land, their estates, their businesses and their country belittled. *"...and they will be abased."* (*Soorah An-Naml* 27:37) That is, upon them will be heaped humiliation, disgrace and ruin. When this was conveyed to them from the Prophet of Allah ﷺ, they had no alternative but to hear and obey. They hastened to answer him in that hour and they went to their queen together in obedience to Sulaiman's command. When Sulaiman ﷺ heard of their delegation, he said to those of the Jinn who were in his presence and who were subjugated to him, *"O, chiefs! Which of you can bring me her throne before they come to me surrendering themselves in obedience?" An* **'Ifreet** *from the Jinn said, "I will bring it to you before you rise from your place (council). And verily, I am indeed strong and trustworthy for such work." One with whom was knowledge of the Scripture said, "I will bring it to you within the twinkling of an eye!" then, when (Sulaiman) saw it placed before him, he said, "This is by the Grace of my Lord to test me whether I am grateful or ungrateful! And whoever is grateful, truly, his gratitude is for (the good of) his ownself, and whoever is ungrateful, certainly, my Lord is Rich (Free of all wants), Bountiful." He said, "Disguise her throne for her that we may see whether she will be guided (to recognize her throne), or she will be one of those not guided." So when she came, it was said (to her), "Is your throne like this?" She said, "(It is) as though it were the very same." And (Sulaiman) said, "Knowledge was bestowed on us before her, and we submitted to Allah (in Islam as Muslims before her)." And that which she used to worship besides Allah has prevented her, for she was of a disbelieving people. It was said to her, "Enter* **as-sarh,** *" (a glass surface with water underneath it or a palace), but when she saw it, she thought it was a pool, and she (tucked up her clothes) uncovering her legs, Sulaiman said, "Verily, it is* **sarh** *(a glass surface with water underneath it or a palace) paved smooth with glass." She said, "My Lord! Verily, I have wronged myself, and I submit (in Islam), together with Sulaiman, to Allah, the Lord of* **Al-'Alameen.** *" (Soorah An-Naml 27:38-44)*

When Sulaiman requested from the jinn that they bring him the throne of Bilqees (Saba'), which was the seat of her kingdom on which she used to sit when passing judgment, before her arrival in Sulaiman's court. *An 'Ifreet from the jinn said, "I will bring it to you before you rise from your place (council)"* (*Soorah An-Naml* 27:39) means, before he could complete his judgments. It was said that this council customarily took place from early in the morning until just before midday; during this council, he would busy himself with the affairs and concerns of Banu Isra'eel. *"And verily, I am indeed strong and trustworthy for such work."* (*Soorah An-Naml* 27:39) That is, I possess the ability to bring it to you and I can be trusted with the precious stones in it. *One with whom was knowledge of the Scripture said...* (*Soorah An-Naml* 27:40) It is well-known that his name was Asif Ibn Barkhiya, who was the maternal cousin of Sulaiman ﷺ. It was also said that he was a man from among the Believers of the jinn who knew the Greatest Name of Allah. It was also said that he was a man from among Banu Isra'eel and that he was one of their scholars. And it was said that he was Sulaiman ﷺ, but this is a very strange claim. It was dismissed as weak by As-Suhaili, on the basis that it was incompatible with the wording. It was also said that there was a fourth opinion, which was that the speaker was Jibraeel. *"I will bring it to you within the twinkling of an eye!"* (*Soorah An-Naml* 27:40) It was said that the meaning is: before you can send a messenger to the farthest point on the Earth which your eye can see and he can return to you. It was also said that it means: before the farthest person you can see can reach you. And it was said that it means: before your glance becomes weary and you blink your eye. It was also said that it means: before you can close your eyes. And it was also said that it means: before your glance can return to you, when you look toward the farthest point from you, then you close your eyes. And this seems most likely of all these sayings. *Then, when (Sulaiman) saw it placed before him...* (*Soorah An-Naml* 27:40) means when he saw the throne of Bilqees placed in front of him in this short space of time from the land of Yemen to Bait Al-Maqdis, in the blink of an eye, *he said, "This is by the Grace of my Lord to test me whether I am grateful*

or ungrateful!" (*Soorah An-Naml* 27:41) That is, this is from
Allah's Favor upon me and upon His slaves, to test us and see
if we are grateful for that Favor or not. *And whoever is grateful,
truly, his gratitude is for (the good of) his ownself.* (*Soorah An-
Naml* 27:40) That is, the benefit of that gratitude will only accrue
to him. *"and whoever is ungrateful, certainly, my Lord is Rich
(Free of all wants), Bountiful."* (*Soorah An-Naml* 27:40) means
that He is in no need of the thanks of those who show gratitude and
He is not harmed by the ingratitude of those who are ungrateful
to Him. Then Sulaiman ﷺ ordered that the throne's adornments
be altered and disguised so that she would not recognize it, in
order to test her understanding and her intelligence, which is why
he said, *"Disguise her throne for her that we may see whether
she will be guided (to recognize her throne), or she will be one
of those not guided." So when she came, it was said (to her),
"Is your throne like this?" She said, "(It is) as though it were
the very same."* (*Soorah An-Naml* 27:41,42) This was due to her
astuteness and deep understanding, because she considered it
unlikely that it could be her throne, since she had left it behind
in the land of Yemen and she knew of no one who was able to
do such an amazing thing. Allah, Most High, says, informing us
about Sulaiman ﷺ and his people, *"Knowledge was bestowed
on us before her, and we submitted to Allah (in Islam as Muslims
before her)." And that which she used to worship besides Allah
has prevented her, for she was of a disbelieving people.* (*Soorah
An-Naml* 27:42,43) That is, the worship of the sun, before which
she and her people used to prostrate, instead of to Allah, prevented
her from embracing Islam. They did this because they followed
the religion of their fathers and their forefathers; no evidence
led them or urged them to do so. Sulaiman ﷺ had ordered the
construction of a palace made of glass and he ordered them to
make a passageway of water, over which a glass floor was placed.
In the water he had placed fish and other aquatic creatures. The
Queen of Saba' was ordered to enter the palace, where she found

Sulaiman ﷺ sitting on his throne. *...But when she saw it, she thought it was a pool, and she (tucked up her clothes) uncovering her legs, Sulaiman said, "Verily, it is sarh (a glass surface with water underneath it or a palace) paved smooth with glass." She said, "My Lord! Verily, I have wronged myself, and I submit (in Islam), together with Sulaiman, to Allah, the Lord of* **Al-'Alameen.** *" (Soorah An-Naml 27:44)*

And He, Most High, says, *And to Dawood We gave Sulaiman. How excellent (a) slave! Verily, he was ever oft-returning in repentance (to Us)! When there were displayed before him in the afternoon, well-trained horses of the highest breed (for* **jihad** *[holy fight in Allah's Cause]). And he said, "I did love the good (these horses) instead of remembering my Lord (in my* **'Asr** *prayer)," till the time was over and it had hidden in the veil (of night). Then he said, "Bring them (horses) back to me." Then he began to pass his hand over their* **sooq** *and their* **a'naq** *(till the end of the display). And indeed We did try Sulaiman and We placed on his throne* **Jasad** *(a devil, so he lost his kingdom for a while) but he did return (to his throne and kingdom by the Grace of Allah and he did return) to Allah with obedience and in repentance. He said, "My Lord! Forgive me and bestow upon me a kingdom such as shall not belong to any other after me: verily, You are the Bestower." So We subjected to him the wind; it blew gently to his order whithersoever he willed, and also the* **Shayateen** *(devils) from the Jinn (including) every kind of builder and diver. And also others bound in fetters. (Saying of Allah to Sulaiman), "This is Our gift, so spend you or withhold, no account will be asked." And verily, he enjoyed a near access to Us and a good final return (Paradise)." (Soorah Sad 38:30-40)*

Allah, Most High, relates how He granted Dawood ﷺ a son, Sulaiman ﷺ, then He praises them both, saying, *How excellent (a) slave! Verily, he was ever oft-returning in repentance (to Us)! (Soorah Sad 38:30)* That is, oft-returning to Allah and obedient to Him. Then Allah relates the story of the horses which were *safinat*, i.e. those which stand on three legs and raise the fourth. They were outstanding horses, lean and swift. *And he said, "I did love the good (these horses) instead of remembering my Lord (in my 'Asr prayer)," till the time was over and it had hidden in the veil (of night) (Soorah Sad* 38:32) means the sun, or it was said, the horses. *"Bring them (horses) back to me." Then he began to pass his hand over their sooq and their a'naq (till the end of the display). (Soorah Sad* 38:33) It was said that their hamstrings and their necks were struck with swords. It was also said that he began patting the horses' heads and legs out of love for them.[1] Most of the *Salaf* supported the first interpretation; they said that he was busily engaged with the presentation of those horses until the time for offering the *'Asr* prayer had departed and the sun had set. This was narrated on the authority of 'Ali Ibn Abi Talib ﷺ and others. What is certain is that he did not intentionally neglect the prayer, without permission, though it was said that he was engaged in watering them and so he delayed the prayer for reasons of *jihad* – and the presentation of the horses was a part of that.

He, Most High, says, *And indeed We did try Sulaiman and We placed on his throne* **Jasad** *(a devil, so he lost his kingdom for a while) and he did return (to Allah with obedience and in repentence, and to his throne and kingdom by the Grace of Allah. (Soorah Sad* 38:34) Ibn Jareer At-Tabari, Ibn Abi Hatim and other scholars of *tafseer* related here a number of traditions from a group of the *Salaf*, but most, if not all of them are taken from *Isra'eeliyyat* – and in many of them there are extremely unacceptable things.

It is reported on the authority of 'Abdullah Ibn 'Amr Ibn Al-'As

---

(1) This is the view that was favored by Ibn Jareer. He said, "Because he would not punish an animal by cutting its hamstrings or destroy his own wealth for no other reason than that he had been distracted from his prayer by looking at it, and it was not the animals' fault."

that he said, "The Messenger of Allah ﷺ said, "When Sulaiman عليه السلام built Bait Al-Maqdis, he asked his Lord, the Almighty, the All-powerful for three things; Allah granted him two of them and we hope that the third will be granted to us. He asked Him for judgment that concurred with His Judgment and He granted him that; he asked Him for a kingdom the like of which no one after him would ever enjoy and He granted him that; He also asked Him that if any man left his house desiring nothing but prayer in this mosque, he would leave behind his sins, like he was on the day on which his mother gave birth to him. And we hope that Allah has granted this to us."[1]

As for the judgment which agreed with Allah's Judgment, Allah has praised him and his father, Dawood عليه السلام in His Words: *And (remember) Dawood and Sulaiman, when they gave judgment in the case of the field in which the sheep of certain people had pastured at night and We were witness to their judgment. And We made Sulaiman to understand (the case), and to each of them We gave* **Hukman** *(right judgment of the affairs and Prophethood) and knowledge. And We subjected the mountains and the birds to glorify Our Praises along with Dawood, And it was We Who was the Doer (of all these things).* (*Soorah Al-Anbiya' 21:78,79*) Shuraih Al-Qadi and more than one of the *Salaf* have mentioned that these people owned grapevines and the sheep of some other people ate them during the night, consuming the whole vine. They took their case to Dawood عليه السلام for judgment and he ruled in favor of the owners of the grapevines, saying that the owners of the sheep must pay them the full value of what their sheep had consumed. When they came out, Sulaiman asked them, "What did the Prophet of Allah judge for you?" They said, "Such-and-such." He said, "Were I the judge, I would have not ruled except that the owners of the sheep hand them over to the owners of the

---

(1)   This is an authentic *Hadith* narrated by Imam Ahmad (2/176, No. 27762),
       An-Nasa'i (694), Ibn Majah (1408), Ibn Khuzaimah in his *Saheeh* (2/228)

grapevines, so that they could benefit from their offspring and milk, until the owners of the sheep had repaired the grapevines and returned them to the condition they were in previously, after which their sheep would be returned to them. When this was conveyed to Dawood عليه السلام, he ruled accordingly.

In *Soorah Sad*, Allah, Most High, says, *So We subjected to him the wind, it blew gently to his order whithersoever he willed and also the* **Shayateen** *(devils) from the Jinn (including) every kind of builder and diver and also others bound in fetters. (Saying of Allah to Sulaiman), "This is Our gift, so spend you or withhold, no account will be asked." And verily, he enjoyed a near access to Us and a good final return (Paradise).* (*Soorah Sad* 38:36-40) When he gave up the horses, seeking thereby Allah's Countenance, Allah replaced them for him with the wind, which is faster, stronger and greater and entailed no trouble or expense for him (unlike the horses). *...it blew gently to his order whithersoever he willed.* (*Soorah Sad* 38:36) That is, wherever he wished from any country; it seems that he had a wooden platform, on which he could place all that he needed, such as erected houses, palaces and tents, goods, horses, camels, loads, men from among mankind and the jinn and other things, such as animals and birds. Then, when he wanted to travel or go on a pleasure trip, or make war on a king or enemies from any land that Allah willed, when the aforementioned things had been loaded on the platform, he would command the wind and it would get underneath it and raise it up. Then, when it was raised up between the heaven and the Earth, he would order it to blow gently and it would proceed with him. If he wanted to go faster than that, he would command the storm and it would carry him at the fastest possible speed and put him down in any place he wished, so that he would set out from Bait Al-Maqdis in the early part of the day and the wind would come and take him to Istakhr (in Persia) and he would remain there throughout the morning hours until midday, then the wind would return him to

Bait Al-Maqdis, as Allah, Most High, says, *And to Sulaiman We subjected the wind, its morning (stride from sunrise till midday) was a month's (journey), and its afternoon (stride from the midday decline of the sun to sunset) was a month's (journey i.e. in one day he could travel two months' journey). And We caused a fount of* **qitr** *to flow for him, and there were Jinn that worked in front of him, by the Leave of his Lord, and whosoever of them turned aside from Our Command, We shall cause him to taste of the punishment of the blazing Fire. They worked for him what he desired, (making) high rooms, images,* **jifan** *like* **jawab** *and* **qudoor rasiyat.** *"Work you, O family of Dawood, with thanks!" But few of My slaves are grateful.* (*Soorah Saba'* 34:12,13) Al-Hasan Al-Basri said, "He used to set out in the morning from Damascus and he would alight at Istakhr, where he would take lunch. From there he would travel to Kabul (in Turkey); and the distance between Damascus and Istakhr was one month's travel, while the distance between Istakhr and Kabul is also one month's travel." I say: The scholars of buildings and towns say that Istakhr was built by the jinn of Sulaiman عليه السلام and that in ancient times, it had been the seat of power of the Turks. They said that likewise, numerous cities, such as Tadmur, Bait Al-Maqdis, Bab Jairoon and Bab Al-Bareed, which are both in Damascus were built by them.

As for *qitr*, according to 'Abdullah Ibn 'Abbas رضي الله عنه, Mujahid, 'Ikrimah, Qatadah and a number of others, it means (molten) copper. Qatadah said, "It was in Yemen that Allah brought it forth for him." As-Suddi said, "In just three days, He extracted for him all that he needed for buildings and other things."

And He, Most High, says, *...and there were Jinn that worked in front of him, by the Leave of his Lord, and whosoever of them turned aside from Our Command, We shall cause him to taste of the punishment of the blazing Fire.* (*Soorah Saba'* 34:12) That is, Allah subjected to him workers from among the

Jinn, who worked for him on whatever he wished and did not disobey him; as for those who did refuse to obey his commands he punished and shackled them. *They worked for him what he desired, (making) high rooms.* (*Soorah Saba'* 34:13) And they are beautiful places, the best and innermost parts of meeting places. This was permissible under their law and their religious code.

jifan. Ibn 'Abbas ﷺ said that a *jafnah* (*jifan* is the plural) is like a pit in the ground, or in another narration on his authority, like a water basin. Mujahid said likewise, as did Al-Hasan, Qatadah, Ad-Dahhak and others. Based on this narration, the word *jawab* would be the plural of *jabiyah*, which is a basin in which water collects, as Al-A'sha said in *Al-Bahr At-Taweel*:

"A pool of water passes by the family of Al-Muhallaq,
Like the reservoir of As-Saih Al-'Iraqi, it fills to overflowing."

As for the *qudoor rasiyat*, 'Ikrimah said that they are fixed cooking cauldrons. Mujahid and others concurred with this, and they were placed thus for the purpose of feeding people and giving charity to mankind and the jinn. Allah, Most High, says, *"Work you, O family of Dawood, with thanks!" But few of My slaves are grateful.* (*Soorah Saba'* 34:13) and He, Most High, says, *And also the* **Shayateen** *(devils) from the jinn, (including) every kind of builder and diver and also others bound in fetters.* (*Soorah Sad* 38:37,38) means, some of them had been subjugated to him as builders, while others had been subjugated to him as divers, whose job it was to dive in the sea and collect precious stones and pearls and other things which were not present with them. *and also others bound in fetters* (*Soorah Sad* 38:38) means that they had disobeyed and so they had been shackled in pairs. All of these were among the things that Allah had prepared for him and subjugated to his will and which were a part of the completeness of his kingdom, the like of which was not given to anyone before him or after him.

And Al-Bukhari narrated on the authority of Abu Hurairah ﷺ from the Prophet ﷺ that he said, "Verily, an *'ifreet* from among the Jinn came to me yesterday suddenly, so as to spoil my prayer, but Allah enabled me to overpower him, and I caught him and intended to tie him to one of the pillars of the Mosque so that all of you might see him, but I remembered the invocation of my brother Sulaiman: *'My Lord! Forgive me, And grant me a kingdom such as shall not belong to any other after me.'* (*Soorah Sad* 38:35) so I let him go cursed."[1]

And more than one of the *Salaf* have mentioned that Sulaiman ﷺ had a thousand wives; seven hundred of them had been wedded to him after the payment of dowries and three hundred had been taken as captives. It was also said that it was the other way around, that they were three hundred free women and seven hundred slaves. It was said that he had a huge appetite for women. Al-Bukhari narrated on the authority of Abu Hurairah ﷺ from the Prophet ﷺ that he said, "Sulaiman, the son of Dawood, said, 'Tonight I will sleep with seventy women each of whom will conceive a child who will be a knight fighting for Allah's Cause.' His companion said, 'if Allah wills.' But Sulaiman did not say so; therefore none of those women got pregnant except one who gave birth to a half child.' The Prophet further said, 'If Prophet Sulaiman had said it (i.e. if Allah wills) he would have begotten children who would have fought in Allah's Cause'." Shu'aib and Ibn Abi Az-Zinad said, "Ninety (women) is more correct (than seventy)."[2] Al-Bukhari was alone in narrating it from this source.

He, Most High, says, *He said, "My Lord! Forgive me, and bestow upon me a kingdom such as shall not belong to any other after me: verily, You are the Bestower."* (*Soorah Sad* 38:35). And Allah gave him all of that, according to the testimony of the

---

(1)   Narrated by Al-Bukhari (3423).

(2)   Narrated by Al-Bukhari (3424).

Prophet ﷺ. And when Allah, Most High, mentioned the great and complete blessings that He had bestowed on him, He said, *"This is Our gift, so spend you or withhold, no account will be asked."* (*Soorah Sad* 38:39) That is, give to whom you will and deny whom you will, for you will not be held accountable for it, i.e. dispose of the wealth as you will, because Allah has permitted whatever you may do with it and He will not ask you to account for it. This was the case with the Prophet-King, unlike the slave-Messenger, who neither gave nor denied without Allah's Permission. And Allah allowed our Prophet ﷺ, to choose between these two situations (slave-Messenger or Prophet-King), and he chose to be a slave-Messenger.

When Allah described what He had granted to His Prophet, Sulaiman ﷺ of the goodness of this life, He described the reward, abundance and beautiful recompense that He has prepared for him in the Hereafter, in addition to the nearness to Him, the great success and the honor that he will enjoy before Him. All of this will be on the Day of Return and Recompense, as He, Most High, says, *And verily, he enjoyed a near access to Us and a good final return (Paradise).* (*Soorah Sad* 38:40)

A Description of His Death

Allah, Most Glorified, Most High, says, *Then ,when We decreed death for him (Sulaiman), nothing informed them (the Jinn) of his death except a crawling creature of the earth, which kept (slowly) gnawing away at his stick, so when he fell down, the Jinn saw clearly that if they had known the Unseen, they would not have stayed in the humiliating punishment.* (*Soorah Sad* 34:14)

And Ibn Jareer At-Tabari, Ibn Abi Hatim and others narrated the *Hadith* of 'Abdullah Ibn 'Abbas ﷺ, in which he reported on the authority of the Prophet ﷺ that he said, "Sulaiman ﷺ, the Prophet of Allah used to see a tree growing before him and he would say to it, "What is your name?" The tree would answer, "So-and-so." He said, "For what purpose are you? If it was for seeds, it would be allowed to go to seed. If it was for medicine, it would be allowed to grow. One day, when he was praying, he saw a tree before him and he said to it, "What is your name?" It said, "Al-Kharroobah." He said, "For what purpose are you?" It replied, "For the destruction of this house." He said, "O, Allah! Keep my death hidden from the jinn until the humans realize that the jinn do not know the unseen." So he carved a stick from it and he leaned on it for a whole year, while the jinn continued working. The stick was eaten by a termite (causing him to fall down), after which it was clear to mankind that if the jinn had known the unseen, they would not have remained for a year in humiliating punishment." [1]

---

(1) Narrated by Ibn Jareer At-Tabari in his *Tafseer* (22/74), by At-Tabarani in *Al-Mu'jam Al-Kabeer* (11/452) and Al-Hakim in *Al-Mustadrak* (4/220, No. 7428).

Mention of a Number of Prophets from Banu Isra'eel after Dawood and Sulaiman and before Zakriyya and Yahya

Among them were those whose lifetime cannot be precisely pinpointed, except to say that they lived after Dawood عليه السلام and before Zakariyya عليه السلام and (Yahya عليه السلام). They included: Sha'ya, son of Amsiya; Muhammad Ibn Ishaq said, "He was before Zakariyya and Yahya (peace be upon them both) and he was one of those who gave the glad tidings of 'Eesa and Muhammad (peace be upon them both)." During his lifetime there was a king over the Children of Isra'eel whose name was Sadeeqah, in the land of Bait Al-Maqdis. He used to listen to Sha'ya عليه السلام and obey whatever he commanded him to do and refrain from whatever he forbade. Affairs had become difficult among the Children of Isra'eel and the king became ill, suffering from an ulcer in his leg.

The king of Babylon set out for Bait Al-Maqdis at that time, and his name was Sanhareeb. Ibn Ishaq said that he had six hundred thousand troops with him.

The people were greatly terrified. The king asked Sha'ya, "What did Allah reveal to you regarding Sanhareeb and his army?" He replied, "He has not yet revealed anything to me." Then the revelation came down for King Sadeeqah to appoint a successor, as he wished, because his end was at hand. When Sha'ya told him this, the king turned to the *Qiblah* (the direction faced in prayer); he prayed, glorified Allah, invoked Him, and wept. Weeping and invoking Allah, the All-Powerful, and majestic with a sincere heart, trust and patience, he said, "O, Lord of lords, and God of gods! O, Benevolent and Merciful One Whom neither sleep nor nodding can overpower, remember me for my deeds and my just judgment over the Children of Isra'eel; and all that was from You, and You know it better than I do, my open acts and my secrets are with You."

Allah answered his prayers had compassion on him. He revealed to Sha'ya to tell him the glad tidings that He had compassion for his weeping and would extend his life for a further fifteen years and save him from the enemy, Sanhareeb. When Sha'ya told this to Sadeeqah, his disease was healed. Evil and sadness departed, and he fell in prostration, saying, "O, Lord, it is You Who grants kingship to whomsoever You wish and dethrones whomsoever You wish and elevates whomsoever You wish and degrades whomsoever You wish, Knower of the Unseen and the evident. And lo! You are the First and the Last; the Manifest and the Perceived; You grant Mercy and answer the prayers of the troubled ones." When he raised his head, Allah revealed to Sha'ya to command the king to extract the juice of the fig and apply it to his ulcer, and he would be whole and cured. He did so and was cured.

Then Allah sent death upon the army of Sanhareeb. In the morning, they were all corpses, except Sanuhareeb and five of his companions, among them Nebuchadnezzar (Bukhtunassar). The king of Isra'eel immediately sent for them, put them in shackles and displayed them in the land for seventy days to spite and insult them. Every day each of them was fed a loaf of barley bread; after seventy days he confined them in prison. Allah then revealed to Sha'ya that the king should send them back to their country so that they might warn their people what would happen to them. When they returned, Sanhareeb gathered his people and told them what had happened to them. The priests and magicians said to him, "We told you about their Lord and their prophets, but you did not listen to us. It is a nation which, with their God, nobody can overcome." So, Sanhareeb was afraid of Allah. He died seven years later.

A Description of the Destruction of Bait Al-Maqdis

Allah, Most High, says, *And We gave Moosa the Scripture and made it a guidance for the Children of Isra'eel (saying), "Take not other than Me as (your)* **Wakil** *(Protector, Lord, or Disposer of your affairs, etc). O offspring of those whom We carried (in the ship) with Nooh (Noah)! Verily, he was a grateful slave." And We decreed for the Children of Isra'eel in the Scripture, that indeed you would do mischief on the earth twice and you will become tyrants and extremely arrogant! So, when the promise came for the first of the two, We sent against you slaves of Ours given to terrible warfare. They entered the very innermost parts of your homes. And it was a promise (completely) fulfilled. Then We gave you once again, a return of victory over them. And We helped you with wealth and children and made you more numerous in manpower. (And We said), "If you do good, you do good for your own selves, and if you do evil (you do it) against yourselves."*

Then, when the second promise came to pass, (We permitted your enemies) to make your faces sorrowful and to enter the mosque (of Jerusalem) as they had entered it before, and to destroy with utter destruction all that fell in their hands. (And We said in the Tawrah,) "It may be that your Lord may show mercy unto you, but if you return (to sins), We shall return (to Our Punishment). And We have made Hell a prison for the disbelievers. (Soorah Al-Isra 17:2-8)

Wahb Ibn Munabbih said, "When sins became prevalent among the Children of Isra'eel, Allah revealed to a Prophet from among them, whose name was 'Armiya (Jeremiah) that he should stand up in the midst of them and inform them that: "You have hearts, yet you do not understand; you have eyes, yet you do not see; and you have ears, yet you do not hear. I thought of the righteousness of their fathers and that made Me feel compassion for their children." (Allah said,) "So ask them, how did they find the outcome of obedience to Me? And was anyone who disobeyed Me made fortunate as a result of his disobedience? And was anyone who obeyed Me made wretched as a result of his obedience? The animals remember their homes and they feel a desire for them, yet these people have abandoned the Religion which I commanded their fathers to follow and sought blessings from other than it. As for their rabbis, they denied My Truth; and as for their (Towrah) reciters, they worshipped other (gods) than Me; and as for their devout, learned men, they did not benefit from what they knew; And as for their rulers, they lied against Me and against My Messengers and they harbored deception in their hearts and accustomed their tongues to lying. I swear by My Majesty and My Might that I will surely incite armies against them whose languages they will not understand and whose faces they will not recognize and they will show no mercy for their tears. And I will surely send to them a tyrannical and cruel king with armies like racing clouds and retinues like mountain trails, as if the flapping of their banners were the wings of eagles, and as if the attacks of their cavalry were the attacks of hawks. They will demolish the buildings and leave the towns deserted, then woe to their inhabitants, how I will subject them to killing and captivity! And I will replace the raised voices in their wedding celebrations with screams and the whinnying of the horses with howling of wolves. And I will turn the galleries of their palaces into the dwellings of beasts of prey. I will replace the lamplight with flames and smoke, might with humiliation and blessings with slavery. And I will surely replace the perfume of their women with dust and their soft carpets will be walked on by their enemies. I will surely make their bodies as fertilizer for the earth and their bones will be bleached by the sun. I will surely humiliate them with all kinds of punishment, then I will surely command the heaven and it will become as a cover of iron, while the earth will become as a copper smelter. If it rains, the earth will not bring forth vegetation. And if anything comes forth from it at that time, it will be by My Mercy toward the grazing animals. Then I will withhold it (the rain) at the time of sowing and send it at the time of harvesting. So if they have grown anything during that time, it will be ruined. And if anything is saved from it, it will be devoid of any blessing. If they call upon Me, I will not answer them and if they ask anything, I will not give it. If they weep, I will not show Mercy to them and if they humble themselves, I will turn My Face away from them."[1] It was narrated by Ibn 'Asakir with this wording.

Hisham Ibn Muhammad Ibn As-Sa'ib Al-Kalbi said, "Then (Bukhtunassar) Nebuchadnezzar advanced upon Bait Al-Maqdis and its king made a peace treaty with him. He was of the family of Dawood ﷺ and he bribed him into leaving the Children of Isra'eel. He took from him captives and set out to return home. When he reached Tabariyyah, word reached him that the Children

---

(1)   See: *Tareekh Ibn 'Asakir* (8/30).

of Isra'eel had rebelled against their king and killed him, because of the peace treaty he had made with him. So he beheaded the captives who were with him and returned to them and took the city by force, killing the fighters and taking the children captive." Hisham said, "We were informed that he found Prophet 'Armiya ﷺ in jail and he set him free…" Then he related his story and his relations with them, how he warned them about these things, and how they belied him and imprisoned him. Bukhtunassar said, "How wretched are a people who disobey the Messenger of Allah ﷺ and abandon his Path!" He treated him well and the weak ones who remained from the Children of Isra'eel gathered to him and they said, "We have done wrong and have been unjust and we turn in repentance to Allah, the Almighty, the All-Powerful for what we have done, so ask Allah to accept our repentance." So he asked his Lord, but Allah revealed to him that He would not do so, and if they were truthful, they should reside with him in that city, and He told him to inform them of what Allah, Most High, had commanded them to do. But they said, "How shall we reside in this city, when it has been destroyed and Allah is Angry with its inhabitants?" So they refused to reside therein.

Ibn Al-Kalbi said, "From that time, the Children of Isra'eel became dispersed throughout the land; a group of them settled in Al-Hijaz, while another group settled in Yathrib (Madinah), still another group settled in Wadi Al-Qura and a small number of them went to Egypt. Bukhtunassar wrote to its king, asking him to return those who had fled there, but he refused and so he set out with his army and fought him, vanquishing him and taking his people captive. Then he rode to the land of Al-Maghrib (Morocco) until he reached the farthest borders of that land. Then he departed therefrom with numerous captives from the land of Al-Maghrib, Egypt, Bait Al-Maqdis, the land of Palestine and Jordan – and included among the captives was Danyal (Daniel ﷺ)."

I say, "It would appear that he was Danyal (Daniel), son of Hizqeel (Ezekiel) – the younger, not the elder – according to what was related by Wahb Ibn Munabbih. And Allah knows better."

Some Details About Danyal (Daniel)

Yoonus Ibn Bukair reported on the authority of Muhammad Ibn Ishaq, who in turn reported on the authority of Abu Khaldah Khalid Ibn Deenar, that he was informed by Abul-'Aliyah: "When we conquered Tustar, we found among the property of Hurmuzan a couch on which there was a dead man and at his head was a book. We took the book and carried it to 'Umar Ibn Al-Khattab ﷺ. He called for Ka'b, who translated it for him into Arabic. I was the first Arab man to read it as I read this Qur'an." (The sub-narrator said,) "I said to Abul-'Aliyah, "What was in it?" He replied, "Your stories, your affairs, your speech and what will be in the future." I said, "What did you do with the (dead) man?" He said, "We dug thirteen different graves by the river and when it was nighttime, we buried him and leveled all of the graves, so that the people should not know where he was buried and dig him up." I said, "And what did they hope from him?" He said, "When rain did not fall on them, they used to bring out his couch and supplicate for rain." I said, "Who do you think the man was?" He said, "A man who was known as Danyal." I asked, "How long ago did he die?" He replied, "Three hundred years ago." I said, "Had nothing changed in him?" He said, "No, except some hairs at the back of his head. Verily, the flesh of the Prophets does not decompose in the earth and it is not eaten by wild beasts." The *isnad* of this narration is authentic up to Abul-'Aliyah, but if it is correct that he had lived three hundred years before them, then he was not a Prophet, but some other righteous man, because there

was no Prophet between 'Eesa ﷺ, the son of Maryam, and the
Messenger of Allah ﷺ, according to the text of a *Hadith* which is
found in *Saheeh Al-Bukhari*.[1]

An Account of the Reconstruction of Bait Al-Maqdis

Allah, Most High, says in His Book – and He is the Most
Truthful of speakers – *Or like the one who passed by a town and
it had tumbled over its rooves. He said, "Oh! How will Allah
ever bring it to life after its death?" So Allah caused him to die
for a hundred years, then raised him up (again). He said, "How
long did you remain (dead)?" He (the man) said, "(Perhaps) I
remained (dead) a day or part of a day." He said, "Nay, you have
remained (dead) for a hundred years, look at your food and your
drink, they show no change; and look at your donkey! And thus
We have made of you a sign for the people. Look at the bones,
how We bring them together and clothe them with flesh." When
this was clearly shown to him, he said, "I know (now) that Allah
is Able to do all things."* (*Soorah Al-Baqarah* 2:259)

Hisham Ibn Al-Kalbi said, "Then Allah, Most High, revealed to
'Armiya ﷺ, according to what has been conveyed to me: I will
rebuild Bait Al-Maqdis, so go out to it and take up quarters there."
So he set out for it and as he approached it and saw it destroyed,
he said to himself, "Glorified be Allah! Allah commanded me to
take up quarters in this city and He informed me that He will
rebuild it. When will Allah rebuild it and when will He revive it
after its death?" Then he laid his head down and slept; with him
was his donkey, and also a basket of food. He remained sleeping
for seventy years until Bukhtunassar had died and his successor,
Lahrasab had ascended to the throne. His reign lasted for a hundred
and twenty years and after him, his son, Bashtasab Ibn Lahrasab

---

(1)   Narrated by Al-Bukhari (3442).

became king. News of the death of Bukhtunassar had reached Bashtasab that Ash-Sham was in utter ruin. The wild beasts had multiplied in Palestine, for it had become empty of men. Bashtasab therefore called to the Children of Isra'eel in Babylon, "Whoever wants to return to Ash-Sham may do so." It was ruled by one from the House of Dawood, who was ordered by Bashtasab to rebuild Jerusalem and its mosque, so they returned and rebuilt it. Then 'Armiya opened his eyes, blinked from the seventy year sleep, and saw how the city was being reconstructed. He remained in that sleep of his until he had completed one hundred years. When Allah awoke him, he thought that he had slept not more than an hour. He had known the city as a devastated land; when he saw it rebuilt and peopled, he said: *"I know (now) that Allah is Able to do all things."* (*Soorah Al-Baqarah* 2:259) Ibn Al-Kalbi said that the Isra'eelites settled in it, and Allah rebuilt their glory. It remained so until Rome vanquished them in the era of the tribal kings; then they lost their community and their authority after the appearance of Christianity. This is how Ibn Jareer tells their story in his *Tareekh*.

The Story of 'Uzair (Ezra)

Ishaq Ibn Bishr reported on the authority of 'Abdullah Ibn 'Abbas ﷺ that he said that 'Uzair (Ezra) عليه السلام was a righteous and wise slave. He went out one day to his own farm, as was his custom. About noon he came to a deserted, ruined place and felt the heat. He entered the ruined town and dismounted his donkey, taking figs and grapes in his basket. He went under the shade of the kharibah tree and ate his food. Then he got up to look at what remained of the ruins. The people had long been lost, and he saw bones. *"Oh! How will Allah ever bring it to life after its death?"* (*Soorah Al-Baqarah* 2:259) He said this not out of doubt but out of curiosity. Allah sent the Angel of Death to take his life. He remained dead for a hundred years. After a hundred years had passed and there had been changes in the affairs of the Children of Isra'eel, Allah sent an angel to 'Uzair عليه السلام to revive his heart and his eyes in order for him to feel and see how Allah revives the dead. The angel said to him, *"How long did you remain (dead)?" He (the man) said, "(Perhaps) I remained (dead) a day or part of a day."* (*Soorah Al-Baqarah* 2:259) He said this because he knew he had slept early in the afternoon and woken up late in the afternoon. The angel said, *Nay, you have remained (dead) for a hundred years, look at your food and your drink.* (*Soorah Al-Baqarah* 2:259) His food was dry bread and his drink was juice that he had pressed in his bowl. When he looked at them, he saw that they had not changed. Likewise, the figs and grapes had not changed and were still fresh. It was as if he doubted in his heart and so the angel said to him, "Do you doubt what I have told you? Look at your donkey." So he looked at his donkey and saw that its bones had become dried and decayed. So the angel called the donkey's bones and they responded and gathered from every side and the angel reconstructed them, while 'Uzair ﷺ looked on. Then he dressed them with veins and nerves, then he clothed them with muscles and then he grew skin and hair over them. Then the angel breathed into the donkey and it stood up and raised its head and its ears to the heaven and brayed, thinking that the Resurrection had begun. This is why he said, *...and look at your donkey! And thus We have made of you a sign for the people. Look at the bones, how We bring them together and clothe them with flesh."* (*Soorah Al-Baqarah* 2:259) That is, look at the bones of your donkey, how they are connected to one another in their joints until they form the skeleton of a donkey, without flesh. Then see how we clothe them in flesh. *When this was clearly shown to him, he said, "I know (now) that Allah is Able to do all things."* (*Soorah Al-Baqarah* 2:259) That is, to give life to the dead and other things. He rode on his donkey and entered his native place, but the people did not recognize him, nor did his household, except the maid, now an old woman. She had been a girl of twenty years of age when he had left. He asked her, "Is this the house of 'Uzair?" She wept and said, "Yes, but I have not seen anyone since the year such-and-such speaking of 'Uzair, and the people have forgotten him." He said, "I am 'Uzair, Allah had taken my life for a hundred years and then he returned it to me." She said: "Glorified be Allah! We had lost 'Uzair a hundred years ago and we have heard no mention of him." He repeated, "I am 'Uzair." She said, "'Uzair used to be answered when he prayed to Allah; he would ask Allah to grant wellbeing and recovery to the sick and those afflicted by disaster. So ask Allah to return my sight to me, so that I may see you. If you are 'Uzair, I will recognize you." So he supplicated for her and massaged her eyes with his hands and she was cured. Then he took her by the hand and said, "Get up, by Allah's Permission," Allah freed her legs and she stood up, cured, as if she had been released from a hobbling rope. She looked and said, "I bear witness that you are 'Uzair," and she rushed to the place of Children of Isra'eel and found them in their assembly. 'Uzair's son was a hundred and eighteen years old, and his children's children now were chiefs of the assembly. She called out to them saying," "This is 'Uzair come to you." They accused her of lying. She said, "I am so-and-so, your old maid. He supplicated his Lord for me, and He has returned my sight to me and cured my lameness. He claims that Allah caused him to do for a hundred years, then He returned him to life." The people stood up and looked at him. His son said, "My father had a black mole between his shoulders." So he uncovered his shoulders and they saw that he was 'Uzair. They said: "None among us memorized the Towrah except 'Uzair, according to what we have been told, and Bukhtunassar burned the Towrah, so nothing remains of it except what the men have memorized. So write it for us." There was only one copy of the Towrah, which was hidden by his father, Sarookh. He buried it in the days of Bukhtunassar in a place none but 'Uzair knows." 'Uzair led the people to the hidden place and took out that copy of the Towrah. Its leaves had rotted, and the book itself crumbled. 'Uzair عليه السلام sat under the shade of a tree surrounded by the Children of Isra'eel and copied out the Towrah for them. And it was said that two shooting stars descended from the heaven and entered him and he recalled the Towrah and copied it out for the Children of Isra'eel. It was from this time that the Jews began to say that 'Uzair عليه السلام is the son of Allah, because of the two shooting stars, his re-copying of the Towrah and his undertaking of the affairs of the Children of Isra'eel.

He had been copying the Towrah for Hizqeel in the rural region, in Dair Hizqeel. The village in which he died was said to be Sayirabaz. 'Abdullah Ibn 'Abbas ﷺ remarked, "So it is as Allah said: *And thus We have made of you a sign for the people."* (*Soorah Al-Baqarah* 2:259) That is, for the Children of Isra'eel, in that he was sitting among his children, and they were old men, while he was a young man, because he died when he was forty years old and so Allah resurrected him as he had been on the day he died. 'Abdullah Ibn 'Abbas ﷺ said, "He was resurrected after Bukhtunassar had died." Al-Hasan concurred with this.

Conclusion

It is well-known that 'Uzair عليه السلام was one of the Prophets sent to the Children of Isra'eel, that his mission was after Dawood and Sulaiman (peace be upon them both) and before Zakariyya and Yahya (peace be upon them both) and that no one remained among the Children of Isra'eel who had memorized the Towrah. Because of this, Allah inspired him with the memorization of it and he recited it to the Children of Isra'eel, as Wahb Ibn Munabbih said, "Allah commanded an angel to descend with a large ladle filled with light; the angel emptied it over 'Uzair عليه السلام and he copied the Towrah, letter by letter, until he had completed it."

Ibn 'Asakir narrated on the authority of 'Abdullah Ibn 'Abbas ﷺ that he asked 'Abdullah Ibn Salam ﷺ about the Words of Allah, Most High: *And the Jews say, " 'Uzair (Ezra) is the son of Allah."* (*Soorah At-Tawbah* 9:30), saying, "Why

did they say this?" Ibn Salam ﷺ then related to him from what
he had memorized of the written Towrah that was in the hands
of the Children of Isra'eel and of how they had said, "Moosa
could not bring us the Towrah except as a book, but 'Uzair
brought it to us without a book." So a group of them claimed
that he was the son of Allah. This is why many of the scholars
say that the continuity of the Towrah was interrupted during
the time of 'Uzair ﷺ.

The Story of Zakariyya and Yahya

Allah says in His Noble Book, **Kaf Ha Ya 'Ain Sad**. *(These letters are one of the miracles of the Qur'an, and none but Allah, Alone, knows their meanings). (This is) a mention of the Mercy of your Lord to His slave Zakariyya. When he called out to his Lord (Allah) a call in secret, saying, "My Lord! Indeed my bones have grown feeble, and grey hair has spread on my head, and I have never been unblessed in my invocation to You, O, my Lord! And Verily! I fear the mawali after me, since my wife is barren. So give me from Yourself an heir, who shall inherit me, and inherit (also) the posterity of Ya'qoob. And make him, my Lord, one with whom You are Well-pleased!" (Allah said), "O Zakariyya! Verily, We give you the glad tidings of a son, his name will be Yahya. We have given that name to none before (him)." He said, "My Lord! How can I have a son, when my wife is barren, and I have reached extreme old age?" He said, "So (it will be). Your Lord says: It is easy for Me. Certainly I have created you before, when you had been nothing!" He (Zakariyya) said, "My Lord! Appoint for me a sign." He said, "Your sign is that you shall not speak unto mankind for three nights, though having no bodily defect." Then* *he came out to his people from* **Al-Mihrab** *(a praying place or a private room, etc.), he revealed to them that they should glorify Allah's Praises in the morning and in the afternoon. (It was said to his son), "O, Yahya! Hold fast to the Scripture (the Tawrah)." And We gave him wisdom while yet a child. And (We gave him) Hanan from Us, and (made him) pure from sins (i.e. Yahya) and he was righteous, and dutiful toward his parents, and he was neither arrogant nor disobedient (to Allah or to his parents). And* **Salamun** *(peace) be on him the day he was born, the day he dies, and the day he will be raised up to life (again)! (Soorah Maryam* 19:1-15)

And He, Most High, says, *So her Lord (Allah) accepted her with goodly acceptance. He made her grow in a good manner and put her under the care of Zakariyya. Every time he entered* **Al-Mihrab** *to (visit) her, he found her supplied with sustenance. He said, "O Maryam! From where have you got this?" She said, "This is from Allah." Verily, Allah provides sustenance to whom He wills, without limit." At that time Zakariyya invoked his Lord, saying, "O my Lord! Grant me from You a good offspring. You are indeed the Hearer of (all) invocations." Then the angels called him, while he was standing in prayer in* **Al-Mihrab**, *(saying), "Allah gives you glad tidings of Yahya, confirming (believing in) the Word from Allah (i.e. the creation of 'Eesa, the Word from Allah ["Be!" – and he was!]), noble,* **hasoor,** *a Prophet, from among the righteous." He said, "O, my Lord! How can I have a son when I am very old, and my wife is barren?" Allah said, "Thus Allah does what He wills." He said, "O, my Lord! Make a sign for me." Allah said, "Your sign is that you shall not speak to mankind for three days except with signals. And remember your Lord much (by praising Him again and again), and glorify (Him) in the afternoon and in the morning." (Soorah Aal 'Imran* 3:37-41)

What is meant by these Verses is that Allah, Most High,

commanded His Messenger 📿 to relate to the people the story of
Zakariyya 📿 and the events that transpired when Allah, Most
High, granted him a son in his old age, when his wife was barren,
due to her advanced age, so that no one should give up hope or
despair of His Bounty and His Mercy. He, Most High, says, *(This
is) a mention of the Mercy of your Lord to His slave Zakariyya.
When he called out to his Lord (Allah) a call in secret.* (*Soorah
Maryam* 19:2,3) Qatadah said in his explanation of these Verses,
"Verily, Allah knows the pure heart and hears the secret call."
Some of the *Salaf* said that he stood up for a part of the night
and called to his Lord in secret, so that those present in the house
should not hear him, saying, "O, my Lord!" His Lord answered,
"I am here, I am here, I am here." He said, *"My Lord! Indeed my
bones have grown feeble…"* (*Soorah Maryam* 19:4) That is, they
have grown weak and declined in vigor, due to old age. *"…and
grey hair has spread on my head."* (*Soorah Maryam* 19:4) That
is, as fire spreads over kindling, i.e. white hair has overcome the
black hair, as Ibn Duraid said in his poetic verses:

"Do you not see my head, how its color resembles,

The sprouting of morning under the tail of night,

And the white has spread through the black,

Like the spreading of fire through hot coals,

And the youthful branch has become dry and withered,

Having formerly been flexible and moist?

He said that weakness has overcome him, both internally and
externally and that was what Zakariyya 📿 said: *"Indeed my
bones have grown feeble and grey hair has spread on my head."*
(*Soorah Maryam* 19:4) And he said, *"…and I have never been
unblessed in my invocation to You, O my Lord!"* (*Soorah Maryam*
19:4) That is, you have accustomed me to naught in supplications

to You, except that You have answered them. What caused him to make this request was that after he became the guardian of Maryam, daughter of Mathan, he found that whenever he entered her room, she had fruits which were not in season and these were among the blessings of Allah's *Awliya'* and he realized that the Provider of something outside its season is Able to provide him with a son, even though he has become old. *At that time Zakariyya invoked his Lord, saying, "O my Lord! Grant me from You, a good offspring. You are indeed the Hearer of (all) invocations."* (*Soorah Aal 'Imran* 3:38)

And He, Most High, says, *"And Verily! I fear the mawali after me, since my wife is barren."* (*Soorah Maryam* 19:5) It is said that what is meant by *mawali* is relatives; it was as if he feared that whoever managed the affairs of the Children of Isra'eel after his death might do so in accordance with ideas that were not consistent with Allah's Law and obedience to Him. So he asked Allah to produce a son for him from his loins, who would be pious and pure and would seek to please his Lord, which is why he said, *"Grant me from Yourself..."* (*Soorah Maryam* 19:5) That is by Your Power and Your Strength. *"...an heir, who shall inherit me"* (*Soorah Maryam* 19:5,6) means in Prophethood and judgment among the Children of Isra'eel. *"...and inherit (also) the posterity of Ya'qoob. And make him, my Lord, one with whom You are Well-pleased!"* (*Soorah Maryam* 19:6) That is, just as his fathers and forefathers from the descendants of Ya'qoob ﷺ were Prophets, make him like them in the Honor that You bestowed upon them by granting them Prophethood and Revelation. This does not refer to the inheritance of wealth, as some of the Shiites have claimed.

And Imam Ahmad narrated on the authority of Abu Hurairah ﷺ that the Messenger of Allah ﷺ said, "Zakariyya was a carpenter." [1]

---

(1) This is an authentic *Hadith* narrated by Ahmad (2/296, No. 7887). It was also narrated by Muslim (2379) and Ibn Majah (2150).

And He, Most High, says, *(Allah said,) "O Zakariya! Verily, We give you the glad tidings of a son, His name will be Yahya. We have given that name to none before (him)."* (*Soorah Maryam* 19:7) This is explained by His Words: *Then the angels called him, while he was standing in prayer in* **Al-Mihrab** *(saying), "Allah gives you glad tidings of Yahya, confirming (believing in) the Word from Allah (i.e. the creation of 'Eesa, the Word from Allah ["Be!" – and he was!]), noble, keeping away from sexual relations with women, a Prophet, from among the righteous."* (*Soorah Aal 'Imran* 3:39). Zakariyya 🙵 was surprised to hear these glad tidings, to hear that a son could be conceived in such circumstances, which is why he said, *"My Lord! How can I have a son, when my wife is barren, and I have reached extreme old age?"* (*Soorah Aal 'Imran* 3:40) That is, how can an old man father a son? It was said that his age at that time was seventy-seven years, but it seems more likely – and Allah knows better – that he was older than that. *"...when my wife is barren"* (*Soorah Aal 'Imran* 3:40) means at the time of her old age, she has become barren and cannot bear a child – and Allah knows better – as *Al-Khaleel* 🙵 said, *"Do you give me glad tidings (of a son) when old age has overtaken me? Of what then is your news?"* (*Soorah Al-Hijr* 15:54) and Sarah said, *She said (in astonishment), "Woe unto me! Shall I bear a child while I am an old woman, and here is my husband, an old man? Verily! This is a strange thing!" They said, "Do you wonder at the Decree of Allah? The Mercy of Allah and His Blessings be on you, O family (of Ibraheem). Surely, He (Allah) is Most Praiseworthy, Most Glorious."* (*Soorah Hood* 11:72,73). And in the same way was Zakariyya 🙵 answered. Said the angel to whom Revelation was given, by the Command of his Lord, *"So (it will be). Your Lord says, "It is easy for Me."* (*Soorah Maryam* 19:9) That is, a simple matter, posing no difficulty for Him. *"Certainly I have created you before, when you had been nothing!"* (*Soorah Maryam* 19:9) That is, His Ability to do all things brought you into being after you had previously not existed, so can He not then produce a son from you, even though you are an old man?

And He, Most High, says, *So We answered his call, and We bestowed upon him Yahya, and cured his wife (to bear a child) for him. Verily, they used to hasten on to do good deeds, and they used to call on Us with hope and fear, and used to humble themselves before Us.* (*Soorah Al-Anbiya'* 21:90) And the meaning of curing his wife is that she had not had menses and how she had them once more.

And He, Most High, says, *He said, "O, my Lord! Make a sign for me."* (*Soorah Aal 'Imran* 3:41) That is, make a sign that alerts me that the child will come. *Allah said, "Your sign is that you shall not speak unto mankind for three nights, though having no bodily defect."* (*Soorah Maryam* 19:10) Allah tells him that his sign is that he will be afflicted by silence, which will leave him unable to speak for three days and that he will only be able to communicate by signs, but that in spite of this, he would be in good health. And He commanded him to mention Allah frequently at this time in his heart and to remember Him much at night and in the morning. When he was given these glad tidings, he went out happily to his people from his *mihrab*. *He revealed to them that they should glorify Allah's Praises in the morning and in the afternoon.* (*Soorah Maryam* 19:11) Revealing here means silently communicating with them, either by writing, as Mujahid and As-Suddi said, or by signs, as Mujahid also said, and Wahb and Qatadah concurred with this. Mujahid, 'Ikrimah, Wahb, As-Suddi and Qatadah said that his tongue was stilled, without him being afflicted by any illness. Ibn Zaid said, "He used to recite and glorify Allah, but he could not speak to anyone."

And Allah, Most High, says, *(It was said to his son), "O, Yahya! Hold fast to the Scripture (the Tawrah)." And We gave him wisdom while yet a child.* (*Soorah Maryam* 19:12) Allah, Most

High, informs us about the birth of the son, in accordance with the Divine Tidings given to, Zakariyya 🕮 and He tells us that He taught him the Scripture and wisdom while he was still a child. 'Abdullah Ibn Al-Mubarak said, "Ma'mar said, "The children said to Yahya, son of Zakariyya, "Come with us and we will play." But he replied, "We were not created for play." This is the explanation of His Words: *And We gave him wisdom while yet a child.* (*Soorah Maryam* 19:12) As for His Saying: *And (We gave him)* **Hanan** *from Us.* (*Soorah Maryam* 19:13) Ibn Jareer At-Tabari narrated on the authority of 'Amr Ibn Deenar, who in turn narrated on the authority of 'Ikrimah, who narrated on the authority of 'Abdullah Ibn 'Abbas 🕮 that he said, "I do not know what *Hanan* is." It was also narrated on the authority of 'Abdullah Ibn 'Abbas 🕮, Mujahid, 'Ikrimah, Qatadah and Ad-Dahhak that *And (We gave him)* **Hanan** *from Us* means: as a Mercy from Us; through it We showed Mercy to Zakariyya 🕮 and blessed him with a son. It was reported on the authority of 'Ikrimah that *Hanan* means: Love. It is possible that this was an attribute to make Yahya 🕮 beloved by the people, in particular, by his parents, who loved him, for he was dutiful and solicitous toward them. As for the purity, it means purity of the heart and freedom from defects and vices. As for the righteousness, it means showing obedience to Allah, by fulfilling His Commands and avoiding the things that He has prohibited. Then He mentioned his dutifulness toward his parents, his obedience to their commands and prohibitions and his avoidance of showing disrespect to them in word and deed. And He, Most High, says, *And dutiful toward his parents, and he was neither an arrogant nor disobedient (to Allah or to his parents).* (*Soorah Maryam* 19:14) Then He says, *And* **Salamun** *(peace) be on him the day he was born, the day he dies, and the day he will be raised up to life (again)!* (*Soorah Maryam* 19:15) These three times are the most difficult for mankind, because in each case, he transfers from one state to another. He loses the first, after he becomes familiar with it and comes to know it and he goes onto another state in which he knows not what is before him, which is why he cries out when he emerges from the womb and leaves it softness and its embrace and comes into this world, where he will endure its anxieties and its sorrows. Likewise, when he departs from this life and goes onto *Al-Barzakh*,[1] which is between the life of this world and the permanent abode of the Hereafter. After living in houses and palaces, he takes up residence among the dead, in the graves. There he waits for the blow of the Trumpet, which will herald the arrival of the Day of Resurrection and Gathering. On that Day, a group will be in Paradise and another will be in the blazing Fire. One of the poets put it well when he said:

When your mother gave birth to you, you were crying and screaming,

And the people around you were laughing and happy,

So take care of yourself, so that when, on the day of your death, they weep,

You will be laughing, happy.

And since these three stages are the most difficult for mankind, Allah sent peace upon Yahya ﷺ in all three of them, saying, *And* **Salamun** *(peace) be on him the day he was born, the day he dies, and the day he will be raised up to life (again)!* (*Soorah Maryam* 19:15) Sa'eed Ibn Abi 'Aroobah reported on the authority of Qatadah that Al-Hasan said, "Yahya and 'Eesa met and 'Eesa said to Yahya, "Ask forgiveness for me, for you are better than I." Yahya said, "Ask forgiveness for me, for you are better than I." 'Eesa answered, "You are better than I, because I invoked peace on myself, but Allah sent peace on you."

---

(1)   *Al-Barzakh*: The period between a person's death and his resurrection on the Day of Judgment.

And He says in another Verse, *"...noble,* **hasoor,** *a Prophet, from among the righteous."* (*Soorah Aal 'Imran* 3:39) What is meant by *hasoor* is that he avoids sexual relations with women. Other explanations have been given for this, but it is similar to His Words: *"Grant me from You a good offspring."* (*Soorah Aal 'Imran* 3:38)

And Imam Ahmad has narrated on the authority of 'Abdullah Ibn 'Abbas ﷺ that the Messenger of Allah ﷺ said, "There is none among the sons of Adam who has not committed a sin or intended to do so except Yahya, son of Zakariyya; and it is not right that anyone should say that I am better than Yoonus, son of Matta." [1]

And Imam Ahmad narrated on the authority of Al-Harith Al-Ash'ari that the Prophet ﷺ said, "Verily, Allah commanded Yahya, son of Zakariyya, to act upon five things and to order the Children of Isra'eel to act upon them. But Yahya was slow in carrying out these commandments. 'Eesa said to Yahya, "You were ordered to implement five commandments and to order the Children of Isra'eel to implement them. So either order it, or I will order it." Yahya said, "My brother! I fear that if you do it before me, I will be punished or the earth will be shaken under my feet." So Yahya called the Children of Isra'eel to Bait Al-Maqdis, until they filled the Mosque. He sat on the balcony, thanked Allah and praised him and then said, "Allah ordered me to implement five commandments and He commanded me to order you to adhere to them. The first is that you worship Allah alone and not associate anyone with Him. The example of this command ment is the example of a man who bought a servant from his money with paper or gold. The servant started to work for the master, but was paying the profits to another person. Who among you would like his servant to do that? Allah created you and sustains you. Therefore, worship Him alone and do not associate anything

---

(1)   This is an authentic *Hadith* narrated by Imam Ahmad (1/254, No. 2294).

with Him. I also command you to pray, for Allah directs His Face toward His servant's face, as long as the servant does not turn away. So when you pray, do not turn your heads to and fro. I also command you to fast. The example of it is the example of a man in a group of men and he has some musk wrapped in a piece of cloth, and consequently, all of the group smells the scent of the wrapped musk. Verily, the odour of the mouth of a fasting person is better before Allah than the scent of musk. I also command you to give charity. The example of this is the example of a man who was captured by the enemy. They tied his hands to his neck and brought him forth to cut off his head. He said to them, "Can I pay a ransom for myself?" He kept ransoming himself with small and large amounts until he liberated himself. I also command you to always remember Allah. The example of this deed is that of a man who the enemy is tirelessly pursuing. He takes refuge in a fortified fort. When the slave remembers Allah, the Almighty, the All-Powerful, he will be resorting to the best refuge from Shaitan." The Messenger of Allah ﷺ said, "And I order you to fulfill five commandments that Allah has ordered me to fulfill. Hold fast to the *Jama'ah* (Community of the Faithful), listen to and obey (your leaders) and perform *hijrah* (migration) and *jihad* for the sake of Allah. Whoever abandons the *Jama'ah*, even the distance of a hand span, will have removed the tie of Islam from his neck, unless he returns. Whoever uses the slogans of *Jahiliyyah* (the pre-Islamic period of ignorance) he will be among those kneeling in *Jahannam* (Hellfire). He said, "O, Messenger of Allah! Even if he prays and fasts?' He said, "Even if he prays, fasts and claims to be Muslim. So call the Muslims with the names with which Allah has called them: the Muslims, the believing slaves of Allah, the Almighty, the All-Powerful." [1]

Explanation of the Cause of Yahya's Killing

---

(1) This is an authentic *Hadith* narrated by Imam Ahmad (4/120, No. 16718).

Scholars have cited numerous reasons for the killing of Yahya ﷺ; among the most well-known of them is that one of the kings at that time in Damascus desired to marry a member of his family who was unlawful to him and Yahya ﷺ forbade him from doing so, but he insisted on marrying her. Dressing attractively, she sang and danced before him. She succeeded in arousing his lust. Embracing her, he offered to fulfill whatever she desired. She then asked for Yahya ﷺ to be killed. The king granted this request and sent men to kill him and bring his head and his blood to her in a bowl. It was said that she died immediately upon holding it. It was also said that the wife of that king loved Yahya ﷺ and so she sent a message to him, but he refused her. When she despaired of him, she requested of the king that he kill him, but he refused. However, she kept on insisting until he agreed; then he sent some men to kill him and bring his head and his blood in a bowl.

Scholars differed regarding the killing of Yahya ﷺ: Did it happen in Al-Aqsa Mosque, or somewhere else? There are two opinions in the matter: Ath-Thawri reported on the authority of Al-A'mash, who in turn reported on the authority of Shimr Ibn 'Atiyyah that he said, "Seventy Prophets were killed on the rock that is in Bait Al-Maqdis, including Yahya, son of Zakariyya (peace be upon them both)."

Abu 'Ubaid Al-Qasim Ibn Sallam said, "We were informed by 'Abdullah Ibn Salih, who reported on the authority of Al-Laith, who in turn reported on the authority of Yahya Ibn Sa'eed, who likewise reported on the authority of Sa'eed Ibn Al-Musayyib that he said, "Bukhtunossar advanced on Damascus and he found the blood of Yahya boiling. He asked about it and they told him about it. On account of his blood, he killed seventy thousand, after which it became still." The *isnad* of this narration is authentic up to Sa'eed Ibn Al-Musayyib and this must mean that he was killed

in Damascus and that the story of Bukhtunassar was after 'Eesa
التَّلاَمُ, as claimed by 'Ata' and Al-Hasan Al-Basri. And Allah knows
better.

Al-Hafiz Ibn 'Asakir narrated by way of Al-Waleed Ibn
Muslim, on the authority of Zaid Ibn Waqid, who said, "I saw the
head of Yahya, son of Zakariyya, when they intended to build the
Damascus Mosque; it was taken from beneath one of the pillars
of the *Qiblah*, which is next to the *mihrab*, adjacent to the east.
The skin and the hair were unaffected by decay and remained
unchanged." In another version, it was stated that: "…it was as if
he had just been killed."

It was reported regarding the building of Damascus Mosque
that it was placed under the pillar which is known as *As-Sakasikah*.
And Allah knows better.

Al-Hafiz Ibn 'Asakir narrated in *Al-Mustaqsa Fi Fada'ilil-Aqsa*
by way of Al-'Abbas Ibn Subh, who reported on the authority
of Marwan, who in turn reported on the authority of Sa'eed Ibn
'Abdul-'Azeez, who likewise reported on the authority of qusaim,
the freed slave of Mu'awiyah that he said, "The king of this city
(i.e. Damascus) was Hadad Ibn Hadad and he had married his
niece, Aryal, Queen of Saida. Included among its territories was
Sooq Al-Mulook in Damascus. He had sworn to divorce her three
times, but then he wished to return her to him and so he sought
a religious verdict from Yahya. Yahya التَّلاَمُ told him, "She is not
lawful for you until she has married another man (and been
divorced by him)." She harbored feelings of hatred toward him
because of this and so she requested from the king that he give her
the head of Yahya. This was at the instigation of her mother, but
he refused her at first, then later he agreed and sent some men to
Jairoon Mosque, where they found him praying; they then killed
him and brought the king his head. The head said to him, "She
will not be lawful to you until she marries another man (and is

subsequently divorced from him).” The woman took the plate and carried it on her head to her mother and it was still repeating the words it had said to the king. When she stood before her mother, the earth opened up at her feet and she sank down to her loins. Her mother began to wail and the servants screamed and slapped their faces. Then she sank down to her shoulders and so her mother ordered the swordsman to strike her neck and cut off her head, so that at least she could keep her head. Then the earth spat out her body. They were then humiliated and destroyed and the blood of Yahya 🙷 continued to boil until Bukhtunassar arrived and killed seventy-five thousand people on account of it.”

The Story of ‘Eesa, Son of Maryam

Allah, Most High, says, *Allah chose Adam, Nooh (Noah), the family of Ibraheem (Abraham) and the family of ‘Imran above* **Al-‘Alameen** *(of their times). Offspring, one of the other; and Allah is the All-Hearing, All-Knowing. (Remember) when the wife of ‘Imran said, “O, my Lord! I have vowed to You what (i.e. the child that) is in my womb to be dedicated for Your services (free from all worldly work; to serve Your Place of worship), so accept this, from me. Verily, You are the All-Hearing, the All-Knowing.” Then, when she delivered her child, she said, “O, my Lord! I have delivered a female child…”* – *and Allah knew better what she had delivered* – *“And the male is not like the female, and I have named her Maryam, and I seek refuge with You (Allah) for her and for her offspring from* **Shaitan,** *the outcast.” So her Lord (Allah) accepted her with goodly acceptance. He made her grow in a good manner and put her under the care of Zakariyya. Every time he entered* **Al-Mihrab** *to (visit) her; he found her supplied with sustenance. He said, “O, Maryam! From where have you got this?” She said, “This is from Allah.” Verily, Allah provides sustenance to whomever He wills, without limit.* (**Soorah Aal**

'*Imran* 3:33-37)

Allah, Most High, describes how He chose Adam 🙶 and the purest of his progeny, who observed His Law and were resolute in their obedience to Him. Then He made a particular specification, saying, "*...the family of Ibraheem.*" (*Soorah Aal 'Imran* 3:33) and He included among them the children of Isma'eel 🙶 and the children of Ishaq 🙶. Then He spoke of the virtue of this pure and noble house, i.e. the family of 'Imran. The 'Imran referred to is the father of Maryam (peace be upon her). Muhammad Ibn Ishaq said, "He was 'Imran, son of Basham, son of Amoon, son of Mansha, son of Hizqiya, son of 'Ahzeeq son of Motham, son of 'Azariya, son of 'Amsiya, son of Yawash, son of 'Ahzeehoo, son of Yaram, son of Yahfashat, son of 'Aish, son of Aban, son of Rahab'am, son of Yaram, son of Dawood (peace be upon them)."

Muhammad Ibn Ishaq and others also said that Mary's mother was unable to conceive. Then one day, she saw a bird feeding its chick and she wanted a child and so she vowed that if she became pregnant, she would surely devote the child to be a servant of Bait Al-Maqdis. It was said that she immediately was afflicted by menses, and that when she became purified from it, her husband was intimate with her and she became pregnant with Maryam (peace be upon her). When she delivered her, she said, "*O, my Lord! I have delivered a female child...*" – *and Allah knew better what she had delivered.* (*Soorah Aal 'Imran* 3:36) This was also recited in a manner that would mean: "And Allah knows better what I have delivered." "*And the male is not like the female.*" (*Soorah Aal 'Imran* 3:36). That is, regarding service to Bait Al-Maqdis; at that time, they used to pledge their sons to the service of Bait Al-Maqdis.

Her saying: "*...and I have named her Maryam.*" (*Soorah Aal 'Imran* 3:36) proves that the naming of a child is done on the day of its birth. Likewise, it has been confirmed in the *Saheehain* on the authority of Anas 🌸 that he went with his (newborn) brother to the Messenger of Allah 🌸, who performed *tahneek*[1] for his brother and named him 'Abdullah.[2] It was also mentioned in the *Hadith* of Al-Hasan from Samurah 🌸 in a *marfoo'* form that: "Every child is held in pledge for his *'aqeeqah* which is sacrificed for him on his seventh day and he is named on it and his head is shaved."[3] This was narrated by Imam Ahmad and the compilers of the *Sunan* and it was declared authentic by At-Tirmidhi. In some versions, it was said, "*tadmiyyah*[4] should be performed on him," instead of: "he is named." And Allah knows better. And she said, "*...and I seek refuge with You (Allah) for her and for her offspring from* **Shaitan,** *the outcast.*" (*Soorah Aal 'Imran* 3:36) This supplication was answered by Allah, just as her pledge was accepted. Imam Ahmad narrated on the authority of Abu Hurairah 🌸 that the Prophet 🌸 said, "Every newborn is touched by *Shaitan* when he is born, causing him to cry out, except Maryam and her son."[5] Then Abu Hurairah 🌸 said, "And recite if you wish: "*...and I seek refuge with You (Allah) for her and for her offspring from* **Shaitan,** *the outcast.*" (*Soorah Aal 'Imran* 3:36)."[6]

Allah, Most High, says, *So her Lord (Allah) accepted her with goodly acceptance. He made her grow in a good manner and put her under the care of Zakariyya.* (*Soorah Aal 'Imran* 3:37). Many

---

(1) *Tahneek*: Chewing a date and then putting the soft paste in the baby's mouth.

(2) Narrated by Al-Bukhari (5470) and Muslim (2144).

(3) This is an authentic *Hadith* narrated by Ahmad (19579), An-Nasa'i (4220), Abu Dawood (2837) and Ibn Majah (3165).

(4) *Tadmiyyah*: According to Ibn Al-Atheer, this was an abrogated practice from the *Jahiliyyah*, in which blood from the slaughtered animal was allowed to drip onto the head of the newborn, after which, the head was washed and shaved.

(5) This is an authentic *Hadith* narrated by Imam Ahmad (7651).

(6) Narrated by Al-Bukhari (4548) and Muslim (2366).

of the scholars of *tafseer* said that when her mother delivered her, she wrapped her in her garments and went out to the mosque with her. She presented her to the worshippers who lived there and because she was the daughter of their *Imam* and prayer leader, they vied with one another to be her guardian.

It would appear that she only presented her to them after she had completed breastfeeding her. Then, when she presented her to them, they vied with one another regarding which of them would be her guardian. Zakariyya 🕮 was their Prophet at that time and he wished to be alone in being her guardian, because his wife was her sister or her maternal aunt, according to two different opinions. But they did not agree to this and so they requested that he allow them to draw lots for her. They did so and Zakariyya 🕮 was the successful one. This was because a maternal aunt is of the same status as a mother.

Allah, Most High, says, *and put her under the care of Zakariyya.* (*Soorah Aal 'Imran* 3:37) That is, because he defeated them in the drawing of lots, as He, Most High, says, *This is a part of the news of the* **ghaib** *(Unseen, i.e. the news of the past nations of which you have no knowledge) which We inspire you with (O Muhammad). You were not with them, when they cast lots with their pens as to which of them should be charged with the care of Maryam; nor were you with them when they disputed.* (*Soorah Aal 'Imran* 3:44) Scholars said that it means that all of them threw their pens, which were recognizable. Then they carried them and placed them in a certain location and ordered a sinless boy to select one of them. He did so and it was the pen of Zakariyya 🕮. They then requested that they might cast their pens again, but that this time, they might throw them into the river and that whichever of them remained still, in spite of the current, its owner would be Mary's guardian. It was Zakariyya's pen that resisted the current. They then requested that they might cast them a third time. This time, they said that whichever pen flowed with the river's current, while the others flowed in a contrary direction, the owner of that pen would win. They did this, and again, it was Zakariyya عليه السلام who was the winner. So he became her guardian, since he had the greatest right, according to the Divine Law and based on numerous (other) reasons. Allah, Most High, says, *Every time he entered Al-Mihrab to (visit) her, he found her supplied with sustenance. He said, "O, Maryam! From where have you got this?" She said, "This is from Allah." Verily, Allah provides sustenance to whomever He wills, without limit.* (*Soorah Aal 'Imran* 3:37) The scholars of *tafseer* said that Zakariyya عليه السلام appointed for her a noble place in the mosque which none but she could enter. There she used to worship Allah and undertake the duties incumbent upon her, such as acting as caretaker of the mosque, when it was her turn to do so. The days and nights she would spend in the worship of Allah, until her name became a byword for devotion among the Children of Isra'eel. She also became known for the miracles with which she was blessed and for her noble character, to such a degree that, whenever the Prophet of Allah, Zakariyya عليه السلام, came to see her in her place of worship, he would find with her strange sustenance which was not in season; he would find with her summer fruits in winter and winter fruits in summer. He asked her, *"From where have you got this?"* (*Soorah Aal 'Imran* 3:37), to which she replied, *"This is from Allah."* (*Soorah Aal 'Imran* 3:37) That is, this is sustenance which Allah has provided for me. *Verily, Allah provides sustenance to whomever He wills, without limit.* (*Soorah Aal 'Imran* 3:37). At this point, Zakariyya عليه السلام conceived a desire for a son of his own, even though he was well advanced in years. He said, *"O, my Lord! Grant me from You a good offspring. You are indeed the All-Hearing of invocation."* (*Soorah Aal 'Imran* 3:38). Some of the scholars said that he said, "O, You Who provides Maryam with fruits that are out of season, grant me a son, even though I am "out of season" (i.e. no longer of the age when one might normally father a child)." And we have already told what happened to him in his story.

Allah, Most High, says, *And (remember) when the angels said, "O Maryam! Verily, Allah has chosen you, purified you (from polytheism and disbelief) and chosen you above the women of Al-'Alameen. O, Maryam! Submit yourself with obedience to your Lord (Allah, by worshipping none but Him Alone) and prostrate yourself, and* **irka'i** *(bow down, etc.) along with* **Ar-Raki'oon** *(those who bow down, etc.)." This is a part of the news of the* **ghaib** *(Unseen, i.e. the news of the past nations of which you have no knowledge) with which We inspire you (O Muhammad). You were not with them when they cast lots with their pens as to which of them should be charged with the care of Maryam; nor were you with them when they disputed. (Remember) when the angels said, "O Maryam! Verily, Allah gives you the glad tidings of a Word ("Be!" - and he was! i.e. 'Eesa the son of Maryam [Mary]) from Him, his name will be the Maseeh, 'Eesa, the son of Maryam, held in honor in this world and in the Hereafter, and will be one of those who are near to Allah. He will speak to the people in the cradle and in manhood, and he will be one of the righteous." She said, "O my Lord! How shall I have a son when no man has touched me." He said, "So (it will be) for Allah creates what He wills. When He has decreed something, He says to it only, "Be!" and it is. And He (Allah) will teach him ('Eesa) the Book and* **Al-Hikmah** *(i.e. the* **Sunnah,** *the faultless speech of the Prophets, wisdom, etc.), (and) the Tawrah and the Injeel. (And He will make him 'Eesa) a Messenger to the Children of Isra'eel (saying), "I have come to you with a sign from your Lord, that I design for you out of clay, as it were, the figure of a bird, and breathe into it, and it becomes a bird by Allah's Leave; and I heal him who was born blind and the leper; and I bring the dead to life by Allah's Leave. And I inform you of what you eat and what you store in your houses. Surely, therein is a sign for you, if you believe. And I have come confirming that which was before me of the Tawrah, and to make lawful to you part of what was forbidden to you, and I have come to you with a proof from your Lord. So fear Allah and*

obey me. Truly! Allah is my Lord and your Lord, so worship Him
(Alone). This is the Straight Path. (*Soorah Aal 'Imran* 3:42-51)

Allah, Most High, says that the angels informed Maryam
(peace be upon her) that Allah had chosen her from among all of
the women of her time to bear a son, without a father. She was
also informed that he would be a noble Prophet. *"He will speak to*
the people in the cradle." (*Soorah Aal 'Imran* 3:46) That is, when
he is an infant, he will call them to the worship of Allah, Alone,
without partners. He will also do so when he is a man of mature
age. This proves that he attained middle age and called the people
to Allah in it. She was commanded to worship Allah much, to be
pious and devout, to prostrate and bow, in order to be deserving
of this generosity and to show gratitude for this blessing. It was
said that she used to stand in prayer until the skin of her feet
split – may Allah be pleased with her and show Mercy to her and
to her mother and father. The angels said, *"O, Maryam! Verily,*
Allah has chosen you." (*Soorah Aal 'Imran* 3:42) That is, He has
selected you and preferred you over the low creatures and given
you beautiful characteristics. *"...and chosen you above the women*
of **Al-'Alameen.***"* (*Soorah Aal 'Imran* 3:42) It is possible that
this means the women of her time, as in Allah's Words to Moosa
🕮: *"I have chosen you above men..."* (*Soorah Al-A'raf* 7:144)
and as in His Words regarding the Children of Isra'eel: *And We*
chose them (the Children of Isra'eel) above **Al-'Alameen** *with*
knowledge. (*Soorah Ad-Dukhan* 44:32). And it is well known
that Ibraheem 🕮 is better than Moosa 🕮 and that Muhammad
🕮 is better than both of them. And likewise, this nation (of Islam)
is better than all of the other nations, greater in numbers, superior
in knowledge and purer in deeds than the Children of Isra'eel and
others.

It is also possible that: *"...and have chosen you above the*
women of **Al-'Alameen.***"* (*Soorah Aal 'Imran* 3:42) is a general
statement, meaning that she is the best of women in this world,

including all those before her and all those after her, because she was a Prophetess, according to those who opine that she, Sarah, the mother of Ishaq 🕮 and the mother of Moosa 🕮 were Prophetesses. Ibn Hazm and others cite as evidence for this the words of the angels and the Revelation given to the mother of Moosa 🕮. According to this, it is not impossible that Maryam might be better than Sarah and the mother of Moosa 🕮, based on the generality of Allah's Words: *"...and have chosen you above the women of Al-'Alameen."* (*Soorah Aal 'Imran* 3:42), if it (the generality) is not contradicted by any other evidence. And Allah knows better. As for the opinion of the majority, according to what has been related by Abul-Hasan Al-Ash'ari and others, on the authority of *Ahl As-Sunnah Wal-Jama'ah*, which states that the Prophethood is conferred exclusively on men and there are no Prophetesses. So the status of Maryam would be as Allah, Most High, says, *The Maseeh ('Eesa, son of Maryam), was no more than a Messenger; many were the Messengers that passed away before him. His mother (Maryam was a* **Siddiqah** *(i.e. she believed in the words of Allah and His Books).* (*Soorah Al-Ma'idah* 5:75) Based on this, it is not impossible that she might be the best of the renowned and celebrated *Siddeeqat* – including those before her and those after her. And Allah knows better. She has been linked with Asiyah Bint Muzahim, Khadeejah Bint Khuwailid and Fatimah Bint Muhammad, may Allah be pleased with them all.

Imam Ahmad, Al-Bukhari and Muslim, At-Tirmidhi and An-Nasa'i narrated on the authority of 'Ali Ibn Abi Talib 🕮 that he said, "The Messenger of Allah 🕮 said, "Maryam, the daughter of 'Imran, was the best among the women (of the world of her time) and Khadeejah is the best amongst the women (of this nation)." [1]

---

(1) Narrated on the authority of Imam Ahmad (1/84, No. 641), Al-Bukhari (3432), Muslim (2430), At-Tirmidhi (38777) and An-Nasa'i in *Al-Kubra* (5/93, No. 8354)

And Imam Ahmad narrated on the authority of Ibn Al-Musayyib that he said, "Abu Hurairah ؓ said that the Prophet ﷺ said, "The best women are the riders of the camels and the righteous among the women of Quraish; and show affection to their children and zealously guard the wealth of their husbands." Abu Hurairah said that Maryam, the daughter of 'Imran, never rode a camel.[1]

And Abu Ya'la Al-Mawsili narrated on the authority of 'Abdullah Ibn 'Abbas ؓ that he said, "The Messenger of Allah ﷺ drew four lines in the earth and he said, "Do you know what this is?" They said, "Allah and His Messenger know better." The Messenger of Allah ﷺ said, "The best among the women of Paradise are Khadeejah Bint Khuwailid, Fatimah Bint Muhammad, Maryam Bint 'Imran and Asiyah Bint Muzahim, the wife of Fir'awn."[2]

As for the *Hadith* narrated by Ibn Marduyayih, on the authority of Shu'bah, who reported on the authority of Mu'awiyah Ibn Qurrah, who in turn reported on the authority of his father that he said, "The Messenger of Allah ﷺ said, "Many men attained perfection, but no women attained perfection except three: Mary, the daughter of 'Imran, Asiyah, the wife of and Khadeejah, the daughter of Khuwailid. And the superiority of 'A'ishah over other women is as the superiority of *thareed* over all other foods."[3]

And likewise, the following *Hadith* narrated by the Jama'ah – aside from Abu Dawood – is also authentic. It was reported on the authority of Abu Moosa Al-Ash'ari ؓ that he said, "The Messenger of Allah ﷺ said, "Many men attained perfection but no women attained perfection except Asiyah, the wife of Fir'awn and Maryam, the daughter of 'Imran; and verily, the superiority

---

(1)   Narrated by Imam Ahmad (2/275) and Muslim (2527).

(2)   This is an authentic *Hadith* narrated by Abu Ya'la in his *Musnad* (5/110, No. 2722).

(3)   The author claimed in his *Tafseer* (1/363) that it was narrated by Ibn Marduyah, by way of Shu'bah, on the authority of his father.

of 'A'ishah over other women is as the superiority of *thareed*
over all other foods."[1] As you see, the *Shaikhain* (Al-Bukhari
and Muslim) agreed upon it. And its wording necessitates that
perfection in women was confined to Maryam and Asiyah; and
it is likely that what is meant by this is in their times, because
each of them was the guardian and protector of a Prophet during
his formative years: Asiyah was the guardian of Moosa 🕮 and
Mary was the guardian of her son, the slave of Allah and His
Messenger, 'Eesa 🕮. And this does not negate the possibility that
other women from this nation, such as Khadeejah and Fatimah
(may Allah be pleased with them) attained perfection. Khadeejah
(may Allah be pleased with her) served the Messenger of Allah 🕮
before his mission started for fifteen years, and after it for more
than ten years. She was his adviser and she devoted herself and
her wealth in the cause of Islam – may Allah be Pleased with her
and gratify her. As for Fatimah (may Allah be Pleased with her),
the daughter of the Messenger of Allah 🕮, she was favored with
greater excellence than her sisters, for she outlived the Prophet
🕮, while all of her sisters died during his lifetime. And as for
'A'ishah (May Allah be Pleased with her), she was the most
beloved wife of the Messenger of Allah 🕮 to him and he did not
marry any virgin except her. In addition, no woman in this nation
– or in any other nation – is known of who was superior to her
in (religious) knowledge and understanding. And Allah protected
her (honor) when the slanderers lied about her, by revealing to the
Prophet 🕮 from above seven heavens that she was innocent. She
lived for about fifty years after the Messenger of Allah 🕮, during
which time she conveyed what she had learned of the Qur'an and
Sunnah from him and acted as peacemaker between those who
differed. She was the noblest of the Mothers of the Faithful, even
Khadeejah, the daughter of Khuwailid (may Allah be Pleased

---

(1) Narrated by Al-Bukhari (3411), Muslim (2431), At-Tirmidhi (1834), An-
Nasa'i in *Al-Kubra* (5/93, No. 8353), Ibn Majah (3280) and Imam Ahmad
(19029).

with her), the mother of the sons and daughters of the Prophet ﷺ, according to the opinion of one group of scholars. But it is better to refrain from making pronouncements regarding which of them was superior. This is because the Prophet's statement: "And the superiority of 'A'ishah over other women is as the superiority of *thareed* over all other foods."[1] – may be understood to be a general statement, including the aforementioned and others, or it may be a general statement with regard to other women only. And Allah knows better.

What is intended here is to discuss matters pertaining to Maryam, (peace be upon her) daughter of 'Imran, for Allah purified her and chose her over the women of her time; and it is also possible that her superiority was over all women, as we have said. It has been reported in a *Hadith* that she will be one of the wives of the Prophet ﷺ in Paradise, along with Asiyah, the daughter of Muzahim.[2] We have related in the *Tafseer* on the authority of some of the *Salaf* that when he said that, he drew support from the Words of Allah: ...*previously married and virgins.* (*Soorah At-Tahreem* 66:5) He said, "The previously married refers to Asiyah, while among the virgins is Maryam, the daughter of 'Imran." And we have spoken of this at the end of *Soorah At-Tahreem*. And Allah knows better.

---

(1) The author claimed in his *Tafseer* (1/363) that it was narrated by Ibn Mar-duyah, by way of Shu'bah, on the authority of his father .

(2) This was related by At-Tabarani (5485) and he said in *Al-Majma'*, "In its chain are some who I do no know. See the *Hadith* which precedes it and the one which proceeds it in *Al-Majma'*." (9/318).

The Description of the Birth of 'Eesa

Allah, Most High, says, *And mention in the Book (the Qur'an, O Muhammad, the story of) Maryam, when she withdrew in seclusion from her family to a place facing east. She placed a barrier (to screen herself) from them; then We sent to her Our Rooh (Angel Jibraeel), and he appeared before her in the form of a man in all respects. She said, "Verily! I seek refuge with the Most Beneficent (Allah) from you, if you are truly taqiyy." He said, "I am only a Messenger from your Lord, to give you a pure boy." She said, "How can I have a son, when no man has touched me, nor am I unchaste?" He said, "So your Lord said; (He said,) "That is easy for Me (Allah). And We will appoint him as a sign to mankind and a Mercy from Us (Allah), and it is a matter (already)*

decreed, (by Allah)." So she conceived him, and she withdrew with him to a far place (i.e. Bethlehem valley about 4-6 miles from Jerusalem). And the pains of childbirth drove her to the trunk of a date-palm. She said, "Would that I had died before this, and had been forgotten and out of sight!" Then he who was below her cried unto her, saying, "Grieve not! Your Lord has provided a water stream under you; and shake the trunk of the date-palm toward you, it will let fall fresh ripe-dates upon you. So eat and drink and be glad, and if you see any human being, say, "Verily! I have vowed a fast unto the Most Beneficent (Allah) so I shall not speak to any human being this day." Then she brought him (the baby) to her people, carrying him. They said, "O, Mary! Indeed you have brought a thing **fariyan.** *O sister of Haroon (Aaron)! Your father was not a man who used to commit adultery, nor was your mother an unchaste woman." Then she pointed to him. They said, "How can we talk to one who is a child in the cradle?" He ('Eesa) said, "Verily! I am a slave of Allah; He has given me the Scripture and made me a Prophet. And He has made me blessed wheresoever I may be, and He has enjoined on me* **salah** *(prayer) and* **zakah** *as long as I live. And dutiful to my mother, and made me not arrogant and unblessed. And* **salam** *(peace) be upon me the day I was born, and the day I die, and the day I shall be raised alive!" Such is 'Eesa, son of Maryam. (It is) a statement of truth, about which they doubt (or dispute). It befits not (the Majesty of) Allah that He should beget a son (this refers to the slander of Christians against Allah, by saying that 'Eesa is the son of Allah). Glorified (and Exalted) be He (above all that they associate with Him). When He decrees a thing, He only says to it, "Be!" and it is. ('Eesa said), "And verily Allah is my Lord and your Lord. So worship Him (Alone). That is the Straight Path (Allah's Religion of Islamic Monotheism which He did ordain for all of His Prophets)."* **(Soorah Maryam** 19:16-37) *(Tafseer At-Tabari)*
Then the sects differed (i.e. they differed regarding 'Eesa), so woe unto the disbelievers (those who gave false witness by saying that

'Eesa is the son of Allah) from the meeting of a great Day (i.e. the Day of Resurrection, when they will be thrown in the blazing Fire).

Allah, Most High tells this story after the story of Zakariyya عليه السلام, which is like an introduction and a preparation before it.

We have already said that when Maryam's mother pledged her to the service of Bait Al-Maqdis, her sister's husband or her maternal aunt's husband, Zakariyya عليه السلام, the Prophet of that time, became her guardian. He appointed for her a *mihrab* in which to worship, and that was a noble place in the Mosque, in which none could visit her except he. Allah also informed us that when she came of age, she devoted herself to worship and she was without equal at that time in all aspects of worship. That which caused Zakariyya عليه السلام to envy her befell her and she was spoken to by the angels, who indicated to her that Allah had chosen her and that He would bestow on her a pure son, who would be a Noble Prophet, purified, venerated and aided by miracles. She was amazed at the idea that she might have a child without a father, because she was not married, nor was she among those who would marry. The angels informed her that Allah is Able to anything that He wills and that when he ordains a thing, He merely says to it, "Be!" and it is. On hearing this, she submitted to it and surrendered herself to Allah's Command. She knew that in this there was a great trial for her, because people would speak about her due to it, for they would be unaware of the truth of the matter. She would simply judge by appearances without reflection or understanding. She only used to leave the Mosque when she was menstruating or in order to fulfill some essential need, such as drawing water or bringing food. One day, when she had left the Mosque to take care of her affairs, *when she withdrew in seclusion* (*Soorah Maryam* 19:17) she went alone to the eastern corner of Al-Aqsa Mosque and lo, Allah sent to her the Angel Jibraeel عليه السلام, the Trustworthy Spirit, *and he appeared before her in the form of a man in all respects.* (*Soorah Maryam* 19:17) When she saw him, *She said, "Verily! I seek refuge with the Most Beneficent (Allah) from you, if you are truly* **taqiyy.***" (Soorah Maryam* 19:18)

Abul-'Aliyah said, "I learned that *taqiyy* means the one who possesses intellect and understanding.[1] This is a reply to those who claimed that among the Children of Isra'eel there was a man who was well known for his immorality and sinfulness and that his name was *taqiyy*, for this claim is false and baseless; indeed, it is ridiculous saying. *He said, "I am only a Messenger from your Lord."* (*Soorah Maryam* 19:19) That is, the angel addressed her, saying, "I am only a Messenger from your Lord, not a human being and He has sent me to you." *"...to give you a pure boy."* (*Soorah Maryam* 19:19) That is, to give you news of a pure and righteous son. *She said, "How can I have a son..."* (*Soorah Maryam* 19:20) This means that Maryam was amazed at this. She said, "How can I have a son..." meaning: "In what way would a son be born to me..." *"...when no man has touched me, nor am I unchaste?"* (*Soorah Maryam* 19:20) That is, I have no husband and I am not a woman who commits sinful acts (i.e. unlawful sexual intercourse). *He said, "So your Lord said; (He said,) "That is easy for Me (Allah)."* (*Soorah Maryam* 19:21) That is, the angel responded to her amazement that she should have a son in such circumstances by saying, *"So your Lord said"* (*Soorah Maryam* 19:21) means He has promised that He will create from you a son, even though you have no husband and you are not among those who commit outrages. *"That is easy for Me (Allah)."* (*Soorah Maryam* 19:21) That is, it is an easy thing for Him to do, because He is Able to do all things.

And He, Most High, says, *"And We will appoint him as a sign to mankind"* (*Soorah Maryam* 19:21) means We will make his

---

(1) According to *Lisan Al-'Arab*, this is because it is the intellect which causes a person to refrain from committing sin. The author of *Al-Lisan* quotes this very narration to prove that *taqiyy* means possessing intellect.

creation in these circumstances a proof for the completeness and perfection of Our Ability to create all kinds of things, for He, Most High, created Adam ﷺ without a male or a female and Eve from a male, without a female. And He created 'Eesa ﷺ from a female, without a male. The rest of the mankind, He created from a male and a female.

And He, Most High, says, *"...and a mercy from Us (Allah)."* (*Soorah Maryam* 19:21) means through him We shall show Mercy to the slaves, by him calling them to Allah in his infachildhood and in his adult life, and in his middle age, asking them to worship Allah, Alone, without partners and to declare Him above taking a wife or having sons, or having partners or equals. *"...and it is a matter (already) decreed, (by Allah)."* (*Soorah Maryam* 19:21) It is possible that these words are part of Jibraeel's dialogue with Maryam, i.e. he informed her that this matter was preordained by Allah's Power and Will. Muhammad Ibn Ishaq gave this interpretation and Ibn Jareer At-Tabari preferred it, but it was not related by anyone besides Ibn Ishaq. And Allah knows better.

It is also possible that His Words: *"...and it is a matter (already) decreed, (by Allah)"* (*Soorah Maryam* 19:21) are an allusion to Jibraeel breathing into her, as He, Most High, says, *Andv (the example of) Maryam, the daughter of 'Imran, who guarded her chastity, so We blew into (her garment) through Our Spirit (i.e. Jibraeel)* (*Soorah At-Tahreem* 66:12) *So she conceived him.* (*Soorah Maryam* 19:22) *...and she withdrew with him to a far place (i.e. Bethlehem valley about 4-6 miles from Jerusalem).* (*Soorah Maryam* 19:22) This was because when Maryam (peace be upon her) conceived, she was unable to bear it, for she knew that many of the people would gossip about her situation. More than one of the *Salaf*, including Wahb Ibn Munabbih said that when the signs of pregnancy became obvious in her, among the first persons to notice it was a man from among the slaves of Banu Isra'eel, whose name was Yoosuf, son of Ya'qoob, the carpenter.

He was her maternal cousin and he expressed great amazement at her state. This was because he knew how religious, decent and devout she was, and yet in spite of this, he observed that she was pregnant when she had no husband. So one day, he confronted her, saying, "O, Maryam! Can there be cultivation without a seed being planted?" She said, "Yes, for who made the first cultivation grow?" Then he asked, "Then can a tree grow without water or rain?" She replied, "Yes, for who created the first tree?" Then he asked her, "Then can there be a son without a male (i.e. a father)?" She answered, "Yes, for verily, Allah created Adam without a male or a female." He said, "Then tell me your news (i.e. how you came to be pregnant)." She said, "Verily, Allah gave me glad tidings. *(Remember) when the angels said, "O Maryam! Verily, Allah gives you the glad tidings of a Word ("Be!" – and he was! i.e. 'Eesa the son of Maryam) from Him, his name will be the Maseeh 'Eesa, the son of Maryam, held in honor in this world and in the Hereafter, and will be one of those who are near to Allah. He will speak to the people in the cradle and in manhood, and he will be one of the righteous."* (*Soorah Aal 'Imran* 3:45,46) And something like this has been narrated about Zakariyya عليه السلام, that he asked her and she answered him in the same way. And Allah knows better.

He, Most High, says, *And the pains of childbirth drove her to the trunk of a date-palm.* (*Soorah Maryam* 19:23) That is, her labor pains caused her to make for the trunk of a date-palm tree and this interpretation is substantiated by a *Hadith* narrated by An-Nasa'i, with a chain of narrators that is not objectionable (i.e. there are no weak narrators in it): It is reported on the authority of Anas ﷺ in a *marfoo'* form and by Al-Baihaqi, with a chain of narrators that he declared to be authentic, on the authority of Shaddad Ibn Aws, which is also in a *marfoo'* form.[1] According to this narration, this took place at Baitlahm (Bethlehem). And Allah knows best. *She*

---

(1)   Narrated by Al-Baihaqi in *Dala'il An-Nubuwwah* (2/255-357).

said, "Would that I had died before this, and had been forgotten and out of sight!" (*Soorah Maryam* 19:23) In this there is evidence that it is permissible to wish for death when afflicted by trial and tribulation. This is because she knew that the people would accuse her (of unlawful sexual intercourse) and they would not believe her. Instead they would accuse her of lying when she came to them with a son in her arms, in spite of the fact that she had been with them in performing acts of worship, religious rites and used to seclude herself in the Mosque. Because of this she wished that she might have died before this or that she had been *"...forgotten and out of sight!"* (*Soorah Maryam* 19:23) means that she had never been created at all. And He, Most High, says, *Then he who was below her cried unto her.* (*Soorah Maryam* 19:2) This was also recited as *Then he called to her from below her.* There are two opinions with regard to who the personal pronoun "he" refers to. One is that it refers to Jibraeel ﷺ. This was said by Al-'Awfi, who reported it on the authority of 'Abdullah Ibn 'Abbas ﷺ. He said, " 'Eesa did not speak except in the presence of the people." Sa'eed Ibn Jubair concurred with this, as did 'Amr Ibn Maimoon, Ad-Dahhak, As-Suddi and Qatadah. Mujahid, Al-Hasan, Ibn Zaid and Sa'eed Ibn Jubair – according to another narration – said that it refers to her son, 'Eesa ﷺ. This was the preferred view of Ibn Jareer At-Tabari and it is authentic.[1]

But the correct interpretation is the first one, based on the Words of Allah, Most High, *"And shake the trunk of date-palm toward you, it will let fall fresh ripe-dates upon you."* (*Soorah Maryam* 19:25) So He mentions food and drink, which is why He says, *"So eat and drink and be glad."* (*Soorah Maryam* 19:26). Then it was said that the trunk of the date-palm was dry. It was also said that the date-palm was bearing fruit. And Allah knows better. It is possible that it was a date-palm, but that it was not bearing fruit at that time, because the time of his birth was in the winter – and

---

(1)   Narrated by At-Tabarani in *Al-Mu'jam Al-Kabeer* (12/346, no. 13303).

that is not the time when date-palms bear fruit. This might be understood from the Words of Allah, Most High, as being a Grace (from Allah): *it will let fall fresh ripe-dates upon you."* (*Soorah Maryam* 19:26) 'Amr Ibn Maimoon said, "There is nothing better for the woman in childbirth than dried dates and fresh dates." Then he recited this Verse. And He, Most High, says, *"...and if you see any human being, say, "Verily! I have vowed a fast unto the Most Beneficent (Allah) so I shall not speak to any human being this day."* (*Soorah Maryam* 19:26) That is, if you see any person, say to him, by mute expression and sign, *"Verily! I have vowed a fast unto the Most Beneficent (Allah)."* (*Soorah Maryam* 19:26) That is, I have vowed to remain silent; according to Qatadah, As-Suddi and Ibn Aslam, it was a part of their religious law that when a person fasted, he would refrain from speaking and from eating. This is proven by the Words of Allah: *"...so I shall not speak to any human being this day."* (*Soorah Maryam* 19:26) But in our religious law, it is disliked for the fasting person to remain silent from morning till night.

And He, Most High, says, *Then she brought him (the baby) to her people, carrying him. They said, "O Mary! Indeed you have brought a thing fariyan. O sister of Haroon! Your father was not a man who used to commit adultery, nor was your mother was an unchaste woman."* (*Soorah Maryam* 19:27,28)

What is meant is that when they saw her carrying her son, *They said, "O Mary! Indeed you have brought a thing **fariyan**."* (*Soorah Maryam* 19:27) The word *fariyah* means a shocking and terrible deed or statement. Then they said, *"O sister of Haroon (Aaron)!"* (*Soorah Maryam* 19:28) It was said that they compared her to one of the devout men of their time, whom she sought to surpass in worship and that his name was Haroon. It was also said that they compared her with an adulterous man of their time, whose name was Haroon. This was said by Sa'eed Ibn Jubair. It was also said that they were referring to Haroon ﷺ, the brother of Moosa ﷺ, and that they were comparing her to him because of her devoutness in worship.

And Imam Ahmad narrated on the authority of Al-Mugheerah Ibn Shu'bah that he said, "The Messenger of Allah ﷺ sent me to Najran and they said, "You read: *"O sister of Haroon..."* (i.e. Maryam) in the Qur'an, whereas Moosa was born much before 'Eesa." When I came back to the Messenger of Allah ﷺ, I asked him about that, whereupon he said, "Did you not inform them that they (the people of former times) used to be named after the Prophets and righteous people who had gone before them?"[1]

What is meant by this is that they (Maryam's people) said, *"O sister of Haroon!"* (*Soorah Maryam* 19:28) and the *Hadith* has prove that she had a brother in lineage whose name was Haroon, and that he was well-known for his devoutness, his righteousness and his charitable deeds, which is why they said, *"Your father was not a man who used to commit adultery, nor was your mother an unchaste woman"* (*Soorah Maryam* 19:28) means you are not from a family who possessed these evil traits, nor were your parents or your brother ever accused of committing such major sins. *Then she pointed to him* (*Soorah Maryam* 19:29) meaning: address him and speak to him, because your answer is his responsibility and that which you seek you may hear from him. When she indicated the baby, those among them who were arrogant and nasty said, *"How can we talk to one who is a child in the cradle?"* (*Soorah Maryam* 19:29) That is, how can you refer us for an answer to a small baby, who is unable to speak, and is a suckling infant in his crib, unable to distinguish between pure milk, unadulterated by water – and buttermilk. And by this suggestion of yours you are merely mocking, ridiculing and belittling us. You are also making light of us, when you do not answer us in words; instead, you

_____

(1) This is an authentic *Hadith* narrated by Imam Ahmad (17736) and by Muslim (2135).

refer us for an answer to a child in his crib. At this point, *He ('Eesa) said, "Verily! I am a slave of Allah; He has given me the Scripture and made me a Prophet. And He has made me blessed wheresoever I may be, and He has enjoined on me* **salah** *(prayer) and* **zakah** *as long as I live."* (*Soorah Maryam* 19:30,31) These were the first words uttered by 'Eesa, the son of Maryam ﷺ, and the very first words he spoke were: *"Verily! I am a slave of Allah."* (*Soorah Maryam* 19:30) – in which he acknowledged that he worships his Lord and that Allah is his Lord, and so he declared himself to be innocent what the unjust people attribute to him, i.e. that he is the son of Allah. Rather, he is His slave and His Messenger, and the son of his people. Then he declared his mother innocent of what the ignorant folk attributed to her and accused her of, saying, *"He has given me the Scripture and made me a Prophet."* (*Soorah Maryam* 19:30), for Allah does not give Prophethood to one who is as they claim, may Allah curse them and disgrace them. He, Most High, says, *And because of their (the Jews') disbelief and (their) uttering against Maryam a grave false charge…* (*Soorah An-Nisa'* 4:156) This was that a group from among the Jews at that time said, "She became pregnant with him due to having committed unlawful sexual intercourse during the time of her menses," may Allah curse them. So Allah declared her innocent of that and informed us that she was honest and upright and that He had taken her child as a Prophet sent by Him, one of the *Ulul-'Azm*, the five greatest Prophets. This is why He says, *"And He has made me blessed wheresoever I may be."* (*Soorah Maryam* 19:31) This is because wherever he was, he used to call the people to the worship of Allah, Alone, without partners and deny the imperfection or deficiency which is implicit in the claim that He had taken a son or a consort. Far above that is He. *"…and He has enjoined on me* **salah** *(prayer) and* **zakah** *as long as I live."* (*Soorah Maryam* 19:31). This is the obligation of slaves (of Allah), to fulfill the rights of the Almighty, Most Praiseworthy, to offer prayers and to do good to His creatures, through *zakah*. The word *zakah* includes the purification of souls from mean, despicable traits and the purification of wealth, by giving to all kinds of needy folk, offering hospitality to guests, providing for wives, slaves and kinfolk, and all acts of obedience (to Allah) and deeds through which one seeks closeness to Him. Then He says, *"And dutiful to my mother, and made me not arrogant and unblessed."* (*Soorah Maryam* 19:32) That is, He has made me dutiful to my mother. This He did by confirming her rights upon him, for he had no parent except her. So Glorified be He Who created all things, showered His Benevolence on them and offered every soul its true guidance. *"...and made me not arrogant and unblessed"* (*Soorah Maryam* 19:32) means I am neither rude nor impolite and no words or deeds that contradict Allah's Commands or the obligation to obey Him ever emanate from me.

Then Allah, Most High, related his true story, made clear his situation and fully explained it, saying, *Such is 'Eesa, son of Maryam. (It is) a statement of truth, about which they doubt (or dispute). It befits not (the Majesty of) Allah that He should beget a son (this refers to the slander of Christians against Allah, by saying that 'Eesa is the son of Allah). Glorified be He (and Exalted above all that they associate with Him). When He decrees a thing, He only says to it, "Be!" and it is.* (*Soorah Maryam* 19:34,35), as He, Most High, says in *Soorah Aal 'Imran*, after relating his story and his situation: *This is (what We recite to you, O Muhammad) of the Verses and the Wise Reminder (i.e. the Qur'an). Verily, the likeness of 'Eesa before Allah is the likeness of Adam. He created him from dust, then (He) said to him, "Be!" – and he was. (This is) the truth from your Lord, so be not of those who doubt. Then whoever disputes with you concerning him ('Eesa) after (all this) knowledge that has come to you, (i.e. 'Eesa being a slave of Allah, and having no share in Divinity) say, (O Muhammad), "Come, let us call our sons and your sons, our women and your women,*

*ourselves and yourselves – then we pray and invoke (sincerely)
the Curse of Allah upon those who lie." Verily! This is the true
narrative (about the story of 'Eesa), and* **La ilaha ill-Allah** *(none
has the right to be worshipped but Allah, the One and the Only
True God, Who has neither a wife nor a son). And indeed, Allah is
the Almighty, Most Wise. And if they turn away (and do not accept
these true proofs and evidences), then surely, Allah is Most Aware
of those who do mischief. (Soorah Aal 'Imran 3:58-63)*

What is meant is that when Allah, Most High, made clear the
situation of the Maseeh ﷺ, He said to His Messenger ﷺ, *"Such
is 'Eesa, son of Maryam. (It is) a statement of truth, about which
they doubt (or dispute). (Soorah Maryam 19:34)* That is, that he
is a created slave, born of a woman from among Allah's slaves,
which is why He says, *"It befits not (the Majesty of) Allah that
He should beget a son (this refers to the slander of Christians
against Allah, by saying that 'Eesa is the son of Allah). Glorified
be He (and Exalted above all that they associate with Him). When
He decrees a thing, He only says to it, "Be!" and it is. (Soorah
Maryam 19:35)* That is, nothing is impossible for Him, nothing
troubles Him and nothing, for He is Omnipotent and the Doer of
whatever He wills. "Verily, His Command, when He intends a
thing, is only that He says to it, "Be!" and it is!" *(Soorah Ya Seen
36:82)* And as for His Saying: *"Truly! Allah is my Lord and your
Lord, so worship Him (Alone). This is the Straight Path" (Soorah
Aal 'Imran 3:51)* it is the completion of 'Eesa's speech to them
in the cradle, in which he informed them that Allah is their Lord,
the God Whom he worshipped and the God Whom they were
obliged to worship and that it was the Straight Path. He, Most
High, says, *Then the sects differed (i.e. regarding 'Eesa), so woe
unto the disbelievers (those who gave false witness by saying that
'Eesa is the son of Allah) from the meeting of a great Day (i.e.
the Day of Resurrection, when they will be thrown in the blazing
Fire). (Soorah Maryam 19:37)* That is, the people of that time and

those after them differed regarding him. Among the Jews there were those who claimed that he was the illegitimate son of an adulteress and persisted in their disbelief and obstinacy. Another group went to the other extreme and claimed that he is the son of Allah. But the true Believers said that he is Allah's slave and His Messenger, the son of his nation and Allah's Word, which He bestowed on Maryam, and a spirit created by Him. These people are the saved ones, who will be rewarded (by Allah) and they are supported and helped (by Him). And those who contradicted them in any of these things are disbelievers, they are astray and they are ignorant. And Allah has warned them (of the punishment that awaits them) in His Words: *So woe unto the disbelievers (those who gave false witness by saying that 'Eesa is the son of Allah) from the meeting of a great Day (i.e. the Day of Resurrection, when they will be thrown in the blazing Fire).* (*Soorah Maryam* 19:37)

And Al-Bukhari narrated on the authority of 'Ubadah Ibn As-Samit, who reported from the Prophet ﷺ that he said, "Whoever bore witness that none has the right to be worshipped but Allah, Alone, Who has no partners, that Muhammad is His slave and His Messenger, and that 'Eesa is Allah's slave and His Messenger and His Word, which He bestowed on Maryam and a Spirit created by Him, that Paradise is true and Hell is true, Allah will admit him into Paradise with the deeds which he had done even if those deeds were few." (Junadah, the sub-narrator said, " 'Ubadah added, "Such a person can enter Paradise through any of its eight gates he likes.")[1]

---

[1]   Narrated by Al-Bukhari (3435).

Chapter on Declaration that Allah, Most High, Has no Son

Allah, Most High, says at the end of this *Soorah*, *And they say, "The Most Beneficent (Allah) has begotten a son (or offspring or children) [as the Jews say: 'Uzair is the son of Allah, the Christians say that He has begotten a son ('Eesa), and the pagan Arabs say that He has begotten daughters (angels, etc.)]. Indeed you have brought forth (said) a thing* **'iddan!** That is, a terrible, evil saying and a lie. *Whereby the heavens are almost torn, and the Earth is split asunder, and the mountains fall in ruins, that they ascribe a son (or offspring or children) to the Most Beneficent (Allah). But it is not suitable for (the Majesty of) the Most Beneficent (Allah) that He should beget a son (or offspring or children). There is none in the heavens and the earth but comes unto the Most Beneficent (Allah) as a slave. Verily, He knows each one of them, and has counted them a full counting. And everyone of them will come to Him alone on the Day of Resurrection (without* *any helper, or protector or defender).* (*Soorah Maryam* 19:88-95) Thus Allah, Most High, has made it clear that it is not fitting that He should have a son, because He is the Creator of all things and the Owner of all things and every thing is in need of Him, submits to Him and is humbled before Him. And all of the inhabitants of the heavens and the Earth are His slaves, while He is their Lord, *La ilaha illa Huwa* (none has the right to be worshipped but He) – and there is no lord but He, as He, Most High, says, *Yet, they join the Jinn as partners in worship with Allah, though He has created them (the Jinn), and they attribute falsely without knowledge sons and daughters to Him. Be He Glorified and Exalted above (all) that they attribute to Him. He is the Originator of the heavens and the Earth. How can He have children when He has no wife? He created all things and He is the Knower of everything. Such is Allah, your Lord!* **La ilaha illa Huwa** *(none has the right to be worshipped but He), the Creator of all things. So worship Him (Alone), and He is the* **Wakil** *(Trustee, Disposer of affairs, Guardian, etc.) over all things. No vision can grasp Him, but His Grasp is over all vision. He is the Most Subtle and Courteous, Well-Acquainted with all things.* (*Soorah Al-An'am* 6:100-103) So He has made clear that He is the Creator of all things, so how can He have a son, when a son cannot be produced except from two like beings – and Allah, Most High, has no like or equal, so He can have no consort and therefore, no son, as He, Most High, says, *Say (O Muhammad, "He is Allah, (the) One.* **Allah-us Samad** *(the Self-Sufficient Master, Whom all creatures need, He neither eats nor drinks). He begets not, nor was He begotten; and there is none coequal or comparable unto Him."* (*Soorah Al-Ikhlas* 112:1-4) He has determined that He is the One, Who has no equal in His Divine Essence, in His Attributes or His Actions. *"***Allah-us Samad** *(the Self-Sufficient Master, Whom all creatures need, He neither eats nor drinks)."* He is the Master, Who is Complete in His Knowledge, His Wisdom, His Mercy and all of His Attributes. *"He begets not."* That is, No son has come from

Him *"...nor was He begotten"* means He was not born to anyone or anything that existed before Him (because nothing existed before Him). *"...and there is none coequal or comparable unto Him."* That is, there is nothing equal to Him, nor anything similar to Him. So He is without equal in all ways and all senses, to it is not possible that he could have a son, since a son can only be begotten of two equal things, or similar things. Far Above that is Allah, Most High.

He, Most High, says, *And they say, "The Most Beneficent (Allah) has begotten a son (or children)." Glory to Him! They (those whom they call children of Allah, i.e. the angels, 'Eesa son of Maryam, 'Uzair, etc.), are but honored slaves. They speak not until He has spoken, and they act on His Command. He knows what is before them, and what is behind them, and they cannot intercede except for him with whom He is Pleased. And they stand in awe for fear of Him. And if anyone of them should say, "Verily, I am an ilah (a god) besides Him (Allah)," such a one We should recompense with Hell. Thus We recompense the zalimoon (polytheists, wrongdoers, etc.).* (*Soorah Al-Anbiya'* 21:26-29)

And He, Most High, says at the beginning of *Soorah Al-Kahf,* which was revealed in Makkah, *All the praises and thanks be to Allah, Who has sent down to His slave (Muhammad) the Book (the Qur'an), and has not placed therein any crookedness. (He has made it) Straight to give warning (to the disbelievers) of a severe punishment from Him, and to give glad tidings to the believers (in the Oneness of Allah, Islamic Monotheism), who work righteous deeds, that they shall have a fair reward (i.e. Paradise). They shall abide therein forever. And to warn those (Jews, Christians, and pagans) who say, "Allah has begotten a son (or offspring or children)." No knowledge have they of such a thing, nor had their fathers. Mighty is the word that comes out of their mouths (i.e. that He begot (took) sons and daughters). They utter nothing but a lie.* (*Soorah Al-Kahf* 18:1-5)

And He, Most High, says, *They (Jews, Christians and pagans) say, "Allah has begotten a son (children)." Glory be to Him! He is Rich (Free of all wants). His is all that is in the heavens and all that is in the Earth. No warrant have you for this. Do you say against Allah what you know not? Say, "Verily, those who invent a lie against Allah will never be successful." – A brief enjoyment in this world! – And then unto Us will be their return, then We shall make them taste the severest torment because they used to disbelieve (in Allah, belie His Messengers, deny and challenge His* **Ayat.***) (Soorah Yoonus* 10:68-70)

The Noble Verses, which were revealed in Makkah include a reply to all of those disbelieving parties, such as the philosophers, the pagan Arabs, the Jews and the Christians, who claimed – without knowledge – that Allah has a son (or children). Glorified be He! He is Far Above what the unjust wrongdoers say.

And since the Christians – may Allah's Curse be on them in perpetuity, until the Day of Resurrection – were among the foremost of those who made this claim, they were mentioned frequently in the Qur'an, in order for Allah to reply to their claims and to expose their contradictions, their lack of knowledge and their deep ignorance.

Their sayings of disbelief take manifold forms and this is because falsehood has a way of diversifying into many branches, varieties and mutual contradictions. As for the truth, it does not vary and it does not suffer from any confusion or contradiction. Allah, Most High, says, *Had it been from other than Allah, they would surely have found therein much contradictions. (Soorah An-Nisa'* 4:82) This proves that truth is one and is in agreement and conformity with itself, while falsehood is contradictory and confused. A party from among their ignorant and misguided folk claimed that the Maseeh ﷺ is Allah, Most High, while another party said that he is the son of Allah, the Almighty, the All-

Powerful. Another group said that he is the third part of a trinity of which they claim that Allah consists. He, Most High, says, *Surely, in disbelief are they who say that Allah is the Maseeh, son of Maryam. Say (O Muhammad), "Who then has the least power against Allah, if He were to destroy the Maseeh, son of Maryam, his mother, and all those who are on the earth together?" And to Allah belongs the dominion of the heavens and the Earth, and all that is between them. He creates what He wills. And Allah is Able to do all things.* (*Soorah Al-Ma'idah* 5:17)

So Allah, Most High, informs us about their disbelief and their ignorance and He makes it clear that He is the Creator, Who is Able to do all things, and it is He Who disposes of the affairs of all things, and He is the Lord of all things, the Owner of all things and the God Who should be worshipped by all things. At the end of *Soorah Al-Ma'idah*, He, Most High, says, *Surely, they have disbelieved who say, "Allah is the Maseeh ('Eesa), son of Maryam." But the Maseeh said, "O, Children of Isra'eel! Worship Allah, my Lord and your Lord." Verily, whosoever sets up partners in worship with Allah, then Allah has forbidden Paradise for him, and the Fire will be his abode. And for the **Zalimoon** there are no helpers. Surely, disbelievers are those who said, "Allah is the third of the three (in a trinity)." But there is no **ilah** (god) (none who has the right to be worshipped) but One **Ilah** (God – Allah). And if they cease not from what they say, verily, a painful torment will befall the disbelievers among them. Will they not repent to Allah and ask His Forgiveness? For Allah is Oft-Forgiving, Most Merciful. The Maseeh, son of Maryam, was no more than a Messenger; many were the Messengers that passed away before him. His mother (Maryam) was a **Siddiqah** (i.e. she believed in the Words of Allah and His Books). They both used to eat food (as any other human being, while Allah does not eat). Look how We make the **Ayat** clear to them, yet look how they are deluded away (from the truth).* (*Soorah Al-Ma'idah* 5:72-75)

Allah, Most High, has delivered His Verdict on their disbelief with good cause and He informs us that this (disbelief) emanated from them, in spite of the fact that the Messenger sent to them, i.e. 'Eesa ﷺ, the son of Maryam, had made clear to them that he was a slave, subject to Allah's Lordship, created and fashioned in the womb and he called the people to the worship of Allah, Alone, without partners. And he warned them that opposing this would lead to punishment in the Hellfire in the Eternal Abode and humiliation, degradation and ignominy in the Hereafter. This is why He says, *Verily, whosoever sets up partners in worship with Allah, then Allah has forbidden Paradise for him, and the Fire will be his abode. And for the* **Zalimoon** *there are no helpers.* (*Soorah Al-Ma'idah* 5:72) Then He says, *Surely, disbelievers are those who said, "Allah is the third of the three (in a trinity)." But there is no* **ilah** *(god) (none who has the right to be worshipped) but One* **Ilah**. (*Soorah Al-Ma'idah* 5:73) Ibn Jareer At-Tabari and others said that what is meant by this is their saying regarding the personages of the trinity, the personage of the Lord, the personage of the son and the personage of the Word sent from the father to the son, according to all the differing sects, including the Melkites to the Jacobites and the Nestorians – may Allah's Curse be on them. And we shall explain how they differed in this and the three councils they held during the reign of Constantine, son of Constantius – three hundred years after 'Eesa ﷺ and three hundred years before the commencement of the Mission of Prophet Muhammad ﷺ. This is why Allah, Most High, says, *But there is no* **ilah** *(god) (none who has the right to be worshipped) but One* **Ilah**. (*Soorah Al-Ma'idah* 5:73). That is, there is no god who has the right to be worshipped, except Allah, Alone, without partners and He has no equal, no like, no consort and no son.

Then He warned them and threatened them, saying, *And if they cease not from what they say, verily, a painful torment will befall the disbelievers among them.* (*Soorah Al-Ma'idah* 5:73) Then

He called upon them, with His Mercy and Kindness, to repent and ask forgiveness for these terrible sins and enormities, which merit the Fire; He says, *Will they not repent to Allah and seek His Forgiveness? For Allah is Oft-Forgiving, Most Merciful.* (*Soorah Al-Ma'idah* 5:74) Then He made clear the situation of the Maseeh ﷺ and his mother and emphasized that he was a slave and Messenger and that his mother was a *Siddiqah*, i.e. she was not an adulteress, as the Jews claim – may Allah's Curse be on them. And in this there is evidence that she was not a Prophet, as a group of scholars have claimed.

And He, Most High, says, *They both used to eat food (as any other human being, while Allah does not eat).* (*Soorah Al-Ma'idah* 5:75) This is an allusion to the fact that food was excreted by them, just as it is excreted by others. That is to say, how can anyone who shares such an attribute be a deity? Far Above their claim and their ignorance is Allah, Most High.

As-Suddi and others said that what is intended by Allah's Saying: *Surely, disbelievers are those who said, "Allah is the third of the three (in a trinity)"* (*Soorah Al-Ma'idah* 5:73) is a reference to their claim that 'Eesa ﷺ and Maryam are deities besides Allah, i.e. as Allah, Most High, made clear regarding their disbelief in this matter, in His Saying: *And (remember) when Allah will say (on the Day of Resurrection), "O 'Eesa, son of Maryam! Did you say unto men, 'Worship me and my mother as two gods besides Allah'?" He will say, "Glory be to You! It was not for me to say what I had no right (to say). Had I said such a thing, You would surely have known it. You know what is in my inner self, though I do not know what is in Yours, truly, You, only You, are the All-Knowing of all that is hidden and unseen. Never did I say to them aught except what You (Allah) did command me to say: 'Worship Allah, my Lord and your Lord.' And I was a witness over them while I dwelt amongst them, but when You* **tawaffaitani,** *You were the Watcher over them, and You are a*

Witness to all things." (This is a great admonition and warning to the Christians of the whole world) "If You punish them, they are Your slaves, and if You forgive them, verily You, only You are the Almighty, the Most Wise." (Soorah Al-Ma'idah 5:116-118)

Allah, Most High, informs us that He will question 'Eesa عليه السلام on the Day of Resurrection, in a manner which honors him and which rebukes and censures those who worshipped him. Those who lie against him and invent a calumny, claiming that he is the son of Allah, or that he is Allah, or that he is His partner – Allah is Far Above all that they ascribe to Him. He will question him, even though He knows that he did not do what he is being asked about. But He will ask in order to rebuke those lied against him; He will say to him, *Did you say unto men, 'Worship me and my mother as two gods besides Allah'?" He will say, "Glory be to You!" (Soorah Al-Ma'idah* 5:116) That is, You are Far Above the partners they ascribe to You. *It was not for me to say what I had no right (to say) (Soorah Al-Ma'idah* 5:116) means no one has this right but You. *"Had I said such a thing, You would surely have known it. You know what is in my inner self, though I do not know what is in Yours, truly, You, only You, are the All-Knowing of all that is hidden and unseen." (Soorah Al-Ma'idah* 5:116) One may note that great courteousness is shown in the question and the answer. *"Never did I say to them aught except what You (Allah) did command me to say" (Soorah Al-Ma'idah* 5:117) means when You sent me to them and revealed to me the Scripture, which I used to recite to them. Then he explained what he used to say to them in his words: *"Worship Allah, my Lord and your Lord." (Soorah Al-Ma'idah* 5:117) That is, my Creator and your Creator, my Sustainer and your Sustainer. *"And I was a witness over them while I dwelt amongst them, but when You tawaffaitani..." (Soorah Al-Ma'idah* 5:117) That is, when You raised me up to You, when they intended to crucify me and kill me, but You had Mercy on me and saved me from them, casting my likeness upon one of them, so that they took their vengeance upon him. And when this happened, *"You were the Watcher over them, and You are a Witness to all things." (This is a great admonition and warning to the Christians of the whole world).* (*Soorah Al-Ma'idah* 5:117) Then he said, in tones indicating submission to the Will of the Lord, the Almighty, the All-Powerful and a declaration of self-exoneration from the claims of the Christians, *"If You punish them, they are Your slaves..."* (*Soorah Al-Ma'idah* 5:118) means they deserve that. *"...and if You forgive them, verily You, only You are the Almighty, the Most Wise."* (*Soorah Al-Ma'idah* 5:118) All matters refer back to Allah, for He does what He Wills and none can question Him about what He does, while He will question them, which is why he said, *"...verily You, only You are the Almighty, the Most Wise."* (*Soorah Al-Ma'idah* 5:118). He did not say, the Most Forgiving, the Most Merciful.

And it has been confirmed in an authentic *Hadith* from the Messenger of Allah ﷺ that he said, "Allah, Most High, says, "The son of Adam has reviled Me and he had no right to do so; he claims that I have a son, when I am the One, *As-Samad*,[1] Who does not beget and Who was not begotten and like unto Whom there is none.""[2]

---

(1)   *As-Samad*: The Self-Sufficient Master, Whom all creatures need, Who neither eats nor drinks.

(2)   Narrated by Al-Bukhari (4974).

Explanation of the Revelation of Four Scriptures and the Times of Their Revelation

Abu Zur'ah Ad-Dimashqi said, 'Abdullah Ibn Saleh told us, "I was told by Mu'awiyah Ibn Saleh, on the authority of the person who informed him, that he said, The Towrah was sent down to Moosa عليه السلام on the sixth night of the month of Ramadan. The *Zaboor* (Psalms) was sent down to Dawood عليه السلام on the twelfth night of the month of Ramadan. This was four hundred and eighty-two years after the Towrah. The *Injeel* (Gospel) was sent down to 'Eesa, عليه السلام on the eighteenth night of the month of Ramadan, one thousand and fifty years after the *Zaboor*. And *Al-Furqan* (the Criterion, i.e. the Qur'an) was sent down to Muhammad ﷺ on the twenty-fourth night of the month of Ramadan."[1]

We have mentioned in the *Tafseer* in the explanation of the Words of Allah, Most High: *The month of Ramadan in which was revealed the Qur'an.* (*Soorah Al-Baqarah* 2:185) the *Ahadeeth* reported to that effect and it is mentioned in them that the *Injeel* was sent down to 'Eesa ﷺ on the eighteenth night of the month of Ramadan.

Ibn Jareer mentioned in his *Tareekh* that it was sent down to him when he was thirty years old and he remained until Allah raised him up to the heaven, when he was thirty-three years old.

Ishaq Ibn Bishr said, "We were informed by Sa'eed Ibn Abi 'Aroobah, who reported on the authority of Qatadah – and Muqatil on his authority – on the authority of 'Abdur-Rahman Ibn Adam, who reported on the authority of Abu Hurairah ﷺ that he said, "Allah, the Almighty, the All-Powerful, revealed to 'Eesa ﷺ, 'O, 'Eesa! Be diligent in (practicing and teaching) My Religion and be tireless; and listen and obey, O son of the pure woman, the chaste, the virgin. You were born without a father, and I created you as a Sign for the worlds. So worship Me Alone and depend upon Me Alone. Take the Scripture (i.e. the *Injeel*) with vigor and zeal and go to the Syriac people and convey to them from what is in your hands, that I am the Truth, the Living, the Everlasting, Who never goes away. Believe in the Unlettered, Arab Prophet, the owner of the camel and the headdress (i.e. the *'imamah* [turban]), the woollen garment, the sandals and the staff, the wide-eyed, the smooth-browed, the smooth-cheeked, the curly-haired, the heavily-bearded, whose eyebrows are joined, the hook-nosed, whose incisors are split, whose *'anfaqah*[2] is free of hair, whose neck is like a silver pitcher, whose clavicles appear to have gold

---

(1)   Narrated by Ibn 'Asakir in *Tareekh Dimashq* (14/42) by way of Abu Zur'ah.

(2)   *Anfaqah*: The area between the lower lip and the lower jaw.

running in them, who has hairs from his throat to his navel, like a branch – and there is no hair on his stomach or on his chest except this. His hands and feet are thick, when he turns (to look), he does so with his whole body and when he walks, it is as if he is walking down from a rock and descending from a hillside (i.e. he walks with confidence). The sweat on his face is like pearls and the scent of musk emanates from it. His like has not been seen before and will not be seen again. He is of fine build and he has a good odour. He will marry many women, but will have only a small number of offspring, His descendants are from a blessed woman (i.e. Khadeejah, may Allah be Pleased with her) and she will have an abode (in Paradise) made from hollowed pearl, in which there will neither be fatigue nor clamor. You will support him, O 'Eesa, at the end of time, just as Zakariyya supported your mother. He will have two offsprings through her (i.e. Khadeejah), both of whom shall be martyred. He will have an abode in Paradise the like of which no other human being will have. His speech is the Qur'an, his Religion is Islam and I am Peace. *Tooba* will be for those who live in his time, witness his days and pay heed to his words'."

'Eesa ﷺ said, "O, my Lord! What is *Tooba*?" He said, "It is a tree which I have planted with My Own Hands; it is for all of the Gardens (of Paradise). Its roots are of *ridwan*, its water is from *tasneem*, whose coldness is like *kafoor* and whose taste is like that of ginger. Anyone who drinks once of that spring shall never be thirsty." 'Eesa said, "O, my Lord! Give me to drink of it." He answered, "It is forbidden for the Prophets to drink from it until that Prophet first drinks of it; it is forbidden for the nations to drink from it until the nation (i.e. followers) of that Prophet first drinks from it. I shall take you up to Me and send you down at the end of time to see wonders from the nation of that Prophet, and that you might assist them against the accursed *Dajjal*. I shall send you down at prayer time that you may pray with them, but then you shall not lead them in prayer, for they are a nation favored with mercy, and no Prophet will come after him."

Hisham Ibn 'Ammar reported on the authority of Al-Waleed Ibn Muslim, who reported on the authority of 'Abdur-Rahman Ibn Zaid, who in turn reported on the authority of his father that 'Eesa ﷺ said, "O, my Lord! Inform me about this nation that is favored with mercy." He said, "It is the nation of Ahmad; they are scholars and men of wisdom, as if they are Prophets. They are pleased with little that they receive from Me and I am Well-Pleased with few deeds from them. I will admit them to Paradise because of (their declaration:) *'La ilaha ill-Allah* (none has the right to be worshipped except Allah)'. O, 'Eesa! They will be the majority of the inhabitants in Paradise, because the tongues of no nation have been humbled by *'La ilaha ill-Allah* (none has the right to be worshipped except Allah)' as their tongues have been humbled. And the necks of no nation have been humbled by prostration as their necks have been humbled." (Narrated by Ibn 'Asakir)

And He, Most High, says, *And when I (Allah) put in the hearts of **Al-Hawariyyoon** (the Disciples of 'Eesa) to believe in Me and My Messenger, they said, "We believe. And bear witness that we are Muslims."* (*Soorah Al-Ma'idah* 5:111) It was said that what is meant by this Revelation is the Revelation of inspiration. That is, Allah led them to it and guided them to it. It was also said that what is meant by it is Revelation through the medium of the Messenger and the reconciliation of their hearts toward the acceptance of the truth. This is why they responded by saying, *we believe in Allah, and bear witness that we are Muslims (i.e. we submit to Allah)."* (*Soorah Ali 'Imran* 3:52)

This is one of the Blessings bestowed by Allah on His slave and Messenger, 'Eesa ﷺ, that He granted him helpers and supporters, who aided him and called with him to the worship of

Allah, Alone, without partners.

The miracles given to each Prophet in his time were suited to the communities in which they lived. It was said that the miracle given to Moosa ﷺ befitted the people of his time, who were skilled magicians, so he was sent with Signs which dazzled the eyes and humbled the necks. And since the magicians were well-versed in the art of magic and its consequences and they witnessed those dazzling occurrences, which they knew could not have been produced by anyone except one who was helped by Allah and given supernatural miracles to prove his truthfulness, they immediately embraced Islam and they did not hesitate.

Likewise, 'Eesa ﷺ was sent at a time when his people excelled in the natural sciences and so he was sent with miracles which they could not emulate and the secrets of which they could not discover, for what could a physician do for the one who was born blind, which is the worst form of blindness, the leper and the one who was afflicted with a chronic illness? And how could any created being acquire the knowledge of how to raise the dead from his grave? As everyone knows, such a miracle proves the truthfulness of the one who performs it and the Omnipotence of the One Who sent him.

Likewise, Muhammad ﷺ, according to the consensus of the scholars, was sent at a time renowned for the eloquence and articulacy of the people. So Allah sent to them the Mighty Qur'an, which falsehood cannot approach from the front or from behind; (it is) sent down by the Most Wise, Worthy of All Praise.[1] Its Words are a miracle, which challenge the mankind and the jinn to produce the like of it, or to produce even ten *Soorahs* like it, or even one *Soorah* like it – and He pronounced definitely that they would not be able to do so, whether at that time or in the future, saying that if they did not do it, and they would never do

---

(1) See: *Soorah Fussilat* 41:42.

it, because it is the Speech of the Creator, the Almighty, the All-Powerful. And there is nothing that resembles Allah, Most High, neither in His Essence, nor in His Attributes, nor in His Actions.

What is meant is that when 'Eesa ﷺ established the arguments and proofs against them, most of them persisted in their disbelief, error, obduracy and oppression, though a righteous group of them dedicated themselves to him and they were his helpers and supporters. They followed him, assisted him and offered sincere advice to him. This was at the time when the Children of Isra'eel became preoccupied with him and denounced him to one of the rulers of that time. They became determined to kill him and crucify him, but Allah saved him from them and raised him up to Him from their midst and cast his likeness on one of his companions and they took him and crucified him to death, believing him to be 'Eesa ﷺ. But they were mistaken in this and contradicted the truth. Many of the Christians believed their claim, but both parties were in error in the matter.

Allah, Most High, says, *And they (the disbelievers) plotted (to kill 'Eesa), and Allah planned too. And Allah is the Best of planners.* (*Soorah Aal 'Imran* 3:54) And He, Most High, says, *And (remember) when 'Eesa, son of Maryam, said, "O, Children of Isra'eel! I am the Messenger of Allah unto you confirming the Tawrah (which came) before me, and giving glad tidings of a Messenger to come after me, whose name shall be Ahmad." But when he (Ahmad i.e. Muhammad) came to them with clear proofs, they said, "This is plain magic." And who does more wrong than the one who invents a lie against Allah, while he is being invited to Islam? And Allah guides not the people who are* **Zalimoon**. *They intend to put out the Light of Allah (i.e. the Religion of Islam, this Qur'an, and Prophet Muhammad) with their mouths. But Allah will complete His Light even though the disbelievers hate (it).* (*Soorah As-Saff* 61:6-8) – up to the Words of Him, Most High after that: *O you who believe! Be you helpers (in the Cause)* *of Allah as said 'Eesa, son of Maryam, to* **Al-Hawariyyoon** *(the Disciples), "Who are my helpers (in the Cause) of Allah?"* **Al-Hawariyyoon** *said, "We are Allah's helpers (i.e. we will strive in His Cause)!" Then a group of the Children of Isra'eel believed and a group disbelieved. So We gave power to those who believed against their enemies, and they became the uppermost.* (*Soorah As-Saff* 61:14)

And something similar to this has been narrated on the authority of Al-'Irbadh Ibn Sariyah and Abu Umamah (may Allah be Pleased with them both) from the Prophet ﷺ and in it he spoke of: "…the supplication of my father, Ibraheem and the glad tidings of 'Eesa." This was because when Ibraheem عليه السلام built the Ka'bah he said, *"Our Lord! Send amongst them a Messenger of their own."* (*Soorah Al-Baqarah* 2:129) When Prophethood among the Children of Isra'eel came to an end with 'Eesa عليه السلام, he addressed them and informed them that Prophethood had been cut off from them and that after him, it would go to the Arabian Prophet, the final Seal of the Prophets, Ahmad, who is Muhammad Ibn 'Abdullah Ibn 'Abdul-Muttalib Ibn Ibn Hisham Hashim, who was of the descendants of Ishmael عليه السلام, son of Ibraheem *Al-Khaleel* عليه السلام.

Allah, Most High, says, *But when he came to them with clear proofs, they said, "This is plain magic."* (*Soorah As-Saff* 61:6)It is possible that the pronoun 'he' refers to 'Eesa عليه السلام and it is also possible that it refers to Muhammad ﷺ.

Then He encouraged His believing slaves to help Islam and its adherents and to assist its Prophet ﷺ and support him in establishing the Religion and propagating it, saying, *O you who believe! Be you helpers (in the Cause) of Allah as said 'Eesa, son of Maryam, to* **Al-Hawariyyoon**, *"Who are my helpers (in the Cause) of Allah?"* (*Soorah As-Saff* 61:14) means who will assist me in calling the people to Allah? **Al-Hawariyyoon** *said, "We* *are Allah's helpers (i.e. we will strive in His Cause)!"* (*Soorah As-Saff* 61:14) This took place in a village known as An-Nasirah, which is why they became known as *Nasara* (Nazarenes). Allah, Most High, says, *Then a group of the Children of Isra'eel believed and a group disbelieved.* (*Soorah As-Saff* 61:14) That is, when 'Eesa ﷺ called the Children of Isra'eel and others to Allah, Most High, some of them believed, while others disbelieved. Among those who believed in him were the people of Antioch in their entirety, according to what has been reported by more than one of the scholars of *Seerah*, history and *tafseer*. He sent three messengers to them, one of whom was Simon the Pure and the people believed and responded positively to their preaching. But it is not they who are referred to in *Soorah Ya Seen*, according to what we have already established in the story of the people of the town. Others from among the Children of Isra'eel disbelieved, and they were the majority of the Jews. Allah supported those who believed in him against those who disbelieved afterward and they became victorious over them and conquered them, as Allah, Most High, says, *And (remember) when Allah said, "O 'Eesa! I will take you and raise you to Myself and clear you (of the forged statement that 'Eesa is Allah's son) of those who disbelieve, and I will make those who follow you (Monotheists, who worship none but Allah) superior to those who disbelieve (in the Oneness of Allah, or disbelieve in some of His Messengers, e.g. Muhammad, 'Eesa, Moosa, etc., or in His Holy Books, e.g. the Tawrah, the Injeel, the Qur'an) till the Day of Resurrection.* (*Soorah Aal 'Imran* 3:55) So those who are closest to the truth will always be victorious over those who are farthest from it. And because the saying of the Muslims about him is the truth, of which there is no doubt, i.e. that he is the slave of Allah and His Messenger, they were victorious against the Christians, who were excessive in their claims regarding him and ascribed to him a status above that which Allah has designated for him.

And because the Christians were closer to the truth regarding him than the Jews – may Allah's Curse be on them – the Christians were victorious over the Jews during the period up to the time of Islam and its followers.

The Story of the Table Spread

Allah, Most High, says, *(Remember) when* **Al-Hawariyyoon** *(the Disciples) said, "O, 'Eesa, son of Maryam! Can your Lord send down to us a table spread (with food) from heaven?" 'Eesa said, "Fear Allah, if you are indeed Believers." They said, "We wish to eat thereof and to be stronger in faith, and to know that you have indeed told us the truth and that we ourselves be its witnesses." 'Eesa, said, "O, Allah, our Lord! Send us from heaven a table spread (with food) that there may be for us – for the first and the last of us – a festival and a sign from You; and provide us sustenance, for You are the Best of sustainers." Allah said, "I am going to send it down unto you, but if anyone of you after that disbelieves, then I will punish him with a punishment such as I have not inflicted on anyone among (all)* **Al-'Alameen.***
(*Soorah Al-Ma'idah* 112-115)

We have already mentioned in the *Tafseer* the traditions reported regarding the descent of *Al-Ma'idah* (the Table Spread) on the authority of 'Abdullah Ibn 'Abbas, Salman Al-Farisi, 'Ammar Ibn Yasir and others from among the *Salaf.* Among those narrations, it was stated that 'Eesa ordered *Al-Hawariyyoon* to fast for thirty days and when they had completed the fast, they requested of 'Eesa ﷺ that a table (spread with food) be sent down from the heaven to them, so that they might eat from it and in order that the faith in their hearts might be strengthened, knowing that Allah had accepted their fast and answered their request, and that they should have an *'Eid* in which they could break their fast and it would be sufficient for the first of them to the last of them, for the wealthy among them and the poor among them. But 'Eesa ﷺ cautioned them against this and feared for them that they would not show gratitude for it, or fulfill the conditions attached to it, but they would not accept from him aught but that he ask this for them from his Lord, the Almighty, the All-Powerful. When they refused to give up this request, he stood up to pray and donned a coarse hair shirt, bowed his head and his eyes filled with tears as he wept and entreated Allah to answer his supplication by granting their request. So Allah sent down to them a table from the heaven. The people saw it descend gradually from between two clouds. It continued to descend by degrees and all the while it was descending, 'Eesa ﷺ was asking his Lord, the Almighty, the All-Powerful to make it a mercy and not an affliction and to make it a (source of) blessing and salvation. It continued to come down until it stood before 'Eesa ﷺ. It was covered with a cloth and so he uncovered it, saying, "In the Name of Allah, the Best of Providers." When it was uncovered, they saw that on it were seven fish and seven loaves. It was also said that there was vinegar and also that there were pomegranates and other fruits. It had a very strong aroma. Allah said to it, "Be!" – and it was. Then 'Eesa ordered them to eat from it. They said, "We will not eat until you eat." He said, "But it was you who asked for it in the first place!" But they refused to eat from it first. So he ordered the poor and needy, the sick and the lame to eat from it. They numbered about one thousand, three hundred and they all ate from it, after which all who were sick, lame or infirm were cured. On seeing the situation of those who had eaten from it, the people regretted not having done likewise. It was said that it then descended once a day and the people would eat from it, the last of them eating as much as the first. It was said that this continued until as many as seven thousand had eaten from it. Then it descended every day, just as the people used to drink from the she-camel of Saleh ﷺ day after day. Then Allah commanded 'Eesa ﷺ to restrict its use to the poor and needy, and not the rich. This upset many people and the hypocrites among them began to gossip about it. This led to the whole table being raised up and those who had spread gossip and tittle-tattle about it were transformed into swine."

And Ibn Abi Hatim and Ibn Jareer both narrated on the authority of 'Ammar Ibn Yasir ◌ from the Prophet ◌ that he said, "The table descended from the heaven with bread and meat and they were commanded not to cheat, hoard the food or keep it for the morrow, but they cheated, hoarded the food and kept it for the morrow and so they were transformed into apes and swine.

Then Ibn Jareer narrated it on the authority of Bundar, who reported on the authority of Ibn Abi 'Adiyy, who in turn reported on the authority of Sa'eed, who likewise reported on the authority of Qatadah, who in turn reported on the authority of Khilas, on the authority of 'Ammar ◌, in a *mawqoof* form. And this is more correct. It was narrated thus by way of Simak, on the authority of a man from Banu 'Ijl, who reported on the authority of 'Ammar ◌, in a *mawqoof* form. And that is the correct view, and Allah knows better.

The narration of Khilas, on the authority of 'Ammar ◌ is *munqati'*.[1] And even if this *Hadith* was authentic in a *marfoo'* form, it would be a decisive criterion in this story, because the scholars have disagreed regarding whether or not the table descended. The majority of scholars hold that it descended, as proven by these traditions and it is also clear from the text of the Qur'an, in particular, His Words: *"I am going to send it down unto you…"* (*Soorah Al-Ma'idah* 5:115), as confirmed by Ibn Jareer At-Tabari. And Allah knows better.

And Ibn Jareer has narrated, with an authentic chain of narrators up to Mujahid and Al-Hasan Ibn Abul-Hasan Al-Basri that they

---

(1)   *Munqati'*: That is, a broken chain.

both said that it did not descend and that they refused its descent when Allah said, *"...but if anyone of you after that disbelieves, then I will punish him with a punishment such as I have not inflicted on anyone among (all)* **Al-'Alameen.***" (Soorah Al-Ma'idah* 5:115), which why it was said that the Christians do not know the story of the Table Spread and why it is not mentioned in their Scripture, although it must have been transmitted by numerous people who witnessed it. And Allah knows better.

Abu Bakr Ibn Abi Ad-Dunya said, "We were informed by a man (whose name is omitted) that he said that Hajjaj Ibn Muhammad was informed by Abu Hilal Muhammad Ibn Sulaiman, who reported on the authority of Bakr Ibn 'Abdullah Al-Muzani that he said, *"Al-Hawarriyyoon* lost their Prophet, 'Eesa ﷺ, and it was said to them, "He has gone to the sea." So they set out in search of him and when they reached the sea, they found him walking on the water, the waves lifting him up and then lowering him again, as they rose and fell. He was wearing a garment, half of which he was using as a lower garment and half of which he was using as an upper garment. He advanced toward them and one of them – Abu Hilal said that he believed he was one of the best of them – said, "Shall I not come to you, Oh, Prophet of Allah?" He said, "Certainly." So he placed one of his feet on the water, then he went to place the other foot, but he said, "O! I am afraid that I will drown, O, Prophet of Allah!" 'Eesa ﷺ said to him, "Give me your hand, Oh, you of little faith! If mankind had as much faith as the equivalent of a single hair, he would be able to walk on water."

This was narrated by Abu Sa'eed Ibn Al-'Arabi, on the authority of Ibraheem Ibn Abil-Jaheem, who reported on the authority of Sulaiman Ibn Harb, who in turn reported on the authority of Abu Hilal, who reported something similar on the authority of Bakr.

Then Ibn Abid-Dunya said, "I was informed by Muhammad Ibn 'Ali Ibn Al-Hasan Ibn Shaqeeq, who said, "I was informed by Ibraheem Ibn Al-Ash'ath, who reported on the authority of Al-Fudail Ibn 'Iyad that he said, "It was said to 'Eesa, the son of Maryam عليها السلام, "O 'Eesa! By what thing do you walk on water?" He said, "By faith and certainty." They said, "We have believed as you have believed and we are certain as you are certain." He said, "Then walk!" So they walked with him on the wave, but they sank. 'Eesa عليه السلام said to them, "What is wrong with you?" They said, "We feared the wave." He said, "Did you not fear the Lord of the wave?" So he took them out and then struck the earth with his hand and took up a handful of it, then he opened his hand and in one of his hands was gold, while in the other was mud or small stones. He asked them, "Which of them is more pleasing to your hearts?" They said, "This gold." He said, "To me, they are equal."

We have mentioned previously in the story of Yahya عليه السلام, son of Zakariyya عليه السلام, on the authority of some of the *Salaf* that 'Eesa عليه السلام used to wear a hair shirt and eat the leaves of the trees and he would not take shelter in a house or with any family and he had no money and he did not store up anything for the morrow. Some of them said that he used to eat from the (earnings of) his mother's spinning (peace be upon them both).

And Ibn 'Asakir narrated on the authority Ash-Sha'bi that he said, "Whenever the Hour was mentioned in the presence of 'Eesa عليه السلام, he would cry out and say, "It is not fitting that the Hour should be mentioned in the presence of the son of Maryam." Then he would be silent.

And it is reported on the authority of 'Abdul Malik Ibn Sa'eed Ibn Abjar that when 'Eesa عليه السلام heard a religious exhortation, he would cry loudly.

It is reported on the authority of 'Abdur-Razzaq that he said,

"Ma'mar informed us that he was told by Ja'afar Ibn Burqan that 'Eesa عليه السلام used to say, "O Allah! I have arrived at a situation where I cannot repel that which I hate and I possess not the ability to acquire what I want. The situation is now in the hands of other than me and I have become pledged to my work, so there is no poor person who is poorer than I. O Allah! Let not my enemy triumph over me and let not my friend be unfortunate because of me. Let me not suffer any affliction in my Religion and let not those who show no mercy or compassion to me gain mastery over me."

Al-Fudail Ibn Iyad reported on the authority of Yoonus Ibn 'Ubaid that he said, "'Eesa عليه السلام used to say, 'No one achieves true faith until he cares not about consuming (the good things in) this world."

Al-Fudail also said, " 'Eesa عليه السلام used to say, 'I thought about the creation and I discovered that He Who was not created is more delightful to me than those who are created'."

Ishaq Ibn Bishr reported on the authority of Hisham Ibn Hassan, who reported on the authority of Al-Hasan that he said, "Verily, 'Eesa عليه السلام will be the head of the ascetics on the Day of Resurrection. He added, "And those who will flee with their sins will be gathered on the Day of Resurrection with 'Eesa عليه السلام."

He said, "One day, while 'Eesa عليه السلام was sleeping on a rock and enjoying his sleep there, Iblees came to him and said, 'O 'Eesa! Do you not claim that you do not desire anything of the material things of this life? Then this rock is one of the material things of this life.' Upon hearing this, 'Eesa عليه السلام took the rock and threw it at him, saying, 'This is for you and the life of this world'."

Mu'tamir Ibn Sulaiman said, " 'Eesa عليه السلام came out to his companions, wearing a woollen cloak, a garment and pants and he was barefoot and weeping. His hair was dishevelled, his skin jaundiced, due to hunger and his lips were dry, due to thirst. He said, "Peace be upon you, Oh, Children of Isra'eel! I am the one who has relegated the life of this world to its true place, by Allah's Permission, without wonder or pride. Do you know where my abode is?" They said, "Where is your abode, oh, Spirit of Allah?" He said, "My abode is the mosques, my perfume is water, my food is hunger, my light is the moon at night, my warmth in the winter is the sun, my sweet basil is the vegetation of the earth, my garments are of wool and my distinguishing characteristic is fear of the Lord of the Might. My companions are the chronically sick and the needy. In the morning, I have nothing and in the evening, I have nothing. But I am in good spirits and have no cares. So who is richer and gets profits more than I? (Narrated by Ibn 'Asakir)

It was narrated in the biography of Muhammad Ibn Al-Waleed Ibn 'Aban Ibn Hibban Abul Hasan Al-'Uqaili Al-Misri that he said, "We were informed by Hani' Ibn Al-Mutawakkil Al-Iskandarani, who reported on the authority of Haiwah Ibn Shuraih that he said, "Al-Waleed Ibn Abil-Waleed informed me on the authority of Shufayy Ibn Mati', who reported on the authority of Abu Hurairah ﷺ from the Prophet ﷺ that he said, "Allah, Most High, revealed to 'Eesa ﷺ, 'O 'Eesa! Move from place to place, so that you are not recognized and subjected to harm, for by My Power and Might, I will give you a thousand *hawra*'[1] as wives and I will surely give you a wedding banquet that will last for four hundred years'." This *Hadith* is *ghareeb*; and it was declared by the narrator to be *marfoo'*. It could be *marfoo'* from the narration of Shufayy Ibn Mati', on the authority of Ka'b Al-Ahbar, or someone else from among the Isra'eelites. And Allah knows better.

Al-Mubarak narrated on the authority of Sufyan Ibn 'Uyainah, who reported on the authority of Khalaf Ibn Hawshab that he said, " 'Eesa ﷺ said to *Al-Hawariyyoon*, 'Just as the kings have left

---

(1) *Hawra'*: Women having eyes with a marked contrast between white and black.

wisdom to you, likewise, leave for them the life of this world'."

said, " 'Eesa ﷺ said, "Ask me, for verily, I am tenderhearted and verily, I am insignificant in my own sight'."

Isma'eel Ibn 'Ayyash reported on the authority of 'Abdullah Ibn Deenar, who reported on the authority of Ibn 'Umar ﷺ that he said, "'Eesa ﷺ said to *Al-Hawariyyoon*, 'Eat barley bread and drink pure water, and depart the world safe and secure. In truth, I say to you that verily, the sweetness of the life of this world is the bitterness of the Hereafter, and the bitterness of the life of this world is the sweetness of the Hereafter. And verily, the slaves of Allah are not those who lead lives of luxury and ease. I truth, I say to you that verily, your evil is like a scholar whose desires affect his knowledge and so he wishes that all of the people were like him. And something like it was narrated on the authority of Abu Hurairah ﷺ.

Abu Mus'ab reported on the authority of Malik that he informed him that 'Eesa ﷺ used to say, "O Children of Isra'eel! It is incumbent on you to drink pure water, eat vegetables, the fruit of the arak tree and barley bread; and beware of wheat bread, because you will not fulfill the gratitude for it."

And Ibn Wahb reported on the authority of Sulaiman Ibn Bilal, who reported on the authority of Yahya Ibn Sa'eed that he said, "'Eesa ﷺ used to say, 'Traverse this world and do not become too comfortable in it.' And he used to say, 'Love of this world is the head of every sin, and looking cultivates desire in the heart'."

Wuhaib Ibn Al-Ward related something similar and he added, "And it may be that desire causes those who have it to inherit long sadness."

And it is reported from 'Eesa ﷺ that he said, "O weak son of Adam! Fear Allah wherever you are and be in this world like a guest. Take the mosques as your abode and teach your eyes to weep, your body to be patient and your heart to contemplate. And do not be preoccupied with tomorrow's sustenance, because it is a sin."

It is also reported from him that he said, "None of you can make a home on a wave of the sea, so do not take this world as an abode."

And regarding this Sabiq Al-Barbari says,

You have houses in Mistan As-Suyool,
And can a house be built on water, whose foundation is mud?

And Sufyan Ath-Thawri said, " 'Eesa ﷺ, the son of Maryam said, 'Love of this world and love of the Hereafter cannot reside together in the heart of a Believer, just as water and fire cannot remain together in a vessel'."

Ibraheem Al-Harbi reported on the authority of Dawood Ibn Rasheed, who reported on the authority of Abu 'Abdullah As-Soofi that he said, " 'Eesa ﷺ said, 'The one who seeks the life of this world is like the one who drinks seawater; the more he drinks, the thirstier he becomes, until it kills him'."

And it is reported from 'Eesa ﷺ that he said, "Verily, Shaitan is with the life of this world, his plot is with wealth, his ability to make evil things seem fair is with desire and his ability to establish himself is with lusts."

Al-A'mash reported on the authority of Khaithamah that he said, " 'Eesa ﷺ used to put food for his companions and he would stand over them and say, 'Thus must you behave toward guests'."

Al-A'mash also narrated that a woman said to 'Eesa ﷺ,

"Blessed be the womb that bore you and the breast that fed you." He said, "Blessed be he who recites the Scripture and pays heed to it."

It was also reported from him that he said, "Blessed be he who weeps when he recalls his sin, guards his tongue and whose abode suffices him."

It was also reported from him that he said, "Blessed be the eye that sleeps and does not speak to itself of sin, but pays attention to that which is not sinful."

And it was reported on the authority of Malik Ibn Deenar that he said, " 'Eesa ﷺ and his companions passed by a corpse and they said, 'How malodorous is its smell!' He said, 'How white are its teeth'!" He said this in order to forbid them from backbiting.

And Abu Bakr Ibn Abi Ad-Dunya said, "Al-Husain Ibn 'Abdir-Rahman related to us on the authority of Zakariyya Ibn 'Adiyy that he said, " 'Eesa ﷺ, said, 'Oh, company of Disciples! Be content with the meanest of this world's provisions, while safeguarding your Religion, as the people of this world are content with the least of Religion, while safeguarding their share of this world's provisions.'

Zakariyya said, and regarding this, the poet said,

"I see men with the least Religion who are content,

But I do not see them content with a life of little provision,

Be satisfied with the Religion over the worldly riches of kings,

As kings are satisfied with their worldly riches over the Religion."

And Abu Mus'ab reported on the authority of Malik that he said, " 'Eesa ﷺ, the son of Maryam said, 'Do not speak excessively about matters other than remembrance of Allah, as it will harden your hearts, for verily, a hard heart is far from Allah, but you know not. And look not at the sins of the slaves, as if you are lords, but instead, look at them as if you are slaves, because the mankind consists of only two types of men: Those who are protected and those who are put to trial. So be compassionate toward those who are put to trial and praise Allah for His Protection.'

And 'Abdullah Ibn Al-Mubarak said, "Sufyan informed us, on the authority of Mansoor, who reported on the authority of Salim Ibn Abul-Ja'd that he said, " 'Eesa ﷺ said, 'Work for Allah and do not work for your stomachs. Look at this bird, how it eats and goes away and it neither tills the soil nor harvests, yet Allah provides it with sustenance. So if you say, 'We have larger stomachs than this bird…', then look at these animals, such as cows and donkeys, for they eat and then go away and they neither till the soil nor harvest, yet Allah provides them with sustenance.'

And Safwan Ibn 'Amr said, "It was reported on the authority of Shuraih Ibn 'Ubaid, who reported on the authority of Yazeed Ibn Maisarah that he said, "*Al-Hawariyyoon* said to the Maseeh ﷺ, "O Maseeh of Allah! Look at the Mosque of Allah, how fine it is! He said, *Ameen, Ameen!* In truth, I say to you, Allah will not leave a single stone of this Mosque standing; He will destroy it because of the sins of its people. Verily, Allah does not do anything because of the gold, silver and stone that so impress you. Verily, righteous hearts are more beloved by Allah than these things. Because of them (the hearts of mankind), Allah makes the earth and because of them, He destroys it, if they are not righteous."

Al-Hafiz Abul-Qasim Ibn 'Asakir reported in his *Tareekh* on the authority of 'Abdullah Ibn 'Abbas ﷺ that he said, " 'Eesa ﷺ passed by a ruined city and the buildings impressed him, so he said, "O my Lord! Command this city to answer me." So Allah revealed to the city, "O you ruined city! Answer 'Eesa!" The city called out, "O 'Eesa, my beloved! What do you want of me?" He said, "What happened to your trees, your rivers and your palaces? And where are your inhabitants?" It replied, "My beloved! The true Promise of your Lord was fulfilled and my trees became dry, my rivers dried up, my palaces were destroyed and my inhabitants died." 'Eesa ﷺ asked, "So where is their wealth?" The city replied, "They gathered it together, including the lawful and the unlawful and placed it in my belly (i.e. they buried it); to Allah belongs the inheritance of the heavens and the Earth." So 'Eesa ﷺ called out, "I am amazed at three persons: **(i)** the one who seeks the life of this world, while death is seeking him, **(ii)** the builder of palaces, when the grave will be his abode and **(iii)** the one who laughs in a loud voice, while the Fire lies before him. Son of Adam, you are not sated by much (wealth), nor are you content with little. You gather your wealth for those who do not praise you and you go to a Lord who will not pardon you. You are no more than a slave of your stomach and your desire. Your stomach will only be filled (i.e. with Fire) when you enter your grave. And you, O son of Adam, will see the piling up of your wealth in the scale of another."

This *Hadith* is very strange, but there is a good admonition in it, which is why we have included it.

Sufyan Ath-Thawri reported on the authority of his father, who reported on the authority of Ibraheem At-Taimi that he said, "'Eesa ﷺ said, "O company of Disciples! Make your treasure in the heaven, because the heart of a man is where he has stored it."

And Thawr Ibn Yazeed reported on the authority of 'Abdul-'Azeez Ibn Zibyan that he said, " 'Eesa ﷺ, the son of Maryam, said, Whoever learned and taught and acted (upon his learning), he will be called great in the Kingdom of Heaven."

And Abu Kuraib said, "It was narrated that 'Eesa ﷺ said,

'There is no goodness in knowledge that does not cross the valley with you, but instead the caller carries you across'."

And Ibn 'Asakir narrated with a chain of narrators that is *ghareeb*, on the authority of 'Abdullah Ibn 'Abbas ﷺ in a *marfoo'* form that 'Eesa ﷺ stood before the Children of Isra'eel and said, "O company of Disciples! Do not speak of the underlying wisdoms (in religious matters) to people who are not qualified to understand them (i.e. the ignorant folk), for you may do injustice thereby to them (the underlying wisdoms) and do not withhold them from those who are qualified to understand them (i.e. the religious scholars), for you will thereby do injustice to them (the scholars). (Religious) matters may be divided into three categories: **(i)** a matter, the integrity of which and the logic behind which is apparent, **(ii)** a matter, the sin and error of which is clear and **(iii)** a matter which is unclear to you; such matters you should refer to Allah, the Almighty, the All-Powerful."

And 'Abdur-Razzaq said, "We were informed by Ma'mar, on the authority of a man who reported on the authority of 'Ikrimah that he said, 'Eesa ﷺ said, 'Do not cast pearls to swine, because swine will not do anything with pearls. And do not give wisdom to one who does not desire it, for wisdom is better than pearls, and those who do not desire it are worse than swine'."

Wahb and others related something similar from him, namely, that he said to his companions, "You are the salt of the earth, so if you go bad, there will be no cure for you; verily, there are two traits of ignorance in you: laughing at things that are not remarkable and early morning without wakefulness."

And that it was said to him, "Who is the worst of people in causing discord and dissent?" He said, "It is the scholar who commits mistakes, for when the scholar errs, many err with him."

It was also reported from him that he said, "O scholars of evil!

You have placed the world above your heads and the Hereafter beneath your feet. Your words are a cure and your deeds are a medicine. Your likeness is as the likeness of an oleander tree: it impresses those who look upon it, but it kills those who eat of it."

And Wahb said, 'Eesa ﷺ said, "O scholars of evil! You have sat at the gates of Paradise, but you will not enter it and you do not call the needy to enter it; verily the wickedest of people with Allah is a scholar who seeks the life of this world through his knowledge."

And Makhool said, "Yahya ﷺ and 'Eesa ﷺ met and 'Eesa ﷺ shook Yahya's hand; he was laughing and Yahya ﷺ said to him, "O son of my aunt! Why do I see you laughing, as if you have been saved?" 'Eesa ﷺ replied, "Why do I see you frowning, as if you have despaired?" So Allah revealed to them both: "The most beloved of you two to Me is the one who is friendliest toward the other."

And Wahb ibn Munabbih said, "'Eesa stood with his companions near a grave, as its occupant was being lowered into it. They began to discuss the grave and its narrowness, and he said, "You were in a place narrower than it: your mothers' wombs. If Allah likes to widen it, He will do so."

And Abu 'Umar Ad-Dareer said, "Whenever 'Eesa ﷺ thought about death, his skin would drip blood."

A Description of 'Eesa's

Ascension to the Heaven, to the Protection of His Lord and Exposition of the Lies of the Jews and Christians, Who Claimed That He Was Crucified

Allah, Most High, says, ❴ And they (the disbelievers) plotted (to kill 'Eesa), but Allah planned too. And Allah is the Best of planners. And (remember) when Allah said, "O, 'Eesa! I will take you and raise you to Myself and clear you (of the forged statement that 'Eesa is Allah's son) of those who disbelieve, and I will make those who follow you (Monotheists, who worship none but Allah) superior to those who disbelieve (in the Oneness of Allah, or disbelieve in some of His Messengers, e.g. Muhammad, 'Eesa, Moosa, etc., or in His Holy Books, e.g. the Tawrah, the

Injeel, the Qur'an) till the Day of Resurrection. Then you will return to Me and I will judge between you in the matters in which you used to dispute." ﴾ (*Soorah Al 'Imran* 3:54,55)

And He, Most High, says, ﴿ Because of their breaking the covenant, and of their rejecting the *Ayat* of Allah, and of their killing of the Prophets unjustly, and of their saying: "Our hearts are wrapped (with coverings, i.e. we do not understand what the Messengers say)" – nay, Allah has set a seal upon their hearts because of their disbelief, so they believe not but a little. And because of their (the Jews') disbelief and uttering against Maryam a grave false charge (that she has committed illegal sexual intercourse); and because of their saying (in boast): "We killed the Messiah, 'Eesa ('Eesa), son of Maryam, the Messenger of Allah," - but they killed him not, nor crucified him, but the resemblance of 'Eesa ('Eesa) was put over another man (and they killed that man), and those who differ therein are full of doubts. They have no (certain) knowledge, they follow nothing but conjecture. For surely, they killed him not (i.e. 'Eesa, son of Maryam). But Allah raised him ('Eesa) up (with his body and soul) unto Himself (and he is in the heavens). And Allah is All-powerful, Most Wise. And there is none of the people of the Scripture (Jews and Christians), but must believe in him ('Eesa, son of Maryam, as only a Messenger of Allah and a human being]), before his ('Eesa's ['Eesa'] or a Jew's or a Christian's death (at the time of the appearance of the Angel of Death). And on the Day of Resurrection, he ('Eesa) will be a witness against them ﴾ (*Soorah An-Nisa'* 4:155-159). Allah, Most High, informs us that He raised him up to the heaven after He had caused him to sleep, according to what has been authentically and decisively reported, saving him from those Jews who wished to harm him and complained of him to one of the disbelieving rulers of that time.

Al-Hasan Al-Basri and Muhammad Ibn shaq said that his

name was Dawood Ibn Yoora and he ordered that 'Eesa ﷺ be killed and crucified. They surrounded him in an abode in Bait Al-Maqdis on a Friday evening/Saturday night. [1] When the time for them to enter came, Allah cast his likeness onto the face of one his companions who was present with him, and He raised 'Eesa ﷺ from the skylight of that house to the heaven, while the people of the house looked on. They entered and found that young man upon whom Allah had cast his likeness. They took him, thinking that he was 'Eesa ﷺ and crucified him. They placed thorns on his head, in order to humiliate him. Most of the Christians, who had not witnessed what happened to 'Eesa ﷺ, accepted the Jews' claim that they had crucified him and because of that, they went far astray. Allah, Most High, informs us in His Words: ❨ And there is none of the people of the Scripture (Jews and Christians), but must believe in him ('Eesa, son of Maryam, as only a Messenger of Allah and a human being), before his ('Eesa's or a Jew's or a Christian's death) at the time of the appearance of the Angel of Death) ❩ (*Soorah An-Nisa'* 4:159). That is, after his descent to the earth at the end of time, before the Day of Resurrection. At that time, he will descend and kill the pigs and break the crosses; he will abrogate the *jizyah* and he will accept naught but Islam (i.e. submission to Allah, Alone, without partners), as we have made clear in the *ahadeeth* accompanying the explanation of this Noble Qur'anic Verse in *Soorah An-Nisa'*. And we shall relate this in detail in the Book of Trials and Battles, in the information pertaining to *Al-Maseeh Ad-Dajjal*; and we shall also mention what has been related regarding the descent of *Al-Maseeh Al-Mahdi* ﷺ from the Owner of Power (Allah), to kill *Al-Maseeh Ad-Dajjal*, the liar, who will call to misguidance and error.

And Ibn Abi Hatim narrated on the authority of 'Abdullah ibn 'Abbas ﷺ that he said, "When Allah intended to raise 'Eesa ﷺ

---

(1)   In Semitic societies, the day ends at sunset and the night is considered part of the next day.

up to the heaven, he came out to visit his companions and in the house he found twelve men, including *Al-Hawariyyoon*, i.e. he came out to them from an opening in the house and his head was dripping with water. He said, "Among you is the one who will deny me twelve times, after having believed in me." Then he said, "Which of you will have my likeness cast upon him and be killed in my place, then he will be with me in my rank (in Paradise)?" On hearing this, a youth, who was among the youngest of them, stood up; but 'Eesa صلى said to him, "Sit down." Then he repeated his request to them, and the young man stood up again, but he said to him once more, "Sit down." Then he repeated his request to them for a third time and the young man stood up again and said, "I." 'Eesa صلى then said, "Let it be you." And so 'Eesa's likeness was cast upon him and 'Eesa صلى was raised up from a skylight in the house to the heaven. The pursuers from among the Jews arrived and they took the young man and killed him. Then they crucified him and one of them rejected him (i.e. 'Eesa صلى) twelve times, after having believed in him. They split into three groups; one of them said, "Allah was among us for as long as He willed, then He ascended to the heaven." These were the Jacobites. A second group said, "The son of Allah was among us for as long as he willed, then Allah raised him up to Him." These were the Nestorians. The third group said, "Allah's slave and His Messenger was among us for as long as He (Allah) willed and then Allah raised him up to Him." These are the Muslims. But the two disbelieving groups prevailed over the Muslim group and they killed them. After that, Islam remained completely effaced until Allah sent Muhammad ﷺ." 'Abdullah ibn 'Abbas ﷺ said, "And that is the meaning of Allah's Words: ﴿ So We gave power to those who believed against their enemies, and they became the uppermost. ﴾ (*Soorah As-Saff* 61:14) [1] This chain of narrators is authentic up to 'Abdullah ibn 'Abbas ﷺ, according to the

---

(1) Narrated by At-Tabari in *Jami'ul-Bayan* (26400) in the explanation of *Soorah As-Saff*.

conditions for acceptance stipulated by Muslim.

Ibn Ishaq said, "Among them there was another man, whose name was (Sergius) and he was concealed by the Christians; it was he on whom the appearance of 'Eesa ﷺ was placed and he was crucified in his place." He said, "Some of the Christians claim that the one who was crucified in place of Maseeh ﷺ and on whom his likeness was cast Yoodus Zakariyya Yoota Judas Iscariot – and Allah knows better."

Al-Hasan Al-Basri said, "The age of 'Eesa ﷺ on the day when he was raised up to the heaven was thirty-four years." And in the *hadeeth* it was stated that: "The people of Paradise will enter it wearing shabby clothes and hairless, wearing kohl on their eyes, and they will be aged thirty-three years." [1] In another *hadeeth*: "….on the birthday of 'Eesa ﷺ and with the good looks of Yoosuf ﷺ." [2]

As for the *hadeeth* narrated by Al-Hakim in his *Mustadrak*, in which it is stated that 'A'ishah (may Allah be Pleased with her) used to say, "Fatimah informed me that the Messenger of Allah ﷺ told her that: "There was no Prophet who was succeeded by another Prophet except that the Prophet who came after him lived for half of his lifespan." He also informed her that: " 'Eesa, the son of Maryam, lived for a hundred and twenty years, so I do not think that I will live beyond sixty years." [3] This is the wording of Al-Fasawi and it is *ghareeb*.

(1) This *hadeeth* is *hasan* and it was narrated by At-Tirmidhi (2545) and Ahmad (21601), on the authority of Mu'az ibn Jabal ﷺ.

(2) Narrated by At-Tabarani in *Al-Mu'jam ul-Kabeer* (20/256, No. 604). Al-Haithami said in *Al-Majma'* (10/334), "Narrated by At-Tabarani; and in its chain is one Yazeed ibn Sinan: Abu Farwah Ar-Rahawi, and he is weak."

(3) Narrated by Al-Fasawi in *Al-Ma'rifah Wat-Tareekh* (3/316) and Ibn 'Asakir in *Tareekh Dimashq* (14/87), by way of Al-Hakim. It was declared *ghareeb* by the author.

Al-Hafiz Ibn 'Asakir said, "The truth is that 'Eesa ﷺ did not attain this age. Sufyan ibn 'Uyainah narrated on the authority of 'Amr Ibn Deenar, who reported on the authority of Yahya Ibn Ja'dah that Fatimah said, "The Messenger of Allah ﷺ said to me, " 'Eesa, the son of Maryam, remained among the Children of Isra'eel for forty years." [1] But this is *munqati'*. Jareer and Ath-Thawri reported on the authority of Al-A'mash that Ibraheem said, " 'Eesa remained among his people for forty years." And it is narrated on the authority of the Commander of the Faithful, 'Ali ﷺ that 'Eesa ﷺ was raised up on the night of the twenty-second of Ramadan; and on the same night, 'Ali died, five days after being stabbed." [2]

A Description of 'Eesa ﷺ*, His Character and His Virtues*

Allah, Most High, says, ﴾ 'Eesa, son of Maryam, was no more than a Messenger; many were the Messengers that passed away before him. His mother (Maryam) was a *Siddiqah* (i.e. she believed in the Words of Allah and His Books [see Verse 66:12]) ﴿ (*Soorah Al-Ma'idah* 5:75)

It was said that he was named Al-Maseeh (the Messiah) because of his *mash* of the earth, i.e. his traveling in it and his flight with his Religion from the trials of that time caused by the Jews' denial of him and the lies they invented against him and his mother (peace be upon them both). It was also said that he was

---

(1)   Narrated by ibn 'Asakir in *Tareekh Dimashq* (14/88); the author said, "It is *munqati'*." (literally broken, i.e. a chain of narrators that is disconnected at any point).

(2)   The *takhreej* of this narration has already been given.

called Al-Maseeh because his feet were anointed.

Allah, Most High, says, ❪ And in their footsteps, We sent 'Eesa ('Eesa), son of Maryam, confirming the *Tawrah* that had come before him, and We gave him the *Injeel* (Gospel), in which was guidance and light ❫ (*Soorah Al-Ma'idah* 5:46). And He, Most High, says, ❪ And indeed, We gave Moosa the Book and followed him up with a succession of Messengers. And We gave 'Eesa ('Eesa), the son of Maryam, clear signs and supported him with *Rooh ul-Quds* (Jibra'eel). ❫ (*Soorah Al-Baqarah* 2:87). And the Verses regarding this are extremely numerous. We have mentioned previously the *hadeeth* confirmed in the *Saheehain*: "There is no child born except that Shaitan stabs its side when it is delivered, causing it to cry out. The only exceptions to this are Maryam and her son; he went to stab him, but the stab struck a barrier protecting him." [1]

We have already related the *hadeeth* of 'Umair ibn Hani', on the authority of Junadah, who reported on the authority of 'Ubadah ⬥, who reported from the Messenger of Allah ﷺ that he said, "Whoever bore witness that '*La Ilaha ill-Allahu Wahdahu la Shareeka Lahu wa Anna Muhammadan 'Abduhu wa Rasooluhu wa Anna 'Eesa 'Abdullahi wa Rasooluhu wa Kalimatuhul-Latee Alqaha Ila Maryama wa Roohun Minhu wal-Jannatu Haqqun, wan-None haqqun* (who testify that none has the right to be worshipped except Allah, Alone, without partners and Muhammad is His slave and His Messenger, and 'Eesa is Allah's slave and His Messenger and His Word, which He cast into Maryam and a Spirit from Him, and that Paradise is true, and the Fire is true),' Allah will admit him to Paradise, according to his deeds." (Narrated by Al-Bukhari (and this is his wording) and Muslim. [2]

And Al-Bukhari and Muslim narrated on the authority of Abu

---

(1)   The *takhreej* of this *hadeeth* has already been given.

(2)   The *takhreej* of this *hadeeth* has already been given.

Moosa ﷺ that he said, "The Messenger of Allah ﷺ said, 'If a person teaches his slave girl good manners, educates her properly, and then manumits and marries her, he will get a double reward. And if a man believes in 'Eesa and then believes in me, he will get a double reward. And if a slave fears his Lord (i.e. Allah) and obeys his masters, he too will get a double reward.' [1]

And 'Abdullah ibn 'Umar ﷺ said, "The Prophet mentioned Al-Maseeh Ad-Dajjal in front of the people saying, Allah is not one-eyed while Al-Maseeh Ad-Dajjal is blind in the right eye and his eye looks like a bulging grape. While sleeping near the *Ka'bah* last night, I saw in my dream a man of brown color, the best one can see amongst brown color and his hair was so long that it fell between his shoulders. His hair was lank and water was dribbling from his head and he was placing his hands on the shoulders of two men while circumambulating the *Ka'bah*. I asked, "Who is this?" They replied, "This is 'Eesa, son of Maryam." Behind him I saw a man who had very curly hair and was blind in the right eye, resembling Ibn Qatan (a pagan Arab) in appearance. He was placing his hands on the shoulders of a person while performing *tawaf* around the *Ka'bah*. I asked, "Who is this?" They replied, "Al-Maseeh Ad-Dajjal." [2]

And it is reported on the authority of 'Abdullah ibn 'Abbas ﷺ that he said, "The Messenger of Allah ﷺ said, "You will be gathered barefoot, naked and uncircumcised." He then recited: ﴿ …as We began the first creation, We shall repeat it, (it is) a promise binding upon Us. Truly, We shall do it. ﴾ (*Soorah Al-Anbiya'* 21:104) He added, "The first to be dressed on the Day of Resurrection, will be Ibraheem, and some of my companions will be taken toward the left side (i.e. to the Hellfire), and I will say, "My Companions! My Companions!" It will be said, "They

---

(1)   Narrated by Al-Bukhari (3446) and Muslim (154).

(2)   Narrated by Al-Bukhari (3440).

reneged against Islam after you left them." Then I will say as the pious slave of Allah (i.e. 'Eesa) said: ﴿ "And I was a witness over them while I dwelt amongst them, but when You took me up, You were the Watcher over them, and You are a Witness to all things. (This is a great admonition and warning to the Christians of the whole world). If You punish them, they are Your slaves, and if You forgive them, verily, You, only You are the Almighty, the Most Wise." ﴾ (*Soorah Al-Ma'idah* 5:117,118) [1]

And Al-Bukhari narrated on the authority of Abu Hurairah ﷺ from the Prophet ﷺ that he said, "None spoke in cradle but three: (The first was) 'Eesa, (the second was) a man from Banu Isra'eel called Juraij. While he was offering his prayers, his mother came and called him. He said (to himself), "Shall I answer her or keep on praying?" (He went on praying) and did not answer her, his mother said, "O, Allah! Do not let him die till he sees the faces of prostitutes." So while he was in his hermitage, a lady came and sought to seduce him, but he refused. So she went to a shepherd and presented herself to him to commit illegal sexual intercourse with her and then later she gave birth to a child and claimed that it belonged to Juraij. The people therefore came to him and dismantled his hermitage and expelled him out of it and abused him. Juraij performed the ablution and offered prayer, and then came to the child and said, "O, child! Who is your father?" The child replied, "The shepherd." (After hearing this) the people said, "We shall rebuild your hermitage of gold," but he said, "No, of nothing but mud." (The third was the hero of the following story:) A lady from Banu Isra'eel was nursing her child at her breast when a handsome rider passed by her. She said, "O, Allah ! Make my child like him." On that, the child left her breast, and facing the rider said, "O, Allah! Do not make me like him." The child then started to suck her breast again. (Abu Hurairah ﷺ further said, it is as if I were now looking at the Prophet ﷺ

---

(1)   Narrated by Al-Bukhari (3447).

sucking his finger [by way of demonstration].") After a while the people passed by, with a slave girl and she (i.e. the child's mother) said, "O, Allah! Do not make my child like this (slave girl)!" On that, the child left her breast and said, "O, Allah! Make me like her." When she asked why, the child replied, "The rider is one of the tyrants while this slave girl is falsely accused of theft and illegal sexual intercourse." [1]

And Al-Bukhari narrated on the authority of Abu Hurairah ﷺ that he said, "I heard the Messenger of Allah ﷺ say, "I am the nearest of all the people to the son of Maryam, and all the Prophets are paternal brothers, and there has been no Prophet between me and him (i.e. 'Eesa)." [2]

And it is reported on the authority of Abu Hurairah ﷺ from the Prophet ﷺ that he said, "The Prophets are paternal brothers; their Religion is one, but their mothers are different. I am the nearest of all the people to 'Eesa, son of Maryam, because there was no Prophet between me and him and he will descend, so if you see him acknowledge him, for he is a well-built man, whose complexion is somewhere between red and white. He will descend while wearing two long, light yellow garments. His head appears to be dripping water, even though no moisture touched it. He will break the cross, kill the pig, and abolish the *jizyah* and will call the people to Islam. During his time, Allah will destroy all religions except Islam and Allah will destroy Al-Maseeh Ad-Dajjal. Safety will then fill the earth, so much so that the lions will mingle with camels, tigers with cattle and wolves with sheep. Children will play with snakes, and they will not harm them. 'Eesa ('Eesa) will remain for forty years and then he will die and the Muslims will offer the funeral prayer over him and bury him." [3]

---

(1)   Narrated by Al-Bukhari (3436) and Muslim (2550).

(2)   Narrated by Al-Bukhari (3442).

(3)   This is an authentic *hadeeth* narrated by Imam Ahmad (9349).

And Hisham ibn 'Urwah narrated on the authority of Saleh, the freed slave of Abu Hurairah ﷺ that the Messenger of Allah ﷺ said, "He will remain in the world for forty years." [1] And details of his descent at the end of time will be given later, insha'Allah, in the *Book of Battles*; we have also explained it in the *Tafseer*, in the explanation of the Words of Allah, Most High, in *Soorah An-Nisa'*: ❴ And there is none of the people of the Scripture (Jews and Christians), but must believe in him ('Eesa, son of Maryam, as only a Messenger of Allah and a human being), before his ('Eesa's or a Jew's or a Christian's) death (at the time of the appearance of the Angel of Death). And on the Day of Resurrection, he ('Eesa) will be a witness against them." ❵ (*Soorah An-Nisa'* 4:159) and His Words: ❴ And he ('Eesa, son of Maryam) shall be a known sign for (the coming of) the Hour (Day of Resurrection) (i.e. 'Eesa's descent to the earth) ❵ (*Soorah Az-Zukhruf* 43:61) and we have explained how he will descend on the White Minaret in Damascus, after the *iqamah* for the *Fajr* prayer will be called, and the *Imam* of the Muslims will say to him, "Advance, O, Spirit of Allah!" But he will reply, "No. Some amongst you are commanders over others. This is the honor from Allah for this *Ummah* (Nation).

---

(1)   This is an authentic *hadeeth* narrated by Imam Ahmad (9017).

The Differing of the Companions of Al-Maseeh عَلَيْهِ السَّلَام (the Messiah)

The companions of Maseeh (the Messiah) disagreed after he had been raised up to the heaven, holding a number of divergent opinions, according to 'Abdullah ibn 'Abbas رَضِيَ اللَّهُ عَنْهُ and others among the *Imams* of the *Salaf*, as we have related in the explanation of the Words of Allah, Most High: ﴿ So We gave power to those who believed against their enemies, and they became the uppermost. ﴾ (*Soorah As-Saff* 61:14). 'Abdullah ibn 'Abbas رَضِيَ اللَّهُ عَنْهُ and others said that some of them said, "His slave and His Messenger was among us, then Allah raised him up to the heaven." Others said, "He is

Allah." Still others said, "He is the son of Allah." [1] But it is the first that is the truth, and the other two sayings are terrible disbelief, as He, Most High, says, ﴾ Then the sects differed (i.e. the Christians about 'Eesa), so woe unto the disbelievers (those who gave false witness by saying that 'Eesa is the son of Allah) from the meeting of a great Day (i.e. the Day of Resurrection, when they will be thrown in the blazing Fire). ﴿ (*Soorah Maryam* 19:37). They also disagreed regarding the transmission of the Gospels, holding four conflicting views in the matter, ranging from exaggeration to understatement and from distortion to alteration. Then three hundred years after Maseeh عليه السلام, the Great Calamity occurred and the four Patriarchs and all of the bishops, the priests, the deacons and the monks differed regarding the Maseeh عليه السلام, holding opinions too numerous to be defined and determined. They held a council and sought judgment from Emperor Constantine, the founder of Constantinople. This was the first council, and the emperor supported the view of the largest sect, who were agreed on one of those opinions. They were known as Melkites. The emperor also refuted the opinions of others and declared them to be apostates. Those who claimed that 'Eesa عليه السلام was a slave from among the slaves of Allah and a Messenger from among His Messengers were isolated and so they settled in the deserts and wildernesses. There they built hermitages, monasteries and religious retreats. They contented themselves with abstemious lives and they did not mix with those other sects. The Melkites built huge churches. They took the buildings erected by the Greeks and altered their *mahareeb* [2] from their original direction, which was toward the North Star, so that they faced toward the east.

Description of the Building of Baitlaham (Bethlehem) and Al-Qumamah

---

(1) See the explanation of this Verse in *Tafseer At-Tabari*.

(2) *Mahareeb*: Prayer niches (sing. *mihrab*).

Emperor Constantine built Bethlehem at the location of the birth of the Maseeh and his mother made Hailanah Al-Qumamah, that is, over the grave of the crucified one, and they accepted the claim of the Jews, that it was the Maseeh 🕮. In fact, both of them were guilty of disbelief. They fabricated laws and religious rulings, including some that contradicted the Tawrah, and they declared lawful things that were unlawful, according to the text of the Tawrah, such as swine flesh. They prayed toward the east, though the Maseeh 🕮 did not pray toward anything except the rock of Bait Al-Maqdis, and all of the Prophets after Moosa 🕮 did likewise. Muhammad 🕮, the Seal of the Prophets prayed toward it after his migration to Al-Madinah, for sixteen or seventeen months. Then he changed the direction of his prayer toward the *Ka'bah*, which was built by Ibraheem, *Al-Khaleel* 🕮. [1] They put images in the churches, and there had been no images in them prior to that. They corrupted the beliefs which are maintained by their children and their men and their womenfolk, and they call this a trust, but in fact, it is the greatest disbelief and betrayal. All of the Melkites and Nestorians are the followers of Nestorius, the organizers of the second council. The Jacobites are the followers of Jacob Baradaeus, the organizers of the third council. They share the same creed, but they differ in their elucidation of it. Here I will describe it – and the one who describes disbelief is not a disbeliever – in order to reveal the weakness of their arguments, the depth of their disbelief and the stupidity which leads the one who proclaims it to the blazing Fire; and they say, "We believe in One God, the Master of all, the Creator of the heavens and the earth – all that is seen and all that is unseen – and (we believe) in one Lord, 'Eesa, the Maseeh, the only begotten son of God, born of the Father, before time, light of light, the God of Truth, from the God of Truth, born not created, equal to the Father in essence, who existed for the sake of us, mankind and in order to save us, he descended from the heaven and took on human

---

(1)   See: *Saheeh Muslim* (525).

form from the Holy Spirit and from the Virgin Maryam, the God Incarnate, who was crucified during the reign of Mulatis, the Nabatean. He suffered and was buried and then he arose on the third day, as is reported in the Scriptures. Then he ascended to the heaven and sat on the right of the Lord. And also he will come in his physical body to order the affairs of the living and the dead. His Kingdom is eternal. And (we believe in) the Holy Spirit, the Life-giving Lord, who proceeded from the Father, with the Father. And (we believe in) the son, before whom all prostrate. And he acknowledged his right to be worshipped, due to his having died for our sins, according to People of the Scriptures.

The Book of the Stories of the People of the Past

We refer to those from the Children of Isra'eel and others up to the end of their time period, excluding the times of the Arabs and their *Jahiliyyah* (Days of Ignorance). We shall present that after we complete this section, if Allah, Most High, wills. He, Most High, says, ❴ Thus We relate to you (O, Muhammad) some information of what happened before. And indeed We have given you from Us a Reminder (this Qur'an). ❵ (*Soorah Ta Ha* 20:99). And He, Most High, says, ❴ We relate unto you (O, Muhammad) the best of stories through Our Revelations unto you, of this Qur'an. And before this (i.e. before the coming of Divine Inspiration to you), you were among those who knew nothing about it (the Qur'an). ❵ (*Soorah Yoosuf* 12:3)

The Story of Dhul-Qarnain

Allah, Most High, says, ❨ And they ask you about Dhul-Qarnain. Say, "I shall recite to you something of his story." Verily, We established him in the earth, and We gave him the means of everything. So he followed a way. Until, when he reached the setting place of the sun, he found it setting in a spring that was *hami'ah*. And he found near it a people. We (Allah) said (by inspiration), "O, Dhul-Qarnain! Either you punish them, or treat them with kindness." He said, "As for him (a disbeliever in the Oneness of Allah) who does wrong, we shall punish him; and then he will be brought back unto his Lord, Who will punish him with a terrible torment (Hell). But as for him who believes (in Allah's Oneness) and works righteousness, he shall have the best reward, (Paradise), and we (Dhul-Qarnain) shall speak unto him mild words (as instructions)." Then he followed another way, until, when he came to the rising place of the sun, he found it rising on a people for whom We (Allah) had provided no shelter against the sun. So (it was)! And We knew all about him (Dhul-Qarnain). Then he followed (another) way, until, when he reached between two mountains, he found, before (near) them (those two mountains), a people who scarcely understood a word. They said, "O, *Dhul-Qarnain*! Verily! (Ya'jooj and Ma'jooj) are doing great mischief in the land. Shall we then pay you a tribute in order that you might erect a barrier between us and them?" He said, "That (wealth, authority and power) in which my Lord had established me is better (than your tribute). So help me with strength (of men), I will erect between you and them a barrier. Give me pieces (blocks) of iron." Then, when he filled up the gap between the two mountain cliffs, he said, "Blow," till when he made it (red as) fire, he said, "Bring me molten copper to pour over it." So they (Ya'jooj and Ma'jooj) were made powerless to scale it or dig through it. (Dhul Qarnain) said, "This is a Mercy from my Lord, but when the Promise of my Lord comes, He will level it down to the ground. And the Promise of my Lord is ever true." 》 (*Soorah Al-Kahf* 18:83-98). Allah, Most High, mentions Dhul-Qarnain and He praises him for his justice and tells how he traveled to the East and to the West and achieved dominion over vast provinces and territories and subdued their inhabitants. He traveled among them dispensing perfect justice and authority confirmed (by Allah), victorious, all-conquering and just. The truth is that he was one of the just kings. It was also said that he was a Prophet and that he was a Messenger. The strongest claim is that he was one of the angels. This was related from the Commander of the Faithful, 'Umar ibn Al-Khattab ﷺ. He heard a man saying to another, "O, Dhul-Qarnain!" On this, he said, "Be silent! Is it not sufficient for you to take the names of the Prophets, but instead you adopt the names of the angels?" This was narrated by As-Suhaili.

And Wakee' narrated on the authority of Isra'eel, who reported on the authority of Jabir, who in turn reported on the authority of Mujahid, who likewise reported on the authority of 'Abdullah ibn 'Amr ﷺ that he said, "Dhul-Qarnain was a Prophet." And Al-Hafiz ibn 'Asakir narrated on the authority of Abu Hurairah ﷺ that he said, "The Messenger of Allah ﷺ said, "I do not know whether Tubba' was a cursed one or not. And, I do not know whether *hudood* (the prescribed penalties) are expiatory for their people or not. And, I do not know whether Dhul-Qarnain was a Prophet or not." [1] From this source, this narration is *ghareeb*.

Scholars have disagreed regarding his name; Az-Zubair ibn Bakkar narrated on the authority of 'Abdullah ibn 'Abbas ﷺ that his name was 'Abdullah ibn Ad-Dahhak ibn Ma'add. And it was said that his name was Mus'ab ibn 'Abdullah ibn Qinan ibn Mansoor ibn 'Abdullah ibn Al-Azad ibn Ghawth ibn Nabt ibn Malik ibn Zaid ibn Kahlan ibn Saba' ibn Qahtan.

---

(1)   Narrated by Ibn 'Asakir in *Tareekh Dimashq* (17/337). It was declared *ghareeb* by the author.

And it has been narrated in a *hadeeth* [1] that he was from Himyar and that his mother was a Roman woman and that he was known as the "Philosopher", because of his intellect. One of the Himyarites composed a poem expressing pride in the fact that he was one of their ancestors; he said:

Dhul-Qarnain my ancestor, was a Muslim,

A king to whom the kings submitted and gathered,

He traveled to the East and to the West,

Seeking to fulfill the Commands of a Wise Guide,

He saw the disappearance of the sun when it set,

In a muddy, black pool of water,

After him came Bilqees and she was my aunt,

She ruled them until the hoopoe came to her.

Regarding the Words of Allah, Most High: ❨And they ask you about Dhul-Qarnain❩ (*Soorah Al-Kahf* 18:83) the reason for them was because Quraish asked the Jews for something with which to test the knowledge of the Messenger of Allah ﷺ and they said to them, "Ask him about a man whoever traveled throughout the Earth and about some young men whose deeds no one knows." So Allah, Most High, revealed the story of the inhabitants of the cave and the story of Dhul-Qarnain; this is why He says, ❨Say, "I shall recite to you something of his story." ❩ (*Soorah Al-Kahf* 18:83). That is, useful and sufficient information in explanation of his affairs and description of his situation. He says, ❨Verily, We established him in the earth and We gave him the means of everything❩ (*Soorah Al-Kahf* 18:84). That is, We made broad his kingdom in the lands and We gave him the tools with which to achieve his great goals and his grand designs. And it is reported on the authority of Habeeb Ibn Hammad that he said, "I was with 'Ali ibn Abi Talib when a man asked him about Dhul-Qarnain

---

(1)   Narrated by Ibn 'Asakir in *Tareekh Dimashq* (7/332).

and how he reached the East and the west, and he said to him, "Allah subjugated the clouds to him and all necessary means were extended to him, and He extended the light for him." Then he said to him. "Shall I tell you more?" But the man remained silent and so 'Ali ﷺ also remained silent.

And it is reported on the authority of Al-Hasan that he said, "Dhul-Qarnain was a king who lived after Nimrod and it is told that he was a righteous Muslim who traveled to the East and to the West. Allah extended his life for him and supported him, so that he subdued the lands, amassed great wealth, conquered the cities and killed (many) men. He roamed throughout the lands and found great citadels. He journeyed on until he reached the farthest points of east and west, which is why Allah says, ❨ And they ask you about Dhul-Qarnain. Say, "I shall recite to you something of his story." ❩ (*Soorah Al-Kahf* 18:83). That is, information (about him). ❨ Verily, We established him in the earth, and We gave him the means of everything ❩ (*Soorah Al-Kahf* 18:84). That is, knowledge with which to find the ways to camping places. ❨ ...and We gave him the means of everything ❩ (*Soorah Al-Kahf* 18:84). That is, knowledge. Qatadah and Matar Al-Warraq said that it means knowledge of the different parts and features of the earth.

And He, Most High, says, ❨ So he followed a way ❩ (*Soorah Al-Kahf* 18:85). ❨ Until, when he reached the setting place of the sun... ❩ (*Soorah Al-Kahf* 18:86). That is, in the earth; he reached a place where no one could proceed further and he stopped on the shore of the western ocean, which is known as Oceanus and in which lie the islands known as *Al-Khalidat*, which are at the beginning of the lines of longitude, according to one of two opinions held by scholars of geography; the second opinion is that they are on the coast of this sea, as we mentioned previously. There he witnessed the setting of the sun, i.e. he followed a route until he reached the furthest point that could be reached in the direction of the sun's setting, which is the west of the Earth. ❨ ... he found it setting in a spring that was *hami'ah* ❩ (*Soorah Al-Kahf* 18:86). What is meant by it is the sea, i.e. he saw the sun as if it were setting in the ocean. This is something which everyone who goes to the coast can see: it looks as if the sun is setting into the sea but in fact it never leaves its path, in which it is fixed. This is why Allah says, ❨ he found ❩ (*Soorah Al-Kahf* 18:86), i.e. it appeared to him and He does not say: "it was setting in a spring that was *hami'ah*, i.e. muddy. Ka'b Al-Ahbar said, "It is black mud." Some recited it as "*hamiyah*", i.e. boiling. This was due to the fierceness of the sun's light and its rays.

A Description of Dhul-Qarnain's Quest For the Spring of Life

Allah, Most High, says, ❨ We (Allah) said (by inspiration), "O, *Dhul-Qarnain*! Either you punish them, or treat them with kindness." He said, "As for him (a disbeliever in the Oneness of Allah) who does wrong, we shall punish him; and then he will be brought back unto his Lord, Who will punish him with a terrible torment (Hell)." ❩ (*Soorah Al-Kahf* 18:86-87). That is, the punishments of this world and the Hereafter will be combined on him. He began with the punishment of this world, because it is a greater deterrent to the disbelievers. ❨ "But as for him who believes (in Allah's Oneness) and works righteousness, he shall have the best reward, (Paradise), and we (*Dhul Qarnain*) shall speak unto him mild words (as instructions)." ❩ (*Soorah Al-Kahf* 18:88). And He began with the most important thing and that is the reward of the Hereafter and He bestowed His Favor on him, and that was justice, knowledge and faith. Allah, Most High, says, ﴾ So he followed a way ﴿ (*Soorah Al-Kahf* 18:85). That is, he followed a path, returning from the West to the East; and it was said that his return spanned twelve years. ﴾ Until, when he came to the rising place of the sun, he found it rising on a people for whom We (Allah) had provided no shelter against the sun ﴿ (*Soorah Al-Kahf* 18:90) That is, they had no houses or shelters to protect them from the heat of the sun. Many of the scholars said, "But when the heat of the sun was intense, they sought refuge in burrows in the ground which they had made, and which resembled graves. Allah, Most High, says, ﴾ So (it was)! And We knew all about him (*Dhul-Qarnain*) ﴿ (*Soorah Al-Kahf* 18:91). That is, We know what he was following and We protected him and preserved him during his travels. All of this was from the West of the land to the east of it.

And He, Most High, says, ﴾ Then he followed (another) way, until, when he reached between two mountains, he found, before (near) them (those two mountains), a people who scarcely understood a word. ﴿ (*Soorah Al-Kahf* 18:92) That is, they did not understand his language because of their isolation from other peoples. It was said that they were the Turks, the sons of Ya'jooj and Ma'jooj's paternal uncle (i.e. their cousins). They informed him that these two tribes had committed acts of aggression against them, spread corruption throughout their land and practiced highway robbery and they paid him a tribute in return for which they asked him to make a barrier which would prevent these two tribes from reaching them. He refused to accept the tribute, being content with the great wealth that Allah had given him. ﴾ He said, "That (wealth, authority and power) in which my Lord had established me is better (than your tribute)." ﴿ (*Soorah Al-Kahf* 18:95). Then he requested that they gather for him men and materials, in order that he might build a barrier between them and their enemies. That barrier took the form of a dam between two mountains which was the only route by which Ya'jooj and

Ma'jooj could attack them. The rest of it was taken up by vast seas and towering mountains. So he built it, as Allah says, from iron and molten copper. It was said that the Arabic word '*qitr*' used in the Verse means lead, but the first interpretation is the correct one. Instead of bricks, he used iron and instead of mud, he used copper. This is why Allah, Most High, says, ❰ So they (Ya'jooj and Ma'jooj) were made powerless to scale it ❱ (*Soorah Al-Kahf* 18:97). That is, they could not climb it with ladders or anything else. ❰ ...or dig through it ❱ (*Soorah Al-Kahf* 18:97). That is, with pickaxes or other digging implements. So He has compared the easiest thing with the easiest thing and the most difficult with the most difficult. ❰ He (*Dhul-Qarnain*) said, "This is a Mercy from my Lord." ❱ (*Soorah Al-Kahf* 18:98). That is, Allah has ordained the barrier's existence in order for it to be a Mercy for His slaves, that it might prevent their enemies from reaching them via that route. ❰ "...but when the Promise of my Lord comes..." ❱ (*Soorah Al-Kahf* 18:98). That is, the time when He has ordained that they shall sally forth against the people at the end of time. ❰ He will level it down to the ground ❱ (*Soorah Al-Kahf* 18:98). That is, He will flatten it; and there is no escaping this event, which is why He says, ❰ "And the Promise of my Lord is ever true." ❱ (*Soorah Al-Kahf* 18:98). This is like His Saying: ❰ Until, when Ya'jooj and Ma'jooj are let loose (from their barrier) and they swiftly swarm from every mound. And the true promise (Day of Resurrection) shall draw near (of fulfillment). Then, (when the mankind is resurrected from their graves), you shall see the eyes of the disbelievers fixedly staring in horror. (They will say), "Woe to us! We were indeed heedless of this; nay, but we were *zalimoon*." ❱ (*Soorah Al-Anbiya*'21:96-97). This is why He says here (in *Soorah Al-Kahf*), ❰ And on that day (i.e. the day when Ya'jooj and Ma'jooj will come out), We shall leave them to surge like waves on one another ❱ (*Soorah Al-Kahf* 18:99). That is, the day when the barrier will be breached, according to the authentic *hadeeth*. ❰ ...and the Trumpet will be blown, and We shall collect them all together ⟫ (*Soorah Al-Kahf* 18:99)

Mention of the Nations of Ya'jooj and Ma'jooj, a Description of Them, What Has Been Related Regarding Them and a Description

It is reported on the authority of Abu Sa'eed Al-Khudri ﷺ that the Messenger of Allah ﷺ said, "Allah, Most High, will say, on the Day of Resurrection, "O, Adam!" Adam will reply, "*Labbaik wa Sa'daik*, and all the good is in Your Hand." Allah will say, "Bring out the people of the fire." Adam will say, "O, Allah! How many are the people of the Fire?" Allah will reply, "From every one thousand, take out nine-hundred and ninety-nine." At that time children will become hoary headed ﴾ and every pregnant woman will drop her load, and you shall see mankind as in a drunken state, yet they will not be drunken, but severe will be the Torment of Allah. ﴿ (*Soorah Al-Hajj* 22:2)." The Companions of the Prophet ﷺ asked, "O, Messenger of Allah! Who is that (excepted) one?" He said, "Rejoice with glad tidings; one person will be from you and one thousand will be from Ya'jooj and Ma'jooj." [1]

In another narration, the Prophet ﷺ said, "Rejoice with glad tidings, for among you there are two nations (i.e. Ya'jooj and Ma'jooj), wherever they go, they defeat the people through strength of numbers." [2]

This proves that their numbers are great and that they outnumber the mankind by many times. They are from the progeny of Nooh ﷺ, because Allah, Most High, informs us that He answered the

---

[1] Narrated by Al-Bukhari (3348) and Muslim (222).

[2] It was narrated by At-Tirmidhi and it is authentic (3169) and An-Nasa'i in *Al-Kubra* (11340).

supplication of His slave, Nooh ﷺ against the people of the Earth, in His Words: ﴿ And Nooh said, "My Lord! Leave not one of the disbelievers on the earth!" ﴾ (*Soorah Nooh* 71:26) and He said ﴿Then we saved him and those with him in this ship﴾ and His statement ﴿And, his progeny, them we made the survivors﴾

As for the claim that Ya'jooj and Ma'jooj were created when Adam ﷺ had a nocturnal emission and his sperm became mixed with the earth and that this resulted in their creation and they are not descended from Eve, this was related by Shaikh Abu Zakariyya An-Nawawi in his explanation of *Saheeh Muslim* and others, but they declared it to be weak – and it is only fitting that it should be so deemed, since there is no evidence for it. Indeed, it contradicts what we have mentioned, which is that all of the people today are descended from Nooh ﷺ, according to the text of the Qur'an.

If it was said, how does the *hadeeth* in the S*aheehain* prove that they are the ransom of the Believers on the Day of Resurrection and that they will be in the Fire, though no Messenger was sent to them and Allah has said, ﴿ And We never punish until We have sent a Messenger (to give warning) ﴾ (*Soorah Al-Isra'* 17:15)' the answer is that they will not be punished until the evidence has been established against them and they have been given a chance to offer their excuses, as Allah, Most High, says, ﴿ And We never punish until We have sent a Messenger (to give warning) ﴾ (*Soorah Al-Isra'* 17:15). So if they lived during the time before the sending of Muhammad ﷺ, then it means that Messengers from among them came to them, in which case, the evidence has been established against them. But if Allah had not sent Messengers to them, then they will fall under the ruling of the people of the *Fatrah* [1] and those whom the call (to Islam) did

---

(1)   The people of the *Fatrah*: According to the Permanent Committee for Research and Religious Verdicts in Saudi Arabia, "As for the one that the call (to Islam) did not reach, then he will be tested on the Day of Resurrec-

not reach. And the *hadeeth* which has been reported from sources on the authority of a number of the Companions ﴾ from the Messenger of Allah ﷺ: "Verily, those who are thus will be tested in the fields of the Resurrection and whoever answered the caller (to Islam) will enter Paradise, while those who refused will enter the Fire." We have recorded the *hadeeth* with its various chains and different wordings and the opinions of the *Imams* regarding it in our *Tafseer*, in the explanation of Allah's Saying: ﴾ And We never punish until We have sent a Messenger (to give warning) ﴿ (*Soorah Al-Isra'* 17:15). It was related by Shaikh Abul-Hasan Al-Ash'ari that there was a consensus (among the scholars) of *AhlAs-Sunnah wal-Jama'ah* regarding this. Their being tested does not necessarily mean that they will be saved, nor does it contradict the information regarding them which states that they are the inhabitants of the Fire, because Allah informs His Messenger ﷺ of what He wills from the knowledge of the unseen, and He has informed him that these people are from among the wretched and that their characteristics prevent them from accepting the truth and acting upon it, so they do not accept the preaching of the caller (to Islam) until the Day of Resurrection. So it is known from this that they are the worst rejecters of the truth in this world, even when it comes to them therein, because in the fields of the Resurrection, some of those who rejected guidance in the life of this world will be guided, for there is even greater reason to believe there, because of the terrors that will be seen (on that Day), than in the life of this world – and Allah knows better – as He, Most High, says, ﴾ And if you only could see when the *mujrimoon* (criminals, disbelievers, polytheists, sinners, etc.) shall hang their heads before their Lord (saying), "Our Lord! We have now seen and heard, so send us back (to the world), we will do righteous good deeds. Verily, we now believe with certainty." ﴿ (*Soorah As-Sajdah* 32:12). And

---

tion according to what has been authentically reported from the *Sunnah* of the Messenger of Allah ﷺ."

He says, ❲ How clearly will they (the polytheists and disbelievers in the Oneness of Allah) see and hear on the Day when they will appear before Us! ❳ (*Soorah Maryam* 19:38). As for the *hadeeth* in which it is stated that the Messenger of Allah ﷺ called them (to Islam) on the night of *Al-Isra'* and that they did not accept his call, it is *munkar*; [1] indeed, it is fabricated, and the person who fabricated it was 'Amr Ibn As-Subh.

As for the barrier, we have mentioned previously that *Dhul-Qarnain* built it from iron and copper and he closed off the path between the towering mountains thereby; and no mightier construction on the face of the Earth is known, nor any more beneficial one to mankind in their earthly life. Al-Bukhari narrated that a man said to the Prophet ﷺ, "I saw the barrier." The Prophet ﷺ asked, "How did you find it (i.e. what was it like)?" The man said, "I found it (i.e. it looked) like *al-burd ul-muhabbar* (a striped cloak)." The Prophet ﷺ said, "You have seen it." This is how Al-Bukhari reported it, in a *mu'allaq* form and in an apocopate form. [2] But I have not seen it with a connected chain of narrators which is acceptable to me, although Ibn Jareer narrated it in his *Tafseer* in a *mursal* form. He said, "Bishr informed us that Yazeed told him, "I was told by Sa'eed, who reported on the authority of Qatadah that he said, "It was mentioned to us that a man said, "O, Messenger of Allah! I have seen the barrier of Ya'jooj and Ma'jooj." The Prophet ﷺ said, "Describe it to me." He said, "It was like *al-burd ul-muhabbar* (a striped cloak), with black and red stripes." On hearing this, the Prophet ﷺ said, "You have seen it." [3]

And if it was asked, then how can we reconcile the Saying of

---

(1) *Munkar*: A narration which contains something that is contrary to what has been authentically reported.

(2) Narrated by Al-Bukhari (3381).

(3) Narrated by ibn Jareer in his *Tafseer* (16/23).

Allah, Most High: ❲ So they (Ya'jooj and Ma'jooj) were made powerless to scale it or dig through it ❳ (*Soorah Al-Kahf* 18:97) and the *hadeeth* narrated by Al-Bukhari on the authority of Zainab Bint Jahsh, the Mother of the Believers (may Allah be Pleased with her), who said, "The Messenger of Allah ﷺ awoke from sleep with a red face and he was saying: There is no god but Allah; there is a destruction in store for the Arabs because of the turmoil which is near at hand as the barrier of Ya'jooj and Ma'jooj has been opened like this," and he (in order to explain it) made a ring with the help of his thumb and forefinger. I said, "O, Messenger of Allah, would we be destroyed even though there are pious people amongst us?" The Prophet ﷺ said, "Yes, when evil predominates." [1]' The answer is: As for the opinion of those who hold that this is an indication of the opening of the gates of evil and trials and that this is simply a metaphor, there is no ambiguity. And as for the opinion of those who consider it to be information about a tangible thing, as appears obvious, then there is also no ambiguity, because His Saying: ❲ So they (Ya'jooj and Ma'jooj) were made powerless to scale it or dig through it ❳ (*Soorah Al-Kahf* 18:97), i.e. in that time, because this wording is in the past tense and so it does not negate the possibility that they might do so in the future, if Allah permits them to penetrate it by degrees, until the appointed time is reached and the (Divine) Ordainment is concluded and they emerge, as Allah, Most High, says, ❲ And they swiftly swarm from every mound ❳ (*Soorah Al-Anbiya'* 21:96). But another *hadeeth* is more detailed than this, and it is that which was narrated by Imam Ahmad in his *Musnad* on the authority of Abu Hurairah ﷺ, who reported from the Messenger of Allah ﷺ that he said, "Ya'jooj and Ma'jooj will excavate the barrier every day until, when they begin to see the rays of the sun, their leader will say, "Return, and you will dig it tomorrow." So they will return to it and when they come back, they will find that the

---

(1)   Narrated by Al-Bukhari (3346) and Muslim (2880).

barrier has become stronger than it was before. This will continue until their time comes and Allah wishes to send them forth. They will dig until they begin to see sunlight, then the one who is in charge of them will say, "Go back; you can carry on digging tomorrow, if Allah wills." In this case, he will make an exception by saying "if Allah wills," thus relating the matter to the Will of Allah. They will return on the following day and find the hole exactly as they left it. They will carry on digging and come out against the people. They will drink all the water, and find the hole exactly as they left it and the people will entrench themselves in their fortresses. Ya'jooj and Ma'jooj will fire their arrows into the sky, and they will fall back to earth with something like blood on them. Ya'jooj and Ma'jooj will say, "We have defeated the people of earth, and overcome the people of Heaven." Then Allah will send a kind of worm in the napes of their necks, and they will be killed by it... "By Him in Whose Hand is the soul of Muhammad, the beasts of the earth will become fat after grazing on their flesh and their blood." [1] So we are informed in this *hadeeth* that: "they (Ya'jooj and Ma'jooj) will excavate the barrier every day until, when they begin to see the rays of the sun," this is due to the thinness of the barrier. Now if it is authentic, it can be understood to mean that this work of theirs will be at the end of time, when their emergence is near, or the meaning of His Words: ﴾ ...or dig through it ﴿ (*Soorah Al-Kahf* 18:97) could be that they have made a small hole in it, and that does not negate the possibility that they dig it, but do not penetrate it. And Allah knows better.

Based on this, it is possible to reconcile this *hadeeth* with what has been recorded in the *Saheehain*, on the authority of Abu Hurairah ﷺ: "...the barrier of (Ya'jooj and Ma'jooj) has been opened like this." That is, a hole has been opened in it. And Allah knows better.

---

[1]   This is an authentic *hadeeth* narrated by Imam Ahmad (10254).

The Story of the Companions of the Cave

Allah, Most High, says, ❰ Do you think that the People of the Cave and the inscription (the news or the names of the People of the Cave) were a wonder among Our Signs? (Remember) when the young men fled for refuge (from their disbelieving folk) to the cave, they said, "Our Lord! Bestow on us mercy from Yourself and facilitate for us our affair in the right way!" Therefore We covered up their (sense of) hearing (causing them to go into a deep sleep) in the cave for a number of years. Then We raised them up (from their sleep), that We might test which of the two parties was best at calculating the time period that they had tarried. We narrate unto you (O, Muhammad) their story with truth: Truly, they were young men who believed in their Lord (Allah) and We increased them in guidance. And We made their hearts firm and strong (with the light of faith in Allah and bestowed upon them patience to bear the separation of their kith and kin and dwellings, etc.) when they stood up and said, "Our Lord is the Lord of the heavens and the Earth, never shall we call upon any *ilah* (god) other than Him; if we did, we should indeed have uttered an enormity in disbelief. These our people have taken for worship *alihah* (gods) other than Him (Allah). Why do they not bring for them a clear authority? And who does more wrong than he who invents a lie against Allah." (The young men said to one another,) "And when you withdraw from them and that which they worship, except Allah, then seek refuge in the cave, your Lord will open a way for you from His Mercy and will make easy for you your affair (i.e. will give you what you will need of provision, dwelling, etc.)." And you might have seen the sun when it rose, declining to the right from their Cave, and when it set, turning away from them to the left, while they lay in the midst of the cave. That is (one) of the *Ayat* (proofs, evidences, signs) of Allah. He whom Allah guides is rightly guided; but he whom He sends astray, for him you will find no *waliyy* (guiding friend) to lead him (to the right Path). And you would have thought them awake, while they were asleep. And We turned them on their right and on their left sides, and their dog stretching forth his two forelegs at the entrance (of the cave or in the space near to the entrance of the cave [as a guard at the gate]). Had you looked at them, you would certainly have turned back from them in flight, and would certainly have been filled with awe of them. Likewise, We awakened them (from their long deep sleep) that they might question one another. A speaker from among them said: "How long have you stayed (here)?" They said, "We have stayed (perhaps) a day or part of a day." They said, "Your Lord (Alone) knows best how long you have stayed (here). So send one of you with this silver coin of yours to the town, and let him find out which is the good lawful food and bring some of that to you. And let him be careful and let no man know of you. For if they come to know of you, they will stone you (to death or abuse and harm you) or turn you back to their religion, and in that case you will never be successful." And thus We made their case known to the people, that they might know that the Promise of Allah is true, and that there can be no doubt about the Hour. (Remember) when they (the people of the city) disputed among themselves about their case, they said, "Construct a building over them, their Lord knows best about them," (then) those who won their point said (most probably the disbelievers), "We verily shall build a *masjid* over them." (Some) say they were three, the dog being the fourth among them; (others) say they were five, the dog being the sixth, guessing at the unseen; (yet others) say they were seven, the dog being the eighth. Say (O, Muhammad), "My Lord knows best their number; none knows them but a few." So debate not (about their number, etc.) except with the clear proof (which We have revealed to you). And consult not any of them (people of the Scripture, Jews and Christians) about (the affair of) the people of the cave. And never say of anything, "I shall do such and such thing tomorrow," except (with the saying): "If Allah wills!" And remember your Lord when you forget and say, "It may be that my Lord guides me unto a nearer way of truth than this." And they stayed in their cave three hundred years, and add nine. Say, "Allah knows best how long they stayed. With Him is the unseen of the heavens and the Earth. How clearly He sees, and hears (everything)! They have no *waliyy* (helper, disposer of affairs, protector, etc.) other than He, and He makes none to share in His Decision and His Rule." 》 (*Soorah Al-Kahf* 18:9-26)

The reason for the sending down of the story of the Companions of the Cave and the information regarding Dhul-Qarnain was, according to what has been reported by Muhammad Ibn Ishaq in his *Seerah* and by others was that Quraish sent a message to the Jews, asking them about matters with which they might test the Messenger of Allah ﷺ and questions that they might ask him, in order to see what his answer might be. The Jews said, "Ask him about people who went out in the past and it is not known what they did. And ask him about a man who traveled throughout the Earth. And (ask him) about the Spirit." So Allah, Most High, revealed: ◀ And they ask you (O, Muhammad) concerning the *Rooh* (the Spirit) 》 (*Soorah Al-Isra'* 17:85) and: ◀ And they ask you about Dhul-Qarnain 》 (*Soorah Al-Kahf* 18:83). [1] And here He says, ◀ Do you think that the people of the cave and the Inscription (the news or the names of the people of the cave) were a wonder among Our Signs? 》 (*Soorah Al-Kahf* 18:9). That is, it is not a great wonder, compared with the information that We have conveyed to you, the clear Signs and the strange wonders. And the Arabic word '*kahf*' means a cavern in a mountain.

It is apparent from the context that their people were polytheists,

---

[1]   See: Ibn Hisham's *Seerah* (2/141).

who worshipped idols. Many of the scholars of *tafseer*, historians and others said that they lived during the era of a king whose name was Daqyanoos (Dacianus) and they were the sons of leading members of society. It was also said that they were the sons of kings. It happened that they gathered on a day that was a religious holiday for their people and they saw their people occupied in prostration to their idols and glorification of their graven images. They looked with discerning eyes and Allah removed the veil of ignorance from their hearts and inspired them with guidance, so they knew that their people were not following guidance and they abandoned their religion and instead worshipped Allah, Alone, without partners. It was said that when Allah inspired each one of them with belief in His Oneness (*Tawheed*), they withdrew from the people. These young men gathered in one place, as confirmed by the *hadeeth* in *Saheeh Al-Bukhari*: "The spirits are massed armies. Those of them that knew one another are friendly. Those that did not know one another disagree." [1] So each of them asked the other about his situation and his circumstances and they informed one another about their own individual conditions. They agreed to withdraw from their people, to wash their hands of them and to flee with their Religion from them – and this is what has been legislated in times of trial and tribulation and the appearance of evil. Allah, Most High, says, ❨ We narrate unto you (O, Muhammad) their story with truth: Truly! They were young men who believed in their Lord (Allah) and We increased them in guidance. And We made their hearts firm and strong (with the light of faith in Allah and bestowed upon them patience to bear the separation of their kith and kin and dwellings, etc.) when they stood up and said, "Our Lord is the Lord of the heavens and the Earth, never shall we call upon any *ilah* (god) other than Him; if we did, we should indeed have uttered an enormity in disbelief. These our people have taken for worship *alihah* (gods) other than

---

(1) Narrated by Al-Bukhari in a *mu'allaq* form in the chapter: "Stories of the Prophets".

Him (Allah). Why do they not bring for them a clear authority?" 〗 (*Soorah Al-Kahf* 18:13-15). That is, a clear evidence for what they are following. ≪ "These our people have taken for worship *alihah* (gods) other than Him (Allah). Why do they not bring for them a clear authority? And who does more wrong than he who invents a lie against Allah. (The young men said to one another,) "And when you withdraw from them and that which they worship, except Allah…" 〗 (*Soorah Al-Kahf* 18:15,16). That is, when you abandon their religion and wash your hands of the idols that they worship besides Allah. This was because they used to associate partners with Allah, as *Al-Khaleel* said, ≪ "Verily, I am innocent of what you worship, except Him (i.e. I worship none but Allah Alone) Who did create me, and verily, He will guide me." 〗 (*Soorah Az-Zukhruf* 43:26,27). Likewise, one of these young men said, "Since you have withdrawn from your people in your religion, remove yourselves physically from their midst, in order to avoid them bringing their evil to you." ≪ "…then seek refuge in the cave, your Lord will open a way for you from His Mercy and will make your affair easy for you (i.e. will give you what you will need of provision, dwelling, etc.)." 〗 (*Soorah Al-Kahf* 18:16). That is, He will cause a veil to descend over you and you will be under His Protection and He will make your end to be good, as stated in the *hadeeth*: "O, Allah! Make the end of all of our affairs us from the humiliation of this world and the punishment of the Hereafter." [1] Then Allah, Most High, describes the cave in which they sought refuge and how its entrance faces toward the north and its interior faced toward the *qiblah*. And that was the most beneficial place, with its interior facing toward the *qiblah* and its entrance facing north. He says, ≪ And you might have seen the sun, when it rose, declining 〗 (*Soorah Al-Kahf* 18:17). The Arabic word (زَوَازَتَ) was also recited (زَوْزَتَ) ≪ to the right from their cave, and when it set,

---

(1) Narrated by Imam Ahmad (4/81, No. 17176) on the authority of Bishr ibn Arta't ﷺ and he said in *Al-Majma'*, One of the *asaneed* of At-Tabarani; (they are) reliable.

turning away from them to the left ⟫ (*Soorah Al-Kahf* 18:17). So He informs us that the sun, i.e. during the summer time or close to it, when it first rose, appeared to those in the cave on the western side of it, then it gradually departed from it. And that is the meaning of its declining toward the right. Then it rose into the sky and departed from the doorway of the cave. Then when it began to set, it entered it little by little from the eastern side, until the time when it set, as may be seen from a similar position. And the wisdom behind the sun's entering at different times is so that the air therein did not become spoiled. ⟪ …while they lay in the midst of the cave. That is (one) of the *Ayat* \of Allah ⟫ (*Soorah Al-Kahf* 18:17). That is, their remaining in this situation for a period lasting many years, during which they did not eat or drink and their bodies did not receive any form of nourishment is one of Allah's *Ayat* and a proof of His Great Omnipotence. ⟪ He whom Allah guides is rightly guided; but he whom He increases in error, for him you will find no *waliyy* (guiding friend) to lead him (to the right Path). And you would have thought them awake, while they were asleep ⟫ (*Soorah Al-Kahf* 18:17,18). Some of the scholars said that this was because their eyes remained open, so that they would not become decayed by being closed for an extended period of time. ⟪ And We turned them on their right and on their left sides ⟫ (*Soorah Al-Kahf* 18:18). It was said that every year they were turned once from one side to the other. It is also possible that they were turned more often than that. And Allah knows better. ⟪ …and their dog stretching forth his two forelegs at the entrance ⟫ (*Soorah Al-Kahf* 18:18). Shu'aib Al-Jaba'i said that the name of their dog was Humran. Others said that the word '*al-waseed*' used in the Verse means the entrance to the cave. What is meant is that the dog that was with them when they withdrew from their people remained with them, but it did not enter the cave with them; instead, it lay down at the cave's entrance and placed its front paws at the threshold. It was his nature and habit to lie down at their door as if guarding them. It was sitting outside the door, because the angels do not enter a house in which there is a dog, as was reported in an authentic *hadeeth*, nor do they enter a house in which there is an image, a person in a state of ritual impurity or a disbeliever, as was narrated in the *hadeeth* that has been graded *hasan*. The blessing they enjoyed extended to their dog, so the sleep that overtook them overtook it too. This is the benefit of accompanying good people, and so this dog attained fame and stature. It was said that it was the hunting dog of one of the people which is the more appropriate view, or that it was the dog of the king's cook, who shared their religious views, and brought his dog with him. And Allah knows better. Much has been related regarding this dog, but most of it was obtained from *Isra'eeliyyat* and most of it is lies and of no benefit, such as their dispute regarding its name and its color.

But Allah has related what is most beneficial regarding their situation and what is most important concerning their affair, and He has described their situation so that it is as if the listener was witnessing and the one who was informed saw the cave as it was described and their situation therein, and how they turned from side to side and how their dog lay with its paws stretched out at the threshold. Allah says, ﴾ Had you looked at them, you would certainly have turned back from them in flight ﴿ (*Soorah Al-Kahf* 18:18). That is, because Allah had made them appear dreadful, so that no one could look at them without being filled with terror, because of the frightening appearance they had been given. This was so that no one would come near them or touch them until the appointed time when their sleep would come to an end as Allah willed, because of the wisdom, clear proof and great mercy involved in that. It is possible that the address in His Words: ﴾ Had you looked at them... ﴿ is to mankind in general and not only to the Messenger of Allah ﷺ, as in His Words: ﴾ Then what (or who) causes you to deny the Recompense (i.e. Day of Resurrection)? ﴿ (*Soorah At-Teen* 95:7). That is, O, mankind. And this is because it is the nature of mankind to flee from the sight of terrifying things in most cases, which is why He says, ❨ Had you looked at them, you would certainly have turned back from them in flight ❩ (*Soorah Al-Kahf* 18:18). This proves that hearing about something is not the same as seeing it, as stated in the *hadeeth*, [1] because the information has been given, but the flight and fear has not occurred. Then Allah informed us that He awakened them from their slumber, after they had slept for three hundred and nine years. And when they awoke, they asked one another, ❨ "How long have you stayed (here)?" They said, "We have stayed (perhaps) a day or part of a day." They said, "Your Lord (Alone) knows best how long you have stayed (here). So send one of you with this silver coin of yours to the town." ❩ (*Soorah Al-Kahf* 18:19). That is, take these *dirhams* of yours, i.e. that you have with you, to the city. It was said that the name of the city was Dafsoos. ❨ "... and let him find out which is the good, lawful food." ❩ (*Soorah Al-Kahf* 18:19). *Azka* means purest. ❨ and bring some of that to you ❩ (*Soorah Al-Kahf* 18:19). That is, some of that food, that you may eat of it. They said this because of their asceticism and their piety. ❨ And let him be careful ❩ (*Soorah Al-Kahf* 18:19). That is, when he enters the city. ❨ and let no man know of you, for if they come to know of you, they will stone you (to death or abuse and harm you) or turn you back to their religion, and in that case you will never be successful." ❩ (*Soorah Al-Kahf* 18:19,20). That is, if you return to their religion after Allah had saved you from it. And all of this is because of their belief that they had slept for a day or part of a day, or more than that, and they did not realise that they had slept for more than three hundred years and that the states and countries and those who ruled them had completely changed, and that the generation among whom they had lived had gone and been replaced by others, who had likewise gone and been replaced by others. And when one of them – whose name, it was said, was

---

(1)   This is an authentic *hadeeth* narrated by Imam Ahmad in his *Musnad* (2/315, 371) and *Al-Ihsan* (6213).

Teedhoosis – set out, he arrived at the city in disguise, so that none of his people should recognize him, based on his belief (that they had only slept for a short while). The country had changed beyond recognition and the inhabitants he met did not recognize him. It was said that he fled from them and it was also said that rather, he informed them about himself and his companions and what had befallen them. The people then went with them, in order that he might show them their place. When they approached the cave, he entered it and went to his brothers and informed them of their true situation and of the length of time they had slept. When he told them, they realized that this had been ordained for them by Allah through His Omnipotence. It was said that they continued to sleep and it was also said that rather, they died after that. As for the people of the city, it was said that they were not guided to their place in the cave and that Allah kept their situation secret from them. It was also said that they were unable to physically enter it and that they were in fear of them.

They differed regarding their case and some of them said: ﴿ "Construct a building over them..." ﴾ (*Soorah Al-Kahf* 18:21). That is, seal up the doorway of the cave over them, so that they may not exit from it, or so that no harm may reach them. Others – and it was their opinion that was implemented – said, ﴿ "We verily shall build a *masjid* over them." ﴾ (*Soorah Al-Kahf* 18:21). That is, a place of worship, so that it might become a blessed place for those righteous people who live around it. This was something well-known to those who came before us. But in our religious law, according to what has been confirmed in the *Saheehain* from the Messenger of Allah ﷺ: "May Allah curse the Jews and Christians for they built the places of worship at the graves of their Prophets." [1] He was warning his Companions ﷺ against doing

---

(1) Narrated by Al-Bukhari (436) and Muslim (531) on the authority of 'A'ishah and 'Abdullah ibn 'Abbas (may Allah be Pleased with them both).

what they had done. As for His Words: ❨ And thus We made their case known to the people, that they might know that the Promise of Allah is true, and that there can be no doubt about the Hour ❩ (*Soorah Al-Kahf* 18:21). That is, We revealed their circumstances to the people. Many of the scholars of *tafseer* said that it means that the people might know that the Promise is true and that there can be no doubt of the Hour, when they knew that these people had slept for more than three hundred years and then woke up as they were before, without any change in them, because He Who caused them to remain as they were is Able to return their bodies, even though they had been eaten by worms and to give life to the dead, even though their bodies and their bones had crumbled. And this is something which the Believers do not doubt. ❨ Verily! Our Word unto a thing when We intend it, is only that We say unto it, "Be!" and it is ❩ (*Soorah An-Nahl* 16:40). It is also possible that the pronoun in His Words: ❨ that they might know ❩ (*Soorah Al-Kahf* 18:21) refers to the Companions of the Cave, because their knowledge of this was deeper and more profound than that of others. It is also possible that it refers to everyone. And Allah knows better. Then He, Most High, says, ❨ (Some) say they were three, the dog being the fourth among them; (others) say they were five, the dog being the sixth, guessing at the unseen; (yet others) say they were seven, the dog being the eighth ❩ (*Soorah Al-Kahf* 18:22). Allah mentions the dispute among the people regarding their number and He relates three sayings. He declares the first two to be weak and He confirms the third and this proves that it is the truth. Since, if there were other opinions, He would have related them. And if this third saying was not the correct one, He would have declared it to be weak. So this proves what we have said. And since there is no avail in disputes such as these and no benefit in them, Allah guided His Prophet ﷺ to the correct behavior in such cases in which the people dispute, telling him to say, "Allah knows better." And this is why He says, ❨ Say (O, Muhammad), "My Lord knows best their number." ❩ (*Soorah*

Al-Kahf 18:22) and He says, ❲ "...none knows them but a few."
❳ (*Soorah Al-Kahf* 18:22). That is, of mankind. ❲ So debate not
(about their number, etc.) except with the clear proof (which We
have revealed to you) ❳ (*Soorah Al-Kahf* 18:22). That is, gently
and politely and do not become engaged in arguments in cases
such as these or seek pronouncements from any person. This is
why Allah, Most High, left their number unclear at the beginning
of the story, saying, ❲ They were young men who believed in
their Lord (Allah) ❳ (*Soorah Al-Kahf* 18:13). And if there was
any great benefit in specifying their number, the Knower of the
unseen and the seen would have mentioned it. And He, Most
High, says, ❲ And never say of anything, "I shall do such and
such thing tomorrow," except (with the saying), "if Allah wills!"
And remember your Lord when you forget and say, "It may be
that my Lord guides me unto a nearer way of truth than this." ❳
(*Soorah Al-Kahf* 18:23,24)

This is a great etiquette to which Allah, Most High, has guided
him and which He has encouraged His creation to follow; and that
is, that if a person says, "I will do such-and-such in the future," it
is legislated that he should not do so without adding, "...if Allah
wills," so that he will achieve his objective, because the slave
does not know what will happen on the morrow and he does not
know if this thing that he intends is ordained for him or not. And
the addition of the words: "...if Allah wills," is not a condition,
rather it is a statement of certainty, which is why, 'Abdullah ibn
'Abbas ⚬ said that a person may say "...if Allah wills," even
if it is a year later, it means that if he forgets to say it when he
makes the oath or when he speaks, and he remembers it later,
even a year later, the *Sunnah* is that he should say it, so that he
will still be following the *Sunnah* of saying "...if Allah wills,"
even if that is after breaking his oath, as we said earlier in the
story of Sulaiman ⚬, when he said, "Tonight I will go around to
seventy women (according to some reports, it was ninety or one

hundred women) so that each one of them will give birth to a son who will fight for the sake of Allah." It was said to him (according to one report, the angel said to him), "Say, 'If Allah wills'," but he did not say it. He went around to the women but none of them gave birth except for one who gave birth to a half-formed child. The Messenger of Allah ﷺ said, "By Him in Whose hand is my soul, had he said, "If Allah wills," he would not have broken his oath, and that would have helped him to attain what he wanted." [1] According to another report, "…they would all have fought as horsemen in the cause of Allah." At the beginning of this *Soorah* we discussed the reason why this *Ayah* was revealed: when the Prophet ﷺ was asked about the story of the People of the Cave, he said, "I will tell you tomorrow." Then the revelation was delayed for fifteen days.

And He, Most High, says, ﴾ And remember your Lord when you forget ﴿ (*Soorah Al-Kahf* 18:24). This is because forgetfulness might be from Shaitan and mentioning Allah repels him from the heart, so that the one who forgets might remember what he had forgotten. And He, Most High, says, ﴾ and say, "It may be that my Lord guides me unto a nearer way of truth than this." ﴿ (*Soorah Al-Kahf* 18:24). That is, when a matter is unclear or a situation is difficult, or the sayings of the people are obscure regarding something, then ask Allah and He will make the matter easy for you and facilitate it for you. Then He says, ﴾ And they stayed in their cave for three hundred years, and add nine ﴿ (*Soorah Al-Kahf* 18:25). Because there is a great benefit in knowing the length of time they remained in the cave, Allah, Most High, informs us about it. The extra nine years referred to means in lunar years, since one hundred solar years equals one hundred and three lunar years and so three hundred solar years is equivalent to three hundred and nine lunar years. ﴾ Say, "Allah knows best how long they stayed." ﴿ (*Soorah Al-Kahf* 18:26). That is, if you are

---

[1] Narrated by Muslim (1654).

asked about a matter similar to this and no information has been conveyed to you, then refer the matter to Allah, the Almighty, the All-Powerful. ﴿ "With Him is the unseen of the heavens and the Earth." ﴾ (*Soorah Al-Kahf* 18:26). That is, He is the Knower of the unseen and no one has access to it except those of His creation whom He wills. ﴿ How clearly He sees, and hears (everything)! ﴾ (*Soorah Al-Kahf* 18:26). Ibn Jareer said, "The language used is an eloquent expression of praise." The phrase may be understood to mean, how much Allah sees of everything that exists and how much He hears of everything that is to be heard, for nothing is hidden from Him! ﴿ They have no *waliyy* (helper, disposer of affairs, protector, etc.) other than He, and He makes none to share in His Decision and His Rule." ﴾ (*Soorah Al-Kahf* 18:26). That is, your Lord, Who is the sole Owner of the Dominion and Disposer of affairs, Alone, without partners.

The Story of the Two Men: The Believer and the Disbeliever

Allah, Most High, says in *Soorah Al-Kahf*, after relating the story of the People of the Cave ﴿ And put forward for them the example of two men; unto one of them We had given two gardens of grapes, and We had surrounded both with date-palms; and had put between them green crops (cultivated fields, etc.). Each of those two gardens brought forth its produce, and failed not in the least therein, and We caused a river to gush forth in the midst of them. And he had property (or fruit) and he said to his companion, in the course of mutual talk, "I am more than you in wealth and stronger in respect of men." (See *Tafseer Qurtubi*, Vol. 10, page 403). And he went into his garden while he was unjust to himself. He said, "I think not that this will ever perish. And I think not the Hour will ever come, and if indeed I am brought back to my Lord, (on the Day of Resurrection), I surely shall find better than this when I return to Him." His companion said to him, during the talk with him, "Do you disbelieve in Him Who created you out of dust (i.e. your father Adam), then out of a *nutfah* (mixed semen drops of male and female discharge), then fashioned you into a man? But as for my part (I believe that) He is Allah, my Lord and none shall I associate as partner with my Lord. It was better for you to say, when you entered your garden, 'That which Allah wills (will come to pass)! There is no power but with Allah.' If you see me less than you in wealth and children, it may be that my Lord will give me something better than your garden, and will send on it *husban* from the sky, then it will be a slippery earth. Or the water thereof (of the gardens) becomes deep-sunken (underground) so that you will never be able to seek it." So his fruits were encircled (with ruin). And he remained clapping his hands with sorrow over what he had spent upon it, while it was all destroyed on its trellises, he could only say, "Would that I had ascribed no partners to my Lord!" (*Tafseer Ibn Katheer*). And he had no group of men to help him against Allah, nor could he defend or save himself. There (on the Day of Resurrection), *Al-Walayah* (the protection, power, authority and kingdom) will be for Allah (Alone), the True God. He (Allah) is the Best for reward and the Best for the final end. (*La ilaha ill-Allah* – none has the right to be worshipped but Allah). ❭ (*Soorah Al-Kahf* 18:32-44)

Some of the people said that this is a parable set forth and it is not necessarily the case that it happened, but the majority are of the opinion that it actually happened. And His Saying: ❬ And put forward for them the example ❭ (*Soorah Al-Kahf* 18:32). That is, for the disbelievers of *Quraish*, regarding their refusal to gather with the weak and the poor and their belittling of them and the arrogance they displayed for them, as He, Most High, says, ❬ And put forward to them a similitude; the (story of the) dwellers of the town, when there came Messengers to them ❭ (*Soorah Ya Seen* 36:13). ❬ "I am more than you in wealth and stronger in respect of men." (See Tafseer Al-Qurtubi, Vol. 10, page 403) 》 (*Soorah Al-Kahf* 18:34). That is, I possess larger gardens; and what he meant by it was that he was better than his companion, i.e. what benefit do you gain from spending what you possess in the way that you do (i.e. giving in charity, etc.)? It would be better for you to do as I have done, so that you might be as I am (i.e. wealthy). So he behaved arrogantly toward his companion. ◀ And he went into his garden while he was unjust to himself 》 (*Soorah Al-Kahf* 18:35). means, he was not following the way that was pleasing to Allah. ◀ He said, "I think not that this will ever perish." 》 (*Soorah Al-Kahf* 18:35). He said this when he saw how vast his lands were, how much water there was and how fine the fruits on its trees were; and if it has perished all of these trees, they would have been replaced by others better than these, which plants are productive, due to the plentiful supply of water. Then he said, ◀ "And I think not the Hour will ever come." 》 (*Soorah Al-Kahf* 18:36). He placed his reliance in the splendor of the transient life of this world and denied the existence of the Hereafter, which everlasting and permanent. Then he said, ◀ "...and if indeed I am brought back to my Lord, (on the Day of Resurrection), I surely shall find better than this when I return to Him." 》 (*Soorah Al-Kahf* 18:36). That is, even if there is a Hereafter and a Return, I will certainly find there something better than this. This was because he deluded by his earthly life and believed that Allah had not given him all that except because of His Love for him and His Benevolence toward him, as Al-'As ibn Wa'il said to Khabbab ibn Al-Aratt, according to the information given to us by Allah in His Words: ◀ Have you seen him who disbelieved in Our *Ayat* (this Qur'an and Muhammad ﷺ) and (yet) says, "I shall certainly be given wealth and children (if I will be alive [again])." Has he known the unseen or has he taken a covenant from the Most Beneficent (Allah)? 》 (*Soorah Maryam* 19:77,78). And Allah, Most High, tells us that when man is given Blessings from Allah, ◀ ...he is sure to say, "This is for me (due to my merit), I think not that the

IIour will be established. But if I am brought back to my Lord, surely, there will be for me the best (wealth, etc.) with Him." 》 (Soorah Fus And when this ignorant man was bedazzled by what he had been granted in this earthly life, denied the Hereafter and claimed that if there was an Afterlife, he would find therein with his Lord something better than that which he had been given in this life. His companion heard his words and 《 (he) said to him, during the talk with him 》 (*Soorah Al-Kahf* 18:37). That is, while he was disputing with him. 《 "Do you disbelieve in Him Who created you out of dust (i.e. your father Adam), then out of a *nutfah* (mixed semen drops of male and female discharge), then fashioned you into a man?" 》 (*Soorah Al-Kahf* 18:37). That is, do you reject the Return, when you know that Allah created you from dust, then from a *nutfah* and then formed you into a man, blessed with hearing and sight, and you have knowledge, strength and understanding? So how can you reject the Return, when Allah is Able to create you from nothing? 《 "But as for my part (I believe) that He is Allah, my Lord." 》 (*Soorah Al-Kahf* 18:38). That is, but I say and believe something contrary to what you say and believe: 《 "He is Allah, my Lord and none shall I associate as partner with my Lord." 》 (*Soorah Al-Kahf* 18:38). That is, I do not worship anything except Him and I believe that He will send forth the bodies (of mankind) after they have rotted away, revive the dead and gather the remaining bones. And I know that Allah has no partners in His Creation or in His Dominion and that there is none worthy of worship but He. Then he guided him toward the thing that was more fitting for him to do whenever he entered his gardens, saying, 《 It was better for you to say, when you entered your garden, 'That which Allah wills (will come to pass)! There is no power but with Allah'." 》 (*Soorah Al-Kahf* 18:39). For this reason, it is preferred for every person who sees something in his wealth, his family or his situation that favorably impresses him to say likewise.

Then the Believer said to the disbeliever, ❲ "It may be that my Lord will give me something better than your garden." ❳ (*Soorah Al-Kahf* 18:40). That is, in the abode of the Hereafter. ❲ "…and will send on it *husban* from the sky." ❳ (*Soorah Al-Kahf* 18:40). 'Abdullah ibn 'Abbas ⸱, Ad-Dahhak and Qatadah said that it means a punishment from the heaven; and it would appear that it refers to blinding, heavy rain, which ruins crops and trees. ❲ "…then it will be a slippery earth." ❳ (*Soorah Al-Kahf* 18:40). And that is smooth ground in which there is no vegetation. ❲ "Or the water thereof (of the gardens) becomes deep-sunken (underground)." ❳ (*Soorah Al-Kahf* 18:41). And that is the opposite of a free-flowing spring. ❲ "…so that you will never be able to seek it." ❳ (*Soorah Al-Kahf* 18:41). That is, you will never be able to reclaim it. Allah, Most High, says, ❲ So his fruits were encircled (with ruin) ❳ (*Soorah Al-Kahf* 18:42). That is, a Command (from Allah) came to him which encircled all of his crops and ruined and destroyed his garden. ❲ And he remained clapping his hands with sorrow over what he had spent upon it, while it was all destroyed on its trellises ❳ (*Soorah Al-Kahf* 18:42). That is, they were totally destroyed and could not be returned. And that was the opposite of what he had expected when he said, ❲ "I think not that this will ever perish." ❳ (*Soorah Al-Kahf* 18:36) and he regretted the words of disbelief in Allah, the Great, that he had spoken, saying, ❲ "Would that I had ascribed no partners to my Lord!" (*Tafseer Ibn Katheer*) ❳ (*Soorah Al-Kahf* 18:42). Allah, Most High, says, ❲ And he had no group of men to help him against Allah, nor could he defend or save himself. There (on the Day of Resurrection ❳ (*Soorah Al-Kahf* 18:43). That is, there was no one who could compensate him for what had befallen him and he himself had no ability to do such a thing, as Allah, Most High, says, ❲ Then will (man) have no power, nor any helper there ❳ (*Soorah At-Tariq* 86:10). And He says, ❲ (On the Day of Resurrection) *Al-Walayah* (the protection, power, authority and kingdom) will be for Allah (Alone), the True God ❳ (*Soorah Al-Kahf* 18:44). Some of them understood this Verse to begin with the word '*Hunalika*' (There), (rather than as the final word of the previous verse) and this is also correct, as He, Most High, says, ❨ The sovereignty on that Day will be the true (sovereignty), belonging to the Most Gracious (Allah), and it will be a hard Day for the disbelievers ❩ (*Soorah Al-Furqan* 25:26). So the Judgment which cannot be repelled, prevented or overcome is in that situation; and in every situation the true Judgment is for Allah. Others recited *Al-Haqqu* rather than *Al-Haqqi*, making the Word an adjective for *Al-Walayah* – and the meanings of both are inseparable. ❨ He (Allah) is the Best for reward and the Best for the final end. (*La ilaha ill-Allah* – none has the right to be worshipped but Allah). ❩ (*Soorah Al-Kahf* 18:44). That is, His Treatment of a person is the best reward for him, which is the Recompense. As for being the Best for the final end, it refers to the end in this life and in the Hereafter. It may be inferred from this story that no one should depend on the life of this world, be misled by it or place one's faith in it. Instead, he should direct his attention toward obedience to Allah and dependence on Him. And that which is in Allah's Hand is more dependable than that which is in his hands. We may also understand from it that whoever gives precedence to something over obedience to Allah and spending in His Cause, he will be punished because of that and it might be taken from him, so that he receives the opposite of that to which he aspired. We may also infer from it that it is obligatory to accept the advice of one's brother, when he is concerned for our wellbeing and that when one opposes good advice, it entails evil consequences and ruin for him. In addition, we can derive from it that regret does not benefit once Allah's Ordainment has been fulfilled. And it is Allah from Whom we seek Help and upon Him we depend.

The Story of the Companions of the Garden

Allah, Most High, says, ❨ Verily, We have tried them as We tried the people of the garden, when they swore to pick them in the morning, without saying, '*Insha'Allah* (if Allah wills)'. Then there passed by on the (garden) something (fire) from your Lord at night and burned it while they were asleep. So the (garden) became black by the morning, like *as-sareem* (in complete ruins). Then they called out to one another as soon as the morning broke, saying, "Go to your tilth in the morning, if you would pick the fruits." So they departed, *yatakhafatoona*, (saying,) "No *miskeen* (poor man) shall enter upon you into it today." And they went in the morning with strong intention, thinking that they have power. But when they saw it, they said, "Verily, we have gone astray," (Then they said), "Nay! Indeed we are deprived!" The best among them said, "Did I not say to you: 'Why do you not glorify?' They said, "Glory to our Lord! Verily, we have been *zalimoon* (wrongdoers, etc.)." Then they turned, one against another, in reproach. They said, "Woe to us! Verily, we were *taghoon* (transgressors, disobedient, etc.) We hope that our Lord will give us in exchange a better (garden) than this. Truly, we turn to our Lord (wishing for good, that He may forgive our sins, and reward us in the Hereafter)." Such is the punishment (in this life), but truly, the punishment of the Hereafter is greater, if they but knew 》 (*Soorah Al-Qalam* 68:17-33). And this is a parable set forth by Allah for the disbelievers of *Quraish*, regarding the Blessing that He bestowed on them, i.e. the sending of the great and noble Messenger ﷺ to them and how they greeted him with denial and opposition, as He, Most High, says, ◀ Have you not seen those who have changed the Blessings of Allah into disbelief (by denying Prophet Muhammad ﷺ and his Message of Islam), and caused their people to dwell in the house of destruction? Hell, in which they will burn – and what an evil place in which to settle! 》 (*Soorah Ibraheem* 14:28,29). 'Abdullah ibn 'Abbas ﷺ said, "They are the disbelievers of Quraish. So Allah, Most High, set forth for them the parable of the Companions of the Garden; their garden contained all kinds of crops and fruits, which were ripe and ready to be harvested. This is why He says, ◀ when they swore... 》 (*Soorah Al-Qalam* 68:17). That is, to one another. ◀ ...to pick them 》 (*Soorah Al-Qalam* 68:17). That is, to harvest the fruits of the garden. ◀ ...in the morning 》 (*Soorah Al-Qalam* 68:17). means, at daybreak, so that no poor or needy person should see them and they would not have to give them anything; and they swore an oath to that effect, but they did not add: '*Insha' Allah*' (if Allah wills) and so Allah invalidated their oath and brought destruction on their garden, burning it and leaving it blackened and ruined, so that nothing useful remained of it, which is why He says, ◀ Then there passed by on the (garden) something (fire) from your Lord at night and burned it while they were asleep. So the (garden) became black by the morning, like *as-sareem* (in complete ruins) 》 (*Soorah Al-Qalam* 68:19-20). That is, like a black night, empty of any light. And this Treatment invalidated their intention. ◀ Then they called out one to another as soon as

the morning broke 》 (*Soorah Al-Qalam* 68:21). means, they woke
up from their sleep and they called out to one another, saying, 《
"Go to your tilth in the morning, if you would pick the fruits."
》 (*Soorah Al-Qalam* 68:22). That is, go to your orchard early in
the morning and pick the fruit before the sun has properly risen
and many questions are asked. 《 So they departed, *yatakhafatoon*
(saying,) 》 (*Soorah Al-Qalam* 68:23). That is, conversing with
one another in low voices, saying, 《 "No *miskeen* (poor man)
shall enter upon you into it today." 》 (*Soorah Al-Qalam* 68:24).
That is, they consulted upon this and agreed upon it. 《 And they
went in the morning with strong intention, thinking that they
have power. 》 (*Soorah Al-Qalam* 68:25) That is, they went out
to gather the fruits, believing that they had strength and power
over their garden and concealing this bad intention in their hearts.
'Ikrimah and Ash-Sha'bi said that 《 and they went in the morning
with strong intention, thinking that they have power 》 (*Soorah
Al-Qalam* 68:25) means that they were angry with the poor. But
As-Suddi erred widely in his interpretation when he said that the
word *hard* was the name of their cultivated land. 《 But when they
saw it... 》 (*Soorah Al-Qalam* 68:26). That is, they reached the
garden and looked at the disaster that had befallen it, after it had
been ripe for harvesting, beautiful and magnificent to behold. And
they had been thus transformed because of their bad intention.
When they saw what had happened, 《 they said, "Verily, we have
gone astray," 》 (*Soorah Al-Qalam* 68:26). That is, we have taken
the wrong path to it. Then they changed their minds and realized
with certainty that it was actually the correct path, so they said,
《 "Nay! Indeed we are deprived!" 》 (*Soorah Al-Qalam* 68:27).
That is, we have been punished because of our bad intention and
deprived of the blessing of our cultivation. 《 The *awsat* among
them said 》 (*Soorah Al-Qalam* 68:28). 'Abdullah ibn 'Abbas ﷺ,
Mujahid and others said that it means: the fairest and the best of
them said, 《 "Did I not say to you: 'Why do you not glorify'?"
》 (*Soorah Al-Qalam* 68:29). It was said by Mujahid, As-Suddi

and Ibn Jareer At-Tabari that this means: Why did you not say, '*Insha' Allah*' (if Allah wills)?" It was also said that it means: Why did you not say something good, instead of the wicked thing that you said? ﴾ They said, "Glory to our Lord! Verily, we have been *zalimoon* (wrongdoers, etc.)." Then they turned, one against another, in reproach. They said, "Woe to us! Verily, we were *taghoon* (transgressors and disobedient, etc.) ﴿ (*Soorah Al-Qalam* 68:29). When it was no longer of any use to them, they expressed their regret and acknowledged their sin after the punishment had been inflicted on them and when it availed them nothing. Allah, Most High, says, ﴾ Such is the punishment (in this life) ﴿ (*Soorah Al-Qalam* 68:30). That is, thus do We punish those who disobey Our Command and show no compassion for the poor and needy among Our creation. ﴾ ...but truly, the punishment of the Hereafter is greater ﴿ (*Soorah Al-Qalam* 68:33). means, more terrible and more severe than the punishment of this world. ﴾ ...if they but knew ﴿ (*Soorah Al-Qalam* 68:33). And the story of these people resembles that of those in the story mentioned by Allah in His Words: ﴾ And Allah puts forward the example of a township (Makkah), that dwelt secure and well content; its provision coming to it in abundance from every place, but it (its people) denied the Favors of Allah (with ungratefulness). So Allah made it taste the extreme of hunger (famine) and fear, because of that (evil, i.e. denying Prophet Muhammad ﷺ) which they (its people) used to do. And verily, there had come unto them a Messenger (Muhammad ﷺ) from among themselves, but they denied him, so the torment overtook them while they were *zalimoon*. ﴿ (*Soorah An-Nahl* 16:112,113). It was said that this parable was set forth for the people of Makkah. It was also said it referred to the people of Makkah themselves and that Allah set forth the parable of them, for them. And this does not contradict the first opinion. And Allah knows better.

The Story of the People of Ailah, Who Transgressed the Laws of Their Sabbath

Allah, Most High, says, (And ask them (O, Muhammad) about the town that was by the sea, when they transgressed in the matter of the Sabbath (i.e. Saturday): when their fish came to them openly on the Sabbath day, and did not come to them on the day they had no Sabbath. Thus We made a trial of them for they used to rebel (*Soorah An-Nisa'* 4:154). And when a community among them said, "Why do you preach to a people whom Allah is about to destroy or to punish with a severe punishment?" (The preachers) said, "In order to be free from guilt before your Lord (Allah), and perhaps they may fear Allah." So when they forgot the reminders that had been given to them, We rescued those who forbade evil, but We seized those who did wrong with a severe punishment because they used to rebel (disobey Allah). So when they exceeded the limits of what they were prohibited, We said to them, "Be you monkeys, despised and rejected." (It is a severe warning to the mankind that they should not disobey what Allah commands them to do, and be far away from what He prohibits them)) (*Soorah Al-A'raf* 7:163-166)

'Abdullah Ibn 'Abbas ﷺ, Mujahid, 'Ikrimah, Qatadah, As-Suddi and others said that they were the people of Ailah. [1] 'Abdullah Ibn 'Abbas ﷺ added that it lies between Madyan and At-Toor (which is in Sinai). They said that they adhered to the religious teachings of the Tawrah, according to which the Sabbath was sacrosanct. The fish were accustomed to being left alone on the Sabbath, because it was unlawful for the Jews to catch them or to undertake any activities on that day, such as trading and business. So the fish were plentiful on that day, swimming near the surface, coming from hither and thither, feeling safe and at ease,

---

(1) Ailah: A village on the Red Sea.

and the Jews did not disturb them or alarm them. ﴾ ...and did not come to them on the day they had no Sabbath ﴿ (*Soorah Al-A'raf* 7:163). This was because they used to try to catch them on days other than the Sabbath. Allah, Most High, says, ﴾ Thus We made a trial of them ﴿ (*Soorah Al-A'raf* 7:163). That is, We tested them through the plentiful fish on the Sabbath. ﴾ ...for they used to rebel (see also *Soorah An-Nisa'* 4:154) ﴿ (*Soorah Al-A'raf* 7:163). That is, because of the sins of disobedience they had previously committed. So when they saw the profusion of fish, they resorted to duplicity, by placing nets, ropes and artificial pools of water on Friday for the purpose of fishing before the Sabbath. When the fish came in abundance on Saturday as usual, they were caught in the ropes and nets for the rest of Saturday. During the night, the Jews collected the fish after the Sabbath ended. Allah was Angry with them and cursed them for their duplicity, which went against His Command and entailed an apparent adherence to the law, while actually circumventing it. So when a group of them did that, the remainder of them split into two factions: (i) those who rebuked them for their deed and their subterfuge, in contravention of Allah's Command and His Law at that time; and (ii) those who did not do it, but did not forbid it, indeed, they rebuked those who forbade it and they said, ﴾ "Why do you preach to a people whom Allah is about to destroy or to punish with a severe punishment?" ﴿ (*Soorah Al-A'raf* 7:164). They said, "What is the benefit of forbidding these people, when they have already merited the Punishment (of Allah) and it is inevitable?" The group which rebuked the sinners replied to them, saying, ﴾ "In order to be free from guilt before your Lord (Allah), and perhaps they may fear Allah." ﴿ (*Soorah Al-'Araf* 6:16). That is, regarding to what He has commanded us to do of ordering that which is good and forbidding that which is evil, and we fulfill it out of fear of His Punishment. ﴾ "...and perhaps they may fear Allah." ﴿ (*Soorah Al-A'raf* 7:164). That is, perhaps these sinners may abandon this deed that they are doing and Allah may preserve them from His

Punishment, if they turn back and listen. Allah, Most High, says, ﴾ So when they forgot the reminders that had been given to them… ﴿ (*Soorah Al-A'raf* 7:165). That is, they paid no heed to those who forbade them from doing this disgraceful and detestable deed. ﴾ We rescued those who forbade evil ﴿ (*Soorah Al-A'raf* 7:165). And they were the group who commanded that which is good and forbade that which is evil. ﴾ …but We seized those who did wrong ﴿ (*Soorah Al-A'raf* 7:165). And they were those who committed the sin. ﴾ …with a severe punishment ﴿ (*Soorah Al-A'raf* 7:165). And that was an extremely painful one. ﴾ …because they used to rebel (disobey Allah) ﴿ (*Soorah Al-A'raf* 7:165). Then He explains the Punishment that befell them in His Words: ﴾ So when they exceeded the limits of what they were prohibited, We said to them, "Be you monkeys, despised and rejected." (It is a severe warning to the mankind that they should not disobey what Allah commands them to do, and be far away from what He prohibits them). ﴿ (*Soorah Al-A'raf* 7:166)

What is meant here is that Allah, Most High, destroyed the wrongdoers and saved the Believers who rebuked the sinners, and He passed over those who remained silent. The scholars divided into two groups regarding them. One held the opinion that they were among those who were saved, while the other opined that they were among those who were destroyed. The correct opinion is the first, according to the investigators and it was the preferred opinion of 'Abdullah ibn 'Abbas ☙, the *Imam* of the Qur'anic exegetes. He reached this opinion as a result of a debate with his freed slave, 'Ikrimah and because of this he clothed him in a garment, as a mark of honor and respect. I say: The only reason why they were not mentioned with those who were saved is because, although they inwardly expressed their disapproval of this sinful act, they did not express any outward censure of it, by verbally condemning it, which is the middle level of the three levels, the highest of which is to express disapproval by one's hand; after that comes verbal condemnation and the third level is to condemn it in one's heart. And since they were not mentioned, it means that they were saved along with the others who were saved, because they did not commit that evil deed; indeed, they censured it.

The Story of Luqman

Allah, Most High, says, ❨ And indeed We bestowed upon Luqman *Al-Hikmah* (wisdom and religious understanding, etc.) saying:, "Give thanks to Allah," and whoever gives thanks, he gives thanks for (the good of) his ownself. And whoever is ungrateful, then verily, Allah is Free of all wants, Worthy of all praise. And (remember) when Luqman said to his son when he was advising him, "O, my son! Join not others in worship with Allah. Verily! Joining others in worship with Allah is a great *zulm* (wrong) indeed. And We have enjoined on man (to be dutiful and good) to his parents. His mother bore him in weakness and hardship upon weakness and hardship, and his weaning is in two years, give thanks to Me and to your parents, unto Me is the final destination. But if they (both) strive with you to make you join in worship with Me others that of which you have no knowledge, then obey them not, but behave with them in the world kindly, and follow the path of him who turns to Me in repentance and in obedience. Then to Me will be your return, and I shall tell you what you used to do. "O, my son! If it be (anything) equal to the weight of a grain of mustard seed, and though it be in a rock, or in the heavens or in the earth, Allah will bring it forth. Verily, Allah is Subtle (in bringing out that grain), Well Aware (of its place). O, my son! *Aqimis-salah* (perform *as-salah* prayers), enjoin (on people) *al-ma'roof* (Islamic Monotheism and all that is good), and forbid (people) from *al-munkar* (i.e. disbelief in the Oneness of Allah, polytheism of all kinds and all that is evil and bad), and bear with patience whatever befalls you. Verily, these are some of the important commandments. And turn not your face away from men, nor walk in insolence through the earth. Verily, Allah likes not each arrogant boaster. And be moderate in your walking, and lower your voice. Verily, the most disagreeable of sounds is the sound (braying) of the ass." ❭ *(Soorah Luqman* 31:12-19)

It is reported on the authority of 'Abdullah Ibn 'Abbas ﷺ that he said, "Luqman was an Abyssinian carpenter." Qatadah reported on the authority of 'Abdullah ibn Az-Zubair that he said, "I said to Jabir Ibn 'Abdullah, "What has come to you regarding the case of Luqman?" He said, "He was of short stature and snub-nosed, and he was from Noobia."

It has been widely reported from the majority of scholars that he was a wise man and a *Waliyy*, but not a Prophet. Allah, Most High, has mentioned him in the Qur'an and praised him and related his words of admonition to his son, who was the most beloved of Allah's creation to him and of all mankind, the person for whose welfare he was most concerned. Among the first words of admonition that he addressed to his son was his saying: ❬ "O, my son! Join not in worship others with Allah. Verily! Joining others in worship with Allah is a great *zulm* (wrong) indeed." ❭ *(Soorah Luqman* 31:13). So he forbade him from such a sin and warned him against it.

Al-Bukhari narrated on the authority of 'Abdullah that he said, "When ❬ It is those who believe (in the Oneness of Allah and worship none but Him Alone) and confuse not their belief with *zulm* (wrong i.e. by worshipping others besides Allah) ﴾ (*Soorah Al-An'am* 6:82) was revealed, the Companions of the Messenger of Allah ﷺ were distressed by this, and said, "Who among us does not confuse his belief with *zulm*?" The Messenger of Allah ﷺ said, "That is not what it means. Have you not heard what Luqman said, ﴾ "O, my son! Join not in worship others with Allah. Verily, joining others in worship with Allah is a great *zulm* (wrong) indeed." ﴿?" It was (also) narrated by Muslim. [1]

Then Allah, Most High, commanded us to be dutiful and kind to our parents and set forth the parents' rights over their children and He confirmed it. He commanded us to treat parents well, even if they be disbelievers; but He told us that they are not to be obeyed if they order us to enter their religion. He then informed us regarding Luqman that he advised his son, ﴾ "O, my son! If it be (anything) equal to the weight of a grain of mustard seed, and though it be in a rock, or in the heavens or in the earth, Allah will bring it forth. Verily, Allah is Subtle (in bringing out that grain), Well Aware (of its place)." ﴿ (*Soorah Luqman* 31:16). He forbids him from being unjust to mankind, even if the injustice is as insignificant as a mustard seed, for Allah, Most High, will ask about it and He will bring it forth at the time of the Reckoning and place it in the scale, as He, Most High, says, ﴾ Surely! Allah wrongs not even of the weight of an atom (or a small ant). ﴿ (*Soorah An-Nisa'* 4:40) and He, Most High, says, ﴾ And We shall set up balances of justice on the Day of Resurrection, then none will be dealt with unjustly in anything. And if there be the weight of a mustard seed, We will bring it. And Sufficient are We as Reckoners. ﴿ (*Soorah Al-Anbiya'* 21:47) He informed him that even if this injustice was as insignificant as a mustard seed and it was concealed within a solid rock, without any door or window in it, or it fell into something in the depths of the earth or it was in the wide expanse of the heavens, Allah would certainly know

---

(1) Narrated by Muslim (124).

its location. ❨ "Verily, Allah is Subtle (in bringing out that grain), Well Aware (of its place)." ❩ (*Soorah Luqman* 31:16). That is, His Knowledge is precise, so the smallest atoms – whether they be apparent or hidden – are known to Him, as He, Most High, says, ❨ And with Him are the keys of the *ghaib* (all that is hidden), none knows them but He. And He knows whatever there is in (or on) the earth and in the sea; not a leaf falls, but He knows it. There is not a grain in the darkness of the earth nor anything fresh or dry, but is written in a Clear Record ❩ (*Soorah Al-An'am* 6:59). And He says, ❨ And there is nothing hidden in the heaven and the earth, but is in a Clear Book (i.e. *Al-Lawh Al-Mahfooz*) ❩ (*Soorah An-Naml* 27:75) and He says, ❨ (Allah, He is) the Knower of the unseen, not even the weight of an atom (or a small ant) or less than that or greater, escapes from His Knowledge in the heavens or in the earth, but it is in a Clear Book (*Al-Lawh Al-Mahfooz*) ❩ (*Soorah Saba'* 34:3)

As for His Saying: ❨ "O, my son! *Aqimis-salah* (perform *as-salah*). ❩ (*Soorah Luqman* 31:17), it means: Perform the prayer with all its obligatory acts regarding its limits, its timings, its bowing, its prostration, its repose, its humility and all that has been legislated therein. And refrain from whatever is prohibited therein. Then he said, ❨ ...enjoin (on people) for *al-ma'roof* (Islamic Monotheism and all that is good), and forbid (people) from *al-munkar* (i.e. disbelief in the Oneness of Allah, polytheism of all kinds and all that is evil and bad) ❩ (*Soorah Luqman* 31:17). That is, (forbid them) with all your power and to the utmost of your ability, i.e. if you are able to do so, by your hand, if not, by verbal censure and if that is not possible, then by expressing hatred for the evil in your heart. Then he commanded him to be patient, saying, ❨ ...and bear with patience whatever befalls you ❩ (*Soorah Luqman* 31:17). This is because the one who enjoins *al-ma'roof* and forbids *al-munkar* may expect to be opposed and suffer harm; but the end result will be in his favor. This is why he ordered him to be patient in the face of that (opposition), for it is well known that the end result of patience is relief from suffering. And He, Most High, says, ﴿ Verily, these are some of the important commandments ﴾ *(Soorah Luqman* 31:17). That is, your enjoining *al-ma'roof* and forbidding *al-munkar* and your patience in the face of harm is among the most important of commandments, which are unavoidable and from which there is no escape. ﴿ "And turn not your face away from men." ﴾ *(Soorah Luqman* 31:18). 'Abdullah ibn 'Abbas ﷺ, Mujahid, 'Ikrimah, Sa'eed ibn Jubair, Ad-Dahhak, Yazeed ibn Al-Asamm, Abul-Jawza' and others said that it means: do not behave arrogantly toward the people, turning your cheek away from them when you speak to them and when they speak to you. According to the scholars of Arabic language, the root meaning of the verb *sa'ara* (used in the Verse) is a disease which afflicts camels in their necks, causing them to twist their heads to one side. So a proud man, who turns his face away when he speaks to people or when they speak to him is compared to the camel afflicted with this disease.

Abu Talib says in his poem:

> *In the past, we did not approve of injustice,*
> *If they arrogantly turned their cheeks,*
> *We would oppose it.*

And 'Amr ibn Hunayy At-Taghlibi said:

> *If a tyrant arrogantly turned his cheek,*
> *We would stand firm against him and oppose him.*

And Luqman said, ﴿ "...nor walk in insolence through the earth. Verily, Allah likes not each arrogant boaster." ﴾ *(Soorah Luqman* 31:18). He forbade his son to walk with a strutting gait out of a sense of self-importance and boastfulness before the people, as He, Most High, says, ﴿ And walk not on the earth with conceit and arrogance. Verily, you can neither rend nor penetrate the earth, nor can you attain a stature like the mountains in height ﴾ (*Soorah Al-Isra'* 17:37). That is, you cannot traverse the lands by the speed of your walk using this gait of yours. Nor by your pounding of the earth with your feet can you penetrate it. Nor by your lofty behavior, your haughtiness and pride can you attain the height of the mountains, so be slow and deliberate, for you cannot outrun your destiny. And it has been confirmed in a *hadeeth* that the Prophet ﷺ said, "While a man was strutting with pride due to his (fine) cloaks, Allah caused the earth to swallow him up and he will continue falling into it until the Day of Resurrection." [1] And in another *hadeeth*, the Prophet ﷺ said, "Beware of letting your *izar* (lower garment) hang down, because it is a form of pride and Allah does not like it." [2] For He, Most High, says in this Verse, ﴾ "Verily, Allah likes not each arrogant boaster." ﴿ (*Soorah Luqman* 31:18). And when he forbade him to display arrogance in his gait, he ordered him to walk moderately, for one must walk and so he prohibited him from evil (when doing so) and ordered him to do good (by walking without pride), saying, ﴾ "And be moderate in your walking." ﴿ (*Soorah Luqman* 31:19). That is, neither walk remarkably slowly, nor exceedingly quickly, but between those two extremes, with an upright posture, as He, Most High, says, ﴾ And the slaves of the Most Beneficent (Allah) are those who walk on the earth in humility and sedateness, and when the foolish address them (with bad words) they reply back with mild words of gentleness ﴿ (*Soorah Al-Furqan* 25:63). Then he said, ﴾ "… and lower your voice." ﴿ (*Soorah Luqman* 31:19). That is, when you speak, do not raise your voice, because the loudest voice and ﴾ Verily, the most disagreeable of sounds is the sound (braying) of the ass. ﴿ (*Soorah Luqman* 31:19)

And it has been confirmed in the *Saheehain* that one should seek Allah's Protection upon hearing the braying of a donkey

---

(1) Narrated by Muslim (2088).

(2) This is an authentic *hadeeth* narrated by Abu Dawood (4084).

at night, because it see a devil. This is why raising one's voice without need is forbidden, especially when one sneezes; in such a case, it is preferred to lower one's voice and cover one's face, as confirmed by the *hadeeth* [1] which describes the action of the Messenger of Allah ﷺ. As for raising the voice when saying the *Adhan* (calling for prayer) when calling a group to fight and at the time of destruction and the like, that is lawful. This is what Allah, Most High, has related concerning Luqman in the Qur'an of wisdoms, admonitions and useful, comprehensive advices to attain goodness and repel evil. Many traditions have been transmitted relating stories pertaining to his life and the admonitions he proffered and there is a book which relates (advices, admonitions, etc.) from him, called *Hikmatu Luqman* (the Wisdom of Luqman); we shall quote from that as much as is easy for us, if Allah wills.

Imam Ahmad narrated on the authority of 'Abdullah ibn 'Umar ؓ that he said, "The Messenger of Allah ﷺ said, "Luqman, the wise, used to say, "Verily, when Allah entrusts something, He protects it." [2]

And Ibn Abi Hatim reported on the authority of Al-Qasim Ibn Mukhaimirah that he said, "The Messenger of Allah ﷺ said, "Luqman said to his son when he was admonishing him, "O, my son! Beware of wearing a mask, for it is deception by night and it is humiliation by day." [3] He also said, "Luqman said to his son, "O, my son! Wisdom has made the poor to sit on the thrones of kings."

---

(1) This is an authentic *hadeeth* narrated by Abu Dawood (5029), At-Tirmidhi (2745) and Ahmad in his *Musnad* (9370).

(2) Narrated by Imam Ahmad in his *Musnad* (5574) and it is authentic, aside from the words: "Verily, Luqman, the wise, used to say…"

(3) Narrated by Ibn Abi Shaibah in his *Musannaf* (5/292, *hadeeth* no. 26213) and Al-Hakim in *Al-Mustadrak* (2/446, *hadeeth* No. 3543).

And on the authority of 'Awn Ibn 'Abdullah said, "Luqman said to his son, "O, my son! If you go to the meeting place of a people, cast the arrow of Islam (i.e. salutation of peace) at them, then sit down in their vicinity and do not speak until you see that they have spoken. Then if you find them observing the remembrance of Allah, cast your arrow with their arrows (i.e. join them). But if they observe anything else, then turn away from them and seek others (who remember Allah)."

It is reported on the authority of Hafs Ibn 'Umar that he said, "Luqman placed a bag of mustard seeds by his side and began to advise his son, giving him a piece of advice for each mustard seed that he withdrew, until he had exhausted the supply of mustard seeds. Then he said, "O, my son! I have given you advice, the like of which, if it was given to a mountain, it would have split open." He (Hafs) said, "Then his son became like one cleft asunder."

The Story of the Companions of the Ditch

Allah, Most High, says, ⟨ By the heaven, holding the big stars. And by the Promised Day (i.e. the Day of Resurrection). And by the witnessing day (i.e. Friday), and by the witnessed day (i.e. the day of 'Arafat [*Hajj*] the ninth of *Dhul-Hijjah*). Cursed were the people of the ditch (the story of the boy and the king). Fire supplied (abundantly) with fuel, when they sat by it (fire), and they witnessed what they were doing against the believers (i.e. burning them). They had nothing against them, except that they believed in Allah, the Almighty, Worthy of all Praise! To Whom belongs the dominion of the heavens and the Earth! And Allah is Witness over everything. Verily, those who put into trial the believing men and believing women (by torturing them and burning them), and then do not turn in repentance, (to Allah), will have the torment of Hell, and they will have the punishment of the burning Fire. ⟩ (*Soorah Al-Burooj* 85:1-10)

We have spoken about this in detail in the *tafseer* of this *Soorah*, all praise and thanks be to Allah. Muhammad Ibn Ishaq claimed that it was after the sending of the Maseeh, but he was contradicted by others. They claimed that they lived before him. More than one mentioned that this deed was perpetrated many times against Believers by disbelieving tyrants. But these mentioned in the Qur'an have been mentioned in a *hadeeth* that is *marfoo'* and a tradition transmitted by Ibn Ishaq, but they both contradict each other; here we present both of them for you to read:

Imam Ahmad narrated on the authority of Suhaib ﷺ that the Messenger of Allah ﷺ said, "Among the people who came before you, there was a king who had a sorcerer, and when that sorcerer became old, he said to the king, "I have become old and my time is nearly over, so please send me a boy whom I can teach magic." So he sent him a boy and the sorcerer taught him magic. Whenever the boy went to the sorcerer, he sat with a monk who was on the way and listened to his speech and admired them. So, when he went to the sorcerer, he passed by the monk and sat there with him; and on visiting the sorcerer the latter would thrash him. The boy complained about this to the monk. The monk said to him, "Whenever you are afraid of the sorcerer, say to him, 'My people kept me busy.' And whenever you are afraid of your people, say to them, 'The sorcerer kept me busy'." The boy continued in this way (for some time). Then a huge terrible creature appeared on the road and the people were unable to pass by. The boy said, "Today I shall know whether the sorcerer is better or the monk is better'." So he took a stone and said, "O, Allah! If the deeds and actions of the monk are more liked by You than those of the sorcerer, then kill this creature so that the people can cross (the road)." Then he struck it with a stone killing it and the people passed by on the road. The boy came to the monk and informed him about it. The monk said to him, "O, my son! Today you are better than I, and you have achieved what I see! You will be put to trial. And in case

354 The Story of the Companions of the Ditch

you are put to trial, do not inform (them) about me." The boy used to treat the people suffering from congenital blindness, leprosy, and other diseases. There was a courtier of the king who had become blind and he heard about the boy. He came and brought a number of gifts for the boy and said, "All these gifts are for you on the condition that you cure me." The boy said, "I do not cure anybody; it is only Allah who cures people. So, if you believe in Allah and supplicate to Him, He will cure you." So he believed and supplicated to Allah and Allah cured him. Later, the courtier came to the king and sat at the place where he used to sit before. The king said, "Who gave you back your sight?" The courtier replied, "My Lord." The king then said, I did?" The courtier said, "No, my Lord and your Lord – Allah." The king said, "Do you have another Lord beside me?" The courtier said, "Yes, your Lord and my Lord is Allah." The king tortured him and did not stop until he told him about the boy. The boy was then brought to the king and he said to him, "O, boy! Has your magic reached to the extent that you cure congenital blindness, leprosy and other diseases?" He said, "I do not cure anyone. Only Allah can cure." The king said, "I?" The boy replied, "No." The king asked, "Do you have a Lord other than me?" The boy answered, "My Lord and your Lord is Allah." So he tortured him also until he told him about the monk. Then the monk was brought to him and the king said to him, "Abandon your religion." The monk refused and so the king ordered a saw to be brought which was placed in the middle of his head and he fell, sawn in two. Then it was said to the man who used to be blind, "Abandon your religion." He refused to do so, and so a saw was brought and placed in the middle of his head and he fell, sawn in two. Then the boy was brought and it was said to him, "Abandon your religion." He refused and so the king sent him to the top of a mountain with some people. He told the people, "Ascend up the mountain with him till you reach its peak, then see if he abandons his religion; otherwise throw him from the top." They took him and when they ascended to the

top, he said, "O, Allah! Save me from them by any means that
You wish." So the mountain shook and they all fell down and
the boy came back walking to the king. The king said, "What did
your companions (the people I sent with you) do?" The boy said,
"Allah saved me from them." So the king ordered some people
to take the boy on a boat into the middle of the sea, saying, "If he
renounces his religion (well and good), if he refuses, drown him."
So, they took him out to sea and he said, "O, Allah! Save me from
them by any means that you wish." So they were all drowned
in the sea. Then the boy returned to the king and the king said,
"What did your companions do?" The boy replied, "Allah, saved
me from them." Then he said to the king, "You will not be able to
kill me until you do as I order you. And if you do as I order you,
you will be able to kill me." The king asked, "And what is that?"
The boy said, "Gather the people in one elevated place and tie
me to the trunk of a tree; then take an arrow from my quiver and
say: 'In the Name of Allah, the Lord of the boy.' If you do this,
you will be able to kill me." So he did this, and placing an arrow
in the bow, he shot it, saying, "In the Name of Allah, the Lord of
the boy." The arrow hit the boy in the temple, and the boy placed
his hand over the arrow wound and died. The people proclaimed,
"We believe in the Lord of the boy!" Then it was said to the king,
"Do you see what has happened? That which you feared has
taken place. By Allah, all the people have believed (in the Lord
of the boy)." So he ordered that ditches be dug at the entrances to
the roads and it was done, and fires were kindled in them. Then
the king said, "Whoever abandons his religion, let him go, and
whoever does not, throw him into the fire." They were struggling
and scuffling in the fire, until a woman and her baby whom she
was breastfeeding came and it was as if she was being somewhat
hesitant of falling into the fire, so her baby said to her, "Be patient
mother, for verily, you are following the truth!") This is how it
was narrated by Imam Ahmad in his Musnad and Muslim also

narrated it in his *Saheeh.* [1]

Some of them claimed that the incident of the ditch was repeated many times throughout the world, as Ibn Abi Hatim reported, on the authority of 'Abdur-Rahman ibn Jubair, who said, "The ditch was in Yemen during the reign of Tubba', in Constantinople, who set the fires in which he threw the Christians who were holding fast to the Religion of 'Eesa ﷺ (Islamic Monotheism). It also took place in Iraq, in the land of Babylon during the lifetime of Bukhthnassar, who erected an idol and ordered the people to prostrate themselves before it. Danyal (Daniel ﷺ) and his two companions refused and thereupon, he set a great fire and threw them into it. However, Allah, Almighty, saved them from the fire and caused the nine men who had oppressed them to fall into the fire they themselves had made. Asbat reported on the authority of As-Suddi that he said regarding Allah's Words: ﴾ Cursed were the people of the ditch ﴿ (*Soorah Al-Burooj* 85:4), "There were three ditches: one in Ash-Sham, another in Iraq and the third in Yemen." (Narrated by ibn Abi Hatim)

---

(1) Narrated by Ahmad in his *Musnad* (6/16 and 17, No. 23413) Muslim (3005) and An-Nasa'i in *Al-Kubra* (6/510, No. 11661).

Chapter Regarding the Permissibility of Narrating and Speaking About the Stories of the Children of Isra'eel

Imam Ahmad narrated on the authority of Abu Sa'eed Al-Khudri ⬥ that he reported from the Prophet ﷺ that he said, "Relate from me, but do not lie about me; and whoever lies about me, let him prepare his seat in the Fire. And relate (the stories) of the Children of Isra'eel, for there is no objection (to that)." [1]

He (Imam Ahmad) also said, "It is reported on the authority of Abu Sa'eed Al-Khudri ⬥ that he reported from the Prophet ﷺ that he said, "Do not write down anything that I say except the Qur'an; and if anyone has written down anything from me aside

_____

(1) This is an authentic *hadeeth* narrated by Imam Ahmad in his *Musnad* (3/49, No. 11032).

from the Qur'an, he should erase it." [1] And he said, "Relate (the stories) of the Children of Isra'eel, for there is no objection (to that). Relate from me and do not lie about me." Hammam said, "I think he said, "...intentionally... then let him prepare his seat in the Fire." This is how it was narrated by Muslim. [2]

And Imam Ahmad narrated on the authority of Jabir Ibn 'Abdullah that 'Umar ibn Al-Khattab ﷺ came to the Prophet ﷺ with a book which he had obtained from one of the People of the Scripture and he read it to the Prophet ﷺ. The Prophet ﷺ became angry and said, "O, Ibn Al-Khattab! Are you all going to fall into chaos? By Him in Whose Hand is my soul, I have brought it (Islam) to you clean and pure. Do not ask them about anything so that they will not tell you of something true which you might declare false, or something false which you might declare true. By Him in Whose Hand is my soul, if Moosa was alive, he would have no alternative but to follow me." (Ahmad was alone in narrating this; and its chain of narrators conforms to the criteria for acceptance stipulated by Muslim). These *ahadeeth* are proof that they had altered, distorted and falsely interpreted the Divine Scriptures that were in their hands, and they omitted parts of it, especially those that were translated into Arabic – for they did not have comprehensive knowledge of them when they were in their own language, so how could they explain them in another language? Due to this, huge errors and baseless beliefs occurred in their translations, in addition to the fact that they had bad intentions and silly notions. This is apparent to anyone who reads the Scriptures that are in their hands and studies the bad interpretations, wicked substitutions and alterations therein. From Allah we seek help, and He is the Best Protector and the Best Helper.

---

(1)　This is an authentic *hadeeth* narrated by Imam Ahmad in his *Musnad* (3/56, No. 11142).

(2)　Narrated by Muslim (3004) and An-Nasa'i in *Al-Kubra* (5/10, No. 8008).

And according to what they have said, the Tawrah, of which they reveal some and conceal much, contains distortions, substitutions, alterations and bad interpretations, which are clear to anyone who reads them and studies what they (the Jews) said, what they revealed and what they concealed and (one may see) how they permit explanations based on unsound foundations and constructions, which are false in meaning and wording. Ka'b Al-Ahbar was one of the best of those who transmitted from them; he embraced Islam during the Caliphate of 'Umar ﷺ and he used to transmit things from the People of the Scripture. 'Umar ﷺ used to approve of some of what he transmitted, because it was in agreement with the truth and also, he wished to strengthen his faith. But many people enlarged on the information that he had and he, himself, overdid it in transmitting these things, many of which are not worth the ink with which they are written, while others are, without doubt, baseless. Others are correct, because they correspond with the truth which is in our hands. Al-Bukhari narrated on the authority of Humaid Ibn 'Abdur-Rahman, who said that he heard Mu'awiyah speaking to a group of Quraish in Al-Madinah and he mentioned Ka'b Al-Ahbar. He said, "Though he is one of the most truthful of those who relate from the People of the Scripture, we found that some of what he said was lies (i.e. he transmitted these lies unintentionally)."

The Story of Juraij, One of the Slaves of Banu Isra'eel

Imam Ahmad narrated on the authority of Abu Hurairah ﷺ that he said, "The Messenger of Allah ﷺ said, "None spoke in the cradle except three: 'Eesa, the son of Maryam, Juraij's companion; Juraij was a man of worship, he had a place of worship and while he was in it, his mother came in and called upon him. He said to himself; 'My Lord, my mother or my prayer?' So he continued praying and she left. The next day also she came and called upon him while he was in prayer. He said to himself; 'My Lord, my mother or my prayer?' So he continued praying and again she left. The following day she came again and called upon him while he was in prayer, he said to himself; 'My Lord, my mother or my prayer?' So he continued praying. She said: 'O, Allah, do not allow him to die until he sees the faces of prostitutes.' The Children of Isra'eel knew of Juraij and his worship. There was a very beautiful prostitute who offered to seduce him. She attempted to do so but he did not pay any attention to her. She then approached a herdsman who used to seek refuge in his place of worship, she offered herself to him and he slept with her. She became pregnant, and when she gave birth she claimed that it was the child of Juraij. The people went to him, invoked curses over him, destroyed his place of worship and attacked him. He said, "Why are you doing this?" They responded, "You fornicated with this woman and she bore you a child." He said, "Where is the child?" So they brought him the child. He said, "Leave me until I pray." When he finished praying he came to the boy and poked him in his stomach. He said, "O, child, who is your father?" The baby boy responded, "So-and-so the herdsman." So the people turned to Juraij, kissing him and asking him for forgiveness. They offered to rebuild his place of worship in gold, but he refused and asked them to rebuild it from mud just as it was before, and so they did. [There was also a baby who was being breastfed by his mother when a rider in fine garments passed by on an agile animal. His mother said, "O, Allah! Make my child like him." The baby stopped suckling and looked at him, then he said, "O, Allah! Do not make me like him." He then continued suckling…" Abu Hurairah ﷺ said, "It is as if I can see Messenger of Allah ﷺ right now, as he is illustrating the scene of the baby's suckling with his forefinger in his mouth." He continued, "They passed by a slave girl who was being beaten by people who were accusing her of committing fornication and theft." She was saying, "Sufficient is Allah for me."

And Al-Bukhari narrated on the authority of 'Abdur-Rahman Al-A'raj that he heard Abu Hurairah ﷺ heard the Messenger of Allah ﷺ say, "While a woman was nursing her child, a rider passed by and she said, "O, Allah! Don't let my child die till he becomes like this (rider)." The child said, "O, Allah! Don't make me like him," and then returned to her breast (sucking it). (After a while) they passed by a lady who was being pulled and teased (by the people). The child's mother said, "O, Allah! Do not make my child like her." The child said, "O, Allah! Make me like her." Then he said, "As for the rider, he is an infidel, while the lady is accused of illegal sexual intercourse (falsely) and she says: "Allah is sufficient for me (i.e. He knows the truth)." And it has been reported regarding those who spoke in the cradle also that Yoosuf's witness did so, [1] and the son of Fir'awn's wife's maidservant. And Allah knows better.

The Story of Barseesa

This is the opposite of the case of Juraij, for he resisted temptation, while Barseesa succumbed to it.

Ibn Jareer narrated on the authority of 'Abdullah Ibn Mas'ood ﷺ regarding this Verse: ﴿ (Their allies deceived them) like *Shaitan* (Satan), when he says to man, "Disbelieve in Allah." But when (man) disbelieves in Allah, *Shaitan* says, "I am free of you, I fear Allah, the Lord of the *'Alameen!*" So the end of both will be that they will be in the Fire, abiding therein. Such is the recompense

---

(1) Translator's note: According to Shaikh Nasiruddeen Al-Albani in *Silsil-atul-Ahadeeth Ad-Da'eefah wal-Mawdoo'ah*, there is no evidence to suggest that this witness was a baby.

of the *zalimoon*. ﴾ (*Soorah Al-Hashr* 59:16,17) – that he said,
"Once there was a woman grazing sheep and goats. She had four
brothers. She used to seek shelter at night at a monk's cell. The
monk committed adultery with her and she got pregnant. Shaitan
came to him and said, "Kill the woman and then bury her for you
are a reputable and highly respected man (i.e. do not risk your
own reputation for such a simple woman)." The monk killed her
and then buried her. Thereupon, Shaitan visited her four brothers
in a dream while they were asleep and said to them, "The monk
committed adultery with your sister and, he killed her and buried
her in such-and-such a location because she got pregnant. In the
morning, one of them said, "By Allah! Last night I dreamt of
something and I do not know whether to relate it to you or just
keep it to myself." They said, "Relate it to us." He did so and one
of them said, "By Allah! I saw the same dream." Another said the
same. And the fourth one said the same thing. They agreed that
there must be something serious about that dream. They went to
the king and appealed for his help against the monk. The king's
troops came to arrest him and he was taken away. On the way,
Shaitan came to the monk (and whispered in his ears), "I caused
you to fall into this. No one else can save you from this. Prostrate
yourself before me just for once and in return, I will save you from
this." Thereupon, the monk prostrated himself before Shaitan.
When they presented themselves before the king, Shaitan said to
him, "I am free of you! Finally, the monk was killed." [1] It was
likewise narrated thus on the authority of 'Abdullah ibn 'Abbas
⬥, Tawoos, Muqatil ibn Hayyan.

And in a narration on the authority of 'Ali Ibn Abi Talib ⬥
that he said, "A monk worshipped Allah, Alone for sixty years.
Shaitan exerted himself to seduce him, but could not. He went to
a woman and touched her with evil (maddened her). The woman
had brothers who were visited by Shaitan, who told them to take

---

(1)   Narrated by Ibn Jareer At-Tabari in his *Tafseer* (28/49, No. 26267).

her to that monk to receive treatment and cure. They took her to the monk and he treated her. Afterwards, she stayed for a while at his cell (house). One day, he was attracted to her and he committed adultery with her. She got pregnant and he killed her (to conceal his first crime). Her brothers came (after knowing the matter) and Shaitan appeared again for the monk and said, "I am your friend, I did not find a solution or way to mislead you, but (finally) I did this to you. So obey me and I will save you from this. Prostrate yourself before me and you will be saved." The monk did so. Then, Shaitan said: ❨ "I am free of you, I fear Allah, the Lord of the *'Alameen!*" ❩ (*Soorah Al-Hashr* 59:16)

The Story of the Three Who Took Refuge in the Cave

Allah's Messenger ﷺ said, "While three persons were traveling, they were overtaken by rain and they took shelter in a cave in a mountain. A big rock fell from the mountain over the mouth of the cave and blocked it. They said to each other. "Think of good (righteous) deeds which you did for Allah's sake only and invoke Allah by giving reference to those deeds so that Allah may relieve you from your difficulty. One of them said, "O, Allah! I had my parents who were very old and I had small children for whose sake I used to work as a shepherd. When I returned to them at night and milked (the sheep), I used to start giving the milk to my parents first before giving to my children. And one day I went far away in search of a grazing place (for my sheep), and did not return home till late at night and found that my parents had slept. I milked (my livestock) as usual and brought the milk vessel and stood at their heads, and I disliked to wake them up from their sleep, and I also disliked to give the milk to my children before my parents, though my children were crying (from hunger) at my feet. So this state of mine and theirs continued till the day dawned. (O, Allah!) If you considered that I had done that only for seeking Your pleasure, then please let there be an opening through which we can see the sky." So Allah made for them an opening through which they could see the sky. Then the second person said, "O, Allah! I had a cousin whom I loved as much as a passionate man loves a woman. I tried to seduce her, but she refused till I paid her one hundred *dinars*. So I worked hard till I collected one hundred *dinars* and went to her with that. But when I sat between her legs (to have sexual intercourse with her), she said, "O, slave of Allah! Be afraid of Allah ! Do not deflower me except legally (by marriage contract)." So I left her. O, Allah! If you considered that I had done that only for seeking Your pleasure, then please let the rock move a little to have a (wider) opening." So Allah moved that rock to make the opening wider for them. And the last (third) person said "O, Allah! I employed a laborer for wages equal to a *faraq* (a certain measure) of rice, and when he finished his job he demanded his wages, but when I presented his due to him, he gave it up and refused to take it. Then I kept on sowing that rice for him (several times) till I managed to buy with the price of the yield some cows and their shepherd. Later on the laborer came to me and said, "(Oh slave of Allah!) Be afraid of Allah, do not be unjust to me and give me my due." I said (to him), "Go and take those cows and their shepherd." So he took them and went away. (So, O, Allah,) if You consider that I did that for the purpose of seeking Your pleasure, then please remove the remaining part of the rock." And so Allah released them (from their difficulty)." [1]

---

[1] Narrated by Al-Bukhari (3465) and Muslim (2743).

The Story of the Three Men: the Blind, the Leper and the Bald

Al-Bukhari and Muslim narrated from more than one source on the authority of Abu Hurairah ⬥ that he heard the Messenger of Allah ⬥ say, "Allah willed to test three men from the Children of Isra'eel, who were a leper, a blind man and a baldheaded man. So He sent them an angel who came to the leper and said, "What thing would you like most?" He replied, "Good color and good skin, for the people have a strong aversion to me." The angel touched him and his illness was cured, and he was given a good color and beautiful skin. The angel asked him, "What kind of property do you like best?" He replied, "Camels (or cows – the narrator is in doubt, for either the leper or the baldheaded man demanded camels and the other demanded cows)." So he (i.e. the leper) was given a pregnant she-camel and the angel said (to him), "May Allah bless you in it." The angel then went to the baldheaded man and said, "What thing would you like most?" He said, "I would like good hair and wish to be cured of this disease, for the people feel repulsion for me." The angel touched him and his illness was cured, and he was given good hair. The angel asked (him), "What kind of property do you like best?" He replied, "Cows." The angel gave him a pregnant cow and said, "May Allah bless you in it." The angel went to the blind man and asked, "What thing would you like best?" He said, "(I would like) that Allah may restore my eyesight to me so that I may see the people." The angel touched his eyes and Allah gave him back his eyesight. The angel asked him, "What kind of property do you like best?" He replied, "Sheep." The angel gave him a pregnant sheep. Afterwards, all the three pregnant animals gave birth to young ones, and multiplied and brought forth so much that one of the (three) men had a herd of camels filling a valley, and one had a herd of cows filling a valley, and one had a flock of sheep filling a valley. Then the angel, disguised in the shape and appearance of a leper, went to the leper and said, "I am a poor man, who has lost all means of livelihood while on a journey. So none can satisfy my need except Allah and then you." In the Name of Him Who has given you such a nice color and beautiful skin, and so much property, I ask you to give me a camel so that I may reach my destination. The man replied, "I have many obligations (so I cannot give you one)." The angel said, "I think I know you; were you not a leper to whom the people had a strong aversion? Were you not a poor man, and then Allah gave you (all this property)?" He replied, "(This is all wrong), I got this property through inheritance from my forefathers." The angel said, "If you are telling a lie, then let Allah make you as you were before." Then the angel, disguised in the shape and appearance of a bald man, went to the bald man and said to him the same as he told the first one, and he too answered the same as the first one did. The angel said, "If you are telling a lie, then let Allah make you as you were before." The angel, disguised in the shape of a blind man, went to the blind man and said, "I am a poor man and a traveler, whose means of livelihood have been exhausted while on a journey. I have nobody to help me except Allah, and after Him, you. I ask you in the Name of Him

Who has given you back your eyesight to give me a sheep, so that with its help, I may complete my journey." The man said, "No doubt, I was blind and Allah gave me back my eyesight; I was poor and Allah made me rich; so take anything you wish from my property. By Allah, I will not stop you from taking anything (you need) of my property which you may take for Allah's sake." The angel replied, "Keep your property with you. You (i.e. three men) have been tested and Allah is pleased with you and is angry with your two companions." [1]

The Hadeeth of the Man Who Borrowed a Thousand Dinars From His Companion and Repaid It

Imam Ahmad narrated on the authority of Abu Hurairah ﷺ from the Messenger of Allah ﷺ that a man from among the Children of Isra'eel asked some of the Children of Isra'eel to lend him a thousand *dinars*. The second man required witnesses. The former replied, "Allah is sufficient as a witness." The second said, "I want a surety." The former replied, "Allah is sufficient as a surety." The second said, "You are right," and lent him the money for a certain period. The debtor then traveled across the sea. When he finished his work, he searched for a ship so that he might reach in time for the repayment of the debt, but he could not find any. So he took a piece of wood and made a hole in it, inserted in it one thousand *dinars* and a letter to the lender and then closed (i.e. sealed) the hole tightly. He took the piece of wood to the sea and said, "O, Allah! You know well that I took a loan of one thousand *dinars* from so-and-so. He demanded a surety from me but I told

---

(1)   Narrated by Al-Bukhari (3464) and Muslim (2964).

him that Allah's Guarantee was sufficient and he accepted Your Guarantee. He then asked for a witness and I told him that Allah was sufficient as a Witness, and he accepted You as a Witness. No doubt, I tried hard to find a ship so that I could pay his money but could not find, so I hand over this money to You." Saying that, he threw the piece of wood into the sea till it went out far into it, and then he went away. Meanwhile, he started searching for a ship in order to reach the creditor's country. One day the lender came out of his house to see whether a ship had arrived bringing his money, and all of a sudden he saw the piece of wood in which his money had been deposited. He took it home to use for fire. When he sawed it, he found his money and the letter inside it. Shortly after that, the debtor came bringing one thousand *dinars* to him and said, "By Allah, I had been trying hard to get a boat so that I could bring you your money, but failed to get one before the one I have come by." The lender asked, "Have you sent something to me?" The debtor replied, "I have told you I could not get a boat other than the one I have come by." The lender said, "Allah has delivered on your behalf the money you sent in the piece of wood. So you may keep your one thousand *dinars* and depart guided on the right path." [1]

Imam Ahmad narrated it thus with a chain of narrators, while Al-Bukhari narrated it in a *mu'allaq* form, in a place other than his *Saheeh*, on the authority of Al-Laith Ibn Sa'd, indicating his firm belief that it is authentic. [2]

---

(1) This is an authentic *hadeeth* narrated by Imam Ahmad in his *Musnad* (348, No. 8381).

(2) This was mentioned by Al-Bukhari in a *mu'allaq* form in *The Book of Zakah* and also in *The Book of Transference of Debt* and in other places.

Another Story Similar to This Story, Regarding Truth and Trustworthiness

Al-Bukhari narrated on the authority of Abu Hurairah ﷺ that he said, "The Messenger of Allah ﷺ said, "A man bought a piece of land from another man, and the buyer found an earthenware jar filled with gold in the land. The buyer said to the seller, "Take your gold, as I have bought only the land from you, but I have not bought the gold from you." The (former) owner of the land said, "I have sold you the land with everything in it." So both of them took their case before a man, who asked, "Do you have children?" One of them said, "I have a boy." The other said, "I have a girl." The man said, "Marry the girl to the boy, spend of the money on both of them and give the rest of it in charity." [1]

Another Story

Al-Bukhari narrated on the authority of Abu Sa'eed Al-Khudri ﷺ from the Prophet ﷺ that he said, "There was a man among the Children of Isra'eel who murdered ninety-nine persons. Then he set out asking (whether his repentance could be accepted or not). He came upon a monk and asked him if his repentance could be accepted. The monk replied in the negative, so the man killed him. He kept on asking till a man advised him to go to such-and-such a village. (So he set out for it) but death overtook him on the way. While dying, he turned his chest toward that village (where he had hoped his repentance would be accepted), and so the angels of mercy and the angels of punishment quarreled among themselves regarding him. Allah ordered the village

---

(1) Narrated by Al-Bukhari (3472) and Muslim (1721).

(toward which he was going) to come closer to him, and ordered the village (from where he had come) to move further away, and then He ordered the angels to measure the distances between his body and the two villages. He was found to be one hand span closer to the village (toward which he was heading) and so he was forgiven." [1]

Another *hadeeth*: Al-Bukhari narrated on the authority of Abu Hurairah ☸ that he said, "The Messenger of Allah ☸ performed the *Fajr* prayer, then he faced the people and said, "While a man was driving a cow, he suddenly mounted it and struck it. The cow said, "We have not been created for this, but we have been created for plowing." On that the people said astonishingly, "Glorified be Allah! A cow speaks!" The Prophet ☸ said, "I believe this, and Abu Bakr and 'Umar believe it too," although neither of them was present there. While a person was amongst his sheep, a wolf attacked and took one of the sheep. The man chased the wolf till he saved it from the wolf, where upon the wolf said, "You have saved it from me; but who will guard it on the day of the wild beasts when there will be no shepherd to guard them except me (because of riots and afflictions)?" The people said surprisingly, "Glorified be Allah! A wolf speaks!" The Prophet said, "I believe this, and Abu Bakr and 'Umar, believe it too," although neither of them was present there." [2]

Another *hadeeth*: Al-Bukhari narrated on the authority of Abu Hurairah ☸ that he reported from the Prophet ☸ that he said, "Amongst the people who came before you there used to be *muhaddithoon* (i.e. persons who can guess things that come true later on, as if those persons have been inspired by a Divine Power), and if there is any such person amongst my followers, it

---

(1)   Narrated by Al-Bukhari (3470) and Muslim (2766).

(2)   Narrated by Al-Bukhari (3471).

is 'Umar ibn Al-Khattab." [1]

Another *hadeeth*. Al-Bukhari narrated in his *Saheeh*, on the authority of Abu Hurairah ﷺ that he said, "The Messenger of Allah ﷺ said, "The Prophet said, "While a dog was going round a well and was about to die of thirst, an Isra'eelite prostitute saw it and took off her shoe and gave it water to drink. So Allah forgave her because of that (good deed)." [2]

Another *hadeeth*: Al-Bukhari narrated on the authority of 'Abdullah ibn 'Umar ﷺ that the Messenger of Allah ﷺ said, "A woman was punished because of a cat which she had imprisoned till it died. She entered the Fire because of it, for she neither gave it food nor water as she had imprisoned it, nor set it free to eat from the vermin of the earth." [3]

Another *hadeeth*: Imam Ahmad narrated on the authority of Abu Sa'eed Al-Khudri ﷺ that the Messenger of Allah ﷺ said, "Among the Children of Isra'eel there was a woman who was short in stature and so she made two sandals out of wood and she used to walk between two short women. She had a gold ring and she placed the best of perfumes and musk underneath its stone and when she passed by the meeting-place, she would shake it and it would diffuse its fragrance." [4]

Another *hadeeth*: Al-Bukhari narrated on the authority of Abu Mas'ood ﷺ that he said, "The Prophet ﷺ said, "One of the sayings of the prophets which the people have got, is: "If you do not feel ashamed, then do whatever you like." [5]

---

(1)   Narrated by Al-Bukhari (3469) and Muslim (2398).

(2)   Narrated by Al-Bukhari (3467) and Muslim (2245).

(3)   Narrated by Al-Bukhari (3482) and Muslim (2242).

(4)   This is an authentic *hadeeth* narrated by Imam Ahmad in his *Musnad* (3/40, No. 10971) and by Muslim (with a similar wording) (2252).

(5)   Narrated by Al-Bukhari (3/484)

Another *hadeeth*: "Imam Ahmad narrated on the authority of Abu Hurairah ⨎ that he said, "A man entered upon his family and when he saw how needy they were, he went out to the desert. When his wife saw that, she went to the millstone and set it up, then she went to the oven and lit it. After that, she said, "O, Allah! Provide us with sustenance." Then she looked, and saw that the *jafnah* [1] had become filled and she went to the oven and saw that it had become filled. Then her husband returned and said, "Did you get something after me?" His wife said, "Yes, from our Lord." He stood up and went to the millstone." This was mentioned to the Prophet ﷺ and he said, "If he had not lifted it up, it would have continued turning until the Day of Resurrection." [2]

---

(1) *Jafnah*: Bowl

(2) This is an authentic *hadeeth* narrated by Imam Ahmad in his *Musnad* (2/513, No. 9168) and the narrators are trustworthy. It was also narrated by Al-Bazzar (3687) and At-Tabarani in *Al-Awsat* (5584) and Al-Baihaqi in *Ad-Dala`il* (6/105) and *Ash-Shu'ab* (1339).

The Story of the two Repentant Kings

Imam Ahmad narrated on the authority of 'Abdullah Ibn Mas'ood ﷺ that he said, "While a man from among those who lived before you was in his kingdom, he began to think, and he realized that all of that would be cut off from him and that his (royal) situation had diverted him from the worship of his Lord, so he stole away from his palace one night and went to a neighboring kingdom. He arrived at the coast and there he found work of brick-making. With the wages he was paid, he sustained himself and gave the remainder as charity. He continued doing this until news of him, his worship and his virtue was conveyed to the king. The king sent a message to him calling for his presence. But he refused to go to him. The king repeated his demand again and again, but he refused to go to him. The king said, "Who is he, and who am I?" So he mounted his horse and rode to him. When the man saw him, he turned away from him and fled. When the king saw this, he raced in pursuit of him but he did not catch up with him, so he called out to him, "O, slave of Allah! You have nothing to fear from me." So the man stood still until the king caught up with him. The king asked him, "Who are you, may Allah have mercy on you?" He replied, "I am so-and-so, the son of so-and-so, the ruler of such-and-such a kingdom. I thought about my situation and I realized that my kingdom would (one day) be cut off from me, and it had diverted me from the worship of my Lord, so I abandoned it and came here, that I might worship my Lord, the Almighty, the All-Powerful." The king said, "You were not in greater need of that which you did than I." Then he dismounted from his horse and set it free. Then he followed him and both of them together worshipped Allah, the Almighty, the All-Powerful and they asked Him to cause them to die together. So they both died." 'Abdullah ؏ said, "If we were in Rumailah, Egypt, I would show You their graves in the location described to me by the Messenger of Allah ﷺ." [1]

Another *hadeeth*: Al-Bukhari narrated on the authority of Abu Sa'eed Al-Khudri ؏ from the Prophet ﷺ, that he said, "Amongst the people who lived before you, there was a man whom Allah had given a lot of money. When he was on his deathbed, he called his sons and said, "What type of father have I been to you?" They replied, "You have been a good father." He said, "I have never done a single good deed; so when I die, burn me, crush my body, and scatter the resulting ashes on a windy day." His sons did accordingly, but Allah gathered the particles and asked (him), "What made you do so?" He replied, "Fear of you." So Allah bestowed His Mercy upon him (i.e. forgave him)." [2]

Another *hadeeth*: It is reported on the authority of Abu Hurairah ؏ from the Prophet ﷺ that he said, "A man used to give loans to the people and used to say to his servant, "If the debtor is poor, forgive him, so that Allah may forgive us." So when he met Allah

---

(1) Narrated by Imam Ahmad in his *Musnad* (1/451, No. 4300), with a *hasan* chain of narrators.

(2) Narrated by Al-Bukhari (3478) and (3452).

(after his death), Allah forgave him." [1]

Another *hadeeth*: Al-Bukhari narrated on the authority of 'Amir ibn Sa'd Ibn Abi Waqqas from his father that he heard him asking Usamah Ibn Zaid ؓ, "What did you hear from the Messenger of Allah ﷺ regarding plague?" Usamah replied, "The Messenger of Allah ﷺ said, "Plague is a calamity which was sent to the Children of Isra'eel or upon those who were before you. So when you hear that it has broken out in a land, do not go to it, and when it has broken out in the land where you are, do not run away from it." [2] It was also narrated by Muslim.

Another *hadeeth*: Al-Bukhari narrated on the authority of 'A'ishah (may Allah be Pleased with her) that the people of Quraish became very worried about the *Makhzoomiyyah* lady who had committed theft. They said, "Nobody can speak (in favor of the lady) to the Messenger of Allah ﷺ and nobody dares do that except Usamah, who is the favorite of Allah's Messenger ﷺ." When Usamah spoke to the Messenger of Allah ﷺ about that matter, he said, "Do you intercede (with me) to violate one of the legal punishments of Allah?" Then he got up and addressed the people, saying, "O, people! The nations before you went astray because if a noble person committed theft, they used to leave him, but if a weak person among them committed theft, they used to inflict the legal punishment on him. By Allah, if Fatimah, the daughter of Muhammad, committed theft, I would cut off her hand!" [3]

Another *hadeeth*: Al-Bukhari narrated on the authority of 'Abdullah Ibn Mas'ood ؓ that he said, "I heard a man reciting a Verse from the Qur'an and I had heard the Messenger of Allah ﷺ

---

(1)   Narrated by Al-Bukhari (3480) and Muslim (1562).

(2)   Narrated by Al-Bukhari (3473) and Muslim (2218).

(3)   Narrated by Al-Bukhari (3475), Muslim (1688), Abu Dawood (4373),
       At-Tirmidhi (1430), An-Nasa'i (4899) and Ibn Majah (2547).

reciting it in a different way and so I took him to the Messenger of Allah ﷺ and informed him (of what I had heard). I recognized in his face signs of dislike and he said, "Both of you are right. Do not differ, for the nations before you differed and perished (because of their differences)." [1]

Another *hadeeth*: Al-Bukhari narrated on the authority of Abu Hurairah ﷺ that he said, "The Messenger of Allah ﷺ said, "The Jews and Christians do not dye (their grey hair), so do the opposite of what they do (i.e. dye your grey hair and beards)." [2] Al-Bukhari was alone in narrating this; Muslim did not narrate it. In Abu Dawood's *Sunan* it is reported : "Pray in your shoes (and by so doing,) be different from the Jews." [3]

Another *hadeeth*: Al-Bukhari narrated on the authority of 'Abdullah Ibn 'Abbas ﷺ that once 'Umar ﷺ was informed that a certain man sold alcohol and he heard him say, "May Allah curse so-and-so! Does he not know that the Messenger of Allah ﷺ said, "May Allah curse the Jews, for Allah had forbidden them to eat the fat of animals but they melted it and sold it." [4]

Another *hadeeth*: Al-Bukhari narrated on the authority of Anas Ibn Malik ﷺ that he said: "The people mentioned the fire and the bell (i.e. they suggested those as signals to indicate the starting of prayers), and by that they mentioned the Jews and the Christians. Then Bilal was ordered to pronounce the *Adhan* for the prayers by repeating its wordings twice; and for the *iqamah* (the call for the actual standing for the prayers in rows) by pronouncing its wordings once. (The *iqamah* is pronounced when the people are ready for the prayer)." [5]

---

(1)   Narrated by Al-Bukhari (3476).

(2)   Narrated by Al-Bukhari (3462).

(3)   Narrated by Abu Dawood (652).

(4)   Narrated by Al-Bukhari (3460).

(5)   Narrated by Al-Bukhari (603) and Muslim (378).

What is meant by this is that we should be different to the People of the Scripture in all manners and characteristics, because when the Messenger of Allah ﷺ arrived in Al-Madinah, the Muslims used to come to prayer without any call to it. Then he ordered someone to call them to prayer (by saying, "The prayer is convened."). Then they wished to be called to prayer with something that the people would recognize, so some of them said, "Let us ring a bell." Others said, "Let us light a fire." But they disliked this, because it was similar to the practices of the People of the Scripture. Then 'Abdullah Ibn Zaid Ibn 'Abd Rabbih Al-Ansari was shown the *Adhan* in a dream. He related this to the Messenger of Allah ﷺ, who ordered Bilal ﷺ to pronounce the *Adhan*, as described in the Chapter on the *Adhan*, in *the Book of Judgments* (in *Saheeh Al-Bukhari*).

Another *hadeeth*: Al-Bukhari narrated on the authority of 'A'ishah (may Allah be Pleased with her) and 'Abdullah Ibn 'Abbas ﷺ that they said that on his deathbed, the Messenger ﷺ would put a sheet over his face and when he felt hot, he would remove it from his face. While in that state (of putting and removing the sheet) he said, "May Allah's Curse be on the Jews and the Christians for they build places of worship at the graves of their prophets." (By that) he intended to warn (Muslims) against what they (i.e. the Jews and Christians) had done. [1]

Another *hadeeth*: Al-Bukhari narrated on the authority of Abu Sa'eed Al-Khudri that the Prophet ﷺ said, "You will follow the ways of those nations who were before you, span by span and cubit by cubit (i.e. inch by inch) so much so that even if they entered a hole of a mastigure, [2] you would follow them." We said, "O, Messenger of Allah! (Are you referring to) the Jews and

---

(1)   Narrated by Al-Bukhari (3454) and Muslim (531).

(2)   Mastigure: Spiny-tailed lizard: a lizard that blocks its burrow with its very spiny tail.

the Christians?" He said, "Whom else?" [1]

What is meant by this is to acquaint us with the sayings and deeds that resemble those of the People of the Scripture who lived before us, which are prohibited according to Islamic Law, and to inform us that Allah and His Messenger ﷺ have prohibited us from copying them in their words and deeds. Even if the intention of the Believer was a good one, if his deed is clearly an imitation of their deeds (it is forbidden). And just as praying at sunrise and sunset is prohibited, in order not to imitate the pagans, who used to prostrate before the sun in those times – even if no such intention occurred to the Believer. Likewise, this is why Allah, Most High, says, ﴿ O, you who believe! Say not (to the Messenger ﷺ), *"Ra'ina,"* but say *"Unzurna,"* (Do make us understand) and hear. And for the disbelievers there is a painful punishment. (See Verse 4:46) ﴾ (*Soorah Al-Baqarah* 2:104). The disbelievers used to say to the Prophet ﷺ, when they spoke with him, *"Ra'ina,"* i.e. direct your gaze toward us and listen to our words. What they actually meant by this was 'joke with us.' So the Believers were prohibited from saying that, even if none of them intended this (evil meaning) by it.

And Imam Ahmad and At-Tirmidhi narrated on the authority of 'Abdullah ibn 'Umar ﷺ from the Prophet ﷺ that he said, "I was sent with the sword just before the Last Hour, so that Allah is worshipped alone without partners. My sustenance was provided for me from under the shadow of my spear. Those who oppose my command were humiliated and made inferior, and whoever imitates a people, he is one of them." [2] So it is not permissible for Muslims to imitate them, whether it be in their religious festivals and holidays, or in their worship, because Allah, Most High, has honored this (Islamic) nation with the Seal of the Prophets, for whom the great, eternal, comprehensive and complete Religion

---

(1)   Narrated by Al-Bukhari (3456) and Muslim (2669).

(2)   Narrated by Imam Ahmad in his *Musnad* (2/50, No. 5093).

was legislated – the Prophet who, if Moosa ﷺ, son of 'Imran – to whom the Tawrah was sent down – and 'Eesa ﷺ, the son of Maryam – to whom the Injeel was revealed – were present, indeed if all of the Prophets were present, they would have no alternative but to follow this pure, noble, exalted and mighty Law. And since Allah, Most High, has blessed us by making us the followers of Muhammad ﷺ, so how can it befit us to imitate a people who have gone astray aforetime, and who have misguided many from the Straight Path? They have altered their religion, distorted it and deliberately misinterpreted it, until it appeared that it was a different religion entirely to that which was originally legislated for them. In addition to this, it is based on adherence to that which has been abrogated; and holding fast to what has been abrogated is unlawful. Allah will accept neither little nor much of it. And there is no difference between it and something that was not legislated (by Allah) at all. And Allah guides whom He wills to the Straight Path.

Another *hadeeth*: Al-Bukhari narrated on the authority of 'Abdullah Ibn 'Umar ﷺ from the Messenger of Allah ﷺ that he said, "Your period (i.e. the Muslims' period) in comparison to the periods of the previous nations is like the period between the *'Asr* prayer and sunset. And your example in comparison to the Jews and the Christians is like the example of a person who employed some laborers and asked them, "Who will work for me till midday for one *qeerat* each?" The Jews worked for half a day for one *qeerat* each. The person asked, "Who will do the work for me from midday to the time of the *'Asr* (prayer) for one *qeerat* each?" The Christians worked from midday till the *'Asr* prayer for one *qeerat*. Then the person asked, "Who will do the work for me from the *'Asr* prayer till sunset for two *qeerats* each?" The Prophet ﷺ said, "It is you (i.e. the Muslims) who are doing the work from the *'Asr* prayer till sunset, so you will have a double reward. The Jews and the Christians got angry and said, "We have

done more work but got less wages." Allah said, "Have I been
unjust to you as regards your rights?" They said, "No." So Allah
said, "Then it is My Blessing which I bestow on whomsoever I
will." [1] In this *hadeeth* there is evidence that the period of this
nation is short, compared to the periods of the nations who came
before us. This is inferred from the saying of the Prophet ﷺ: "Your
period (i.e. the Muslims' period) in comparison to the periods of
the previous nations is like the period between the *'Asr* prayer
and sunset." And none knows the past except Allah, just as none
but He knows the future. But it is short in comparison to what has
passed; and none knows precisely how much time remains except
Allah, the Almighty, the All-Powerful, as He, Most High, says,
❴ None can reveal its time but He ❵ (*Soorah Al-A'raf* 7:187) and
He, Most High, says, ❴ They ask you (o, Muhammad) about the
Hour – when will be its appointed time? You have no knowledge
to say anything about it. To your Lord belongs (the knowledge
of) the term thereof ❵ (*Soorah An-Nazi'at* 79:42-44). As for the
hadeeth that some of the people mention, which is well-known
to the common folk, and which states: "He has no knowledge
of the unseen," it is baseless and is not to be found in the books
of *ahadeeth*. A *hadeeth* has been related which states that the
life of this world is one Friday of the Fridays of the Hereafter.
[2] But there is doubt about its authenticity. What is meant by this
comparison between the workers is to point out the dissimilarity
in their rewards and that this is not dependent on abundance of
deeds or paucity of deeds. Rather, it is dependent on other matters
which Allah, Most High, deems important. And how often are
few deeds more useful or advantageous than abundant deeds?
Deeds performed on *Lailatul-Qadr*, for example, are better

---

(1) Narrated by Al-Bukhari (3459).

(2) Narrated by At-Tabari in *At-Tareekh* (1/15), on the authority of 'Abdullah
     Ibn 'Abbas ﷺ in a *mawqoof* form and by Ibn Abi 'Asim in *Az-Zuhd*, on
     the authority of Sa'eed Ibn Jubair ﷺ. But as the author points out, there is
     doubt about its authenticity.

than a thousand nights of worship performed at any other time. The Companions of Muhammad ﷺ spent (in Allah's Cause) and if someone in our time were to spend the same amount in gold as they spent in dates, it would not be equivalent to it. And Allah sent the Messenger of Allah ﷺ when he was forty years old and took him when he was sixty-three, according to what is widely accepted. During these twenty-three years, he excelled in beneficial knowledge and righteous deeds over all of the Prophets who came before him, including even Nooh ﷺ, who remained among his people for nine hundred and fifty years, calling them to the worship of Allah, Alone, without partners and working day and night in obedience to Allah. May the Blessings and Peace of Allah be upon all of the Prophets. This nation was only honored and had its reward multiplied because of the blessed leadership of the Prophet ﷺ, his nobility and his greatness, as Allah, Most High, says, ﴾ O, you who believe (in Moosa i.e. the Jews and 'Eesa i.e. the Christians)! Fear Allah and believe too in His Messenger (Muhammad). He will give you a double portion of His Mercy, and He will give you a light by which you shall walk (straight), and He will forgive you. And Allah is Oft-Forgiving, Most Merciful. So that the people of the Scripture (the Jews and Christians) may know that they have no power whatsoever over the Grace of Allah and that (His) Grace is (entirely) in His Hand to bestow on whomsoever He wills. And Allah is the Owner of Great Bounty. ﴿ (*Soorah Al-Hadeed* 57:28,29)

Section:

The stories of the Children of Isra'eel are extremely numerous in the Qur'an and the Prophetic *Sunnah*, and were we to make an exhaustive study of them, the book would be very long. But we have mentioned what Imam Abu 'Abdullah Al-Bukhari has mentioned in this book and in that there is sufficiency, and they are a reminder and examples for this chapter. And Allah knows better.

As for the Isra'eelites' stories, according to what has been mentioned by the scholars of *tafseer* and the scholars of history, they are extremely numerous. Some of them are authentic and agree with what has been related in the Qur'an and *Sunnah*. But a lot of the stories they mention – indeed, most of them – are lies and inventions fabricated by their disbelievers and those who had gone astray. These narrations fall into three categories: (i) Those that are authentic, because they agree with what Allah has related in His Book or with what the Messenger of Allah ﷺ has reported; (ii) those whose falseness is known, because they contradict the Book of Allah and the *Sunnah* of His Messenger ﷺ; and (iii) those which may be true, or they may be false. Concerning this latter category, we are commanded to remain non-committal. We neither believe them nor belie them, as confirmed in the authentic *hadeeth*: "If the People of the Scripture relate something to you, neither believe them, nor disbelieve them; instead, say, "We believe in what has been revealed to us and in what has been revealed to you." [1] And it is permissible to report it, according to the aforementioned *hadeeth*, which states: "Relate from the Children of Isra'eel, and there is no objection." [2]

---

(1) Narrated by Imam Ahmad (2/159, No. 16774) and by Abu Dawood (3644).

(2) Narrated by Imam Ahmad (2/474) and it has been mentioned previously, on page 360 (of the Arabic original).

Mention of the Alterations and Substitutions Made by the People of the Scripture in their Religion

As for the Jews, Allah had sent down to them the Tawrah, by the hand of Moosa, son of 'Imran, and it was as Allah says: ❲ Then, We gave Moosa the Book (the Tawrah), to complete (Our Favor) upon those who would do right, and explaining all things in detail ❳ (*Soorah Al-An'am* 6:154) and He, Most High, says, ❲ Verily, We did send down the Tawrah (to Moosa), therein was guidance and light, by which the Prophets, who submitted themselves to Allah's Will, judged the Jews. And the rabbis and the priests (too judged the Jews by the Tawrah after those Prophets) for to them was entrusted the protection of Allah's Book, and they were witnesses thereto. Therefore fear not men but fear Me (O, Jews) and sell not My Verses for a miserable price. And whosoever does not judge by what Allah has revealed, such are the *kafiroon* (i.e. disbelievers of a lesser degree, as they do not act on Allah's

Laws) ﴾ (*Soorah Al-Ma'idah* 5:44). They used to judge by them and they held fast to them for a while, but then they began to distort them, alter them, misconstrue them and declare things that were not from them, as Allah, Most High, says, ﴾ And verily, among them is a party who distort the Book with their tongues (as they read), so that you may think it is from the Book, but it is not from the Book, and they say, "This is from Allah," but it is not from Allah; and they speak a lie against Allah while they know it ﴿ (*Soorah Ali 'Imran* 3:78). So Allah, Most High, informs us that they explained it, misconstrued it and quoted things out of context – and there is no disagreement in this matter among the scholars, i.e. that they interpreted its meanings freely (according to their whims) and attributed false implications to it, such as when they changed the ruling of stoning to flogging and blackening of the face with charcoal, without altering the word for stoning in it. In addition, when an eminent person among them committed theft, they would overlook his offense, but when a weak or unimportant person among them committed theft, they would inflict the prescribed punishment on him, in spite of the fact that they were commanded to inflict all prescribed punishments on the eminent and the lowly, without distinction.

As for their alteration of its wordings, some said that it means that all of the words were altered. Others said that the whole of the Tawrah was not altered and they cited as evidence the Words of Allah: ﴾ But how do they come to you for decision while they have the Tawrah, in which is the (plain) Decision of Allah ﴿ (*Soorah Al-Ma'idah* 5:43) and: ﴾ Whom they find written with them in the Tawrah (Deuteronomy, xviii, 15) and the *Injeel* (Gospel) (John xiv, 16) – he commands them to implement *al-ma'roof* (i.e. Islamic Monotheism and all that Islam has ordained); and forbids them from *al-munkar* (i.e. disbelief, polytheism of all kinds, and all that Islam has forbidden); he allows them as lawful *at-tayyibat* ([i.e. everything good and lawful] as regards things, deeds, beliefs, persons, foods, etc.) ❩ (*Soorah Al-A 'raf* 7:157) and also: ❨ Say (O, Muhammad), "Bring here the Tawrah and recite it, if you are truthful." ❩ (*Soorah Ali 'Imran* 3:93).

And there is the story of the stoning, as confirmed in the *Saheehain*, on the authority of 'Abdullah Ibn 'Umar ﷺ, [1] in *Saheeh Muslim*, [2] on the authority of Al-Bara' Ibn 'Azib ﷺ, of Jabir ibn 'Abdillah ﷺ and in the *Sunan*, [3] on the authority of Abu Hurairah ﷺ and others, when they sought judgment from the Messenger of Allah ﷺ with regard to the case of the Jew and the Jewess who committed adultery, A Jew and a Jewess were brought to the Messenger of Allah on a charge of committing an illegal sexual intercourse. The Prophet ﷺ asked them. "What is the legal punishment (for this sin) in the Tawrah." They replied, "We blacken their faces with charcoal and flog them." So the Messenger of Allah ﷺ ordered them to bring the Tawrah. The Tawrah was brought, and 'Abdullah ibn Sooria (one of the Jews) put his hand over the Verse of *ar-rajm* (stoning to death) and started reading what preceded and what followed it. On that, the Messenger of Allah ﷺ said to the Jew, "Lift up your hand." So he lifted his hand and in it (the Tawrah) was the Verse of *ar-rajm*. The Messenger of Allah ﷺ then ordered that the two (sinners) be stoned to death and he said, "O, Allah! I am the first one to revive Your Commandment after they (the Jews) had suppressed it." And in Abu Dawood's *Sunan*, it was stated that they placed a cushion for the Messenger of Allah ﷺ who sat on it and said, "Bring the Tawrah." They brought it. Then he withdrew the cushion from beneath him and placed the Tawrah on it saying, "I believe in you and in Him Who revealed you." [4] Some of them said that he stood for it, but I have not read its *sanad*. And Allah knows better.

---

(1)   Narrated by Al-Bukhari (6819) and Muslim (1699).

(2)   Narrated by Muslim (1700 and 1701).

(3)   Narrated by Abu Dawood (4450 and 4451).

(4)   Narrated by Abu Dawood (4449).

Many of the religious scholars and others have said that the *tawatur*[1] of the Tawrah was cut off during the era of Bukhtunassar, and that none remained who had memorised it except Uzair (Ezra عليه السلام). But Uzair عليه السلام was a Prophet and was thus protected from error (by Allah) and *tawatur* up to a person who is protected from error is sufficient. Although it was said that it was not *mutawatir*[2] up to him. But after him came Zakariyya, Yahya and 'Eesa (peace be upon them all) – and all of them held fast to the Tawrah; now if it had not been authentic and valid, they would not have depended on it, since they were Prophets, protected from error. In addition, Allah, Most High, has stated in the Revelation sent down to His Messenger, Muhammad, the Seal of the Prophets – may the Peace and Blessings of Allah be upon him and upon all of the Prophets – which rebukes the Jews for their evil intentions, because they turned away from that which they knew to be true (i.e. the Tawrah) and which they were commanded to follow, in favor of seeking judgment from the Messenger of Allah ﷺ, even though they rejected what he had brought. But in reality, they were seeking a judgment that concurred with their heresy, i.e. flogging and blackening of the face, which was contrary to what Allah had Commanded them to do. And they said, "If he rules that you should flog them and blacken their faces, then accept it, and on the Day of Resurrection, when you stand before Allah, you will be able to plead in your defence that you were given a ruling by a Prophet. But if he does not make this ruling for you, then beware of accepting it from him." So Allah, Most High, rebuked them for their evil intention, which was prompted by the desire to attain a corrupt objective, and accorded with their own inclinations and desires, not the true Religion, which is why Allah, Most High, says, ❴ But how do they come to you

---

(1) *Tawatur*: Continuity, i.e. being transmitted by so many people, from a variety of sources, that it would be impossible for them to have conspired together to produce falsehood.

(2) *Mutawatir*: Possessing *tawatur*.

for decision while they have the Tawrah, in which is the (plain) Decision of Allah; yet even after that, they turn away. For they are not (really) Believers. Verily, We did send down the Tawrah (to Moosa), therein was guidance and light, by which the Prophets, who submitted themselves to Allah's Will, judged the Jews. And the rabbis and the priests (too judged the Jews by the Tawrah after those Prophets) for to them was entrusted the protection of Allah's Book, and they were witnesses thereto. Therefore fear not men but fear Me (O, Jews) and sell not My Verses for a miserable price. And whosoever does not judge by what Allah has revealed, such are the *kafiroon* (i.e. disbelievers – of a lesser degree, as they do not act on Allah's Laws 》 (*Soorah Al-Ma'idah* 5:43,44). This is why, when the Prophet ﷺ ruled that they be stoned, he said, "O, Allah! I am the first one to revive Your Commandment after they (the Jews) had suppressed it." He asked them what caused them to do this and why they had abandoned Allah's Command which was in their hands. They replied: "Unlawful sexual intercourse had become widespread among our nobles and we were unable to enforce the legal punishment against them, so we used to stone the weak among us. So we said, "Let us resort to a just solution between the noble and the humble," so we agreed that we would flog them and blacken their faces." This was a part of their distortion, substitution, alteration and false interpretation. They only altered the meaning, not the wording of *ar-rajm*, which they left in their Scripture, as proven by the *hadeeth* whose authenticity is agreed upon by Al-Bukhari and Muslim. [1] This is why some claimed that the substitution only occurred in the meanings and that the wordings remained, and that is a proof against them, for if they had implemented what was in their Scripture in full, it would have led them to follow the truth and to obey the Messenger, Muhammad ﷺ, as He, Most High, says, 《 Those who follow the Messenger, the Prophet, who can neither read nor write (i.e. Muhammad) whom they find written

---

[1]   The *takhreej* for it was given previously on P. 374 (of the Arabic original).

with them in the Tawrah (Deuteronomy xviii, 15) and the Injeel (John xiv, 16) – he commands them for *al-ma'roof*; and forbids them from *al-munkar* he allows them as lawful *at-tayyibat* , and prohibits them as unlawful *al-khaba'ith* (i.e. all evil and unlawful as regards things, deeds, beliefs, persons, foods, etc.), he releases them from their heavy burdens (of Allah's Covenant), and from the fetters that were upon them ❩ (*Soorah Al-A'raf* 7:157). And He, Most High, says, ❨ And if only they had acted according to the Tawrah, the Injeel, and what has (now) been sent down to them from their Lord (the Qur'an), they would surely have gotten provision from above them and from underneath their feet. There are from among them people who are on the right course (i.e. they act on the revelation and believe in Prophet Muhammad ﷺ like 'Abdullah Ibn Salam). ❩ (*Soorah Al-Ma'idah* 5:66). And He, Most High, says, ❨ Say (O, Muhammad), "O, people of the Scripture (Jews and Christians)! You have nothing (as regards guidance) till you act according to the Tawrah, the Injeel, and what has (now) been sent down to you from your Lord (the Qur'an)." Verily, that which has been sent down to you (O, Muhammad) from your Lord increases in many of them their obstinate rebellion and disbelief ❩ (*Soorah Al-Ma'idah* 5:68). And this is the opinion, i.e. the one which states that the substitution only occurred in the meanings and not in the wordings, was expressed by Al-Bukhari, on the authority of 'Abdullah ibn 'Abbas ﷺ at the end of his *Saheeh*[1] and he acknowledged it and did not reject it. Al-Fakhr Ar-Razi also related it in his *Tafseer*, on the authority of most of the religious scholars.

I say: As for what is in their hands of the Arabic translation of the Tawrah, no rational person doubts that substitution has occurred in it, that many of its wordings have been distorted and that stories have been changed, along with wordings and that obvious and clear additions and omissions have occurred. In

---

(1)   Narrated by Al-Bukhari (7541).

addition, it contains manifest lies and many monstrous errors. As for what they recite with their mouths and write down with their pens, we are not privy to it, but it is presumed that they are lying, treacherous and make many fabrications against their Messengers and their Scriptures.

As for the Christians, their four Gospels, narrated by way of Mark, Luke, Matthew and John, contain more contradictions, additions and omissions and more monstrous disparities than the Tawrah and contradict the rulings of the Tawrah and the Injeel in many matters. They have legislated many things in it according to their own will, including praying to the East, for there is no evidence for it and no command to do it in any place in the four Gospels. Likewise, their embellishment of their churches with pictures and images is without foundation, as is their abandonment of circumcision and their transfer of their fast from the spring season and their lengthening of it to fifty days. In addition, they eat pork and have instituted something totally without foundation, which is monasticism, involving the abandonment of marriage for those who wish to devote themselves to worship and they have declared it unlawful for them. And their priests have laid down three hundred and eighteen laws for them. All of these things were innovated and fabricated by them during the era of Constantine, son of Constantius, builder of Constantinople. He reigned three hundred years after the time of 'Eesa عليه السلام.

Comprehensive Book of the Stories of Previous Prophets

Allah, Most High, says, ❮ Those Messengers! We preferred some to others; to some of them Allah spoke (directly); others He raised to degrees (of honor); and to 'Eesa, the son of Maryam, We gave clear proofs and evidences, and supported him with *Rooh Al-Quds* Jibra'eel ❯ (*Soorah Al-Baqarah* 2:253)

And He, Most High, says, ❮ Verily, We have inspired you (O, Muhammad) as We inspired Nooh and the Prophets after him; We (also) inspired Ibraheem (Abraham), Isma'eel (Ishmael), Ishaq (Isaac), Ya'qoob, and *Al-Asbat* (the twelve sons of Ya'qoob [Jacob]), 'Eesa, Ayyoob (Job), Yoonus (Jonah), Haroon (Aaron), and Sulaiman (Solomon), and to Dawood (David) We gave the *Zaboor* (Psalms). And Messengers We have mentioned to you before, and Messengers We have not mentioned to you – and to Moosa Allah spoke directly. Messengers as bearers of good news as well as of warning in order that the mankind should have no plea against Allah after the Messengers. And Allah is Ever All-Powerful, Most Wise ❯ (*Soorah An-Nisa'* 4:163-165)

And it has been narrated on the authority of Jabir Ibn 'Abdullah that he said, "The Messenger of Allah ﷺ said, "I am the Seal of a thousand Prophets or more and there was no Prophet among them who did not warn his people against the Dajjal. And that which has not been made clear to any of those before me regarding him has been made clear to me: He is one-eyed, and your Lord is not one-eyed." The *isnad* of this *hadeeth* is *hasan* and the *hadeeth* is understood to refer to the number of Prophets who warned their people against the Dajjal. However, another *hadeeth* states: "There is no Prophet who did not warn his nation against the Dajjal." [1] So Allah knows better.

And Al-Bukhari narrated on the authority of Abu Hazim that he said, "I sat with Abu Hurairah for five years and I heard him narrate from the Prophet ﷺ that: "The Prophets used to rule the Children of Isra'eel. Whenever a Prophet died another Prophet succeeded him, but there will be no Prophets after me; instead there will be *Khulafa'* (Caliphs) and they will number many." They asked, "What then do you order us to do?" He said, "Fulfill your allegiance to them, one after the other. Give them their dues. Verily Allah will ask them about that with which he entrusted them." [2]

And 'Abdullah Ibn Mas'ood said, "It is as if I am looking at the Messenger of Allah ﷺ relating the story of one of the Prophets whose people have beaten and wounded him, and he was wiping the blood off his face and saying, "O, Lord! Forgive my people, for they do not know'." [3]

---

(1) It was narrated with this wording by Ibn Hibban in his *Saheeh* (15/183, *hadeeth* No. 6780). It was also narrated by Al-Bukhari (7131), Muslim (2933), Abu Dawood (4316), At-Tirmidhi (2245) and Imam Ahmad in his *Musnad* (11593) – and in their versions (except that of Abu Dawood) it was stated: "...the one-eyed", rather than: "...the Dajjal".

(2) Narrated by Al-Bukhari (3455) and Muslim (1842).

(3) Narrated by Al-Bukhari (3477) and Muslim (1792).

And Imam Ahmad narrated on the authority of Abu Sa'eed Al-Khudri ⸎ that he said, "A man put his right hand on the Prophet ﷺ and said, "By Allah! I am unable to put my hand on you due to the severity of your fever." The Prophet ﷺ said, "For us, the community of the Prophets, the severity of the affliction is increased many times over, just as the reward for us is multiplied. If a Prophet from among the Prophets is afflicted with *qummal*, [1] they afflict him so severely that it kills him. If one of the Prophets is afflicted with poverty, he may take his cloak and cut it (in order to fashion a kind of pocket for it). But they rejoice in their afflictions as they rejoice in ease and comfort." [2]

And Imam Ahmad narrated on the authority of Abu Mus'ab Ibn Sa'd, who reported on the authority of his father, that he said, "I said, "O, Messenger of Allah! Which of the people are most severely afflicted by trials?" He said, "The Prophets, then the righteous people, then those who are nearest to them in perfection, then those among the people who are nearest to them in perfection. A man is tried in accordance with his religiousness; if his faith is strong, his test is increased and if he is weak in religion, his test is reduced. A Believer will be tested until he walks on the earth sinless (i.e. until his sins have been erased by the series of afflictions that he has endured)." [3]

And we have already mentioned the *hadeeth* which states: "We, the community of the Prophets, are paternal brothers and their Religion is one; but their mothers are different." [4] This means that the Law given to them is one Law, even though there might be differences in the applied Jurisprudence given to each Prophet,

---

(1) *Qummal*: According to *Lisan Al-'Arab*, they are lice, or ticks.

(2) This is an authentic *hadeeth* narrated by Imam Ahmad in his *Musnad* (3/94, No. 11483).

(3) This is an authentic *hadeeth* narrated by Imam Ahmad in his *Musnad* (1/172, No. 1484)

(4) Narrated by Al-Bukhari (3442) and Muslim (2365).

and some of them abrogated others, until all of them ended in the Law that Allah gave to Muhammad (peace be upon him and upon all of them). But the Religion of every Prophet whom Allah sent was Islam, and that is to affirm Allah's Oneness (*Tawheed*) and to worship Him, Alone, without ascribing partners to Him, as He, Most High, says, ﴾ And We did not send any Messenger before you (O, Muhammad) but We inspired him (saying), *La ilaha illa Ana* (there is none who has the right to be worshipped but I [Allah]), so worship Me (Alone and no one else)." ﴿ (*Soorah Al-Anbiya'* 21:25). And He, Most High, says, ﴾ And ask (O, Muhammad) those of Our Messengers whom We sent before you, "Did We ever appoint *alihah* (gods) to be worshipped besides the Most Beneficent (Allah)?" ﴿ (*Soorah Az-Zukhruf* 43:45). And He, Most High, says, ﴾ And verily, We have sent among every *Ummah* (community, nation) a Messenger (proclaiming), "Worship Allah (Alone), and avoid (or keep away from) the *taghoot* (all false deities, etc. (i.e. do not worship the *taghoot* besides Allah)." Then of them were some whom Allah guided and of them were some upon whom the straying was justified. So travel through the land and see what was the end of those who denied (the truth) ﴿ (*Soorah An-Nahl* 16:36). Paternal brothers means that they share the same father, but their mothers are different. So the father represents the Religion, and that is to affirm the Oneness of Allah (*Tawheed*). The mothers represent the Divine Laws, which differ in matters of jurisprudence, as He, Most High, says, ﴾ To each among you, We have prescribed a Law and a Clear Way ﴿ (*Soorah Al-Ma'idah* 5:48). And He, Most High, says, ﴾ For every nation We have ordained religious ceremonies (e.g. slaughtering of the sacrificial beasts during the three days of stay at Mina (in Makkah) during the *Hajj* [pilgrimage]) which they must follow ﴿ (*Soorah Al-Hajj* 21:67). And He says, ﴾ For every nation there is a direction to which they face ﴿ (*Soorah Al-Baqarah* 2:148) – according to one of the two sayings regarding its explanation. And what is meant is that the Laws, though they differed in the times at which they were revealed, all of them commanded that Allah be worshipped Alone, without partners – and that is the Religion of Islam, which Allah ordained for all of the Prophets; and it is the Religion besides which Allah will accept none on the Day of Resurrection, as He, Most High, says, ❴ And whoever seeks a religion other than Islam, it will never be accepted of him, and in the Hereafter he will be one of the losers ❵ (*Soorah Ali 'Imran* 3:85). And He, Most High, says, ❴ And who turns away from the religion of Ibraheem (i.e. Islamic Monotheism) except he who befools himself? Truly, We chose him in this world and verily, in the Hereafter he will be among the righteous. When his Lord said to him, "Submit (i.e. be a Muslim)," he said, "I have submitted myself (as a Muslim) to the Lord of the *'Alameen*." ❵ (*Soorah Al-Baqarah* 2:130,131). And He, Most High, says, ❴ Verily, We did send down the Tawrah (to Moosa), therein was guidance and light, by which the Prophets, who submitted themselves to Allah's Will, judged the Jews ❵ (*Soorah Al-Ma'idah* 5:44). So the Religion of Islam is the worship of Allah, Alone, without partners; and that is sincere devotion to Him, Alone, without any other besides Him, and *ihsan* means to do so in the manner legislated (by Allah) at that time. This is why Allah, Most High, does not accept a deed from anyone which is contrary to what Allah ordained for Muhammad ﷺ after He has sent him, as He, Most High, says, ❴ Say (O, Muhammad), "O, mankind! Verily, I am sent to you all as the Messenger of Allah." ❵ (*Soorah Al-A'raf* 7:158). And He, Most High, says, ❴ "And this Qur'an has been revealed to me that I may therewith warn you and whomsoever it may reach." ❵ (*Soorah Al-An'am* 6:19). And He, Most High, says, ❴ and before it came the Book of Moosa, a guidance and a mercy, they believe therein, but those of the sects (Jews, Christians and all the other non-Muslim nations) that reject it (the Qur'an), the Fire will be their promised meeting place. ❵ (*Soorah Hood* 11:17) And the Messenger of Allah ﷺ said, "I have been sent to the red and the black." [1] It was said that the red and the black refers to the Arabs

---

(1)   Narrated by Muslim (521), on the authority of Jabir Ibn 'Abdullah ﷺ.

and the non-Arabs. It was also said that it refers to mankind and the *jinn*. The Prophet ﷺ also said, "By Him in Whose Hand is my soul, if Moosa ﷺ appeared among you, then you followed him and abandoned me, you would surely have gone astray." [1] The *ahadeeth* bearing this meaning are very numerous. And what is meant is that the brotherhood of *al-'allat* means that they are from one father, but their mothers are different. The word is derived from the expression: "…drinking from *al-'alal* (the tributaries) after (drinking from) the source. As for the brotherhood of *al-akhyaf*, it is the opposite of that, i.e. that their mothers are one, but their fathers are different. The brotherhood of *al-a'yan* means they are brothers from the same father and mother. And Allah, Most High, knows better.

In another *hadeeth*, the Prophet ﷺ said, "We, the community of the Prophets, do not bequeath what we leave, for it is (given in) charity." [2] This is one of the special characteristics of the Prophets, that they do not bequeath anything. The reason for this is that the material things of this world are held in too much contempt by the Prophets for them to bequeath their worldly goods. In addition, their trust in Allah, the Almighty, the All-Powerful regarding their offspring is too great and too positive for them to need to leave their property to their heirs, to the exclusion of the rest of the mankind. Rather, all of what they leave is a charity for the poor people, to alleviate their poverty and fulfill their needs. We shall mention all of the characteristics peculiar to the Prophets, including the characteristics of our Prophet (peace be upon all of them) at the beginning of *the Book of Marriage*, in *the Great Book of Rulings*, where the *Imams* usually write them, in emulation of Imam Abu 'Abdullah Ash-Shafi'i (may Allah have mercy on all of them).

---

(1)   Narrated by Imam Ahmad in his *Musnad* (15437); in its chain of narrators is Jabir Al-Ju'fi, who is weak.

(2)   Narrated by An-Nasa'i in *Al-Kubra* (6309).

Information Regarding the Arabs

It has been said that all of the Arabs can trace their lineage to Isma'eel, son of Ibraheem (peace be upon them both). What is correct and well-known is that there were pure Arabs before Isma'eel ﷺ. And we have mentioned previously that pure Arabs included 'Ad, Thamood, Tasm, Jadees, Umaim, Jurhum, the Amalekites and others known to none except Allah. They were before *Al-Khaleel* (Ibraheem ﷺ) and during his time also. As for those who were assimilated into the Arabs, they are the Arabs of Al-Hijaz and they are the descendants of Isma'eel ﷺ. As for the Arabs of Yemen, they are Himyar and it is well-known that they are from Qahtan, whose name was Muharrim, according to Ibn Makoola. It was said that they were four brothers: Qahtan, Qahit, Miqhat and Faligh. Qahtan was the son of Hood. It was also said that he was Hood ﷺ and it was said that Hood ﷺ was his brother, and also that he was from his progeny and that Qahtan was from among the progeny of Isma'eel ﷺ. This last was related by Ibn Ishaq and others. Some said that he was Qahtan Ibn Al-Hamaisa', son of Taiman, son of Qaizar, son of Nabt, son of Isma'eel ﷺ. Other claims were also made regarding his lineage to Isma'eel ﷺ. And Allah knows better.

Al-Bukhari has written regarding his biography in his *Saheeh*, under the "Chapter: The Relationship of Yemen to Isma'eel ﷺ, on the authority of Salamah ﷺ that he said, "The Messenger of Allah ﷺ passed by some people from the tribe of Aslam practicing archery. He said, "O, children of Isma'eel! Fire (your arrows), for your father was an archer. I am on the side of Banu so-and-so," meaning one of the two teams. The other team stopped firing, whereupon the Prophet said, "What has happened to them?" They replied, "How shall we throw while you are with Banu so-and-so?" He said, "Fire, for I am with all of you." [1]

And Al-Bukhari said, "And Aslam Ibn Afsa Ibn Harithah Ibn 'Amr ibn 'Amir from Khuza'ah refers to Khuza'ah, a group from among those who split from the tribes of Saba', when Allah sent upon them the great flood, as we shall explain later. Al-Aws and Al-Khazraj were also from them. The Prophet ﷺ said to them, "O, children of Isma'eel! Fire (your arrows), which proves that they were from his progeny. Others interpreted it as meaning the Arab race, but it is a far-fetched interpretation, since it contradicts the apparent meaning without any proof. However, the majority hold that the Qahtani Arabs are from the Arabs of Yemen and the others are not from the progeny of Isma'eel ﷺ. They also contend that all of the Arabs may be divided into two categories: Qahtani and 'Adnani. The Qahtanis are two tribes: Saba' and Hadramawt. The 'Adnanis are also two tribes: Rabee'ah and Mudar; they were the sons of Nizar Ibn Ma'add Ibn 'Adnan. There is a difference of opinion regarding the fifth tribe, Quda'ah. It was said that they were 'Adnanis; Ibn 'Abdul-Barr said, "And that is the opinion of the majority." Muhammad Ibn Salam Al-Basri An-Nassabah

---

(1) Narrated by Al-Bukhari (3507).

said, "The Arabs have (descended from) three roots: 'Adnanis, Qahtanis and Quda'ah." It was said to him, "Then which of them are the majority, the 'Adnanis or the Qahtanis?" It depends on what Quda'ah says; if they say that they are from Yemen, then the Qahtanis will be the majority. But if they say that they are from the tribe of Ma'add, then they will be 'Adnanis." This proves that they are undecided regarding their origins. And if the aforementioned *hadeeth* of Ibn Lahee'ah is authentic, then it is a proof that they are from the Qahtanis. And Allah knows better. Allah, Most High, says, ‹ O, mankind! We have created you from a male and a female, and made you into nations and tribes, that you may know one another. Verily, the most honorable of you with Allah is that (Believer) who has *at-taqwa* (i.e. one of the *muttaqoon* (pious – see V. 2:2) › (*Soorah Al-Hujurat* 49:13). The scholars of genealogy said that it is said: nations and then tribes, then *'ama'ir*, then *butoon*, then *afkhadh*, then families, then kin. And kin are the closest of people to a man and there is nothing after it.

Let us begin first with a mention of the Qahtanis, then after them, we shall mention the Arabs of the Hijaz, who are the 'Adnanis, and matters pertaining to the *Jahiliyyah*, in order that that may be connected to the *Seerah* of the Messenger of Allah ﷺ, if Allah wills – and it is Him in Whom we place our trust.

Al-Bukhari said under the "Chapter: Mention of Qahtan, it is reported on the authority of Abu Hurairah ﷺ from the Prophet ﷺ that he said, "The Hour will not be established until a man emerges from Qahtan and he drives the people with his stick." [1]

The Story of Saba'

Allah, Most High, says, ‹ Indeed there was for Saba' (Sheba) a sign in their dwelling place – two gardens on the right hand and

---

(1)   Narrated by Al-Bukhari (3517) and by Muslim (2910).

on the left (and it was said to them,) "Eat of the provision of your Lord, and be grateful to Him, a fair land and an Oft-Forgiving Lord. But they turned away (from the obedience of Allah), so We sent against them *Sail Al-'Arim* (the flood released from the dam), and We converted their two gardens into gardens producing bitter, bad fruit and tamarisks, and a few lote trees. In this way We requited them because they were ungrateful disbelievers. And never do We requite in such a way except those who are ungrateful (disbelievers). And We placed between them and the towns which We had blessed, towns easy to be seen, and We made the stages (of journey) between them easy (saying,) "Travel in them safely both by night and day." But they said, "Our Lord! Make the stages between our journey longer." And they wronged themselves, so We made them as tales (in the land), and We dispersed them all, totally. Verily, in this are indeed signs for every steadfast grateful (person). ❩ (*Soorah Saba'* 34:15-19)

The scholars of genealogy, including Ibn Ishaq, said that the name of Saba' was 'Abd Shams Ibn Yashjub Ibn Ya'rub Ibn Qahtan. They said that he was the first of the Arabs from Saba' and so he was called Saba'. He was known as Ar-Ra'ish because he used to give the people from his property. As-Suhaili said, "It was said that he was the first to be crowned king. Some said that he was a Muslim and that he had poetry in which he gave tidings of the coming of the Messenger of Allah ﷺ; this included the following words:

A Prophet will rule after us a great kingdom,

And he will not permit the unlawful,

And after him, from among them will be kings,

Who will treat the slaves without disparagement,

And after them, kings from among us will rule,

And the kingdom will be divided up among us,

And after Qahtan a Prophet will rule,

Who is pure of brow, the best of mankind,

He will be called Ahmad, how I wish that I,

Could live after he is sent for but a year,

I would support him and give him my help,

Will all my arms and all of my spearmen,

When he appears, be his supporters,

And whoever meets him, convey my salutations to him.

This was related by Ibn Dihyah in his book *At-Tanweer Fee Mawlid Al-Basheer An-Nadheer.*

And Imam Ahmad narrated on the authority of As-Saba'i 'Abdur-Rahman Ibn Wa'lah (that he said,) "I heard 'Abdullah ibn Al-'Abbas ⬥ say, "A man asked the Prophet ﷺ about Saba', was it a man, or a woman or a land? He said, "Nay, it was a man. He fathered ten sons and six of them took up residence in Yemen and the other four took up residence in Ash-Sham. As for the Yemenis, (they were) Madhhij, Kindah, Al-Azd, Al-Ash'ariyyoon, Anmar and Himyar. As for the Shamites, (they were) Lakhm, Judham, 'Amilah and Ghassan." [1]

What is meant is that Saba' includes all of these tribes. Among them were *At-Tababi'ah* in Yemen (the singular is *Tubba'*) and their kings had crowns that they wore at the time of delivering judgments, just as the Kisras of Persia used to do. The Arabs used to call every king who ruled Yemen, including Ash-Shihr [2] and Hadramawt, "*Tubba'*", just as they referred to every ruler of Ash-Sham and Al-Jazeerah as "*Qaisar*" (Ceasar), while every ruler of Persia was known as *Kisra* (Kisra). Every ruler of Egypt

---

(1) Narrated by Imam Ahmad (2893) and Al-Haithami said in *Al-Majma'* (7/94), "In its chain is Ibn Lahee'ah, in whom there is weakness; but the remainder of the narrators are trustworthy."

(2) Ash-Shihr: A crossing point on the coast of the Indian Ocean, on the south coast of Yemen. (*Mu'jam Al-Buldan*).

was known as "*Fir'awn*" (Pharaoh) and every ruler of Abyssinia was known as "*An-Najashi*" (the Negus) and every ruler of India was known as "*Batlaimoos*" (Ptolemy). Among the rulers of Himyar, in the land of Yemen was Bilqees, whose story with that of Sulaiman ﷺ we have already told. They enjoyed great good fortune and abundant provisions and plentiful fruits and crops. In addition to this, they were rightly guided and followed the path of righteousness. But when they repaid Allah's Blessing with disbelief, their land became uncultivable.

Muhammad Ibn Ishaq narrated on the authority of Wahb Ibn Munabbih that Allah sent thirteen Prophets to them. As-Suddi claimed that he sent twelve thousand Prophets to them. And Allah knows better. What is meant is that they turned away from guidance in favor of error and prostrated before the sun, instead of Allah – and that was during the reign of Bilqees and before it also – and this continued until Allah sent *Sail Al-'Arim* against them, as He, Most High, says, ❨ But they turned away (from the obedience of Allah), so We sent against them *Sail Al-'Arim* (the flood released from the dam), and We converted their two gardens into gardens producing bitter, bad fruit and tamarisks and a few lote trees. In this way We requited them because they were ungrateful disbelievers. And never do We requite in such a way except those who are ungrateful (disbelievers) ❩ (*Soorah Saba'* 34:16,17)

More than one of the earlier and the later scholars from among the scholars of *tafseer* and others said that the reason for the building of the dam of Ma'rib was because the waters used to run between two mountains and so in the far distant past, they built a very strong dam between the two mountains, so that the water rose and the dam held it back to the tops of the mountains. Then they planted orchards and trees and got the best fruits that could ever be harvested, plentiful and beautiful and they grew bountiful crops. It was said that the first person to build the dam was Saba'

Ibn Ya'rub and that seventy rivers ran into it, while it had thirty openings from which the water emerged (to irrigate the land). He died when the construction of the dam was not yet finished and so it was completed after him by Himyar. It was many *farsakhs* [1] wide and they enjoyed great wealth and lived lives of enviable luxury, to such a degree that, according to Qatadah and others, a woman would walk with a large basket on her head and it would be filled with fruits that fell into it, due to their ripeness and their profusion. They also said that there were no fleas or harmful creatures in their lands, due to the healthy climate and the good health they enjoyed, as He, Most High, says, ﴿ Indeed there was for Saba' a sign in their dwelling place – two gardens on the right hand and on the left (and it was said to them,) "Eat of the provision of your Lord, and be grateful to Him, a fair land and an Oft-Forgiving Lord ﴾ (*Soorah Saba'* 34:15) and as He, Most High, says, ﴿ And (remember) when your Lord proclaimed, "If you give thanks (by accepting faith and worshipping none but Allah), I will give you more (of My Blessings), but if you are thankless (i.e. disbelievers), verily! My Punishment is indeed severe." ﴾ (*Soorah Ibraheem* 14:7). So they worshipped (false) deities besides Allah and disregarded His Blessings and asked Allah to make the stages between their journey longer and to make their journeys longer and more difficult and tiresome. And they asked that He replace goodness with evil, just as the Children of Isra'eel asked for manna and quails to be replaced with herbs, cucumbers, *foom* (wheat or garlic), lentils and onions. So they were deprived of this great Blessing and the widespread Benevolence by the destruction of the land and the scattering of the slaves throughout the lands, as He, Most High, says, ﴿ But they turned away (from the obedience of Allah), so We sent against them *Sail Al-'Arim.* ﴾ (*Soorah Saba'* 34:16)

---

(1)   *Farsakh*: Parasang, an ancient Persian measurement of how far a man could walk in a day.

More than one of the scholars said that Allah sent rats to the
foundations of the dam, i.e. desert rats. It was also said that they
were moles. When they realized this, they brought cats to counter
the rats, but this did not benefit them at all once the Divine
Decree had come to pass. Their vigilance was to no avail. No!
There is no refuge! When the rats took hold of the foundations,
the dam collapsed and the water gushed forth and rushed through
the bottom of the valley and destroyed everything in their path
– buildings, trees, etc. As the water drained from the trees that
were on the mountains, to the right and the left, those trees dried
up and were destroyed. Those beautiful, fruit-bearing trees were
replaced with something altogether different, as Allah says, ﴾ and
We converted their two gardens into gardens producing bitter, bad
fruit, and tamarisks. ﴿ (*Soorah Saba'* 34:16)

'Abdullah Ibn 'Abbas ﷺ, Mujahid and others said that it was
the *arak* tree, [1] whose fruit is known as *bareer* and tamarisk,
which is *at-tarfa'*. [2] It was also said that it resembles it and that
it is dry wood has no fruit. ﴾ and some few lote trees ﴿ (*Soorah
Saba'* 34:16). This was because it bore lotus fruit and so there
were only a few of them, although it has many thorns and its fruit
is, as it is said in the parable, "The meat of a lean camel is on the
top of a high mountain and there is no easy path to it and (if you
could reach it,) there is little meat to be had from it." This is why
Allah, Most High, says, ﴾ Like this We requited them because they
were ungrateful disbelievers. And never do We requite in such a
way except those who are ungrateful (disbelievers). ﴿ (*Soorah
Saba'* 34:17). That is, We only inflict this severe punishment on
those who disbelieve in Us, belie Our Messengers, disobey Our
Commandments and violate Our Prohibitions. And He, Most
High, says, ﴾ So We made them as tales (in the land), and We

---

(1)   *Arak* tree: A tree from whose roots the *miswak* (tooth cleaning stick) is
      obtained.

(2)   *At-Tarfa'*: A genus of plants, which includes trees such as the tamarisk.

dispersed them all, totally 》 (*Soorah Saba'* 34:19). That is, when their wealth was destroyed and their land was ruined, they had to depart from it and so they were widely dispersed throughout the lands.

The Story of Rabee'ah Ibn Nasr Ibn Abi Harithah Ibn 'Amr Ibn 'Amir

Muhammad Ibn Ishaq said, "Rabee'ah Ibn Nasr was the king of Yemen, one among many of the *Tabab'ah*. He saw a vision which terrified and shocked him and he gathered every soothsayer, magician, *'a'if* [1] and astrologer from among his people and said to them, "I have seen a vision that terrified me and shocked me, so inform me about it and explain it to me." They said, "Relate it to us and we will inform you of its explanation." He said, "If I inform you of it, I am not sure that you will be able to explain it to me, because none can know its meaning except who knows it (the vision) before I inform him of it." One of them said, "If the king desires this, then let him send word to Shiqq and Sateeh, because no one is more knowledgeable than they; they will inform about that which he asks." So he sent word to them and Sateeh came to him before Shiqq and he said to him, "I have seen a vision that terrified me and shocked me; inform me about it and if you get it right, you will be able to correctly explain it." He said, "I will do so. You saw something that had been burned in the fire emerging from blackness and it arrived in Tahamah and there it ate every living creature." The king said to him, "You have not erred in any detail of it, O, Sateeh! Now what is your explanation of it?" He said, "I swear by that which is between the two lava fields of Hanash, your land will be brought down by the Abyssinians and they will certainly rule that which lies between Abyan and Jurash."

---

(1)   *'A 'if*: One who bases his prognostications on the flight of birds.

The king said to him, "O, Sateeh! Verily, this is distressing and painful to us. When will it happen? Will it be in my time, or after it?" He said, "Nay! It will be a long time after it – more than sixty or seventy years." He asked, "Will their rule continue, or will it be terminated?" He said, "Nay! It will be terminated after seventy-odd years, and then they will be killed and expelled from it and put to flight." The king said, "And who will come after their killing and expulsion?" He replied, "They will be followed by Iram Dhee Yazan. He will attack them from Adan and he will not leave a single one of them in Yemen." The king asked, "Will his rule continue, or will it be terminated?" He said, "Nay! It will be terminated." The king said, "And who will terminate it?" Sateeh said, "A pure Prophet, who will receive Revelation from the Supreme (Allah)." The king asked, "And from whom is this Prophet?" He replied, "A man from the sons of Ghalib ibn Fihr ibn Malik ibn An-Nadr. The kingdom will remain in the hands of his people until the end of time." The king asked, "Does time have an end, then?" Sateeh said, "Yes, a Day on which the first and the last generations will be gathered; on that Day, those who used to do good deeds will be happy, while those who did evil will be wretched." The king asked, "Is it true, what you have told me?" He said, "Yes, by the afterglow of sunset, by the twilight, by the daybreak in its fullness, verily, that which I impart to you is the truth."

The Story of Tubba'

Abu Karib Tubban As 'ad, king of Yemen and the People of Al-Madinah, and How He Intended to Attack the Sacred House, Then He Honoured and Glorified it and He Draped it With a Covering and He Was the First Person to Do So

Ibn Ishaq said, "It was Tubban As'ad Abu Karib, king of Yemen, who came to Al-Madinah and took two of the Jewish

rabbis to Yemen. He also rebuilt the Sacred House and draped it
with a covering. His reign was before that of Rabee'ah Ibn Nasr.
He had selected his route through Al-Madinah when he returned
from fighting in the lands of the east. He had passed by it on the
outward journey and he did not burn its inhabitants. He appointed
one of his sons to govern them, but he was assassinated. So
when he arrived in the city, he resolved to destroy it, annihilate
its inhabitants and burn down its date-palms. So he gathered to
himself the tribe of the *Ansar*, whose chief was 'Amr Ibn Talhah,
the confederate of Banu An-Najjar, then one of Banu 'Amr Ibn
Mabdhool. The name of Mabdhool was 'Amir ibn Malik Ibn An-
Najjar. And the name of An-Najjar was Taimullah Ibn Tha'labah
Ibn 'Amr Ibn Al-Khazraj Ibn Harithah Ibn Tha'labah Ibn 'Amr
Ibn 'Amir."

Ibn Ishaq added, "A man from Banu 'Adiyy Ibn An-Najjar,
whose name was Ahmar, attacked a man from among the
companions of Tubba' whom he found taking a bunch of his
dates, striking him with his scythe and killing him. He said, "The
dates are only for the one who pollinated them." This served to
increase the anger of Tubba' against them and so they fought. The
Ansar said that they used to fight him during the daylight and at
night they would offer him their hospitality. This impressed him
and he said, "By Allah, they are a generous people!"

Ibn Ishaq said, "While Tubba' was engaged in fighting them,
two Jewish rabbis from Banu Quraizah, who were firmly grounded
in knowledge came to him, when they heard that he intended to
destroy Al-Madinah and annihilate its inhabitants. They said to
him, 'O, king! Do not do this, for if you insist on carrying out
your intention, you will be prevented from doing so, and we fear
that a swift punishment may descend upon you.' He said, 'And
why should that be?' They said, 'It is the place of refuge for a
Prophet who will depart from the Sacred Precincts (Makkah),
fleeing from Quraish at the end of time. This will be his abode and

his settlement.' And so he desisted from attacking it. He realized that they were knowledgeable men and he was impressed by what he heard and so he left Al-Madinah and adopted their religion."

We have already mentioned in the *Tafseer* the *hadeeth* that was reported from the Prophet 鏐 in which he said, "Do not curse Tubba' for he embraced Islam." [1] And As-Suhaili narrated on the authority of Abu Hurairah 鏐 that the Messenger of Allah 鏐 said, "Do not curse As'ad Al-Himyari, for he was the first to drape the *Ka'bah*." [2] As-Suhaili said, "When the two rabbis informed Tubba' about the Messenger of Allah 鏐, he recited the following poetic verses:

I bear witness that Ahmad is a Messenger from Allah, pure of soul,

And if my life was prolonged till his time, I would be his vizier and his nephew,

And I would perform jihad with my sword against his enemies,

And I would endeavor to free his heart from all cares.

And this poem continued to be passed down through generations of the *Ansar* and memorized by them; it was known to Abu Ayyoob Al-Ansari 鏐.

---

(1) This *hadeeth* has been designated as being raised to the level of *hasan*, due to other supporting narrations. It was narrated by Imam Ahmad in his *Musnad* (5/240, No. 22373) and it is recorded *Silsilah Al-Ahadeeth As-Saheehah* (2423) and it was narrated by Al-Baghawi in his *Tafseer* (4/153).

(2) See: *Al-Kamil Fid-Du'afa'* by ibn 'Adiyy (6/241) and *Meezan Al-I'tidal* (6/274). In its chain of narrators is Al-Waqidi (who is acknowledged by scholars of *hadeeth*, such as Imam Ahmad and Ibn Al-Madani as a narrator of fabricated *ahadeeth*).

The Cause of Abrahah's Determination to Destroy the Ka'bah With an Elephant

Allah, Most High, says, ❴ Have you (O, Muhammad) not seen how your Lord dealt with the Owners of the Elephant (The elephant army which came from Yemen under the command of Abrahah Al-Ashram intending to destroy the Ka'bah at Makkah)? Did He not make their plot go astray, and send against them birds in flocks, striking them with stones of *sijjeel*? And He made them like an empty field of stalks (of which the corn has been eaten up by cattle) ❵ (*Soorah Al-Feel* 105:1-5). He was the first person to put saddles on horses. As for the first person to tame horses and ride them, it was Tahmoorith, who was the third king in this world. It was also said that the first person to ride them was Isma'eel ﷺ, and it is possible that he was the first person from among the Arabs to ride them. And Allah knows better.

It is said that the elephant, in spite of its great size and strength, flees from cats. [1] Some generals employed cats in war against the Indians (who used elephants), releasing them during the turmoil of the battles and the elephants fled.

Ibn Ishaq said, "Then Abrahah built *Al-Qullais* in *San'a'*; it was a church the like of which had never been seen on earth at that time. He wrote to the Negus of Abyssinia saying, "I have built for you a church the like of which no king before you has ever built, but I will not be content until I have diverted the Arab pilgrims to it." As-Suhaili mentioned that Abrahah humiliated the people of Yemen during the building of this infamous church and forced them to labor on its construction. Those who arrived after sunrise to work on its construction would have one of their hands cut off. He transferred marble, stones and wonderful furnishings to it from the palace of Bilqees and he erected in it crosses of gold and silver. He also placed in it pulpits made from ivory and ebony and made it extremely high and very vast in width. After Abrahah had been killed and the Abyssinians had fled, anyone who tried to take anything from its furnishings would be afflicted with evil by the jinn. This was because the church was built over two idols: Ku'aib and his wife. The height of each of them was sixty cubits and so the people of Yemen left the church as it was and it remained so until the era of As-Saffah, the first Caliph of the Abbasid dynasty. He sent a group of resolute men of learning to it and they demolished it stone by stone, and all traces of it have remained hidden to this day.

Ibn Ishaq said, "When the Arabs heard about the letter that

---

(1)   This claim was probably first made by Pliny the Elder in his *Naturalis Historia*, book VIII, in which he said, "Of all other living creatures, they (elephants) cannot abide a mouse or a rat." Modern studies have shown this to be a myth. The truth behind the myth is most likely that elephants are made nervous by nearby sounds or movements they cannot identify, such as those made by dogs, cats, rats, mice, etc.

Abrahah had sent to the Negus, a man from *An-Nasa'ah*, who belonged to the tribe of Kinanah, became angry. They were known as *An-Nasa'ah* because they used to defer the sanctity of the month of Muharram until Safar (*nasa'a* is the Arabic verb to defer or postpone), announcing its deferment in Makkah, upon the completion of the Hajj rites, as we established in the explanation of the Words of Allah, Most High: ﴿ The postponing (of a Sacred Month) is indeed an addition to disbelief. ﴾ (*Soorah At-Tawbah* 9:37) Ibn Ishaq said, "So the Kinani man set out and traveled to *Al-Qullais* and he sat in it, i.e. relieved himself in it, in a place where no one could see him, after which he left the church and returned to his own land. On discovering this, Abrahah was furious and he swore to march on the House (of Allah) and destroy it, then he ordered the Abyssinians to prepare for the march to Makkah and they did so."

Ibn Ishaq added, "When Abrahah camped at Al-Mughammis, he sent a man from Abyssinia whose name was Al-Aswad Ibn Maqsood on horseback to Makkah. There he captured the property of the Makkan people from Quraish and other tribes, including two hundred camels belonging to 'Abdul-Muttalib Ibn Hashim, who was at that time the leader of Quraish and its chief. Quraish, Kinanah, Hudhail and those from other tribes and peoples who were in the Sacred Precincts desired to fight Abrahah, but then they realized that they did not have the ability to do so and they abandoned the idea. Abrahah sent Hunatah Al-Himyari to Makkah and he said to him, "Ask for the leader of this city." Then say to him, "The king says to you, "I have not come to fight you, I have only come to destroy this House, and as long as you do not try to prevent us from doing so by fighting us, I have no desire to shed your blood. If he does not desire to fight, then bring him to me." When Hunatah entered Makkah, he asked for the leader of Quraish and he was told, "He is 'Abdul-Muttalib Ibn Hashim." So he went to him and conveyed the message that

Abrahah had ordered him to give. 'Abdul-Muttalib said to him, "By Allah, we do not wish to fight him and we do not have the ability to do so. This is Allah's Sacred House and the House of His Khaleel, Ibraheem ﷺ. So if He prevents him, then it is His Sacred Place and His House, and if He lets him approach it, by Allah, We have no means to defend it from him." So Hunatah told him, "Come with me to him (Abrahah)." And so 'Abdul-Muttalib went with him, accompanied by some of his sons. When Abrahah saw him, he was impressed by him, because 'Abdul-Muttalib was a large and handsome man. So Abrahah descended from his seat and sat with him on a carpet on the ground. Then he asked his translator to say to him, "What do you need?" 'Abdul-Muttalib replied to the translator, "I want the king to return my camels that he has taken from me, which are two hundred in number." Abrahah then told his translator to tell him, "I was impressed by you when I first saw you, but now I withdraw from you after you have spoken to me. You are asking me about two hundred camels which I have taken from you and you leave the matter of a House which is (the foundation of) your religion and the religion of your fathers, and which I have come to destroy and you do not speak to me about it!" 'Abdul-Muttalib said to him, "Verily, I am the lord of the camels. As for the House, it has its Lord Who will defend it." Abrahah said, "I cannot be prevented (from destroying it)." 'Abdul-Muttalib answered, "Then do so." It is said that a number of the chiefs of the Arabs accompanied 'Abdul-Muttalib and offered Abrahah a third of the wealth of the tribe of Tihamah if he would withdraw from the House, but he refused and returned 'Abdul-Muttalib's camels to him. 'Abdul-Muttalib then returned to his people and ordered them to leave Makkah and seek shelter at the top of the mountains, fearful of the excesses which might be committed by the army against them. Then he took hold of the metal ring of the door of the Ka'bah, and along with a number of Quraish, he called upon Allah to give them victory over Abrahah and his army. 'Abdul-Muttalib said, while hanging onto the ring of the door of the Ka'bah:

> *There is no matter more important to any man right now,*
> *Than the defence of his livestock and property,*
> *So defend Your Property,*
> *Their cross and their cunning will not be victorious,*
> *Over Your Astuteness by the time morning comes.*

Ibn Hisham said, "This is what has been authentically reported from him." According to Ibn Ishaq, then 'Abdul-Muttalib let go of the metal ring of the door of the Ka'bah, and they left Makkah and ascended to the mountain tops. Muqatil Ibn Sulaiman mentioned that they left one hundred animals (camels) tied near the Ka'bah hoping that some of the army would take some of them without a right to do so, and thus bring about the vengeance of Allah upon themselves. When morning came, Abrahah prepared to enter the sacred city of Makkah. He prepared the elephant named Mahmood. He mobilized his army, and they turned the elephant toward the Ka'bah. At that moment Nufail Ibn Habeeb approached it and stood next to it, and taking it by its ear, he said, "Kneel, Mahmood! Then turn around and return directly to whence you came, for verily, you are in the Sacred City of Allah." Then he released the elephant's ear and it knelt, after which Nufail Ibn Habeeb left and hastened to the mountains. Abrahah's men beat the elephant in an attempt to make it rise, but it refused. They beat it on its head with axes and used hooked staffs to pull it out of its resistance and make it stand, but it refused. So they turned him toward Yemen, and he rose and walked quickly. Then they turned him toward Ash-Sham and he did likewise. Then they turned him toward the East and he did the same thing. Then they turned him toward Makkah and he knelt down again. Then Allah sent against them the birds from the sea, like swallows and herons. Each bird carried three stones the size of chickpeas and lentils, one in each claw and one in its beak. Everyone who was hit by them was destroyed, though not all of them were hit. They fled in panic along the road asking about the whereabouts of Nufail that he might point out to them the way home. Nufail, however, was at the top of the mountain with Quraish and the Arabs of the Hijaz observing the wrath which Allah had caused to descend on the People of the Elephant. Nufail then began to say:

Where will they flee when the One True God is the Pursuer, For Al-Ashram is defeated and not the victor?

Ibn Ishaq reported that Nufail said these lines of poetry at that time:

O, Rudaina! Did you not live with continued support?

We favored you all with a revolving eye in the morning (i.e., a guide along the way),

If you saw, but you did not see it at the side of the rock covered mountain that which we saw,

Then you will excuse me and praise my affair,

And do not grieve over what is lost between us,

I praised Allah when I saw the birds, and I feared that the stones might be thrown down upon us,

So all the people are asking about the whereabouts of Nufail,

As if I have some debt that I owe the Abyssinians.

Ibn Ishaq said that they left (Makkah) being struck down and destroyed along every path and at every water spring. Abrahah's body was afflicted by the pestilence of the stones and his army carried him away with them as he was falling apart piece by piece, until they arrived back in San'a'. When they arrived there he was but like the baby chick of a bird. And he did not die until his heart

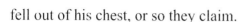
fell out of his chest, or so they claim.

Ibn Ishaq said that when Allah sent Muhammad with the Prophethood, among the things that he used to recount to Quraish as blessings that Allah had favored them with of His bounties, was His defending them from the attack of the Abyssinians. Due to this they (Quraish) were allowed to remain (safely in Makkah) for a period of time. Thus, Allah says, ﴿ Have you (O, Muhammad) not seen how your Lord dealt with the Owners of the Elephant (The elephant army which came from Yemen under the command of Abrahah Al-Ashram intending to destroy the Ka'bah at Makkah)? Did He not make their plot go astray, and send against them birds in flocks, striking them with stones of *sijjeel*? And He made them like an empty field of stalks (of which the corn has been eaten up by cattle). ﴾ (*Soorah Al-Feel* 105:1-5)

Ibn Hisham said that "*ababeel*" is the word used for hosts, and the Arabs do not speak of just one (bird). He also said, "As for *sijjeel*, Yoonus An-Nahwi and Abu 'Ubaidah have informed me that according to the Arabs, it means something hard and solid." He then said, "Some of the commentators have mentioned that it is actually two Persian words that the Arabs have made into one word. The two words are '*sang*' and '*gill*', '*sang*' meaning stones, and '*geel*' meaning clay. The rocks are of these two types: stone and clay." He continued, saying, "' *'asf*' are the leaves of the crops that are not gathered. One of them is called ' *'asfah*'." Al-Kisa'i said, "I have heard some of the scholars of Arabic grammar (*nahw*) say that the singular of '*ababeel*' is '*Ibbeel*'." Many of the *Salaf* said that "*ababeel*" means different groups, some of them following others, from hither and thither. And it is reported on the authority of 'Abdullah Ibn 'Abbas ﷺ that they had beaks like those of birds and feet like those of dogs." On the authority of 'Ikrimah that he said, "They had heads like the heads of predatory animals and they emerged from the sea and were green in color." 'Ubaid Ibn 'Umair said, "They were black birds of the sea that had stones in their beaks and claws." And it is reported on the authority of 'Abdullah ibn 'Abbas ☙ that he said, "They were shap like strange griffons." [1] It was also said by 'Abdullah ibn 'Abbas ☙ that the smallest stone held by them was the size of a man's head, while some of them were as large as camels. Yoonus ibn Bukair also mentioned this on the authority of Ibn Ishaq. It was also said that they were (all) small. And Allah knows better.

Ibn Abi Hatim narrated on the authority of 'Ubaid Ibn 'Umair that he said, "When Allah willed to destroy the People of the Elephant, He sent birds against them that came from the sea, like terns. Each of the birds was carrying three small stones – two stones in its claws and one stone in its beak. They came until they gathered in rows over their heads. Then they gave a loud cry and threw what was in their claws and beaks. Thus, no stone fell upon the head of any man except that it came out of his behind (i.e. it went through him), and it did not fall on any part of his body except that it came out from the opposite side. Then Allah sent a severe wind that struck the stones and increased them in force. Thus, they were all destroyed."

I say: In that year the Messenger of Allah ﷺ was born, according to what is widely accepted. It was also said that it happened some years before his birth, as we shall mention, if Allah, Most High, wills, and in Him we place our trust.

Then Ibn Ishaq mentioned the poetry that the Arabs recited regarding this great incident, in which Allah saved His Sacred House, which it was His Will to ennoble, purify and revere by sending Muhammad ﷺ with the true Religion that He had ordained for him, one of whose pillars is prayer; indeed it is a foundation of His Religion. And he would make the purified Ka'bah its *Qiblah*. So what He did to the People of the Elephant was not to help Quraish, for they were the Abyssinian Christians, whose

---

(1)   Huge, unknown birds, with a large wingspan.

religion at that time was closer to the true Religion than that of the pagan Quraish. Nay, His Help was for the Sacred House and in preparation for the advent of Muhammad ﷺ.

Ibn Hisham said, "It was narrated by Umayyah Ibn Abi As-Salt in *Al-Bahr Al-Khafeef*:

"Verily, the Signs of our Lord are everlasting,

No one disputes regarding them except the disbelievers,

He created the night and the day,

And the measure of each of them is plainly ordained,

Then a Merciful Lord reveals the day,

With a sun whose rays are widely diffused,

He halted the elephant at Al-Mughammis,

Until it began to creep, as if it was wounded,

Like a camel held back by reins,

As if it were an overturned, fallen rock,

Around it were the brave rulers of Kindah,

Stained with the dust of war, falcons,

They allowed it to lead, then they all raced ahead,

As if its leg bone was broken,

Every religion on the Day of Resurrection,

Will be held as falsehood in Allah's Sight,

Except the Haneef Religion."

This incident occurred in the month of Muharram, in the Year 886, according to the calendar of Dhul-Qarnain.

The Story of the Persian Involvement in Yemen

Ibn Hisham said, "Then Wahriz died and Kisra appointed

Wahriz's son, Al-Marzuban as governor of Yemen. Then Al-Marzuban died and so Kisra appointed Marzuban's son, At-Tainujan as governor. After At-Tainujan died, he (kisra) appointed Tainujan's son. Then he deposed him from the governorate of Yemen and appointed Badhan as its governor. During his era, the Messenger of Allah 🌼 was sent." Ibn Hisham said, "It was conveyed to me on the authority of Az-Zuhri that he said, Khosrau wrote to Badhan informing him that a man from Quraish had appeared in Makkah, claiming that he was a Prophet and he ordered him to proceed there and tell him to repent. If he refused, he told Badhan to send his head to him. Badhan sent a messenger to the Messenger of Allah 🌼 with Kisra's letter. The Messenger of Allah 🌼 wrote to him, saying, "Verily, Allah has promised me that Kisra will be killed on such-and-such a day, in such-and-such a month.' When the letter reached Badhan, he paused to think and then he said, "If he is a Prophet, then what he says will come to pass." Then Allah killed Kisra on the day specified by the Prophet 🌼." [1] ibn Hisham said, "(He was killed) by the hand of his son, Sheerawaih." [2] I say: Some said that his sons all took part in his murder. This Kisra's name was Abraweez, son of Hurmuz, son of Anushirwan, son of Qubaz; and he is the defeater of Rome mentioned in Allah's Words: ﴾ Alif-Lam-Meem. The Romans have been defeated in the nearer land (Syria, Iraq, Jordan, and Palestine). ﴿ (*Soorah Ar-Room* 30:1-3)

As-Suhaili said, "His murder occurred on the night of Tuesday, the tenth of Jumad Al-Oola, in the Year 9 A.H. It is said that when the Messenger of Allah 🌼 wrote to him, he invited him to embrace Islam, but Kisra was enraged and tore up the letter. He then wrote to his representative in Yemen with the aforementioned orders. And Allah knows better. In some narrations, it was stated that the Messenger of Allah 🌼 said to

---

(1)   See: *As-Seerah An-Nabawiyyah* (1/191) by Ibn Hisham.

(2)   See: *As-Seerah An-Nabawiyyah* (1/191) by Ibn Hisham.

Badhan's messenger, "Verily, my Lord has killed your lord this night." [1] And it transpired that the Messenger of Allah ﷺ had spoken truthfully; he had been killed on that very night by his sons because of his injustice and wrongdoings, having previously been a just ruler. After they had deposed him, they replaced him with his son, Sheerawaih; but he only remained alive for six months or less, after the death of his father. Regarding this incident, Khalid Ibn Hiqq Ash-Shaibani said:

And remember when Kisra was cut up,

By his sons with their swords,

As a piece of meat is dismembered,

For every person there is an appointed time.

Az-Zuhri said, "When Badhan was informed of this, he sent word to the Messenger of Allah ﷺ that he and those with him had embraced Islam. The messengers said, "To whom do we belong, O, Messenger of Allah?" He said, "You are from us and you belong to us, *Ahl Al-Bait.* [2] Az-Zuhri said, "And for that reason the Messenger of Allah ﷺ said, "Salman is from us, *Ahl Al-Bait.*" [3]

I say: It is apparent that this was after the Messenger of Allah ﷺ migrated to Al-Madinah, which is why he sent governors to Yemen to teach the people goodness and call them to Allah, the Almighty, the All-Powerful. First, he sent Khalid Ibn Al-Waleed

---

(1) This is an authentic hadeeth narrated by Imam Ahmad in his *Musnad* (19925).

(2) *Ahl Al-Bait*: Within the Islamic tradition, the term refers to the family of Muhammad ﷺ. Muslims venerate Muhammad's household as it is given a special significance in the Qur'an and the *hadeeth*.

(3) Narrated by Al-Hakim in *Al-Mustadrak* (3/691, No. 6539) and At-Tabarani in *Al-Kabeer* (6/212, No. 6040) and it is weak, indeed, it has been said that it is extremely weak.

and 'Ali Ibn Abi Talib ⚬, then he sent after them Abu Moosa Al-Ash'ari ⚬ and Mu'adh Ibn Jabal ⚬, and Yemen and its people embraced the Religion of Islam. Then Badhan died and after him, Shahr, son of Badhan, took his place. It was he who was murdered by Al-Aswad Al-'Ansi, when he claimed to be a prophet and he took his wife, as we shall explain, if Allah wills. He also ousted all of the vicegerents appointed by the Messenger of Allah ⚬. But after he had been killed, Islamic rule returned to Yemen. Ibn Hisham said, "And it was he who was referred to by Sateeh when he said, "A pure Prophet, who will receive Revelation from the Supreme (Allah)." And it was he who was referred to by Shiqq in his words: "Nay, it will be cut off by a Messenger sent (by Allah); he will bring truth and dispense with justice to the people of religion and virtue and the rule shall remain among his people until the Day of Decision."

The Story of As-Satiroon, Owner of Al-Hadhr

'Abdul-Malik Ibn Hisham mentioned his story here because of what some of the scholars of lineage have said, which was that it was An-Nu'man Ibn Al-Mundhir who, as mentioned previously, was from the offspring of As-Satiroon, ruler of Al-Hadr. And we have related previously from Ibn Ishaq that An-Nu'man Ibn Al-Mundhir descended from Rabee'ah Ibn Nasr and he narrated on the authority of Jubair Ibn Mut'im that he was one of the descendents of Qunus Ibn Ma'add ibn 'Adnan. These are three opinions regarding his lineage. Ibn Hisham proceeded to describe the ruler of Al-Hadr. Al-Hadr was a massive fortress built by king, i.e. As-Satiroon, on the banks of the Euphrates. It was a towering, elevated structure, vast in breadth, with a huge courtyard; and its perimeter was like that of a great city. It was of the utmost perfection, magnificence, beauty and splendor. And all of the surrounding towns and villages owed fealty to it. As-Satiroon's name was Ad-Daizan Ibn Mu'awiyah Ibn 'Ubaid Ibn Ajram, from the tribe of Banu Sulaih Ibn Halwan ibn Al-Haf Ibn Quda'ah, according to the lineage attributed to him by ibn Al-Kalbi. Others said that he was from Al-Jaramiqah and that he was one of the kings of At-Tawa'if and that he used to lead them whenever they gathered for war against their enemies. His fortress lay between the Tigris and the Euphrates.

Ibn Hisham said, "Kisra Saboor, Zul Aktaf made war on As-Satiroon, king of Al-Hadr." Others said that the person who made war on him was none other than Saboor, son of Ardasheer, son of Babak, the first of the Sassanid kings. He subdued the kings of At-Tawa'if and returned sovereignty of their lands to the Kisras. As for Saboor Zul Aktaf, son of Hurmuz, he lived many years after that. And Allah knows better. This was mentioned by As-Suhaili.

The Story of the Kings of At-Tawa'if

As for the ruler of Al-Hadr, he was As-Satiroon, and as we have said, he used to lead the other kings of At-Tawa'if. He lived in the time of Alexander, son of Philip II of Macedon, in Greece. The reason for this was because after Alexander had conquered the Persian King, Dara, son of Dara, subdued his kingdom, destroyed his lands, taken his people's property as booty, plundered his granaries and divided Persia, scattering the people in all directions. He resolved that no force should ever assemble against them again and that no one should unite against them and so he appointed kings over small groups of people (tawa'if), ruling over small parcels of land occupied by Arabs and non-Arabs. Each king would protect his territory and profit from his position, and when he died, his son or one of his people would succeed him. The situation continued thus for about five hundred years, until Azdasheer, son of Babak from the tribe of Sasan, son of Bahman, son of Isfandyar, son of Yashtasib, son of Lahrasib. He returned their kingdom to its former state and restored the empire. He abolished the petty kingdoms of At-Tawa'if and nothing of them remained. The siege of the ruler of Al-Hadr delayed him, for he was the greatest of them, the most powerful of them and the mightiest of them, being their leader. But when Azdasheer died, he was succeeded by his son, Saboor, who besieged the fortress until he captured the king, as we mentioned previously. And Allah, Most Glorified, Most High, knows better.

The Story of Khuza'ah and 'Amr Ibn Luhayy and His Worship of the Idols in the Land of the Arabs

Ibn Ishaq said, "Ghubshan was from Khuza'ah, who took over responsibility for the House from Banu Bakr Ibn 'Abd Manat. The person who took over from them was 'Amr ibn Al-Harith Al-Ghubshani. Quraish at that time were scattered, separated and lived in abodes dispersed between the people of Kinanah. It was said that they were known as Khuza'ah because they left the sons of 'Amr Ibn 'Amir and when they arrived from Yemen, they were en route to Ash-Sham, but they stopped at Marr Az-Zahran and took up residence there. 'Awn Ibn Ayyoob Al-Ansari, then Al-Khazraji, said regarding this:

> *When we settled at Batn Marr,*
> *Khuza'ah left us on fast horses,*
> *Every wadi in Tihamah fought,*
> *With pointed spears and sharpened swords.*

So Khuza'ah took on responsibility for the House and it was

passed down from father to son, until the last of them, Hulail Ibn Hubshiyyah Ibn Salool Ibn Ka'b Ibn 'Amr Ibn Rabee'ah Al-Khuza'i. His daughter, Hubba, married Qusayy ibn Kilab. She bore him four sons: 'Abdud-Dar, 'Abd Manaf, 'Abdul-'Uzza and 'Abd. Then the responsibility of the House passed to him, as we shall explain in detail in the relevant place, if Allah, Most High, wills – and in Him we place our trust.

Khuza'ah continued to be responsible for the House for around three hundred years, or it was said, five hundred years. And Allah knows better. Ibn Hisham said, "I was informed by one of the scholars that 'Amr Ibn Luhayy set out from Makkah for Ash-Sham on business and when he arrived at Ma'ab in the land of Al-Balqa', which was at that time in the hands of the Amalekites, who were the descendants of 'Imlaq, or it was said, 'Imleeq Ibn Lawadh Ibn Sam, Ibn Nooh. He saw them worshipping idols and he said to them, "What are these idols that I see you worshipping?" They said to him, "We worship these idols and ask them for rain and they grant us rain, and we seek help from them and they help us." He said to them, "Will you not give me an idol from among them and I will take it to the land of the Arabs, that they may worship it?" So they gave him an idol named Hubal and he brought it to Makkah and erected it there and ordered the people to worship and glorify it."

Ibn Ishaq said, "They claim that the beginning of idol worship among the descendants of Isma'eel ﷺ was that whenever they departed from Makkah and they were traveling in the wide open spaces and were feeling uneasy, they would take with them a stone from the stones of the Sacred Precincts in glorification of them and wherever they camped, they would place it on the ground and circumambulate it, as they circumambulated the Ka'bah until this led them to worship the stones and their descendants forgot the religion that they had formerly followed.

It is reported in *Saheeh Al-Bukhari* on the authority of Abu Raja' Al-'Utaridi ﷺ that he said, "During the *Jahiliyyah* (days of ignorance), if we could not find a stone, we would collect a handful of dust, then we would bring a sheep and milk it over it, then we would circumambulate it." [1]

Based on this, we may infer that there were some remnants of the rites practiced during the time of Ibraheem عليه السلام to which they adhered, i.e. glorification of the House and circumambulation of it, Hajj and 'Umrah, standing on 'Arafat, visiting Muzdalifah, slaughtering a sacrificial animal, making the *ihlal* [2] for Hajj and 'Umrah, though they added to them things to them which were not a part of them. When Kinanah and Quraish made *ihlal*, they would say, "*Labbaik Allahumma Labbaik, Labbaika La Shareeka Laka Labbaik, Illa Shareekan Huwa Lak, Tamlikuhi Wa Ma Malak* (O, Allah! I respond to Your Call, I respond to Your Call and You have no partner except a partner whom You have and You own all that he owns)." So they would declare His Oneness in the *talbiyyah*, then they would insert into it their idols and they would place their ownership in His Hand. Allah, Most High, said to Muhammad ﷺ: ﴿ And most of them believe not in Allah except that they attribute partners unto Him (i.e. they are *mushrikoon* [polytheists].﴾ See also *Soorah Al-An'am* 6:121) (*Soorah Yoosuf* 12:106). That is, they do not affirm My Oneness except that they ascribe partners to Me from among My creation.

And it has been confirmed in the *Saheeh* that when the Messenger of Allah ﷺ heard them saying, "*Labbaika La Shareeka Laka Labbaik* (I respond to Your Call and You have no partner," he said, "*Qad, Qad* (Enough, enough)." [3]

---

(1) Narrated by Al-Bukhari (4376).

(2) *Ihlal*: Announcing one's intention to perform Hajj or 'Umrah by means of the *talbiyyah*, when assuming *ihram*.

(3) Narrated by Muslim (1185), on the authority of 'Abdullah Ibn 'Abbas ﷺ.

And 'Abdullah Ibn Ahmad narrated on the authority of 'Abdullah ibn Mas'ood ﷺ, who reported from the Prophet ﷺ that he said, "The first person to let animals roam free for the idols was the father of Khuza'ah, 'Amr Ibn 'Amir and I saw him dragging his entrails in the Fire." [1]

And Al-Bukhari narrated on the authority of 'A'ishah (may Allah be Pleased with her) that she said, "The Messenger of Allah ﷺ said, "I saw the Hellfire and its different portions were consuming each other and saw 'Amr dragging his intestines (in it), and he was the first person to establish the tradition of letting animals loose (for the idols)." [2]

What is meant is that 'Amr Ibn Luhayy – may Allah Curse him – introduced heresies to them in their religion by which he changed the Religion of *Al-Khaleel* ﷺ and the Arabs followed him in that, which caused them to stray far from the truth. And Allah, Most High, rebuked them in His Noble Book in more than one Verse, such as His Words: ﴿ And say not concerning that which your tongues put forth falsely: "This is lawful and this is forbidden," so as to invent lies against Allah. ﴾ (*Soorah An-Nahl* 16:116) and His Words: ﴿ Allah has not instituted things like *baheerah* (a she-camel whose milk was spared for the idols and nobody was allowed to milk it) or a *sa'ibah* (a she-camel let loose for free pasture for their false gods, idols, etc. and nothing was allowed to be carried on it), or a *waseelah* (a she-camel set free for idols because it has given birth to a she-camel at its first delivery and then again gives birth to a she-camel at its second delivery) or a *ham* (a male camel freed from work for their idols, after it had finished a number of matings assigned for it. All these animals were liberated in honor of idols as practiced by pagan Arabs in the pre-Islamic period). But those who disbelieve invent lies against

---

(1)   Narrated by Al-Bukhari (3520) and by Imam Ahmad (4246).

(2)   Narrated by Al-Bukhari (4624).

Allah and most of them have no understanding 》 (*Soorah Al-Ma'idah* 5:103). We have discussed this in detail and we made clear the difference of opinion among the *Salaf* regarding its *tafseer*. So whoever wishes to read it may find it there, all praise and thanks be to Allah. And He, Most High, says, 《 And they assign a portion of that which We have provided them unto what they know not (i.e. false deities). By Allah, you shall certainly be questioned about (all of) that which you used to fabricate. 》 (*Soorah An-Nahl* 16:56)

And He, Most High, says, 《 And they assign to Allah a share of the tilth and cattle which He has created, and they say, "This is for Allah according to their pretending, and this is for our (Allah's so-called) partners." But the share of their (Allah's so-called) "partners" reaches not Allah, while the share of Allah reaches their (Allah's so-called) "partners"! Evil is the way they judge! And so to many of the *mushrikoon* (polytheists - see v. 2:105) their (Allah's so-called) "partners" have made fair-seeming the killing of their children, in order to lead them to their own destruction and cause confusion in their religion. And if Allah had willed they would not have done so. So leave them alone with their fabrications. And according to their pretending, they say, "such-and-such cattle and crops are forbidden, and none should eat of them except those whom we allow." And (they say) there are cattle forbidden to be used for burden or any other work, and cattle on which (at slaughtering) the Name of Allah is not pronounced, lying against Him (Allah). He will recompense them for what they used to fabricate. And they say: "What is in the bellies of such-and-such cattle (milk or fetus) is for our males alone, and forbidden to our females (girls and women), but if it is born dead, then all have shares therein." He will punish them for their attribution (of such false orders to Allah). Verily, He is Most Wise, All-Knowing. (*Tafseer At-Tabari,* Vol. 8, page 49). Indeed lost are those who have killed their children from folly, without knowledge, and have forbidden that which Allah has provided for them, inventing a lie against Allah. They have indeed gone astray and were not guided. 》 (*Soorah Al-An'am* 6:136-140)

And Al-Bukhari narrated in his *Saheeh* on the authority of 'Abdullah Ibn 'Abbas ﷺ that he said, "If you wish to know about the ignorance of the Arabs, refer to *Soorah Al-An'am* after Verse No. 130: 《 Indeed lost are those who have killed their children from folly, without knowledge and have forbidden that which Allah has provided for them, inventing a lie against Allah. They have indeed gone astray and were not guided 》 (*Soorah Al-An'am* 6:140). We have already given the explanation of this Verse and the heresies they introduced into the Religion, which were false and wicked, and which their leader, 'Amr ibn Luhayy – may Allah Curse him – thought were beneficial and a mercy to the cattle and camels, but he was a liar and fabricator in this. And in spite of his ignorance and misguidance the foolish, common people followed him. Indeed, they followed him in something far worse than that, i.e. the worship of idols besides Allah, the Almighty, the All-Powerful. And they altered the True Religion and the Straight path with which Allah sent Ibraheem, His *Khaleel* 緻元ﷺ and perverted the religious knowledge, when they themselves had no knowledge and no evidence – be it authentic or weak. And in doing so, they followed those pagan nations who came before them, imitating the people of Nooh ﷺ, who were the first people to associate partners with Allah and to worship idols, which is why Allah sent Nooh ﷺ to them. He was the first Messenger who prohibited the worship of idols, as we made clear earlier, in the story of Nooh ﷺ, 《 And they said, "You shall not leave your gods, nor shall you leave *Wadd,* nor *Suwa',* nor *Yaghooth,* nor *Ya'ooq,* nor *Nasr* (names of the idols). And indeed they have led many astray." 》 (*Soorah Nooh* 71:23,24). 'Abdullah ibn 'Abbas ﷺ said, "They (the idols) were righteous persons from among the people of Nooh ﷺ and when they died, they used to sit around their graves, then after a long period of time had passed, they began to worship them." And we have explained how they used to worship them previously in such detail, that there is no necessity to repeat it here.

The Story of 'Adnan, the Father of the Arabs of Al-Hijaz

There is no difference regarding the fact that 'Adnan was one of the descendants of Isma'eel, son of Ibraheem, *Al-Khaleel* (peace be upon them both), but there are several opinions regarding the number of forefathers there were between him and Isma'eel ﷺ. The greatest number of forefathers mentioned is forty, which is the number stated by the People of the Scripture. They took it from the Books of Rakhya, as we shall make clear. It was also said that there were thirty forefathers and also that there were twenty and that there were fifteen, and also ten and nine. The smallest number claimed was four, according to the narration of Moosa Ibn Ya'qoob, who reported on the authority of 'Abdullah Ibn Wahb Ibn Zam'ah Az-Zam'i, who reported on the authority of his paternal aunt that she reported on the authority of Umm Salamah (may Allah be Pleased with her), that she reported from the Prophet ﷺ that he said, "Ma'add was the son of 'Adnan Ibn Udad Ibn Zand ibn Yara Ibn A'raq Ath-Thara." [1] Umm Salamah (may Allah be Pleased with her) said, "Zand is Al-Hamaisa', Al-Yara is Nabt and A'raquth – Thara is Isma'eel ﷺ, because he is the son of Ibraheem ﷺ – and Ibraheem ﷺ was not consumed by the fire, just as fire does not consume '*ath-thara*'." [2] Ad-Daraqutni said, "We do not know Zand except in this *hadeeth* and

---

(1)   Narrated by Al-Hakim in *Al-Mustadrak* (2/437, No. 3519) and At-Tabarani in his *Tareekh* (1/516), both of them via Moosa Ibn Ya'qoob.

(2)   *Ath-Thara*: Moist earth.

Zand ibn Al-Jawn is Abu Dulamah, the poet."

Abu 'Umar said, "There were a number of people from among the *Salaf*, including 'Abdullah Ibn Mas'ood, Amr Ibn Maimoon Al-Azdi and Muhammad Ibn Ka'b Al-Qurazi, who, when they recited the Words of Allah: ❨And those after them? None knows them but Allah ❩ (*Soorah Ibraheem* 14:9), would add, "The scholars of lineage have lied."

Abu 'Umar – may Allah have Mercy on him – said, "The meaning, as we understand it, is different from what they have understood; it is that whoever claimed to know the number of Adam's descendants, (they should know that) none knows it except Allah, Who created them. As for the lineages of the Arabs, the scholars know them, including times and ancestries and they have memorized their groups and the origins of their tribes, though have differed regarding some of the branches of those tribes."

Abu 'Umar also said, "The opinion of the scholars of this discipline regarding the lineage of 'Adnan is that he is 'Adnan Ibn Udad Ibn Muqawwam Ibn Nahoor Ibn Tairah Ibn Ya'rub ibn Yashjub ibn Nabit ibn Isma'ccl ibn Ibraheem *Al-Khaleel* (peace be upon them both). This is how it was related by Muhammad Ibn Ishaq Ibn Yasar in his *Seerah*."

What Has Been Said Regarding the Lineage of Quraish, Its Origins and Its Virtues – and They Are Banu An-Nadr ibn Kinanah

Ibn Hisham said, "An-Nadr is Quraish and the one who is descended from him is a Quraishite; those who are not descended from him are not Quraishites. Abu 'Ubaid and Ibn 'Abdul-Barr said, "The opinion of the majority is that he is An-Nadr Ibn

Kinanah, based on the *hadeeth* of Al-Ash'ath Ibn Qais." I say: This is what was cited by Hisham Ibn Muhammad ibn As-Sa'ib Al-Kalbi and Abu 'Ubaidah Ma'mar Ibn Al-Muthanna and it is the opinion of Ash-Shafi'i (may Allah be pleased with him). Abu 'Umar's preferred opinion was that he was Fihr Ibn Malik and he cited as evidence that there is no one today who claims descent from Quraish except that he traces his lineage from Fihr Ibn Malik."

And Al-Bukhari narrated on the authority of Kulaib Ibn Wa'il that he said, "I said to the stepdaughter of the Prophet ﷺ (i.e. Zainab Bint Abi Salamah), "Tell me about the Prophet, did he belong to the tribe of Mudar?" She replied, "Yes, he belonged to the tribe of Mudar and was from the offspring of An-Nadr Ibn Kinanah." [1]

And At-Tabarani said, "on the authority of Al-Jufsheesh Al-Kindi that he said, 'A people from Kindah came to the Messenger of Allah ﷺ and they said, You are from us,' and they claimed him (as one of them). But he said, 'No, we are Banu An-Nadr Ibn Kinanah; we do not follow our mother and we do not deny our father'." [2]

And Imam Ahmad narrated on the authority of Muslim from Al-Haisam Ibn Al-Ash'ath Ibn Qais ؓ that he said, "I went to

---

(1) Narrated by Al-Bukhari (3491).

(2) Narrated by At-Tabarani in *Al-Kabeer* (2/285, No. 2190) and in *As-Sagheer* (1/144, No. 219). Al-Haithami said in '*Al-Majma*' (1/195), "In its chain of narrators is Isma'eel Ibn 'Amr Al-Bajali, who was declared weak by Abu Hatim and Ad-Daraqutni, though he was declared trustworthy by Ibn Hibban. The rest of its narrators are trustworthy." (Translator's note: In such cases, it is necessary to accept the negative report, since the scholars of *hadeeth* would not declare a person to be weak without cause, while those who declared him trustworthy may have done so because they were not privy to the information which caused the other scholars to deem him weak).

the Messenger of Allah ﷺ with a delegation from Kindah and I said, "O, Messenger of Allah! We claim that you are from us.' But the Messenger of Allah ﷺ said, 'We are Banu An-Nadr ibn Kinanah; we do not follow our mother and we do not deny our father." Al-Ash'ath ibn Qais said, "By Allah, I do not hear anyone denying that Quraish are from An-Nadr except that I inflict on him a flogging.' [1] And this is the decisive proof in this matter, so no regard should be paid to those who contradict it. And Allah knows better. A person from Quraish is known as a Qurashi or a Quraishi. Al-Jawhari said, This is a comparison; the poet said:

Every Quraishi is honorable,

He hastens to answer the call of the caller and he is generous.

He said, "If one intends by Quraish the clan, then it will be inflected (i.e. *Quraishun*), but if one intends by it the tribe, then it will be uninflected (i.e. *Quraishu*). The poet said regarding its being uninflected:

And Quraish's support sufficed them against their problems.

And Muslim narrated in his *Saheeh*, on the authority of Wathilah Ibn Al-Asqa' that he said, "The Messenger of Allah ﷺ said, "Verily, Allah chose Kinanah from the sons of Isma'eel, He chose *Quraishan* from Kinanah, He chose Hashim from *Quraishin* and He chose me from Banu Hashim." [2]

Ibn Ishaq said, "A person whose integrity I do not doubt informed me that 'Umar Ibn Al-Khattab said to some men, among whom were men from Banu Murrah, "If you wish to refer to your lineages, then do so." Ibn Ishaq said, "They were eminent people among Ghatafan and they were masters and leaders of them, a people possessing fame amongst all of Ghatafan and Qais. They

---

(1) This is an authentic *hadeeth* narrated by Imam Ahmad in his *Musnad* (5/313, No. 21338). It was also narrated by Ibn Majah (2612).

(2) Narrated by Muslim (2276).

held fast to their lineage and they said, "Whenever their lineage was mentioned, they would say, "We do not disavow or reject them and it is the dearest lineage to us." Then he mentioned their poems regarding their claim of descent from Lu'ayy. He added, "They followed a practice known as *al-basl*, which was the designation of eight months in each year as sacred months; and the other Arabs accepted this from them and they would guarantee their safety in them." I say: Rabee'ah and Mudar accepted the sanctity of only four months in the year: Dhul-Qa'dah, Dhul-Hijjah, Muharram – and Rabee'ah and Mudar disagreed as to the fourth, but it is Rajab. Mudar said that it is the month that is between Jumada and Sha'ban, while Rabee'ah said that it is the month between Sha'ban and Shawwal. And it has been confirmed in the *Saheehain* on the authority of Abu Bakrah ﷺ that the Messenger of Allah ﷺ said in the sermon that he delivered in his Farewell Pilgrimage: "The division of time has turned to its original form which was current when Allah created the heavens and the earths. The year is of twelve months, out of which four months are sacred: Three are in succession Dhul-Qa'dah, Dhul-Hijjah and Muharram, and (the fourth is) Rajab of (the tribe of) Mudar which comes between Jumada Ath-Thaniyah and Sha'ban." [1] This lends more weight to the saying of Mudar, as opposed to that of Rabee'ah; and Allah, Most High, says ﴾ Verily, the number of months with Allah is twelve months (in a year), so was it ordained by Allah on the Day when He created the heavens and the Earth; of them four are sacred, (i.e. the 1st, the 7th, the 11th and the 12th months of the Islamic calendar). ﴿ (*Soorah At-Tawbah* 9:36). This is a reply to Banu 'Awf Ibn Lu'ayy and their designation of eight sacred months, for they increased thereby what Allah had ordained and included in it that which is not from it. As for the saying of the Prophet ﷺ in the *hadeeth*: "Three are in succession," it is a reply to the people of *An-Nasi'*, who used to defer the sanctity of Muharram until Safar. As for his saying: "and (the fourth is)

_____

(1)   Narrated by Al-Bukhari (1679).

Rajab of (the tribe of) Mudar," it is a reply to Rabee'ah.

The Story of Qusayy Ibn Kilab

Qusayy was a master and leader among his people, a man whose commands were obeyed and who was venerated (by them). What is meant is that he gathered Quraish from their dispersed locations throughout the Arabian Gulf. He sought support from those Arab clans who obeyed him in his war against Khuza'ah, their expulsion from the Sacred House and the handing over of it to Qusayy. There was much fighting and bloodshed between them, then they called for a ruling and they sought that ruling from Ya'mur Ibn 'Awf Ibn Ka'b Ibn 'Amir Ibn Laith Ibn Bakr Ibn 'Abd Manat ibn Kinanah. Ya'mur subsequently ruled that Qusayy had more right than Khuza'ah to take responsibility for the House. He also ruled that Qusayy was not responsible for the bloodshed inflicted by him on Khuza'ah and Banu Bakr, while Khuza'ah and Banu Bakr were obligated to pay bloodwit for the bloodshed that they had inflicted on Quraish, Kinanah and Qudha'ah. Finally, the area of Makkah, including the Ka'bah was to be vacated for Qusayy and his people. Thenceforth, Ya'mur became known as Ash-Shaddakh (the Crusher).

Ibn Ishaq said, "So Qusayy took over the custodianship of the Ka'bah and the affairs of Makkah and he gathered his people from their homes and made them take up residence in Makkah. He also became ruler of his people and of Makkah. But he confirmed the Arabs in what they were following, for he considered that it was the true religion and that it did not require any alteration. He confirmed the family of Safwan, 'Adwan, An-Nasa`ah and Murrah Ibn 'Awf in what they were doing and the matter remained thus until the advent of Islam, by which Allah destroyed all of that." ibn Ishaq said, "Qusayy was the first of Banu Ka'b to become the ruler of Makkah, obeyed by all of his people. He was responsible for *Al-Hijabah*, [1] *As-Siqayah*, [2] *Ar-Rifadah*, [3] *An-Nadwah* [4] and *Al-Liwa'*. [5] He divided Makkah into four regions which he then allocated to Quraish as their homes."

I say: Custodianship of the House became established as the right of Quraish, while Khuza'ah were dispossessed of it because of the heresies they introduced there, such as their worship of idols, their erection of them around the Ka'bah, the animals they sacrificed to them, the humility they displayed toward them, the help they sought from them and the sustenance they requested from them. Qusayy apportioned the valleys of Makkah to the tribes of Quraish and he settled a group of them in its outskirts. All matters pertaining to leadership were in the hands of Qusayy Ibn Kilab, such as the maintenance and custodianship of the House and leadership in all military matters. He built a house for the resolution of disputes, which he called *Dar An-Nadwah*. When a problem arose, the leaders of all the tribes would meet therein and they would resolve it. But no military covenants or marriage contracts were enacted except in *Dar An-Nadwah*. The door of this meeting place was opposite the Sacred Mosque. Then this meeting place became the responsibility of Hakeem Ibn Hizam, after Banu 'Abdud-Dar and he sold it during the era of Mu'awiyah ﷺ for a hundred thousand *dirhams*. Mu'awiyah ﷺ rebuked him for selling it, saying, "You have sold the honor of your people for a hundred thousand?" He replied, "By Allah, honor this day is only in piety. I purchased it in the *Jahiliyyah* for

---

(1)　*Al-Hijabah*: Maintenance of the Ka'bah and the guardianship of its keys.

(2)　*As-Siqayah*: Provision of water for the pilgrims coming to Makkah.

(3)　*Ar-Rifadah*: A tax collected from the people of Makkah with which food for the pilgrims was purchased.

(4)　*An-Nadwah*: This was the meeting place established by Qusayy, where the Arabs met to discuss their affairs; Qusayy held the chairmanship of these meetings.

(5)　*Al-Liwa'*: Literally, the flag or standard; this implied leadership in all military matters.

a skin of wine and look now, I have sold it for a hundred thousand *dirhams* and I call upon you to bear witness that its price is given in charity in Allah's Cause. So which of us is deceived?" This was mentioned by Ad-Daraqutni in his discussion of the narrators in *Al-Muwatta'*.

The responsibility for providing water to the pilgrims was in the hands of Qusayy and they would not drink except from his water basins. *Zamzam* was at that time lost and had been like that since the time of Jurhum and knowledge of it had been forgotten and they were unable to find its location.

Ibn Ishaq said, "This was because Qusayy obliged them to do so; he said to them, "O, people of Quraish! You are Allah's neighbors, the people of Makkah and the people of the Sacred Precincts and the pilgrims are Allah's guests and the visitors to His House and they are most worthy of hospitality. So prepare for them food and drink during the days of Hajj until they leave you." So they did this, and every year they would pay a tax from their wealth to him and he would use it to prepare food for the people during the days of Mina. Matters continued thus during the *Jahiliyyah* until the advent of Islam. Then matters continued in Islam and they have remained like this until this day, and that is the food which is prepared by the Sultan every year for the people until the Hajj is completed."

I say: Then this ended after Ibn Ishaq's time. Later, a group from *Bait Al-Mal* (the Treasury) were ordered to carry food and drink to people traveling to Makkah to perform Hajj. This is a good deed for reasons too numerous to be mentioned, but it should really be the sole responsibility of *Bait Al-Mal*, because they have the resources to do it. And it would be better if it were taken from the Jews and Christians, because they do not perform pilgrimage to the Ancient House; and it has been stated in the *hadeeth*, "Whoever is able to perform Hajj and does not do so, then let him die if he wishes as a Jew or a Christian." [1]

Section

Then, when Qusayy became old, he passed the matter of these responsibilities which had been in his hands, such as the leadership of Quraish, *Ar-rifadah*, *As-siqayah*, *Al-hijabah*, *Al-liwa'* and *an-nadwah*, to his son, 'Abdud-Dar, who was his eldest son. He selected him to bear all of these responsibilities because his other brothers, 'Abd Manaf, 'Abdul-'Uzza and 'Abd had been honored during their father's lifetime and had achieved their greatest potential and so Qusayy wanted 'Abdud-Dar to attain the same level of leadership as they had. His brothers did not dispute this, but after they had passed away, their sons fell into dispute regarding it. They said, "Qusayy only chose 'Abdud-Dar for this responsibility because he wanted to bring him up to the same level as his brothers, but we deserve what our fathers deserved." The sons of 'Abdud-Dar said, "This is a matter that was decided for us by Qusayy, so we have more right to it." So they disagreed profoundly and the clans of Quraish divided into two groups, one of them pledged their loyalty to 'Abdud-Dar and entered into an alliance with him, while the other group pledged their loyalty to Banu 'Abd Manaf and made an alliance with them. To signify this, they placed their hands in a bowl of perfume, then when they stood up, they wiped their hands on the corners of the Ka'bah, for which reason the alliance became known as the Alliance of the Perfumers. Among the tribes of Quraish who did so were Banu Asad Ibn 'Abdul-'Uzza Ibn Qusayy, Banu Zuhrah, Banu Taim and Banul-Harith ibn Fihr. With Banu 'Abdud-Dar were Banu Makhzoom, Banu Sahm, Banu Jumah and Banu 'Adiyy. Banu

---

(1)   Narrated by At-Tirmidhi (812), but it is weak and there is contention among the scholars regarding its *isnad*.

'Amir ibn Lu'ayy and Muharib ibn Fihr abstained and did not side with either group. Then they held peace talks and agreed that *Ar-Rifadah* and *As-Siqayah* should be the responsibility of Banu 'Abd Manaf and that *Al-Hijabah*, *Al-Liwa'* and *An-Nadwah* should remain in the hands of Banu 'Abdud-Dar, and the matter was settled in this way and continued thus.

Chapter: Mention of a Group Who Were Renowned in the Jahiliyyah

The Story of Khalid Ibn Sinan Al-'Absi Who Lived During the Era of Al-Fatrah

Some claimed that he was a Prophet, and Allah knows better.

Al-Hafiz Abul-Qasim At-Tabarani said, "on the authority of 'Abdullah Ibn 'Abbas ﷺ that he said, "The daughter of Khalid Ibn Sinan came to the Prophet ﷺ and he spread out his garment for her and said, "The daughter of a Prophet whose people neglected him." [1]

And it was narrated by Al-Hafiz Abu Bakr Al-Bazzar ﷺ on the authority of 'Abdullah Ibn 'Abbas ﷺ that he said, "Khalid ibn Sinan was mentioned in the presence of the Messenger of Allah ﷺ and he said, "That was a Prophet whose people neglected him." [2] Then he said, "We do not know of any *marfoo'* version

---

[1]   Narrated by At-Tabarani in *Al-Kabeer* (11/441, *hadeeth* No. 12250). Al-Haithami said in *Al-Majma'* (8/214), "In its chain is Qais Ibn Ar-Rabee', who was declared trustworthy by Shu'bah and Ath-Thawri, but declared weak by Imam Ahmad – in spite of his piety – and Ibn Ma'een."

[2]   It was mentioned by Al-Haithami in *Al-Majma'* (8/214) and he said, "Al-Bazzar said, "It was narrated by Ath-Thawri on the authority of Salim, who reported on the authority of Salim, who in turn reported on the au-

of it except from this source; and Qais Ibn Ar-Rabee' was a trustworthy person, except that he had a poor memory; and he had a son who used to insert things into his *ahadeeth* that did not belong in them. And Allah knows better. It would appear most likely that he was a righteous man who was virtuous and noble, for if he lived during *al-fatrah*, [1] it has been confirmed in *Saheeh Al-Bukhari* that the Messenger of Allah ﷺ said, "I am the nearest of all the people to the son of Maryam, and all the Prophets are paternal brothers, and there has been no Prophet between me and him (i.e. 'Eesa)." [2] If he lived before it, then it is impossible that he could have been a Prophet, because Allah, Most High, says, ﴾ to give warning to a people to whom no warner had come before you. ﴿ (*Soorah Al-Qasas* 28:46). And more than scholar has said that Allah, Most High, did not send any Prophet to the Arabs after Isma'eel عليه السلام except Muhammad ﷺ, the Seal of the Prophets, to whom Ibraheem, *Al-Khaleel*, builder of the venerable Ka'bah (which was ordained by Allah as the *Qiblah* for the people of the world) called, and whose advent the Prophets foretold to their peoples, until the last Prophet to foretell of his advent came, i.e. 'Eesa, the son of Maryam عليه السلام. And by this very means one may refute the argument propounded by As-Suhaili and others – which holds that a Prophet from the Arabs, whose name was Shu'aib ibn Dhee Mahzam ibn Shu'aib ibn Safwan of Madyan was sent and that Hanzalah ibn Safwan was also sent to the Arabs, but that they belied them and so Allah made Bukhtunassar victorious over them, and that he killed some of them and took others captive, which was similar to the punishment inflicted on the Children of Isra'eel. They also claim that this occurred during the era of Ma'add ibn 'Adnan. But it would appear that these people were

---

thority of Sa'eed ibn Jubair in a *mursal* form."

(1)   *Al-Fatrah*: The time period between two Messengers or Prophets, in this case, the ascension of 'Eesa عليه السلام and the advent of the Messenger of Allah ﷺ.

(2)   Narrated by Al-Bukhari (3443).

righteous men who called to goodness. And Allah knows better. We have already told the story of 'Amr Ibn Luhayy Ibn Qama'ah ibn Khindif in the stories of Khuza'ah, after Jurhum.

Mention of the Story of Hatim At-Ta'i, One of the Generous Folk in the Jahiliyyah

Al-Hafiz Abu Bakr Al-Bazzar said in his *Musnad*, "on the authority of 'Abdullah Ibn 'Umar ☜ that he said, "Hatim was mentioned in the presence of the Prophet ﷺ and he said, "That (man) intended something and he attained it." This *hadeeth* is *ghareeb*; Ad-Daraqutni said, "[1]

And Imam Ahmad narrated on the authority of 'Adiyy Ibn Hatim ☜ that he said, "I said to the Messenger of Allah ﷺ, "My father used to maintain the ties of kinship and do such-and-such; will he have the reward of that?" He replied, "Your father sought something and he attained it." [2]

And in another *hadeeth* in the *Saheeh*, that they asked the Messenger of Allah ﷺ about 'Abdullah Ibn Jud'an Ibn 'Amr Ibn Ka'b Ibn Sa'd Ibn Taim Ibn Murrah and they said to him, "He used to be hospitable toward his guests and he would free slaves and give charity; will that benefit him?" He said, "It would be of no avail to him as he did not ever say: "O, my Lord, pardon my sins on the Day of Resurrection." [3] This was in spite of the fact that he was renowned as one of most generous people in the *Jahiliyyah* and also one of those who fed the poor during the years of drought and in times of sandstorms.

---

(1) This was narrated by Imam Ahmad in his *Musnad* (18897).

(2) This is an authentic *hadeeth* narrated by Imam Ahmad in his *Musnad* (18896).

(3) Narrated by Muslim (214).

And Al-Hafiz Abu Bakr Al-Baihaqi reported on the authority of 'Ali Ibn Abi Talib ❀ that he said, "Glorified be Allah! I wonder at a Muslim who does not do benefit to his brother Muslim who stands in need of it. If he hopes for rewards and fears punishment, he should hasten toward good conduct as it shows the path of salvation." On hearing this, a man stood up and said to him, "May my father and mother be ransomed for you, O, Commander of the Faithful! Did you hear it from the Messenger of Allah ❀?" 'Ali ❀ replied, "Yes, and (I heard) that which is better than it, when the captives of Tai' were brought to him, a girl with a rosy complexion, red lips, a fine nose, with a good stature and head, trim ankles, straight legs, good thighs, wide hips and a trim waist arrived and when I saw her, I admired her, so I said, "I will ask the Messenger of Allah ❀ to make her a part of my share of the spoils, but when she spoke, her eloquence caused me to forget her beauty; she said, "O, Muhammad! If you wish, release me, but don't dishonor me before the Arab clans. I am the daughter of the leader of my people and my father was the caretaker of my people. He used to set free the captives, feed the hungry, spread peace and never refused any beggar in his time of need. I am the daughter of Hatim Ta'i." The Prophet ❀ said, "O girl! What you have mentioned about his qualities are the attributes of a true Believer. If your father had been a Believer, we would have treated him with compassion. Set her free, for her father used to love good character and conduct and Allah, Most High, loves good character and conduct." Then Abu Burdah Ibn Niyar stood up and said, "O, Messenger of Allah! Does Allah love good character and conduct?" The Messenger of Allah ❀ replied, "By Him in Whose Hand is my soul, No one will enter Paradise unless he has a good character."

Among the poems composed by Hatim is the following:

If I continued to drink more than my thirst demanded,

Because of an intoxicant in the drink, then I would not quench my thirst,

If I continued to cheat

Should I dishonor my neighbor's wife and deceive my neighbor?

By Allah, I will not do so as long as I live.

Also from his poetry is the following (*Al-Bahr Al-Kamil*):

No neighbor of mine has been harmed,

By not having a screen for his doorway,

I should close my eyes if my neighbor's wife appeared,

Until she was concealed by the curtain.

Also from the poetry of Hatim (*Al-Bahr ul-Wafir*) is:

It is not in my nature to malign my cousin,

Nor do I disappoint one who puts his hope in me,

And the word of an envier without cause,

I heard and said (to it), "Pass by and go through me,"

And they found fault with me for it, but it did not hurt me,

And it did not cause sweat on my brow at all,

And a hypocrite met me face-to-face,

And when he was absent, it did not worry me,

And I triumphed over his accusation and was forbearing toward him,

In order to protect my dignity and my religion."

Also from his poetry (*Al-Bahr ut-Taweel*) is:

O, Umm Malik! Ask the cold and wretched person,

When he came to me, between my fire and my meat,

Did I not smile at him, as if he was the first guest,

And extend my benevolence to him, without rebuke?

And he also said (*Al-Bahrut-Taweel*):

And verily, if you gave your stomach its desire,

And also your loins, they would both receive the utmost censure.

And Al-Qadi Abul-Faraj Al-Mu'afa Ibn Zakariyya Al-Jareeri said, "Al-Husain Ibn Al-Qasim Al-Kawkabi told me, "Abul-'Abbas Al-Mubarrid told me, "Ath-Thawri informed me on the authority of 'Ubaidah that he said, When the following words of Al-Mutalammis reached Hatim At-Ta'i:

If you have but little money and you use it well, it will last,

And much money will not last if you waste it,

And saving money is better than finishing it,

And reckless expenditure, leaving one without provision.

He said, "What is wrong with him? May Allah cut off his tongue! He encourages the people to be miserly; why did he not say (*Al-Bahrut-Taweel*):

Generosity does not exhaust wealth before its time,

Nor does the miser's niggardliness increase it,

So do not seek wealth by living a frugal life,

For every tomorrow there is a provision that will return anew,

Do you not see that wealth departs and disappears,

And that the One Who give it to you is not far away?

And Al-Qadi Abul-Faraj said, "He spoke well when he said,

"And that the One Who gives it to you is not far away?"

If he had been a Muslim, it might have been hoped that he might have a good end in the Hereafter; and Allah, Most High, says in His Book, ❴ ...and ask Allah of His Bounty ❵ (*Soorah An-Nisa'* 4:32), and He, Most High, says, ❴ And when My slaves ask you (O, Muhammad) concerning Me, then (answer them), I am indeed near (to them by My Knowledge). I respond to the invocations of the supplicant when he calls on Me (without any mediator or intercessor) ❵ (*Soorah Al-Baqarah* 2:186).

Mention of Something of the Story of 'Abdullah ibn Jud'an

He was 'Abdullah Ibn Jud'an Ibn 'Amr Ibn Ka'b Ibn Sa'd Ibn Taim Ibn Murrah, the chief of Banu Taim and he was the son of Abu Bakr As-Siddeeq's great-uncle. He was one of the generous and kind folk in the *Jahiliyyah*, who used to feed the poor and needy.

Ibn Qutaibah and others mentioned that the Messenger of Allah ﷺ said, "I used to get shelter under the water trough of 'Abdullah Ibn Jud'an at noontime." [1]

---

(1) See *An-Nihayah Fee Ghareebil-Athar* (3/43), where it is mentioned without any *isnad*.

In the *hadeeth* of the killing of Abu Jahl it was mentioned that the Messenger of Allah ﷺ said to his Companions ﷺ, "Search for him among the dead; you will recognize him by a wound on his knee, for he and I argued regarding a banquet for Ibn Jud'an and I pushed him and he fell on his knee and it fractured, and the scar of it remains on his knee." So they found him like that. [1]

It was also said that he used to feed people with dates and *saweeq* [2] and he would give them milk until he heard the words of Umayyah Ibn Abis-Salt:

I have seen the doers and their deeds,

*And I have seen that the most generous of them are
Banu Ad-Dayyan,*

Their food is wheat mixed with honey,

Not like what Banu Jud'an give to us.

So Ibn Jud'an sent two thousand camels bearing wheat, honey and clarified butter to Ash-Sham and he ordered a caller to invite the people every night from the roof of the Ka'bah to drink from the water trough of Ibn Jud'an. Umayyah said regarding this:

He has a swift caller in Makkah,

And another atop the Ka'bah calling,

To bowls full of wheat mixed with honey.

But in spite of all this, it has been confirmed in *Saheeh Muslim* that 'A'ishah (may Allah be Pleased with her) said, "O, Messenger of Allah! Verily, Ibn Jud'an used to give food and offer hospitality to the guests; will that benefit him on the Day of the Resurrection?" The Prophet ﷺ replied, "No, for he never even once said, "My

---

(1)   I have not found it in the sources of *hadeeth* and history, even though they are numerous.

(2)   *Saweeq*: Barley porridge.

Lord! Forgive me my sins on the Day of Judgment." [1]

Mention of Imru'ul-Qais Ibn Hujr Al-Kindi, the Author of One of Al-Mu'allaqat

It is one of the most excellent and most famous of them and it begins thus:

Stop and let us weep at the memory of a beloved person and his status.

And Imam Ahmad narrated on the authority of Abu Hurairah ﷺ that he said, "The Messenger of Allah ﷺ said, "Imra'ul-Qais is the bearer of the flag of the poets to the Fire." [2]

Al-Kalbi mentioned that Imra'ul-Qais came forward with a banner, intending to fight Banu Asad after they had killed his father and he passed by Tabalah, where an idol called Dhul-Khalasah was located. The Arabs used to use divining arrows before it and so he cast the divining arrows and the arrow of prohibition came out. Then he cast them a second time and then a third time, with the same result, so he broke the arrows and struck the face of Dhul-Khalasah with them and said, "I bite your father's penis! Had it been your father who was murdered, you would not have forbidden me from avenging him. Then he attacked Banu Asad and annihilated them." Ibn Al-Kalbi said, "And he did not use divining arrows before Dhul-Khalasah after that until the advent of Islam."

Some said that he celebrated Qaisar, the emperor of Rome, in his poetry and that he supported him in some of the wars that he fought, but that when he requested support from him, he did not receive what he had hoped for from him and so he disparaged him

---

(1) Its *takhreej* has already been given.

(2) Narrated by Ahmad in his *Musnad* (7087) and it is very weak.

after that. It was said that Caesar had him poisoned as a result of this and that death approached him when he was beside the grave of a woman near to a mountain known as 'Aseeb and there he wrote:

O, my neighbor, verily, the sanctuary is near,
And I will reside where 'Aseeb resided,
O, my neighbor, verily, we are both strangers here,
And every stranger is to a fellow stranger a kinsman.

It was said that the seven *Mu'allaqat* were attached to the Ka'bah [1] and this was because when one of the Arabs composed a *qaseedah*, [2] he would present it to Quraish and if they approved of it, they would affix it to the Ka'bah in order to honor and venerate it and so the seven *Mu'allaqat*, the first of which was by Imru'ul-Qais Ibn Hujr Al-Kindi, were collected from these.

Mention of Something of the Story of Umayyah Ibn Abis-Salt Ath-Thaqafi, Who Was One of the Poets of the Jahiliyyah and Who Lived During the Era of Islam

Al-Hafiz ibn 'Asakir said, "He was Umayyah Ibn Abis-Salt 'Abdullah Ibn Abi Rabee'ah ibn 'Awf Ibn 'Uqdah Ibn 'Ghiyarah Ibn 'Awf Ibn Thaqeef Ibn Munabbih Ibn Bakr Ibn Hawazin Abu 'Uthman." It was said that he was a righteous man and that at first, he had faith, but later, he deviated from it and that it was he who was referred to in the Words of Allah, Most High: ❨ And recite

---

(1) The word *mu'allaqah* means something that is attached.

(2) *Qaseedah*: An ancient Arabic poem having as a rule, a rigid tripartite structure.

(O, Muhammad) to them the story of him to whom We gave Our *Ayat*, but he threw them away, so *Shaitan* (Satan) followed him up, and he became of those who went astray 〗 (*Soorah Al-A'raf* 7:175)

And 'Abdur-Razzaq said that Ath-Thawri said, "Habeeb Ibn Abi Thabit informed me that 'Abdullah Ibn 'Amr said regarding the Words of Allah, Most High: 〖 And recite (O, Muhammad) to them the story of him to whom We gave Our *Ayat*, but he threw them away, so *Shaitan* followed him up, and he became of those who went astray 〗 (*Soorah Al-A'raf* 7:175), "He was Umayyah Ibn Abu As-Salt. on the authority of Nafi' Ibn 'Asim Ibn Mas'ood that he said, "I was in a gathering which included 'Abdullah Ibn 'Amr and a man from among the people recited the verse which is in *Soorah Al-A'raf*: 〖 And recite (O, Muhammad) to them the story of him to whom We gave Our *Ayat*, but he threw them away 〗 (*Soorah Al-A'raf* 7:175) and he said, "Do you know who he is?" One of them said, "He is Saifi Ibn Ar-Rahib." Another said, "Nay, he is Bal'am, a man from Banu Isra'eel." He said, No." They asked, "Then who?" He replied, "Umayyah Ibn Abis-Salt." This was also said by Abu Salih and Al-Kalbi and Qatadah transmitted it from some of them.

And Al-Hafiz Ibn 'Asakir narrated on the authority of Az-Zuhri that he said, "Umayyah ibn Abis-Salt said:

Will not a Messenger come to us from among us, informing us, About what is after our destination, and (who is) from our tribe."

He said, "Then Umayyah Ibn Abis-Salt set out for Bahrain and the Messenger of Allah ﷺ announced his Prophethood, and Umayyah Ibn Abis-Salt remained in Bahrain for eight years. After that, he traveled to At-Ta'if and he said to them, what does Muhammad Ibn 'Abdullah say?" They said, "He said, "He claims that he is a Prophet and that he is the one you were hoping for."

So he set out for Makkah and met with him and he said to him, "O, son of 'Abdul-Muttalib! What is it that you are saying?" He said, "I say that I am the Messenger of Allah and that none has the right to be worshipped but He." He said, "I wish to speak to you, so meet me tomorrow." The Prophet ﷺ said, "Your appointment is on the morrow." Umayyah said, "Do you desire that I come to you alone, or with a group of my Companions? Or will you come to me alone, or with a group of your companions?" The Messenger of Allah ﷺ replied, "Whatever you wish." He said, "Then I will come to you in a group." Ibn 'Asakir said, "So the next morning, Umayyah came with a group from Quraish and a number of the Companions of the Messenger of Allah ﷺ also came to him and they sat in the shade of the Ka'bah. Umayyah began to speak and then he began to compose some poetry and to recite it aloud. After he finished reciting it, he said, "Answer me, O, son of 'Abdul-Muttalib!" The Messenger of Allah ﷺ recited: " ﴿ In the Name of Allah, the Most Beneficent, the Most Merciful, *Ya Seen.* (These letters are one of the miracles of the Qur'an, and none but Allah [Alone] knows their meanings). By the Qur'an, full of wisdom (i.e. full of laws, evidences, and proofs) ﴾ (*Soorah Ya Seen* 36:1,2) – until the end of the *Soorah.* Then Umayyah leapt up and Quraish followed him, saying, "What do you say, O, Umayyah?" He said, "I bear witness that he is following the truth." They asked, "Will you follow him?" He said, "Until I have considered his case." Ibn 'Asakir said, "Umayyah departed for Ash-Sham and the Messenger of Allah ﷺ went to Al-Madinah. When the participants in the Battle of Badr were killed, Umayyah came from Ash-Sham and camped at Badr. Then he set out in search of the Messenger of Allah ﷺ and someone asked him, "What do you want, O, Abus-Salt?" He said, "I want Muhammad." The questioner asked him, "And what will you do?" He said, "I will declare my belief in him and place my fate in his hands." The questioner asked him, "Do you know who is in the well?" Umayyah said, "No." He said, "In it are 'Utbah Ibn Rabee'ah

and Shaibah Ibn Rabec'ah, who are your maternal uncle's sons
and his (your uncle's) mother is Rabee'ah Bint 'Abd Shams." On
hearing this, he cut off the ears and tail of his she-camel, then he
stood beside the well and recited a long poem, lamenting the loss
of life:

> *What was in Badr? It was as a valley full of people,*
>> *Who are ready and willing to rush to one's aid,*
>> *Badr was a battle where swords were flashing,*
>> *As the warriors moved across the sands,*
> *The warriors were of all ages and sizes and very strong,*
> *Can you not see what I see? The battle was very clear,*
> *Can you not see that Makkah has become strong and*
>> *ferocious?*
> *Warriors were like friends who loved one another,*
>> *They were like kings during the battle,*
>> *They were tall, muscular and very strong,*
> *And they did whatever they wanted during the battle,*
>> *Everything they said and did was good,*
>> *They were generous and used to feed people,*
>> *From the best food available to them,*
>> *There were giant pans full of food,*
>> *And they had food for whoever wanted it,*
> *Their homes were always open and welcoming to guests,*
>> *They gave them anything that they needed,*
> *And they gave them camels from the valley of Baladih,*
>> *Their generosity is more than any in the world,*
>> *They gave to people without counting the cost,*
> *They are betrayed by people and they are the defenders,*
>> *When they fight with their swords,*

They compete to be first on the battlefield,
I was sad when I heard them screaming on the battlefield,
May Allah bless the married and the single ones among them,
When they approached, the enemy would retreat in fear,
They advanced on their horses and ate up the distance,
And galloped for a long time, their heads held High,
These horses are like lions, strong and aggressive,
When the armies met with each other face to face,
They were as close as people shaking hands,
They were magnificent, thousand upon thousand,
Including those wearing armor and those bearing spears.

Then he returned to Makkah and At-Ta'if and abandoned Islam.

Some said that he used to study the languages of animals and that while on a journey, he passed by a bird and he said to his companions, "This bird says such-and-such." And they said, "We do not know the truth of what he is saying," until they passed by a flock of sheep and they saw that an ewe and its lamb had become detached from the rest of the flock. He looked toward it and it bleated, as if it was prompting it to hasten and he said, "Do you know what it is saying to its lamb?" They said, "No." He said, "It is saying, "Let us hasten, so that the wolf does not come and eat you, just as it ate your brother last year." So they hurried on until they met the shepherd and they asked him if a wolf had eaten one of his sheep last year in that place, and he said, "Yes." It was also said that one day he passed by a camel being ridden by a woman and it was raising its head toward her and foaming at the mouth. He said, "It is saying to her, "You are riding me and under the saddle there is a needle." So they made the woman dismount and they removed the saddle and found underneath it a needle, as he had said.

And it has been confirmed in an authentic *hadeeth* on the authority of Abu Hurairah ﷺ that he said, "The Messenger of Allah ﷺ said, "The truest word spoken by a poet was the saying of Labeed:

Verily, everything except Allah is perishable.
– and Umayyah Ibn Abis-Salt almost embraced Islam." [1]

And Imam Ahmad narrated on the authority of Ash-Shareed ﷺ that he said, "I was riding mounted behind the Messenger of Allah ﷺ and he said to me, "Do you know any of Umayyah Ibn Abis-Salt's poetry?" I replied, "Yes." He said, "Then recite it to me." So I recited a verse to him and after each verse I recited to him, he would say, "Yes," until I had recited a hundred verses to him. Then the Prophet ﷺ remained silent, so I became silent." [2]

It was also narrated thus by Imam Muslim, [3] and in some narrations, it was stated, "Then the Messenger of Allah ﷺ said, Be it that he almost embraced Islam." [4]

And it was narrated on the authority of Al-Asma'i that he used to recite from the poetry of Umayyah:

Praise Allah, for He is Worthy of praise,
Our Lord is in the highest place,
(He is praised) highly in the evening,
In the highest edifice, which preceded,
The creation of mankind and He fashioned,
Above the heaven a Throne which is carried,

---

(1) Narrated by Al-Bukhari (6147) and Muslim (2255).

(2) This is an authentic *hadeeth* narrated by Imam Ahmad in his *Musnad* (18973).

(3) Narrated by Muslim (2255).

(4) Narrated by Muslim (2255), Ibn Majah (3758) and Ahmad in his *Musnad* (18963).

No eye has seen it, even the angels who bear it,
Avert their gaze from it.

Also from the admirable poetry of Umayyah is:

They do not violate the earth when they ask,
As if they are searching for excuses with sticks,
Rather, their faces shine and you see them,
When they ask, in the best color,
And when the poor man rises in the midst of their steeds,
They refer him to the Lord of the horses and the slaves,
And if you called them to every misfortune,
They would block the rays of the sun with their horses.

This is the end of the biography of Umayyah Ibn Abis-Salt. Mention of Quss Ibn Sa'idah Al-Iyadi

It is reported on the authority of 'Ubadah Ibn As-Samit that he said, "A delegation visted the Prophet ﷺ from Iyad and he said to them, "O, members of the delegation of Iyad! What has happened to Quss Ibn Sa'idah Al-Iyadi?" They replied, "He has died, O, Messenger of Allah." He said, "I witnessed him one day on the market of 'Ukaz, on a red camel, speaking admirable and elegant words, which I find myself unable to remember." Then a Bedouin from among the most remote people stood up and said, "I remember them, O, Messenger of Allah!" On hearing this, the Messenger of Allah ﷺ looked pleased. The Bedouin said, "He was in the market of 'Ukaz, on a red camel and he said:

O, assembly of people! Gather round,
for all those who pass away have gone, And everything that

is to come will come,

A dark night, a starry evening and a roaring sea,

Stars that shine, firmly fixed mountains and flowing rivers,

Verily, in the heaven there is a message,

And in the earth there is a warning,

Why do I see the people going and not returning?

Are they happy to stand in prayer and so they pray?

Or do they abandon it and sleep?

Quss swears an oath to Allah,

Of which there is no doubt,

Verily, Allah's Religion is more pleasing,

Than this religion if yours.

Then he recited these verses:

In those of the earlier generations who have gone,

There are insights for us,

When I saw the destinations of the dead,

Without origins,

And I saw my people like them,

The great and small depart,

None of those who have departed come to you,

And none of those who remain have departed,

I am certain that it is inevitable,

That I shall go where they have gone. [1]

---

(1) It was narrated by At-Tabarani in *Al-Kabeer* (12/88,89) and it was mentioned by Al-Haithami in *Al-Majma'* (9/697), who said, "It was narrated by At-Tabarani and Al-Bazzar, but in its *sanad* there is one Muhammad Ibn Al-Hajjaj Al-Lakhmi and he is a liar." The author declared it to be *ghareeb*. It was narrated from a number of other sources, but all of them are weak, according to Ibn Hajar Al-'Asqalani.

Its *isnad* is *ghareeb* from this source.

Al-Jarood Ibn Al-Mu'alla Ibn Hanash Ibn Mu'alla Al-'Abdi was a Christian who was renowned for his explanation and exegesis of the Scriptures and he was knowledgeable regarding the history and parables of Persia. He was also a learned philosopher and physician, shrewd, well mannered and handsome in appearance. He possessed great wealth and property and he was one of a delegation from 'Abdul-Qais, all of whom were intelligent and eloquent men, who visited the Prophet ﷺ and when he met the Prophet ﷺ, he stood in front of him and began to declaim:

O, Prophet of guidance! Men have come to you,

Having crossed vast tracts of desert,

And traversed barren lands to reach you,

And they did not consider tiredness,

In their eagerness to see you,

All of Bahma' avert their eyes from them,

As they spurred on their steeds,

They raced to traverse it,

In armor, like twinkling stars,

Seeking to avert the harm of a great Day,

Terrible, paining the hearts and frightening,

When all of creation will be gathered,

Estranged and separated,

For those who persisted in error,

They rode toward Light from the Deity,

And in order to find proof and piety,

Allah has chosen you, o, son of Aminah,

For goodness, since clouds filled with rain have come,

So let great good come from you, o, Proof of Allah,

For there is no good for one who stays behind.

After he finished, the Prophet ﷺ approached him and sat close to him, then he said to him, "O, Jarood! The promise for you and your people has been delayed." Al-Jarood replied, "May my father and mother be ransomed for you! Has not whoever delayed in coming to you lost his opportunity? And that would be the greatest sin and the worst punishment. I am not among those who have seen you or heard of you and then opposed you and followed someone other than you. I am presently a follower of the faith that you know (i.e. Christianity). I have come to you and here and now, I abandon it in favor of your Religion. Does that purify the sins, misdeeds and offenses that I have committed, and does such an action from the slave please the Lord?" The Messenger of Allah ﷺ said to him, "I guarantee that for you; now devote yourself to belief in Allah's Oneness and leave behind you the religion of Christianity." Al-Jarood replied, "May my father and mother be ransomed for you! Extend your hand, for I bear witness that none is worthy of worship except Allah, Alone, without partners and I bear witness that you, Muhammad, are His slave and His Messenger." So he embraced Islam and those with him from his people also embraced Islam. The Prophet ﷺ was happy with their Islam and showed them such hospitality as pleased them and delighted them. Then the Messenger of Allah ﷺ came to them and said, "Is there anyone among you who is acquainted with Quss Ibn Sa'idah Al-Iyadi?" Al-Jarood replied, "May my father and mother be ransomed for you! All of us know him and I am the best acquainted of all of them with him and his circumstances. Quss, O, Messenger of Allah, was one of the sons of the Arabs; he lived for six hundred years, of which five were spent in the deserts and wastelands, raising his voice in glorification (of Allah), in imitation of the Messiah, during which time he remained unsettled, had no home to shelter him and heard not the sound of any neighbor. He used to wear hair shirts and travel alone for the purpose of worship and he never tired of his monasticism. He used to drink from ostrich eggs and keep the company of reptiles and vermin. He enjoyed the darkness. He would look and reflect and he would think and seek information. As a result of all this, his name became a byword for wisdom and terrors were removed through him. He was a contemporary of the head of the Disciples, Sam'an (Simon) and he was the first person from among the Arabs to believe in Allah's Oneness and devote himself to His service and to declare his certain belief in the Resurrection and the Reckoning. He warned the people against an evil return (i.e. the Hellfire) and he ordered them to do good deeds before it was too late and warned them against death. He submitted to Allah's Divine Decree – whether in times of ease or in times of hardship – and he composed laments in poetic verse and he used to visit graves. He reminded them of the Resurrection and contemplated Allah's Divine Ordainments. He demonstrated his knowledge and wisdom in numerous ways, pointing out to the people the many proofs of Allah's existence in creation: in the heavens and the Earth, in the rotation of night and day, in the sun and the moon, in the wind and the rain, the land and the seas, in the existence of male and female throughout nature and many more signs too numerous to mention. He declared that Allah is One God, that He was not born and that He has no father, that He gives life and causes death. He called upon them to dwell on the fate of 'Ad and Thamood and the fate of their fathers and their forefathers. He told them that all of them would have their just deserts in the Hereafter, good for good and evil for evil." And it is he who said:

Remembrance of Allah fills the heart with love,

As night is followed by day,

And dark clouds filled with rain,

Pour down water, and inside them is fire,

Its light blinds the eyes and,

Violent thunder causes hearts to flutter,
And lofty palaces are filled with goodness,
While others are empty and devoid of it,
And high mountains are firmly anchored,
And seas whose waters are abundant,
And stars that shine in the darkness of night,
We see them every day revolving,
Then a sun that is urged on by the evening moon,
And each follows the other in succession,
And young, grey-haired and old,
All of them will be equal on a Day that is coming,
And their minds will be unable to imagine,
And all of these things that I have mentioned,
Show the hearts the way to Allah,
  Those that are rightly-guided and reflect.

The Messenger of Allah ﷺ said, "No matter what I forget, I will never forget him in the market of 'Ukaz, sitting on his red camel and addressing the people thus: "Gather and listen, and if you hear, remember it and if you remember it, then benefit from it. And speak, and if you speak, speak the truth. Whoever lives will die and whoever dies will pass away. And everything that comes comes, rain and plants and the living and the dead." [1]

---

(1)   This was narrated by Ibn 'Asakir in his *Tareekh* (3/431) and it was mentioned by Ibn 'Adiyy in *Al-Kamil* in his biography of Zarbi Ibn 'Abdullah (No. 730) and he said, "Zarbi had few *ahadeeth* other than those that I have mentioned; and his *ahadeeth* and the texts of some of his *ahadeeth* are rejected." It was also mentioned by As-Suyooti in *Al-La'ali Al-Masnoo'ah* (1/167-173) and he said, "There are clear signs that this is a fabrication." And Allah, Most High, knows better.

Mention of Zaid Ibn 'Amr Ibn Nufail ﷺ

It is reported on the authority of Asma' Bint Abu Bakr (may Allah be Pleased with them both) that she said, "I saw Zaid Ibn 'Amr Ibn Nufail leaning his back against the Ka'bah and he was saying, "O, assembly of Quraish! By Him in Whose Hand is Zaid's soul, none of you is following the Religion of Ibraheem but I." Then he said, "O, Allah! If I but knew the most beloved way to You, I would worship You thereby, but I do not know." Then he prostrated on his camel." This is how it was narrated also by Abu Usamah, on the authority of Hisham. He added, "He used to pray toward the Ka'bah and he would say, "My God is the God of Ibraheem and my Religion is the Religion of Ibraheem." And he used to save girls from being buried alive, saying to the man who intended to kill his daughter, "Do not kill her. Give her to me and I will be her guardian. Then, when she had grown up, he would say, "If you wish, take her and if you wish, leave her." This was narrated by An-Nasa'i by way of Usamah [1] and Al-Bukhari included it in a *mu'allaq* form. [2]

And Abu Dawood At-Tayalisi [3] said, "I was informed by Al-Mas'oodi on the authority of Nufail Ibn Hisham Ibn Sa'eed Ibn Zaid Ibn 'Amr Ibn Nufail Al-'Adawi, on the authority of his father, who in turn reported on the authority of his grandfather, that Zaid Ibn 'Amr and Waraqah Ibn Nawfal set out in search of the (true) Religion and they traveled until they reached a monk in Al-Mawsil. The monk said to Zaid Ibn 'Amr, "From where have you come, O, owner of the camel?" He replied, "From the sons of Ibraheem." He asked, "And for what are you searching?" He said, "I am searching for the (true) Religion." He said, "Return,

---

(1)   This is an authentic *hadeeth* narrated by An-Nasa'i in *'Al-Kubra'* (5/54, no. 8187).

(2)   Narrated by Al-Bukhari in a *mu'allaq* form (3828).

(3)   Narrated by Abu Dawood At-Tayalisi in his *Musnad* (No. 234).

for it is about to appear in your land." He said, "As for Waraqah, he became a Christian, and as for myself, I decided to follow Christianity, but it did not suit me." So he returned, reciting:

Here I am, at Your service in truth,

Worshipping and as a slave,

It is piety that I desire and I seek not to beguile,

So should I migrate, like the one who said,

"I have believed in that in which Ibraheem believed,"

O, Allah I shall remain obedient to You,

No matter what hardships I may undergo,

I shall certainly bear them.

Then he fell down and prostrated. The narrator said, "Then his son, i.e. Sa'eed Ibn Zaid ﷺ, one of the ten who were promised Paradise came and said, "O, Messenger of Allah! If my father was as I have seen and as you have been informed, then ask forgiveness for him." He said, "Yes, for he will be sent forth on the Day of Resurrection as a nation of one." [1]

Zaid Ibn 'Amr came to the Messenger of Allah ﷺ, and with him was Zaid Ibn Harithah ﷺ and they were eating from a table belonging to them. They invited him to eat their food, but Zaid Ibn 'Amr said, "O, my nephew! I do not eat of that which has been slaughtered on stone altars." [2]

And Al-Bukhari narrated in his *Saheeh* on the authority of 'Abdullah Ibn 'Umar ﷺ that the Prophet ﷺ met Zaid Ibn 'Amr Ibn

---

(1)   This *hadeeth* is *hasan*; it was narrated by Al-Hakim in his *Mustadrak* (4956).

(2)   Translator's note: This narration would suggest that the Prophet ﷺ used to eat the meat of animals that had been sacrificed to Quraish's idols and only ceased to do so when Zaid Ibn 'Amr rebuked him for it! This alone proves that the narration is weak, since it has been authentically reported that even before Revelation came to him, the Prophet ﷺ abhorred idolatry.

Nufail at the bottom of (the valley of) Baldah [1] before any Divine Inspiration came to the Prophet 🕮. A meal was presented to the Prophet 🕮 but he refused to eat from it. (Then it was presented to Zaid 🕮) who said, "I do not eat anything which you slaughter in the name of your stone idols. I eat none but those things on which Allah's Name has been mentioned at the time of slaughtering." Zaid Ibn 'Amr used to criticize the way Quraish slaughtered their animals, and he used to say, "Allah has created the sheep and He has sent the water for it from the sky, and He has grown the grass for it from the earth, yet you slaughter it in other than the Name of Allah." He used to say this because he rejected that practice and considered it as something abominable." [2]

And Ibn 'Asakir cited here a number of *ahadeeth* which are very strange and in some of them there are extremely objectionable things. Then he related from numerous sources from the Messenger of Allah 🕮 that he said, "He will be sent forth on the Day of Resurrection as a nation of one." Among them was the narration of Muhammad Ibn 'Uthman Ibn Abi Shaibah: on the authority of Jabir that he said, "The Messenger of Allah 🕮 was asked if Zaid Ibn 'Amr Ibn Nufail used to face the *Qiblah* in the *Jahiliyyah* and he said, "That man will be brought forth as a nation of one, between me and 'Eesa, the son of Maryam." [3] Its *isnad* is *jayyid*, (good) *hasan* (sound).

And Al-Baghandi narrated on the authority of 'A'ishah (may Allah be Pleased with her) that she said, "The Messenger of Allah 🕮 I entered Paradise and I saw two tall trees with many branches for Zaid Ibn 'Amr Ibn Nufail." [4] Its *isnad* is *jayyid* and it is not in any of the books.

---

(1)   Baldah: A valley near Makkah.

(2)   Narrated by Al-Bukhari (3826 and 3828).

(3)   As mentioned above from *'Al-Majma"* (9/416, no. 16177).

(4)   This *hadeeth* was narrated by Ibn 'Asakir in his *'Tareekh'* (19/512).

And from the poetry of Zaid Ibn 'Amr Ibn Nufail is the following:

> *To Allah my praise and extolment are directed,*
>
> *And pleasing words which time does naught to diminish,*
>
> *To the Highest King, above Whom there is no god,*
>
> *Nor any lord that approximates Him.*

Also from his poetry affirming Allah's Oneness are the following verses related by Muhammad Ibn Ishaq, Az-Zubair Ibn Bakkar and others:

> *I have submitted my countenance to the One to Whom,*
>
> *The earth, which bears heavy rocks, has submitted,*
>
> *He spread it and when it was leveled,*
>
> *He made it firm and anchored the mountains,*
>
> *And I have submitted my countenance to the One to Whom,*
>
> *The clouds, which bear sweet, cold water, have submitted,*
>
> *If they are sent to a land, they obey and pour abundant rain on it,*
>
> *And I have submitted my countenance to the One to Whom,*
>
> *The wind has submitted, when it is directed hither and thither.*

The Story of the Re-Excavation of Zamzam

'Abdul-Muttalib said, "While I was sleeping in my room, someone came to me, saying, "Dig Teebah." I said, "What is Teebah?" Then he went away. The next day, I retired to my bed and while I was sleeping, he came to me saying, "Dig Barrah." I said, "What is Barrah?" Then he left me and on the next day, I retired to my bed and while I was sleeping, he came to me and said, "Dig Al-Madnoonah." I asked, "What is Al-Madnoonah?" Then he left me and on the following day, I retired to my bed and while

I was sleeping, he came to me and said, "Dig Zamzam." I asked, "What is Zamzam?" He replied, "It will never be depleted, nor will its water decrease. It is to provide water for the Hajj pilgrims. It is between the blood and the entrails, where the white-footed raven raps, near the ants' nest." He said, "When he had made its situation clear to me and directed me to its location I knew that he had spoken the truth." He then took his *adze* and accompanied by his son, Al-Harith Ibn 'Abdul-Muttalib – who was his only son at that time – and he dug until he found what had been concealed, upon which he called out, "*Allahu Akbar!*" Immediately, Quraish realized that he had found what he was looking for." Ibn Ishaq said, "This is what was conveyed to me on the authority of 'Ali Ibn Abi Talib ﷺ regarding Zamzam." He added, "And I have heard one who spoke regarding 'Abdul-Muttalib saying that it was said to him when he ordered the digging of Zamzam,

Then call for sweet water, not muddy,
To provide water for Allah's Hajj pilgrims in every place,
That no person need fear, as long as it lasts.

He said, "When this was said to 'Abdul-Muttalib, he came out to Quraish and said, "Do you know that I was ordered to excavate Zamzam?" They said, "Was it made clear to you where it was?" He said, "No." They said, "Then return to your bed where you saw what you saw and if it is the truth from Allah, he will make it clear to you, but if it is from Shaitan, he will not return to you." So he returned home and slept and someone came to him and it was said to him, "Excavate Zamzam; if you excavate it, you will not regret it. It is an inheritance from your illustrious forefather. It will never be depleted, nor will its water decrease and it will provide water for the mass of pilgrims. It is like a shying ostrich and it is not shared. Let a person vow (to water them with it) and it will flow generously. It will be an inheritance and firm covenant. It does not belong to some, as you know; and it is between the blood and the entrails.

And Ibn Ishaq and others mentioned that during the time of 'Abdul-Muttalib, there were many wells in Makkah prior to the appearance of Zamzam. Ibn Ishaq enumerated them, named them and mentioned their locations in Makkah, along with the names of those who dug them. Then he said, "Then Zamzam eliminated all of the wells and all of the people turned to it because of its location in the Sacred Mosque and its superiority over waters, for it was the well of Isma'eel, son of Ibraheem (peace be upon them both). Banu 'Abd Manaf vaunted their superiority over all of Quraish and all of the other Arabs because of it. And it has been confirmed in *Saheeh Muslim* in a *hadeeth* relating the story of how Abu Dharr ﷺ embraced Islam, that the Messenger of Allah ﷺ said of Zamzam, "It serves as a food and it is a cure for the sick." [1] And in another narration, "The water of Zamzam is for whatever purpose it was drunk for." [2]

The Story of 'Abdul-Muttalib's Vow to Sacrifice One of His Sons

Ibn Ishaq said, "According to what is claimed, due to the attitude of Quraish toward his digging of Zamzam, 'Abdul-Muttalib vowed that if ten sons were born to him and they all survived to reach manhood, he would sacrifice one of them to Allah beside the Ka'bah. When his sons numbered ten, he knew that Quraish would try to prevent him – and they were Al-Harith, Az-Zubair,

---

(1)   Narrated by Muslim (2473), without the words: "…and it is a cure for the sick." This addidtion was narrated by At-Tabarani in *As-Sagheer* (1/186, No. 295), by Al-Bazzar in his *Musnad* (9/361, No. 3929) and by Al-Baihaqi in *Al-Kubra* (5/147, No. 9441), on the authority of Abu Dharr ﷺ – and it is an authentic addition.

(2)   This *hadeeth* has been deemed authentic due to the other narrations supporting it. It was narrated by Imam Ahmad in his *Musnad* (14578).

Hajl, Dirar, Al-Muqawam, Abu Lahab, Al-'Abbas, Hamzah, Abu Talib, and 'Abdullah – he gathered them and informed them of his vow and he called upon them to fulfill it for Allah, the Almighty, the All-Powerful and they obeyed him, asking him, "What will you do?" He replied, "Each of you will take a divining arrow and then he will write his name on it, then all of you come to me." They did as he asked and then they came to him and he went with them to the idol, Hubal, which was inside the Ka'bah. Hubal was near a well inside the Ka'bah. It was at this well that donations to the Ka'bah were stored. Beside Hubal there were seven divining arrows, which they used to use to seek judgments when any matter was difficult for them, such as bloodwit, paternity or any other problem. They would go there and cast their arrows and whatever the arrows ordered or forbade, they would fulfill it.

What is meant is that when 'Abdul-Muttalib came and cast the divining arrows beside Hubal, the arrow on which 'Abdullah's name was written came up. He was his youngest son and the most beloved of them to him. But he took 'Abdullah by the hand and took his knife and approached Isaf and Na'ilah, [1] with the intention of sacrificing his son before them. But Quraish left their assemblies and tried to prevent him, saying, "What do you intend, O, 'Abdul-Muttalib?" He said, "(I intend to) sacrifice him." Quraish and his sons – the brothers of 'Abdullah – said to him, "By Allah, you shall never sacrifice him unless there is some valid reason for it! If you do so, men will continue to come and sacrifice their sons and the people cannot remain upon such a custom."

---

(1)   Isaf and Na'ilah: Two idols inside the Ka'bah.

The Story of 'Abdullah's Giving of His Son, 'Abdullah in Marriage to Aminah Bint Wahb Az-Zuhriyyah

Ibn Ishaq said, "Then 'Abdul-Muttalib left, taking his son, 'Abdullah by the hand and according to what is claimed, he passed by a woman from Banu Asad Ibn 'Abdul-'Uzza Ibn Qusayy, whose name was Umm Qannal; she was the sister of Waraqah Ibn Nawfal Ibn Asad Ibn 'Abdul-'Uzza Ibn Qusayy and she was beside the Ka'bah. She looked at his face and she asked, "Where are you going, o, 'Abdullah?" He said, "With my father." She said, "You can have the like of the camels that were slaughtered in your stead if you will have intimate relations with me." But he said, "I am with my father and I cannot disobey him or leave him." So 'Abdul-Muttalib departed with him and went to Wahb Ibn 'Abd Manaf Ibn Zuhrah Ibn Kilab Ibn Murrah Ibn Ka'b Ibn Lu'ayy Ibn Ghalib Ibn Fihr, who was at that time the leader of Banu Zuhrah, being the oldest of them and the noblest, and he gave 'Abdullah to his daughter, Aminah Bint Wahb in marriage, who at that time was the head of the women of her tribe. It is claimed that he consummated his marriage to her as soon as he had transferred her to his home and that she became pregnant with the Messenger of Allah ﷺ. Then he left her and went to the woman who had offered herself to him and he said to her, "Why do you not offer to me today what you offered me yesterday?" She said to him, "The light that was with you yesterday has left you and so I have no need of you." She used to hear from her brother, Waraqah Ibn Nawfal, who had embraced Christianity and read the Scriptures, that there would be a Prophet from this nation and so she desired that he should be born to her. But Allah made him to be from the finest and noblest stock, as Allah, Most High, says, ﴿ Allah knows best with whom to place His Message. ﴾ (*Soorah Al-An'am* 6:124)